T0369078

T0369021

Dialogues with EMERGING SPIRITUAL TEACHERS

JOHN W. PARKER

Second Edition

iUniverse, Inc.
New York   Bloomington

Dialogues With Emerging Spiritual Teachers

iUniverse books may be ordered through booksellers or by contacting:

iUniverse
1663 Liberty Drive
Bloomington, IN 47403
www.iuniverse.com
1-800-Authors (1-800-288-4677)

ISBN: 978-1-4401-1631-5 (pbk)
ISBN: 978-1-4401-1632-2 (ebk)

Library of Congress Control Number: 2009921500

Printed in the United States of America

iUniverse rev. date: 1/23/09

Contents

INTRODUCTION

I remember a hot, humid summer night when I was nine years old. I sat on my bed staring intently into the endless sky, looking for anything that would give me a sign that "God" or "Spirit" existed, not knowing exactly what I was looking for. Enveloped in total stillness I whispered, "O.K. I'm ready. If you're out there just give me a sign, any sign: a shooting star, an angel flying by, a bearded old guy from The Ten Commandments movie, ANYTHING! Are you out there?" Nothing happened for what seemed like hours. I wasn't giving up. I just kept gazing out the window, focusing on deeper and deeper layers of indigo emptiness dotted with flickering celestial bodies.

My mind was churning a million miles an hour. "Am I just a blob of meat spinning on a speck of dust and that's all there is to life? What are we doing here on this planet anyway? Maybe I should be looking for God in church like everybody else, but it's so boring and hot in there. Maybe I'm looking in the wrong place! Is it in books? I'll bet Jerry (the kid who lived down the street) knows. I'll ask him tomorrow. Why am I thinking about all this stuff anyway? I must be going nuts! Nobody else I know cares about it! All anybody else thinks about is baseball, fishing and swimming at the river. Bob (another neighborhood buddy) is the one to ask! He's Catholic and his parents are always dragging him off to church. What about the guy next door? He's in the tile business and knows everything! I'll ask him."

My brain continued to boil over in a cul de sac of nonsense. Finally total exhaustion set in and I slumped under the sheets burying myself in utter disappointment. I muttered to myself, "There is no God. There are no angels, otherwise they'd be here by now! Ask and you shall receive. Baloney! There is nothing. NOTHING!"

Within a split second of self-pitying defeat, while drifting into the twilight of deep sleep, I felt a warm, ethereal light enveloping me, bathing every cell of my body with a feeling of love and tenderness. I took a long, deep breath and muttered, "Wow, what is this? Is this IT?" For no apparent reason I found myself grinning from ear to ear as I nodded off, thanking whomever or whatever was responsible for giving me this wonderful experience. Something spoke to my heart without words and said, "Yes, I am here." From then on, I knew at some fundamental level that life was infinitely more than I ever imagined.

As karmic whirlpools of adolescent and early adult narcissism ensued, the graceful epiphany bestowed upon me faded into the porous nature of unconsciousness. However, despite my many expeditions deep into maya (the great master of illusion and delusion), I never fully lost the "Presence." An infinitesimal heart-flame of pure Light burned like a tiny ember buried under the ashes. Over the years, the "fire" for truth was strengthened and intensified through my association with various spiritual teachers and teachings who have been most graciously given to me precisely at the right time.

For thirty years I have been inexplicably drawn into the flame of love and eternal beauty that was my childhood experience. It still remains my primary passion to this day.

The purpose of this book is two fold: to serve your natural inquisitiveness into reality or truth and to introduce you to fourteen "emerging" spiritual teachers. What is an "emerging spiritual teacher"? The word "emerging" in this context means "to come into view." Originally I considered naming the book "Dialogues With Emerging Spiritual Teachers and Extraordinary Students," or "Dialogues with Emerging Spiritual Teachers, Guides and Friends." However, in the end both titles were too wordy and I made it less complicated. In actuality the content more accurately reflects the original title ideas.

These dialogues reveal that there is an increasing number of less well-known, unadorned "spiritual teachers, guides and friends" sharing with us powerful insights into eternal Truth and Light. This was once thought to be the exclusive domain of celebrated, highly visible gurus.

These "Emerging Spiritual Teachers" are in many respects ordinary people. They are also spiritual emissaries of notable veracity, bringing forth in their own unique manner the underlying indivisibility of flesh and spirit. They have worked, or are working in a variety of occupations: a forest firefighter, a prosthetic shoemaker, a tour guide, school teachers, a federal prison inmate who was once on the "Ten Most Wanted" list, a housewife, and others. To lend some balance, I also included an adjunct professor of theology and two Ivy League graduates.

Each teacher is uniquely suited to serve as a transformative spiritual agent. I want to comment briefly on the word "spiritual." As Jack Kornfield puts it, "It's a delusion to say that this is the spiritual part of one's life, this is the financial part, this is the psychological part. That's insane. Spirituality isn't about any particular realm or dimension to be liberated. It means liberation in the heavens and hells, in the monastery and in the marketplace. It means liberation of the body, the emotions, and relationships with all other beings." In other words, we don't have to worry so much about whether we're being "spiritual" or not. Again Jack Kornfield, "The lesson of spiritual life is not about gaining knowledge, but about how we love. Are we able to love what is given to us, love in the midst of all things, love ourselves and others?" If the answer is no, then Kornfield suggests we move with our body, heart and mind to open and rest in the natural perfection that is always here, now.

Whether or not these teachers, guides or friends are appropriate in your own case is for you to discover as you journey through these dialogues. Over the decades I have observed that many spiritual seekers feel less intimidated by teachers who are not so towering and are more accessible on a one-to-one basis. The absence of celebrity provides fertile ground for seekers to open up to, be with, and absorb honored teachings.

Another observation is that the spiritual potency of a teacher has little or nothing to do with public notoriety. Throughout history, there have been many examples of inconspicuous teachers who have had an enormous effect on those who were fortunate enough to meet them. These obscure teachers, for whatever reason, were not interested in becoming highly visible world figures, and some cases never did. On the other hand, teachers like Neem Karoli Baba, and more recently H.W.L. Poonja (Papaji), became highly visible as their students spread the word throughout the world about their powerful presence and accessibility.

How did I go about selecting these particular "emerging" teachers? The task was simultaneously daunting and exhilarating. Through decades of spiritual inquiry, I have had the good fortune of meeting dozens of well known and lesser-known teachers. There were literally hundreds of candidates to choose from. I intentionally did not include teachers such as His Holiness the Dalai Lama, Ram Das, Deepak Chopra, Thich Nhat Hanh and others, who have simply transcended the "emerging" phase. Numerous interviews have been conducted with this luminous population. At this juncture, I felt it was imperative to reveal the potency of grass-root sages, teachers, spiritual friends and guides who are serving in a superb and powerful way but are not yet famous.

In some instances, teacher selection was simply driven by accessibility, availability, geographical proximity and timing. What I observed while conducting these dialogues is a benevolence of spirit coming forth with unprecedented intensity and simplicity through relatively unknown, downright obscure human instruments. I could put together another ten volumes of dialogues and not scratch the surface of the flourishing numbers of truly awesome "emerging spiritual teachers" now populating the planet. It is a boon to us all that we have such a wonderful variety from which to chose. Once people discovered this project, recommendations came pouring in. Even after I had finished interviewing this collection of teachers, others implored me to include their teachers. For those not included my sincere apologies.

How can we know if these teachers are truly "awakened" or "enlightened" and can help us on our spiritual journey? This determination is left entirely up to you with respect to the relative importance or unimportance of this question. As you progress through these dialogues, various qualities, flavors or levels of resonance will make themselves known to you. As Suzuki Roshi pointed out, "Strictly speaking, there are no enlightened people, there is only enlightened activity." In other words, enlightenment simply cannot be contained or owned by anyone. It may in fact only reside within the context and essence of freedom itself. If you need to inquire further into a teacher's quality or level of "enlightenment," I highly recommend a new book titled *Halfway Up The Mountain: The Error of Premature Claims to Enlightenment* by Mariana Caplan. This book is a marvelous collection of wisdom about the foibles and folly of traversing the spiritual terrain. As mentioned in the book, it is a "blueprint for [just this sort of] self-examination and honest dialogue." In my view, this is a beneficial publication for both spiritual aspirants and teachers alike.

There are two points (out of dozens) made in Mariana's book that I would like to reference. One concerns being a student, the other selecting an appropriate teacher. From a student perspective, she quotes Indries Shah who says, "If you seek a teacher, try to become a real student." Awakening to reality requires complete mutuality. Regarding the topic of undiminished enlightenment as a prerequisite to teach, Mariana quotes the skillful adept Lee Losowick who says, "If you're not enlightened you teach what you know—that's all. And if you do that with integrity and commitment to your path, you can be a source of transmission as much as anybody else."

Mariana continues on with an inquiry into the question, "Can a real student benefit from a false teacher?" The answer is an overwhelming "yes" which may surprise some. Mariana points out after some discussion on the subject, "[But] there also is a whole group of teachers who are sincere in their intent, and maybe even spiritually mature to a large degree, who range anywhere from slightly limited in their teaching capacities to grossly mistaken about their own abilities as a teacher. Sincere students do seem to extract enormous benefit from such teachers." Again quoting Jack Kornfield from Mariana's book, "Sometimes it takes a misguided or a false teacher to create a wise student." There is no ultimate "scorecard" for such matters. It's much more of a mystery than we can possibly imagine.

What I looked for in teachers for this book was the integrity and commitment that Losowick so adeptly points to. However, I have purposely avoided teacher-endorsements other than to share a few minor subjective impressions and experiences. I also intentionally wrote sparse introductions to avoid over-coloring the interviews themselves so they could fundamentally stand on their own.

Throughout the book I use the words "dialogue" and "interview" interchangeably although technically they are different in some respects. In either case, the intention was to create a casual, informal conversation fostering a fundamental exchange of ideas or perspectives.

The interviews were conducted (usually one-on-one) and recorded. I then transcribed the interviews and sent copies to teachers who edited them for accuracy. The interview questions and answers were left in tact as much as possible from the original taped transcript, although some editing was necessary to render further clarity. Please remember that these are verbal, not written, dialogues so there are incomplete sentences and other grammatical anomalies. The underlying intention is for you to engage these teachers as they are, based on their own merits. Again, my own personal opinions regarding teachers is entirely irrelevant. The invitation is for you to remain fully open and honest about what is reflected back to you, and see if any change of heart or consciousness comes about as a result.

Note: It is good to leave time for reflection and integration after reading each dialogue before moving on to the next. Reading in this manner should help you to avoid confusion.

The length of each interview was a result of available time afforded by each teacher, and the natural flow of dialogue that came about. Some interviews are quite short, others are tome-like. In either case, interview length is not an indication of bias one way or the other. It just so happened that it turned out the way it did. In all cases, I opted for content inclusion rather than edited exclusions.

The questions selected for each teacher are relatively generic, although some highlight circumstances unique to a specific teacher or teaching. Some questions selected were given as "teasers" in an attempt to urge readers to pursue further interests on their own. Other questions are quite esoteric. Many questions simply popped up during our dialogues. In some instances I asked the same questions of almost all teachers. I did this to serve those who approach the subject in a more comparative, analytical manner, and are keen to explore various forms of congruity. I also asked some of the same questions because of their broad subject appeal. Many more questions could have, and probably should have been asked, but then we would have fourteen books instead of one. If you feel drawn to do so, I encourage you to pursue additional lines of inquiry with teachers of your choosing. Please refer to the teacher-contact information provided. In some cases, we honor their desire not to have it published at this time.

It is with great joy that this fourteen course spiritual meal is presented for your consumption. Dig in and savor each morsel.

JOHN SHERMAN

I met John Sherman while attending a public lecture given by Gangaji, a respected female Western spiritual teacher. Gangaji invited John (pictured together above) to come before the audience and share his spiritual sojourn. What a truly amazing person John turned out to be! Sitting before us was a man who spent eighteen years in the Federal Prison system, and yet by some miracle was cajoling us with laughter, wit and exquisite spiritual presence. We were deeply moved by the experience. John's metamorphosis from the Ten Most Wanted List to a person filled with love and heart is not unlike a water-breathing amphibian crawling out of the water and being transformed into an air-breathing warm-blooded mammal.

In the mid-1990's, Gangaji started doing work with prisoners. As you will discover, John was resistant to Gangaji and what she was trying to do. However, through a fortuitous personal encounter with her, the obstructions to his true essence were directly penetrated and transcended. After meeting Gangaji, John wrote to her often which developed into a rich dialogue. She began sharing John's letters with participants who attended her public gatherings. The outpouring of love between John and Gangaji is an awesome example of the benevolence of grace. It was a few more years after John's initial meetings with Gangaji that he was finally released from prison.

I interviewed John in Novato, California, at Gangaji's administrative office where he was working at the time. Over the past few years, the Ganga River Foundation has been created to support John's work. John is actively teaching throughout the United States. He has recently written a book titled *Meetings with Ramana Maharshi: Conversations with John Sherman* that can be downloaded from his web site.

It's a great joy to share John's story with you.

ʒʘ·ʒʘ·ʒʘ

John, thank you very much for meeting with us this morning. You have such an incredible story to share. Where did you grow up, and how did it affect your overall perspective on life?

I grew up in Camden, New Jersey. I was born in 1942. I was a difficult child. You know, I have since come to the opinion that when I was about four years old, my grandmother began teaching me to read, using the Bible as a text. My grandmother was a Pentecostal Christian and quite fervent and enthusiastic in her religious beliefs. And when I was four she started teaching me to read using the gospels as a text. Since that time I have found it not so untrue to say that hearing the words of this teacher Jesus at that age, when the normal strategies for dealing with such extreme and outrageous demands that he calls upon us to meet, crippled me, ruined me for life.

You know, when you're four years old and you hear such things as, "Take no thought for your life," or "Love your neighbor as yourself," these lessons hit home, because the mind isn't formed enough to strategize and defend itself against the extremity of what he's saying. It may be that nothing else measures up, nothing in the world measures up to what he called upon us to embrace.

So in the time since meeting Gangaji I've often kind of reflected on what effect that had on me. I know that as a child, as a teenager, as an adult that nothing measured up. It was my continuous experience throughout life, that nothing was real, nothing was authentic enough to give one's life to.

As you grew up to be an adult and assumed more responsibility for different kinds of activity, you ran into some difficulty with the law. Can you give us some details of your life during this period of time and what happened as a result?

Well, you know from the beginning I found that I was always having difficulty with the law no matter what law it might have been. Like with everything else the rules and regulations seemed to have no basis in reality. And it's my sense that throughout this life I was honoring an idea that a life had to be lived to the fullest, and that something had to be found to which the life could be totally given. And certainly obeying the rules and regulations did not meet that criterion. So that from the beginning I ignored the rules, from the beginning I was in trouble. I was in trouble throughout school. I was finally expelled from high school in tenth grade.

Finally, in the late sixties, in 1968 I was arrested in Oregon for interstate transportation of a stolen car and I was sent directly to the penitentiary for three years. And in the penitentiary I found the thoughts of Marx and Lenin and Engels and the Communists and was quite taken by them and thought that I had found something that explained why the world was as crazy and as painful and as horrifying as it obviously was. And not only explained why it was that way but what could be done about it. The level of commitment necessary to play any role in this transformation of the world was total. So it seemed at that time to be exactly what I was looking for, something to which I could give my life without reservation.

When I was released from prison in 1971 I immediately began pursuing this ideology. Even in prison, I spent 18 months in the "hole" as a result of organizing a strike at McNeal Island, a federal prison in Seattle. And from that time on, for years my life was given over to finding a way to give myself completely to this idea, give myself completely to this activity. Clearly it was all I could see that held out the promise of transformation, that held out the promise of changing the world from a horror to a paradise.

One thing led to another. In 1975 I developed a friendship with a fellow named Ed at McNeal Island (penitentiary). He and I were kind of partners in this adventure. As time went on after we were released from prison our paths parted and I became much more dedicated to the orthodox Communist philosophies and the orthodox Communist ways of doing things. And it diverted into more craziness, more anarchistic "total-freedom" type of activities.

Radical political means to an end?
Yes, but without a strategy, plan or idea of what was to be done. In 1975 I was to meet Ed again. He had put a bomb in a Safeway store in Seattle, in a poor neighborhood.

For the purpose of . . . .
Well, he wasn't sure what the purpose was, that was the whole point. Safeway was a prime mover and into anti-union activities. And the farm workers struggle was also taking place at that time. So in his mind Safeway was a target and therefore any Safeway was fair game. But after this bomb exploded in a Safeway store that was in a poor neighborhood, and no one was hurt, just by luck, he began to see that there was something missing here. He finally came to me and asked me what I thought that he should be doing. I told him, well, if I was going to do something of this nature, I would probably—there was at that time a year long strike by the Electrical Workers Union in Seattle, the municipal electrical workers. They were out of money and were still holding fast and determined to continue. And I told him if I was going to do such a thing at all I would probably find the richest neighborhood in Seattle and shut off their lights and let them see to what extent they depended on these workers. One thing led to another and on New Year's Eve in 1975 I found myself crawling into a park in Laurelhurst, Seattle, which is a rich neighborhood, dragging a pipe bomb with another guy. And we did shut off the lights in that neighborhood and it was quite effective and quite successful.

Did you actually go to the power plant itself?
We just blew up the transformer that served this one neighborhood. And it was quite dramatic. We had called the police and the

police came out and set up barricades. The people in the neighborhood were out celebrating New Years. There was this huge explosion and it was all quite spectacular on TV. Of course the next morning they all woke up and had no hot water and no coffee and no toast and . . . .

No coffee after New Year's Eve—that's pretty tough! [Laughter]
Yes, that was pretty tough. And within a month or so the strike was settled. So there I was. I had been dissatisfied with what I was doing before. I now thought I had something to do that was true. Certainly we never had any thought of hurting anybody. Our view was that the destruction of property in support of struggles that are ongoing where the people already basically know where the problem is, could show them that there were other tactics that they could use besides the tactics that were imposed upon them by the law.

About a month after that bombing we had decided that we had to rob banks to keep ourselves going because, you know, you're doing this kind of stuff and you don't have the time or energy to work for a living. We were caught in the first bank robbery we ever did. I was shot and a friend of mine was killed in the bank. I was shot in the jaw. My mouth was wired closed for six weeks, and six weeks later on a trip to the hospital to get the wires removed, the people who were still remaining outside came and took me away from the authorities. A police officer was shot in the parking lot. I've spoken to him since and he thinks it's the best thing that ever happened to him. He got a medical retirement and owns an apple orchard in Walla Walla (Washington). At least twenty years ago when I last talked with him he was quite happy with his life.

This of course removed any possibility that I could see of extracting myself from this course that I had chosen. Too much had happened. Too much action had taken place. Too many consequences were in place. Although I have to say that it didn't take, as with everything I have tried in this life - it really didn't take any time at all to see that it was another dead-end. However, with this as with most of the activities that I've embraced in this life there is—once you take some action about something, then there's this web of cause and effect that you've enacted and this web of consequence and karma that you've hooked yourself up to. And it has to play out.

There's no way to short-circuit it; there's no way to do anything about it, it has to play out. You can add to it, you can be miserable while it's happening, you can suffer, but nevertheless the consequences have to play out.

So I spent the next two years as a fugitive with what remained of the group of people, robbing banks and blowing things up in the name of freedom and justice. About two years after that escape I was caught again and went through several extremely highly visible media trials.

What did you get caught doing after two years into it again?

We were charged with an eighteen-count conspiracy indictment that involved all of the banks, all of the bombings and the escape. We had a possible sentence of two hundred eighty years. We represented ourselves with attorney advisors. By the time the trial was over the jury recommended that we not go to prison. And the judge sentenced me to twenty years. At a subsequent trial I was sentenced to an thirty years, but not an additional thirty years, thirty years to run along with the twenty years. And when the trials were over I married the woman who was the court appointed investigator for the defense in the Federal courthouse.

That's an ironic twist.

Yes. We went to Lompoc, California to the prison at Lompoc to begin this sentence. We had already decided that I would escape. We were not going to stay there. So I think four months after I got to Lompoc I escaped with the help of my wife at the time. This time they put me on the "Ten Most Wanted" list. We ended up in Denver, where I worked for a company called Sunstrand, which is a big aerospace manufacturer. I am a journeyman machinist and was able to find work there. After about six months of working there, I found myself dealing with the machinist union trying to bring a union into that plant in the midst of real anti-union sentiment. Denver at the time was a real anti-union area. I eventually got fired for union activity. We filed with the national labor relations board. I found myself in the strange position of going down to the Federal Building to attend hearings with the NLRB in the same building where the FBI had me on the "Ten Most Wanted List."

Eventually, through a story that's complicated and beside the point, they caught me in Denver after two years. I pleaded guilty to escape and the judge gave me a five-year concurrent sentence, which added nothing to my time. This time I went to Marion (penitentiary) which was at the time known as the "New Alcatraz." I began a sentence that was to be fourteen years before meeting Gangaji.

Marion is located in Illinois?

Yes. I was at Marion for about a year and a half and then went through all the other penitentiaries. The Federal system has gradations of security levels. The penitentiaries are the highest and then there are FCI's and camps. I never made it to a camp. And I have since thought of that fourteen years as a time when all of the remaining misunderstandings about where satisfaction can be found, whether in status or position, or pleasure were worn away, kind of abraded away against the wall of no possibility of satisfying. I spent that time involved in the same kind of intrigues and nonsense that prisoners get themselves involved in. It was all just mind seeking to make itself necessary, seeking to make itself something.

By the time I met Gangaji, I had found a state of despair so profound that I did not even think of it as despair. I thought of it as clear seeing. It had become quite obvious to me that life was a false promise, that the universe was structured in such a way as to grind us into the dirt and cause pain and misery. And that there was no escape from that. Nor was there any hope of mitigating it.

So a real deep sense of hopelessness.

Hopelessness yes, but I was happy for it. It was like now finally I see things clearly. It's all garbage, all meaningless, all foolishness.

But it didn't lead you to become suicidal and want to end your life?

No. It didn't. It was something more profound than that. There was no point in ending the life; there was no point in continuing life. I saw myself as waiting either for the sentence to be over or the life to be over and it really didn't matter much to me which it was, or so I thought.

At that point in time did you feel that some kind of "spiritual awakening" had taken place?

No, in fact I would have said the opposite. I would have said that all of the spiritual practices, and all of the ideas about God were the biggest false promise of all, that they are stories we tell each other to divert our attention from the essential hopelessness and misery of life. They were obviously that, and there was no point looking into them any further.

Then what happened?

I had no interest in spiritual practice at that time.

How long had you been in prison at that point?

Fourteen years. That was in 1993 and I was in the fourteenth year. And actually, as I said, I saw my state as being a clear seeing. You know it's interesting. Herman Hesse said something. He says that any attempt to live a life that's true and virtuous must lead to despair. He says that children live on one side of that despair, and the awakened live on the other. This is, I think, the despair that he's talking about. It is a despair that doesn't even look like despair.

So you hadn't been reading anything that had to do with the "spirit" or done any spiritual activity at all?

Nothing.

Were you a reader? Did you go to the library?

I was an addicted reader for all of my life. I read philosophy. It had come to my attention, interestingly, that it seemed like all of the philosophers eventually ended up with God, no matter how they made it appear, no matter how it looked. Nevertheless it was clear that they ended up with this unspeakableness. And I thought that was just an indication of their misunderstanding, their weakness.

I've told this story pretty often, but I'm going to tell it one more time. In September of 1993, a friend of mine came to me and said there was a spiritual teacher coming into the chapel by the name of Gangaji. He described her to me a little bit and gave me some indication of what she was about, this beautiful American woman, Southern woman, and asked me if I wanted to come. It seemed exotic. It seemed like it might be entertaining, some way to spend a couple of hours. So I said, sure, I'll come.

On the day she came to Englewood, which was her second visit, I was on my way to the chapel to see her, to entertain myself with some cynicism and the usual pursuits of mind. And as I was walking across the upper compound, I without warning was struck with a terror so huge that I couldn't move. I couldn't even stand; I had to sit down on a bench. It's tempting to connect this terror with her visit. I actually have no sense that it had any connection with anything, but nevertheless it happened as she was entering the prison. I could barely breathe; my heart was pounding; I was sweating; I couldn't stand. I knew that I was going to die. And in the knowing that I was going to die I discovered that maybe I wasn't quite so blasé about the idea of dying as I had thought myself to be. I didn't go. I couldn't go anywhere.

I sat there for awhile, and as time went by the experience of terror began to subside as experiences always do. Again the mind began operating as it does with its strategies to handle such an overwhelming occurrence, explain it, deny it, "Oh that wasn't really so bad, it's O.K. now." By the time the meeting with her was finished, I was O.K. I had already gone a long way toward forgetting the whole episode and burying it wherever we bury these things. My friend came to me and said, "What happened to you?" and I said "Oh I had something better to do."

I'm sure there was some story I was telling to explain why I was doing this but I don't recall what it was. Eventually I found myself going to the Tibetan Buddhists, the people from Naropa, from Trungpa Rinpoche.

Did they have a prison program?

Yes. They were coming into Englewood every week. I found, quite to my utter surprise, that what they were teaching I already knew.

At some fundamental level?

Yes, that I already knew it, that it was some pre-existing fundamental pool of knowledge, of knowing that was being tapped by this teaching but that knowing was always present. I was profoundly affected by it and the people who were coming in saw this to be the case.

They brought in a Tibetan Llama who gave me refuge in Bodisattva vows. It was obvious to me then that I was a Buddhist and that I had always been a Buddhist and that "Ah, one more time, this is it!" I became quite a rigorous and devoted practitioner of Buddhist meditation techniques. I became quite proud of my experiences in this pursuit.

And at the same time, for reasons that I can't imagine now, I was also going to the people who were bringing Gangaji videos into the prison. They were also coming in every week. When I would watch these videos, I had a deep sense that I knew this woman, that I had known her for some time. It wasn't spiritual or romantic or anything like that. It was more as if I hadn't seen somebody for ten or twenty years and then saw them in some unexpected context, I might very well recognize them, their phrasing, their gestures, the way they carried themselves without being able to place them. And given my background it didn't bode really well for her that I thought that she was someone I had run across in the past.

I was deeply of the opinion that she was a fraud. I didn't know what she was up to, but obviously what she was saying was foolishness, was poison. And I would tell the men who attended those meetings that this woman is a fraud, pay her no mind, she's poison. I would speak to them at some length about how the Buddhists have been at this for 2,500 years and they know what they're doing. It takes a lifetime, or lifetimes of devoted, rigorous, careful meditation practice to weaken and make fragile a mind that is so strong and so shaped by ancient conditioning and ancient habits of behavior and reaction. It takes this time, it takes these practices, it takes this technique in order to weaken it enough that the truth can break through.

And here this woman comes in and says that you need do nothing. That you are what you seek. This is foolishness. Don't listen to her. Stay away from her. And when they would come in, Dyanand was the name of the man who was coming in from Gangaji, he would bring a Gangaji videotape and I would say, "Not another fucking Gangaji tape!" [Laughter]

And somehow - and neither she nor I nor Dyanand to this day know what caused him to do this, but he would go to her and tell her there's this man in Englewood that you've got to meet, his name is John. And I didn't know this. All I knew was that I despised her, not despised her, I didn't have that much feeling about her at all except that she was wrong.

She wasn't a Buddhist in the traditional sense of the word. . . .

Not a Buddhist. She was scheduled to visit in June of 1994, six months after I was unable to go see her. By that time the guy who had initially invited me to see her, and who had been the prisoner liaison between the chapel administration and all the Eastern spiritual types, was transferred to another institution. By whatever mechanism these things happen, I found myself in his role. When it was time for her to come into the prison again, it was I who was responsible for setting it up with the chapel, making the arrangements, and informing the people in the prison when she was coming. I did so.

The night she was to come, all the men who were going to meet with her had gone into the chapel. I was waiting outside the chapel. I was leaning against a wrought-iron table that was bolted to the concrete that people can sit at. I was leaning against this table waiting for her and her entourage to show up so I could explain to them what the arrangements were. I kind of wanted to get this done with because I had other things to do. I had no intention of going to the meeting.

She came in and there's a long sidewalk that they have to walk down to get from the administration building to the chapel. And I saw her and her group walking down the sidewalk. She walked up to me and she took my hand and she looked into my eyes and she said, "You must be John." And everything stopped. All the strategies, all the opinions, all the movement of the mind stopped. [John paused briefly as he looked at a picture of Gangaji on his desk] I'm looking at her picture here. So of course I accompanied her in and sat with her for that two hours. And during that whole time nothing happened. Nothing moved. And when she was finished she went around and was talking with some of the prisoners, and I went up to her and said, "You know I always hated your video tapes." And she laughed and said, "Yeah I know, they told me."

A little while later she was talking to another friend of mine and I was standing there just watching her and my friend had said to her, "You know I feel like I've known you from somewhere." They talked as you will in a case like that to see where their paths might have crossed and concluded that it was unlikely. And when they finished that conversation I said to her, "You know, I too have always thought that I've known you." And she spun on me and looked at me and she said, "Of course you do. This love cannot be denied." Then she asked me to write to her. Then she left and I walked down the sidewalk with her. There's a place you come to where the outside people go one way and you go the other way back into the main institution. She put her hand on my heart and she said, "Always." Then she left and I felt like my heart had been torn out of my chest. If I had known how, I would have wailed.

I started writing to her. The first letter I wrote to her she read in Marin. It was a very long letter. And I told her how I was torn apart, I was torn asunder. I would talk to her picture. I paced the cell. I couldn't eat, I couldn't sleep. A friend of mine, Kenny Johnson, who you may have heard of, took care of me during that period. I was really unsuited for prison life. I couldn't get myself to where I was supposed to be and do the things I was supposed to do, the little simple things you have to do in prison. And Kenny would come and make sure I got to where I was supposed to go and got to the mess hall. He took care of me for that time. He later said he was really pissed and jealous that he had spent all these years meditating and I hadn't even wanted it and "got it."

I wrote her almost every day. She read my letters all over the world. She was travelling more in those days than she is now. And people got to know who "John" was and I started receiving letters from people. She came in September again and I saw her then. When she left in September it would be three and a half years before I'd see her again. I was transferred to Florence.

That's in Colorado?

That's also in Colorado.

Is that a minimum-security prison?

It's a medium security prison. Those three and a half years; you know Papaji (Gangaji's teacher) has said that "inquiry" stirs the snakes. And Gangaji has spoken often of how when the mind is finally humiliated and brought to its knees that the demons come. And they come to be free. They are your children; they are your self. And so all of the

ancient tendencies, the ancient sufferings, the ancient misunderstandings, the ancient masks that we wear, that we pretend to be, come in full
force to be seen, to be released, to be set free. And this life, its nature,
produced a lot of demon masks. So that three and a half years was just
the right amount of time. It was just exactly perfect for all that had to
be seen to be seen, all that had to be recognized and acknowledged to
be recognized and acknowledged. And I don't want to give the impression that there's some process involved in this. That's not the case. I
said they "have to be seen," but that's not really true.

*They just spontaneously arose, as if on a lit stage and paraded in front
of the audience. You were there to observe that.*
   And to be caught up in it and to suffer in it.

*And you had support there through your letter writing I would sus-
pect? In some sense you received some kind of feedback from. . . .*
   Not for a single nanosecond was she ever absent.

During that time?
   During that time. There was a time I have to say that I would have
given anything never to have met her.

It was excruciating then at various points in time?
   I would have given anything never to have met her. And that did-
n't help! [Laughter]

*You said during that time she was "always with you," not only in terms
of her feedback from letters, but also in some sense in your heart?*
   She was always with me. That's right. She was never absent. The
letters are one aspect of her presence, but actually the letters are the
least of it. The truth is she is your Self. There is nothing other than
your Self. And how that is ignored is the great mystery. The truth is
not a mystery. Reality is not a mystery. This is permanently present.
The mystery is that we can deny it and ignore it. So that she, as her, as
Self, as nothing, was never absent in the entire time. She's not absent
now. She's never been absent, not even throughout the life.

So at some point you must have felt like the demons, or the stuff that was coming up, the tendencies and so forth - that you really didn't know what they were, but they were feeling pretty excruciating. Did it reach a point, a critical mass that allowed you to move past it or to transcend it or have it revealed to you what that actually was?

My actual sense of it John, is that there is this story that plays in mind that has to do with what is done in order for this to be finished with. But it's just a story.

Yes.

The truth is that there is nothing to them at all. There's nothing to the story either. It's all thought. It's all made up. And saying that, I will say also that I can remember times when I would sit on my bed in Florence holding this thought, this experience of a "me." And like a mantra, I would say over and over again, "die," "die," "die." And then there came a point in this incredibly dramatic story that I had managed to give myself to, when in an instant it became obvious that it wasn't going to die. The truth was that there is no escape. That there's no escape from hell. And in that moment, in the moment of seeing that nothing is going to change, hell was not going to go away, ego is not going to die, in that moment—I laughed, I howled with laughter at how ridiculous I was, at how arrogant.

So it was in the total acceptance of that revelation that the hellishness of the ego and everything that you had seen from that level was in a sense not going to go away by fighting against it? It was a form of total acceptance then?

Yes that's right—and not a problem.

And not making it a problem. And in that sense the actual drama was seen for "what it is."

That's right, which is just a story. And one of the most predacious stories that we tell ourselves is the spiritual story, the spiritual melodrama.

Help us get into that a little bit more.

The very idea that there is someone here who is caught up in suffering, who has found the key to being released from suffering, that idea itself is ego. That idea itself is the problem that is not a problem at all. When we become spiritually inclined, then we construct and concoct, we kind of bring in the whole sphere of spiritual story-telling that has developed over the 2,500-3,000 years that human beings have been talking about these things and writing about these things. And we bring the whole thing in and we are sinners, and we have to do something in order to be free of our sin, and the consequences of our sin. We have to cleanse ourselves, purify ourselves, kill ego. There's such a wide range of ways in which to tell this story. But it all comes down to the same thing, and that is: there's something I have to do in order to be free. This is the spiritual melodrama. And that somehow it will be revealed to me, somewhere, what it is that I actually have to do to be free.

Some technique, some process, some method. . . .

That's right, some technique, some process, some method, some magic, some transmission, some initiation—something has to happen in order for me to be free. This, of course, is only the strategy of mind that says, "I am something about which something needs to be done." You know, there's nothing to mind except survival, except survival of mind. That's all it does. Everything it does is to that end.

And it's incredibly pernicious in its desire to maintain its own existence.

That's right. And its existence is absurd. And the truth is that you are always and forever free. That's the truth. You've never, ever not been free. Not for the slightest hair's breadth of time have you ever not been free. All that is ever going on is lies, stories that say I am not free.

Coming from the mind.

It is mind. The truth is there's nothing but mind. Even the most profound, the most subtle, the most spacious spiritual experiences, awakening experiences are only mind. How can they be anything else? Quite clearly the seer of all of this cannot be seen, cannot be experienced. The vast, simple, plain truth of who you are cannot be experienced. So that the whole business surrounding the spiritual melodrama is mind. It's making something of experience, of experience that comes and goes. Hell comes and goes. The experience of hell comes and goes. The experience of heaven comes and goes. The experience of awakening comes and goes. The experience of "Oh, this huge opening and emptiness" comes and goes. And Gangaji has said often, "it's not reliable."

Is there any practical function, then, to the mind?
Why, yes, the whole universe is the mind. [Laughter]

Talk about the ultimate practicality!
The whole universe is mind. How could it be anything else? And it seems, you know, this too is a story, but if there's anything to it, it's love. If there's anything to it, it's the impossibility of being not to experience itself in the context of the impossibility of the "One" to experience itself. There cannot be the experience of Self unless there's a "you" and a "me." It's not possible. And yet experienced as "you" and "me," it cannot be the truth. This is the heart of the paradox and the energy that gives rise to all of it.

So it's almost like the impossibility of the eye seeing itself.
That's right. That's exactly right. And yet the impossibility for the eye not to see itself. There's nothing to it; there's nothing to Being except this desire to see, to touch.

To know itself.
To know, to love. It's love. Not love as the weak metaphor of human love is to this ruthless uncompromising, unconditional love of Self. Of love. And I don't know whether that counts as practicality, but it seems to me that's the energy of Being, that's the energy of existence. Nothing's excluded from that, including our inclination as individuals to be children of the lie and to suffer in the belief that we are individuals. That we are something separate. That too. Just more ways in which Self can experience itself.

So nothing is excluded from this, high or low, good or bad. It's all-inclusive then.
Yes. There's nothing. There's nothing but love.

If you were to go back and give us the contrast between how you saw the world before you met Gangaji and had this revelation, and how you perceive reality now, what would it look like? Maybe there's some analogy or metaphor or something that comes to mind just in reflecting directly on what your experience was.

You know that's an interesting question. It's a good question. It's very difficult because in a sense nothing has changed. I think that's what I was getting at. It's also true that nothing will ever be the same.

It reminds me of a Zen story where the Zen monk said, "Before enlightenment I saw the mountains as mountains, and afterwards I saw the mountains as mountains."

That's right. Yes, and in between he saw the mountains as shining, huge vast open space, and then he saw mountains and rivers as mountains and rivers. The difference is that if there's a difference— Ramana says in an often quoted and often overlooked powerful statement—he says, "The only thing standing between you and Self-realization is the belief that you are not already realized." So if there is a difference, that belief has disappeared. You are Self just as you are. The truth is: Nothing needs to be changed. Nothing needs to be kept from changing.

It seems like the belief you previously held about reality got translated, and that it was revealed to you over time. But in a way it never really took place in time.

That's right.

You went through sort of the "dark night of the soul;" you met the snakes and all of those "shadows" that were moving in some way, and they may not necessarily have been "real" in terms of what it is that was making those shadows, but. . . .

Of course they're not real, but they are real as shadows. And shadows are a good metaphor for them. It's that which seems to block the light. And the interesting thing about shadows is that if you are caught in the shadow, then there's nothing but shadow. But if you just for a moment see it as "shadow," then it absolutely indicates the existence of the Light. Because there cannot be shadow without Light. So the shadows persist. So what?

But in some way they are also revealing and confirming the fact that there is Light.
Yes, that's right. And so what? Who can be hurt by shadows? [Laughter]

Yes, that's good. That completely destroys the "belief" then.
Yes, that's right.

I want to switch gears a little bit and then go back to what we have been discussing here in just the last few minutes. If I were a prisoner right now, what would your message be to me?
I would say to you, "You are already and forever free." And somehow life has unfolded for you to produce a circumstance in which . . . this business of imprisonment is a huge gift. It is an unbelievable gift. We are placed in prison; even the idea that anything we do has any meaning is denied and suppressed by the ones who run the prison. The idea that we are individuals is denied and suppressed. The idea that there's anything we need to do is denied and suppressed. The gift of imprisonment is huge. It's like a monastery. You don't have to be concerned about feeding yourself or clothing yourself, or finding shelter from the weather. There is nothing worth doing in life other than discovering the truth of who you are. And in prison you're placed in a circumstance where that's encouraged. You are already and forever free. Whether to prisoners or to "prisoners of whatever stripe," you know the mind is the prison. The mind is the bars. And the mind which is nothing cannot be found upon investigation.

Even corporate executives could be in the same situation, that is, being imprisoned but within their own context . . . .
And the only thing that needs to be seen is that there's nothing that needs to be seen. There's nothing to get. There's nothing to do. Just to stop. Just to be finished with looking anywhere for anything that you think you need. And you are free in this moment to do that. This is perhaps the only choice. The universe knows nothing of choice. The uni-

verse is a web of cause and effect that is universal from which nothing escapes. The universe can't know anything of choice. You, perhaps, have one choice in life, and that's the choice to stop. To just stop, stop looking, stop searching, stop doing. And in that choice, when news of that choice breaks into the universe, the whole universe rejoices.

Can you make a few comments on the current prison system and challenges that need to be overcome?

I don't think there's anything that needs to be overcome anywhere. You know, I have a very hard time with things like that. The universe is like a "given." The universe that includes the prisons as they are, and the political systems as they are is a "given." I have no interest in looking at what needs to be done to anything in particular in the world of circumstance. I know from deep personal experience that all that ever has to happen is to stop doing that. That's a misunderstanding.

That's quite a switch between what you did before when you were thinking that you may want to reform the world as a Communist or someone working within the Union system.

It seems that way, like quite a change, but . . . .

It's sort of a realization of the misunderstandings of those kinds of perspectives . . . .

But really it's not quite that. Gangaji talks a lot about how difficult it is to speak of these things. And it's not quite that because—"you are," "I am" nothing whatsoever, nothing in particular, nothing that has enacted any kind of strategies or philosophies or ideas whatever. These things take place within "who you are." So that I can't say that I ever thought anything should be done. There certainly was a story running about this in which I somehow got believed to be "me."

You identified with it.

Yes, I said, "That's me." And there's a common metaphor for these things that have these kinds of thoughts. This core thought, the core assumption that is the only one that really needs to be brought to question is the assumption that "I am something." And what seems to happen is that thought appears that is so exquisitely rendered to look and feel like what we imagine Self looks and feels. So exquisitely, so perfectly rendered. It's the most perfect thought in the universe. Somehow the energy of identification says, "Oh, that's me!" In some traditions the "I" thought is called a mirror because it perfectly mimics the "feel" that we expect Self to feel like. So all of this goes on, but has nothing to do with me. It had nothing to do with me then. The only thing was, then I thought it did. Then there was this belief.

That misidentification.
   Yes.

I want to move on to the Prison Programs that are currently being done by the Gangaji Foundation. Can you tell us a little bit about what's happening with that and what your role and responsibility has been? I know that the Foundation received a private grant recently.
   I actually have little involvement with the prison program now. I'll tell you about the grant. It was a fluke that I was involved with that. However, the Foundation, the person who coordinates the Prison Program is in Boulder. And we send books and videos and audios to a number of prisons all over the country. We visit prisons in California and in Colorado, and write and correspond to many prisoners. There has been a number of prisoners who have awakened in this meeting with Gangaji. Very beautifully. A Foundation, just by sheer coincidence, was looking for places where they could give money to spiritual programs that operate in prisons and found us by our website. Just by sheer coincidence the woman who was involved in that called and I answered the phone. She told me what she wanted and I met with her. In the response to that, we decided that we would love to have some money and we would love to expand the prison program to this extent. We don't have a lot of interest in affirmatively or aggressively reaching out. We have nothing to give people. We have no belief on anything to give them. And it is our continuous experience that people come. That they draw themselves, somehow. But we decided that we would like to announce to every prisoner in the country, if it were possible, just the simple good news that you already and forever free. And see what happens when such an outrageous statement is made.

We designed a plan for beginning to do just that; beginning to do mailings to the prisoners through the chapels of just this simple message that you are already free, permanently, completely. Unconditionally free. We submitted that plan and ended up with a $20,000 grant with which this program will begin, I think, the first of August (1999). We hired a part-time staff member in Boulder to administer this program. And we'll see what happens.

You are now holding your own Satsangs in the Bay Area. Please share with us what your experience has been in taking on this activity.

My experience is that in the first place I've resisted this for the last year that I've been out of prison. And finally Gangaji came to me not long ago because people had been asking. She said to me, "Well, you must do this. You must do this as much as you can, as much as you have physical energy for." Thereby removing all of my resistances, all of my foolishness about it.

My experience in it is that I do this because she told me to. That's not entirely true. Really I have no idea why I do this. But her telling me to provides some resting-place for the mind so it doesn't have to go through all of its usual activities in explaining it. My experience is that in Satsang, and I have elected not to call it Satsang—but in these meetings, in these conversations with people, it is I who am the recipient, it is I who am receiving everything there is to receive. That there is such peacefulness and such a beauty when people come together in the acknowledgement and the recognition that there is nothing but love, that there is no "other." Never has been. As far as what I find myself saying to people, my experience is that I have never said anything that was the least useful or clear to anybody at anytime. And yet here I am speaking still with you, with whoever wants to meet with me.

If there were one summary message that you'd like to leave us with this morning about realizing the truth in this lifetime, what would it be?

Stop. Stop. Stop. Stop believing that you don't realize the Truth. The Truth is ever present. It's permanently here. It can't be missed. It takes just one instant of stopping your looking. And then you will see that That, what you have been searching for, is always here. You will immediately recognize it. It is instantly recognizable as that Presence which is permanently present. So stop.

John, thank you very much for meeting with us and congratulations on your recent marriage. I understand you're a married man of 30 days now?

Maybe six weeks, June 9th.

We wish you all the best.

That's another thing. We were just taken in that. We had nothing to do with that.

We very much appreciate your time, and wish you all the best and hopefully we'll be able to get with you sometime in the future and get some updates on what's happening with you and the Self.

O.K. Nothing's happening I can tell you that. [Laughter]

Contact information:

John Sherman
www.riverganga.org

AUDREY KITAGAWA

I was first introduced to Audrey Kitagawa through What is Enlightenment? magazine's web site. As soon as I saw a short video interview with Audrey conducted at the 2004 World Parliament of Religions in Spain, I knew I wanted to share more of her with everyone. Audrey is an incredible blend of attorney, spiritual teacher and humanitarian.

Audrey met Flora Nomi, known as "Divine Mother" in Hawaii before attending law school. Audrey said of Divine Mother, "Though she rarely left her kitchen, she was a God-realized being." In 1996, Audrey gave up her law practice to fulfill a request Divine Mother made of her shortly before she passed away in May, 1992. She chose Audrey to lead the spiritual family that had grown around Divine Mother.

In addition to spiritual work, Audrey is an Advisor to the Office Of The Special Representative Of The Secretary General For Children And Armed Conflict at the United Nations*, and is a member of several organizations that focus on spirituality, consciousness transformation, and pathways to peace. Please enjoy Audrey as she takes us on a wonderful journey through the depths of householder practicality, spiritual wisdom and love that she so beautifully embodies through her presence. This interview was conducted May 12, 2005.

಄ ಄ ಄

Thank you Audrey for spending time with us today. We are honored to have the opportunity to speak with you.
Thank you, John.

Can you briefly share with us what major events took place that led you to become a spiritual teacher?
Shortly before my spiritual master left her body in May of 1992, she chose me to carry on with her works, and to lead the spiritual family which had grown around her over the years. She asked me to carry Sri Ramakrishna's Light to the world for her.

Sri Ramakrishna was an Avatar, who lived a brief life in India from 1836-1886. He was a forerunner to the interfaith and multi-faith movements which are becoming more prevalent today, and taught that we must respect the various pathways to the Divine. He demonstrated through his own life, that through one's intense love and devotion to God, one could attain to God Realization.

Divine Mother said that the teacher and the student is in the human plane, and that is not the level at which she was in relationship to us. Rather, she said she worked with the Light, and she was transmitting directly to us, "spirit to spirit, heart to heart, infinite to infinite and not mind to mind." Therefore, she was not communicating with us in the dialogic modality that implies a dualistic state, but rather, was transmitting to us from the seamless, undivided One.

How would you characterize your connection with Ramakrishna? Do you have any direct affiliation with his organization?

Sri Ramakrishna is my Chosen Ideal, and Divine Mother pointed our hearts to Him, as representing and embracing the Wholeness of the Divine, while simultaneously acknowledging and respecting the various pathways that lead to the Divine.

Divine Mother gave us what she called the "liberal doctrine," and freed us from rituals so we could move directly to our hearts in the cultivation of our love and devotion to God. Her transmissions were spontaneous, endless outpourings of the most powerful expositions on the Divine that I was privileged to hear.

Our spiritual family has no direct or formal affiliation with his organizations.

Is there anything you can recall that happened during your childhood that would translate into what we could refer to as a "spiritual experience"? Some people had some wonderful experiences early on, and for others nothing happened until later on in their lives.

I've had many spiritual experiences along the way from early childhood. It would take a long time to tell you about them. I'll just select one. I was a shy, withdrawn child. I did not have an outgoing, bubbly personality. I cried at the drop of a hat, and was uncomfortable around those who were not in my immediate family. I admired children who could join the Brownies or Girl Scouts, and freely participate in group activities. I dreaded the thought of having to attend parties, events, or even go to school. Changes did not sit well with me, and I liked the certainty of familiar faces and routines.

By the time I reached the sixth grade, I was still in the same condition, and facing a lot of anxiety about having to attend an upcoming orientation to acquaint us with the new intermediate school some of us would have to attend. I did not relish the thought of being with new students, new teachers, and on a new campus, all in one fell swoop.

It was recess, and I was standing outside of the classroom under the eaves of a covered outdoor corridor. My teacher was to my right and was busy talking to another student. I was filled with anxiety, thinking about this upcoming orientation, and thought to myself, "Am I going to be this way for the rest of my life?" Suddenly, I shot out of my body and in microseconds went through these rapid transformations and shot back into my body. It was a completely unexpected, spontaneous, quick experience. I knew I had come back into my body a different person. My worldview had been transformed from a closed perspective, to an expansive, open one. Life was no longer filled with anxiety and fear, but rather was now filled with a sense of wonderment and adventure.

Suddenly, I looked forward to going to a new school, and meeting new students and teachers. I couldn't wait to see if other people had witnessed what had happened to me. I looked around. It seemed as if everything had continued on as if nothing had happened. The teacher was still talking to the student. No one seemed to even know that I had undergone a most remarkable experience. I couldn't wait to go home because I wanted to see if my family could see the change in me. When I got home, everyone just continued on with their regular business, and no one seemed to notice that I was different.

However, not too long ago my mother was sitting with me at her kitchen table and said, "You know, I could never understand how a 'nakimiso' like you, (which is slang for 'crybaby' in Japanese), ever became a lawyer." (Laughter)

This was an intensely personal, internal experience which I did not share with my family or anyone else at that time, but it changed my life, how I embraced it, perceived it, and moved through it. I call that whole experience the Grace of God. I firmly believe that God's Grace flows to us in unexpected, mysterious and wondrous ways.

So it was really an internal experience you had that over time developed as you matured, and became a very big part of your presence, your essence and how you have showed up in the world.

It changed an inner core within me instantaneously. I was transformed from a closed, shy and anxious person to one who now saw life as a beautiful, unfolding adventure that was not to be feared. I welcomed life rather than receded from it. This happened in microseconds. It was something I did not expect, and could not have planned. It arose out of the question, "Am I going to be this way for the rest of my life?"

That was a key question wasn't it? A major inquiry!

It was a serious inquiry, and the Grace of God instantly responded.

What do you feel is the most important thing people should know about you and what you do as a spiritual teacher?

It's not so important what people should know about me. Everyone should understand that their lives are precious and each person is traveling on a sacred journey. The journey is filled with challenges, but God is always with us. Each person should get to know him/herself more intimately, and embrace life with equanimity and courage. We are here to realize our eternal union with the Divine, and to deepen our hearts with compassion, love and understanding for ourselves and others. Divine Mother often said that where we are is the holy ground, and we must find God here.

Since God is love, we actualize the Divine by living love, and being that love itself in our daily thoughts, speech and conduct. We mustn't think that God is far away in a heavenly abode out of our present reach. God is everywhere around us presenting His myriad of forms in the eternal here and now so we can learn how to become that love itself, whether through selfless service, speaking kindly to your spouse, lending a listening ear to someone in distress, respecting our environment, forgiving someone who has hurt you. The ways in which we can put love in action daily are numerous, and each little action, like a constant drop of water on a rock, will eventually carve the rock.

Neither Sri Ramakrishna nor Divine Mother believed in calling anyone a "sinner," or focusing the consciousness on "sin," and all of the ramifications which that word conjures up. At my very first meeting with Divine Mother, she said to me, "You are a perfect child of God, immortal, eternal, and already in God's Light." She wanted to stabilize our consciousness in that Divine Reality.

In the Self-discovery process, are there any techniques, tools or spiritual practices in developing or deepening enlightenment? How does it come about?

The longing of the heart to know God ripens you to experience God, and draws the necessary assistance to help you along the way.

We've often heard the phrase, "When the student is ready, the teacher appears." I believe in this, and experienced this. A true teacher will always direct you back to your Self. I feel very privileged to have been with an enlightened master. Divine Mother always said, "The true Guru is within you, the Kingdom of God is within you. All of the infinite wisdom, scriptures, knowledge and wealth are already within you. God, Who makes your heart beat, is within you the closest of all." This was her way of pointing us back to ourselves that we may cultivate a direct relationship with God Who is already within us.

Daily meditation helps us to focus and point the mind within. It is important that we set aside this quiet time. Being in the company of spiritual people can help to elevate the mind toward higher purposes. Practicing daily, loving thoughts, speech and conduct will also make you a better person. Being a sincere seeker after God will surely bring forth God's Grace. Divine Mother said, "You can till the soil, and till the soil, but in the end, it is the Grace of God."

We hear the term "enlightenment" bantered around so much now days. How would you define enlightenment, and why does there seem to be so much confusion about the term? From your perspective is there a difference between having an "awakening" and true "enlightenment?

We have moments where veils are lifted, and those moments of awakening become milestones in our spiritual growth and awareness. These milestones become stepping stones toward our ultimate goal, which is God Realization. The God realized person is said to be "enlightened," and is permanently freed from the veils of ignorance.

When I was in my first year of law school, I had a very beautiful spiritual experience, a visitation from the living Christ. The living Christ is the Christ Consciousness which is the Consciousness of Illumination. What I experienced in this visitation was an unspeakable love. It was so perfect, so exquisitely beautiful. There are really no words in any language that can describe the magnitude and beauty of God's love. I was filled with that love. I was shown that even though the Christ Consciousness is right here with us, people are often unaware of its presence, and they go about their daily lives oblivious to it. My master likened it to being in the state of a "sleeping zombie." So we are walking around, unaware that this magnificent, perfect love and light are all around us, within us, ever-present, and the essence of who we are.

Yes, and it's getting in touch with this presence that seems to be important. Currently there is quite a bit of discussion about the apparent divide between the spiritual and the material, heaven and earth, nirvana and samsara. In many instances people who identify themselves as "spiritual" have a hard time relating fully to the world. Historically they have used various means of disassociating themselves from the world through marginalizing or trivializing worldly, material, bodily existence, and tend to get stuck in absolutism. On the other hand, another part of society remains essentially narcissistic and nihilistic about material life. They appear to have lost their connection with the vast spiritual context that holds, and transcends material existence. Help us understand what there is to know about the dynamics involved, and how a more holistic perspective can be realized?

When Swami Vevikananda came to the West and saw its material wealth, he inherently understood that we must learn how to merge the great spiritual traditions and teachings of the East with the material progress of the West. We must be able to strike a balance: being in the world, but not of it. Being clothed in the body, but knowing in the back of it that the reality of who we are is not the body. Being surrounded by the material, but not attaching to it. Attachment causes suffering because we want to hold onto what is inherently impermanent as if it is permanent. And, everything in creation changes, so we are in a constant dynamic flux in the material world.

In creation, we also confront the pairs of opposites, the good, the bad, the happy, the sad, the positive, the negative, the male, the female, and so forth. The two hemispheres of the physical brain is the physical manifestation of the dual nature of the mind. Yet, God is beyond the mind and thoughts.

The great masters impart to us the universal truths to stabilize our consciousness in the Divine while we go about our daily lives. It is difficult for householders because we have children, we work, we live in society, we are constantly immersed in relationships, and carry the concerns of family, and livelihood. Divine Mother said she came for the householders, who carry all of these burdens and need to know how to move through life with their consciousness firmly centered on God.

Her own life was a prime example of how one can attain to enlightenment while living as a householder. She was married, and had five children. She was a housewife, and only had an eighth grade education. She fulfilled completely her duties and responsibilities as a wife, mother, and grandmother. From a young age, she was prayerful, committed to spiritual practices and disciplines, and endured many hardships. She said she had to suffer to have compassion for others. She was chosen to be that pure vessel of transmission of Divine love. People came from all over to experience the nectar of this love.

When one cultivates love and devotion to God first, all things are given, including the holistic perspective you mentioned because you are united with that unified field of consciousness from which we all arise.

Some people say that there is only God and thus the material world is also God. It's the flip side of the coin of God as absolute which appears as relative. Some people have referred to it as "non-dual multiplicity" where both are present at the same time and recognized as God in its completeness and totality. In that sense, nothing is missing.

Nothing is ever missing. However, in the beginning stages you have to discriminate, "neti neti" ("not this, not this") the Real from the unreal. The spiritual masters help you to understand where your focus should be. They equip you with various tools that are appropriate for you. Along the way it is up to the individual to utilize the tools, and to do the spiritual practice with sincerity. However long it may take, we are ultimately going to end up in the same place by whatever path we have traveled to get there. We are all evolving back to the Godhead.

What message would you have for seekers who have struggled with awakening and enlightenment for years or possibly decades, and have mostly experienced a series of major disappointments along the way leading to a feeling of hopelessness?

Don't give up. Though the moods go up and down, inspiration abounds for God is always with you. I was moved when I recently heard a monk who lives in a beautiful, 1,000 year old monastery in Montserrat, Spain, describe his most difficult challenge as those times when "God disappears."

My work at the UN involves children affected by armed conflict. People often ask me, "How is it that you don't get depressed, over-whelmed and filled with a sense of hopelessness to see the tragedy and

suffering that wars bring, especially to innocent children?" When you know that hundreds of thousands of children, some as young as eight years old, have been conscripted to fight in adult wars, have been exploited sexually and for their labor, have been maimed, killed, orphaned and displaced by the millions because of war, it is daunting and heart wrenching.

At the same time I am continuously humbled, amazed and uplifted by the indomitability of the human spirit that has the capacity to share exquisite moments of love, caring and concern for others in the midst of great personal tragedy, sacrifice and suffering. There are many people around the world who work quietly and tirelessly day in and day out under the most dire conditions, in the most dangerous circumstances, and without acknowledgement of any kind, to help others in need. There is continuous confirmation of the inherent goodness of the human heart and spirit that can only come from a Divine Source.

One of the fastest ways to overcome preoccupation with the little self is to do selfless service. Serve God in His myriad forms disguised as the poor, the sick, the hungry. As we experience the suffering of others, we are also tapping into the greater compassion, love and understanding that already exists within our own hearts. As we experience the many challenges in life the struggle too becomes part of the sacred journey, and serves to make us deeper, more caring and humble human beings.

We touched on this subject before, but I want to get into it a bit deeper. If a person wants to find an authentic spiritual teacher, what should they be looking for, and what should they be wary of?

Each person should trust his/her own inner self. Everyone is blessed with Divine intelligence and intuition. Some people are very vulnerable and must be careful not to be taken advantage of in their vulnerability.

I also believe that if a person is a sincere seeker after God they will be appropriately guided. An authentic spiritual teacher would not take you away from yourself, but will bring you back to yourself that you may know yourself, and blossom into the fullness of your own beautiful potential.

A spiritual family has formed around your teaching. Can you share with us what its purpose is, some of its activities, and how it's structured?

The spiritual family arose from Divine Mother. People were drawn to her. She started meditations at her home in Honolulu because so many people started to come and wanted to receive her powerful transmissions. She held meditations six days a week at certain times. When she was not having group meditations, people came to see her privately. We have spiritual family in many places, and growing.

People open their homes to others for meditation on a weekly basis. It is a time for the community to come together and share how God works in our daily lives, and how we can move through challenges with a God centered focus. We help each other and care for each other whenever the need arises. Whether it's providing transportation, home care, home cooking or whatever the person may need during times of illness or crises, we are a loving community that stands ready to assist one another. In this manner, we practice love in action within the community.

We also do humanitarian outreach, and take shipping containers of clothing, school, and medical supplies to communities in developing countries that are needful of these supplies. We also do a cultural exchange as a part of our visits abroad, and bring the songs, dances and costumes of Hawaii to these communities. They, in turn, have been so wonderful to share with us their native songs, dances and costumes. The children from these countries who participate in their native dances and costumes are especially adorable, and are a source of great joy. These cross cultural exchanges and visits overseas have broadened our horizons. It is always a privilege to share our love and goodwill with others.

Wonderful! I would like to shift gears a bit and talk about some of the pragmatic events you have going on in your life. You have had a highly distinguished career as an attorney and work as an advisor to the Secretary General's Special Representative for Children and Armed Conflict at the United Nations. Please share with us some of your insights about how you manage the challenges of integrating your spiritual perspective with the ongoing events that take place in the world of complex international dynamics?

It's all a reflection of consciousness. I would like to see spirituality move more and more into the core of not only our daily lives but into the lives of international organizations as well. The Preamble to the United Nations Charter is a very spiritual, inspired and inspiring document.

It talks about fundamental human rights, the dignity and worth of each person, equal rights for men and women. It arose out of two world wars, and the commitment of the world's leaders that we should unite to maintain international peace and security. However, we must bring these inspired words into a living reality. We must put into practice respecting each other and honoring the dignity that is in each person because life is sacred. It's about living that reality individually as well as collectively. The institutions we create give us an opportunity to put into practice on a global scale those loving spiritual practices that we should be implementing in our daily lives. One reflects the micro, the other, the macro, but they both give us the opportunity to live elevated, dignified lives.

You're also doing work with the Toda Institute for Global Peace and Policy Research. How is this work different from what you're doing at the United Nations?

They are related. Both organizations advocate and work for peace. The Toda Institute brings together peace researchers, policy makers and community activists who study the global landscape and look at ways that conflicts can be resolved.

You've written numerous articles, some published in the World Affairs Journal of International Issues. I was particularly intrigued with the article titled, "Practical Spirituality." Could you share with us some of the main points of this article?

Primarily, it addresses the global landscape and the importance of living a spiritual life. Where we are is the holy ground, and we must be able to share our love, compassion and understanding with others right where we are. I highlight the examples of Mahatma Ghandi and Mother Theresa because they lived their messages. Their lives were filled with suffering and great sacrifice, but they never gave up.

In the spiritual arena, a large number of traditional and non-traditional interpretive maps have come about in the form of Christianity, Buddhism, Hinduism, Islam, various New Age Paradigms, post-modern integral approaches and so on. To various degrees and depths, these interpretive maps color or frame the taste of awakening experiences, enlightenment experiences, finding God, seeing God, being one with God, and so on which are not easily conveyed or translated. It seems then that how enlightenment gets translated is as important as the experience itself.

Given the increasing number of interpretive maps, is there a way to embody "enlightenment" without falling into the malaise of it being perceived as only a collection of relative truths based on one's individual experience, and the interpretive maps that are employed?

One should not get mired in the various interpretive maps. The reason why there are increasing numbers of interpretive maps is because we have increasing numbers of people, and the maps are diverse because people are diverse. People will be drawn to the map that is most suitable for them. There are six billion plus people in the world and six billion plus pathways to God. Ultimately, however, the interpretive map cannot be a substitute for the actual experience. Enlightenment is, and cannot be embodied. Our own limitations seek to encapsulate what is limitless, to place parameters around what is boundless, to give form to what is formless.

So there is a basic Truth, Presence or Essence that transcends all relative truths, and given that this is so, how does it relate to all of the different interpretations and maps?

The maps are guides. But ultimately you have to be the one to undergo the experience. The maps can point the way but you actually have to undertake the journey and arrive at the destination. The maps can show the way, but the maps are not the journey, nor the experiencer of the journey. The map can show you how to get there by many different routes or directions because it plots a huge landscape. However, you alone are the undertaker of the journey, and the experiencer of the journey.

Do you feel that one of the roles of a spiritual teacher is to allow someone to more easily recognize what path or way the nature of the tran-

scendent is best communicated and translated according to how they show up as a student?

Yes, I think the spiritual teacher is very helpful as a guide. A spiritual teacher moves with you in a variety of ways, and supports and guides you along the way. But, you must still experience for yourself. It's like trying to explain to someone who has never seen or eaten an orange what an orange is. You describe as best as you can what it looks, smells, feels, and tastes like, where you can go to obtain it, and so forth, but no matter how much you explain, the person has to actually see and eat the orange to know for him/herself what an orange is.

Do you feel there is a transmission of Essence or Presence from a spiritual teacher that allows someone to taste something that is transcendent?

Yes. Through direct transmission, the spiritual teacher can give the devotee transcendent experiences. Those can be imparted.

It appears those experiences were something that you received from Divine Mother.

Absolutely. She had the gift to quiet our minds. When we were with her, our minds were still. I experienced such pure love from her. She herself was radiant in that love, and I often found myself staring at her. She was so radiantly beautiful. She was nurturing, supportive, generous, and always there for us. She burned off a lot of the dross that can weigh you down, and when you left her, you felt lighter, cleaner, and everything seemed brighter, clearer and more crisp. After being with her I could understand scriptures from deep within my heart, and prior mental machinations over them had completely abated. There were many beautiful, profound and transformative experiences with her.

Audrey, what would you like to leave us with that would sum up the primary message of your teaching?

First, we should cultivate our love and devotion to God within the sacred chamber of our own hearts. As God is love, we must actualize God in our daily lives by living and being that love itself in our thoughts, speech and actions. Love then becomes a living reality and not just a philosophy or a mental concept about which we have wistful musings. May we also express daily, our gratitude, praise and thanksgiving to God, Who alone is the Doer, Creator, and Giver of Life.

Thank you Audrey for your time and wisdom. We wish you all the best with the many endeavors you are involved with.
Thank you very much. It was lovely talking with you John.

At the conclusion of the interview, Audrey gifted me with the singing of the Gayatri Mantra. As she began to sing, it was immediately clear that this beautiful song was coming from a very deep spiritual place within Audrey. It resonated at the core of my heart and soul. Blessings to you dear Audrey for this Divine gift of love and beauty.

Contact Information:
dmaudrey@aek9.net

* Note: The comments and opinions expressed in this article are strictly those of the author, and do not purport in any way to represent the views of the United Nations or any other organization.

BILL BAUMAN

I met Bill Bauman in 2004. He left an immediate impression as a brilliant, wise and seasoned spiritual teacher. He gifts us with humor, and great insights into the human and spiritual condition. His sheer Presence along with great clarity of mind and intuition gives us the means to see through and move beyond who we might erroneously conceive ourselves to be. Bill brings with him an extensive background in both spiritual and psychological disciplines, and a unique and powerful blend of East and West wisdom rarely encountered in these times. Bill's God-given gifts allow us to step into a vast space of love, beauty and joy. It sets the stage to land deeply in the Essence of who we are. As Bill puts it in his new book "Oz Power", "Listen closely to your heart—it speaks to you about how to love." Enjoy Bill, and what he graciously brings to all of us.

Bill, thank you for spending time with us today. We are honored to have the opportunity to speak with you.

Thank you very much. It's absolutely my pleasure, my privilege and my delight.

I would like to start out by asking you to share with us a little bit about your background, and what led you to become a spiritual teacher?

My background has been a bit varied in that it's been characterized by a number of phases and focuses. I started out being raised as a Catholic and at age thirteen heard the first inner voice in my life, which said, "Bill I want you to be my priest." Of course, after I got over the initial shock of it, I realized strongly that something deep in me, some deep spiritual force that I'd never felt before, was calling me to exactly that. It was a voice that I felt compelled to follow, bewildered as I was, so from that point on I moved from home and began studies to become a Catholic priest.

In my early twenties, John, I had the privilege of studying Theology at the University of Louvain in Belgium for four years. That experience really opened me up to life in its bigger sense. In that it was the first time I had experienced life outside the United States, I found myself quickly becoming a world citizen. Also, being outside of traditional American Catholicism, I could open myself to the essential meaning of both Christianity and God. At that point, just as I was ordained a Catholic priest, I felt like I had truly captured within my core not only the essence of Christianity but a deep, deep soul level connection with the Divine—in a way that was far beyond the usual definitions of the Church. Of course, within a couple of years I felt "done" with the Church and experienced a deep inner urge to move on. At that point, I met my beautiful wife Donna, who was a nun. She and I left the Church together and have truly "lived happily ever after."

I then got a doctorate in Psychology because I felt strongly compelled to know the deepest dynamics of the human experience and of human functioning. In short, I had to grasp the totality of human living. Psychology offered me my next perspective in that quest. I was a practicing psychologist for many years specializing mostly in psychotherapy and depth psychology. In that mode, I could explore, discover, and learn all the ways we were put together as human beings. In my view, I went from this intimate bond with God into an intimate bond with the human psyche.

After many years as a therapist—just when I was thinking, "Hmm, there's got to be more to life than what I've learned"—spirituality "struck" me. When I say it "struck," John, I mean that a powerful, compelling, dynamic universal force—let's just call it God—just took me over. It called me, from the depths of my entire being, to a much more expansive connection to and unity with life—universal life, divine life, human life, earth life, all life.

It was at this point that many spiritual gifts began to show up in my life: the gifts of seeing people's light and energy; of knowing a person's essence, of having a true connection with people's souls. Also, the gift of healing—healing far beyond what I had experienced before. Keep in mind, John, that I was never looking for any of this; I had not been searching for enlightenment, giftedness or God. In fact, I had spent a fair amount of time running from those qualities; I simply wanted to be a regular, real-life human being. You can imagine, then, how this experience really blew me away. In my true resistant form, I spent a few years struggling against these changes, hoping the gifts would go away, and trying to keep God at arms length, only to realize that this force was much bigger than the "me" that I was so desperately trying to hang on to.

How old were you when this happened?

I was born in 1940, so I was around forty years old. From that point on, I shifted my whole psychological approach, which was already quite holistic, to one that blended the psychological with the spiritual, more what is called the Transpersonal. In truth, I shifted to become more of a spiritual leader.

It was at that point I became a minister in the Church of Religious Science, a capacity I served for only a few years. In this ministerial function, in my private sessions and in seminars that I led, I quickly became a spiritual leader helping people attune spiritually to their soulful essence and deepest inspiration.

After several years, John, I moved into another phase, at about age fifty. I've come to call it my "Oneness" phase. It was precipitated by a gripping, transformational event, similar to a near-death experience, in which I experienced the last remnants of my "human" self leave my body and be replaced with an unidentifiable, yet totally internalized, Divine Presence. In one fell swoop, I was one with the Divine as never before. From that moment on, my whole experience of life became one of Unity—I was one with every aspect of life; one with God, one with humanity, one with nature, one with the air that I breathed, just one with every moment of existence.

Throughout this "Oneness" phase, my wife and I lived in Washington D.C. and started and operated a non-profit organization called World Peace Institute. As you might expect, the Institute was based on the philosophy or consciousness of oneness. It was my way of sharing the power and blessings of this mighty consciousness with the world.

Then, in the late 1990's, it became obvious to me that it was time to take the next step—to whatever lay beyond oneness. So, my wife and I just let go of everything. I took three years off—a joyous time of non-service, non-focus and non-involvement in the world. It was my "nirvana" time, and in it I discovered what lay beyond the experience of oneness. I stepped into and felt powerfully immersed in what I call the essence of the divine, in a state of being. Historically we call this state enlightenment. So from that time on, I began living in a state of bliss, a state of inner peace. I experienced not so much the adjectival or qualitative aspects of God, but the essence and "is-ness" of the Divine. And I discovered that in this simple state everything simply is, nothing else is needed, all meaning and purpose cease, in short, all there is is God.

Then, toward the end of 2001, God called me back out into the world to serve people. So, here I am, helping people resonate with their truth, hear their soulful inspiration, and be moved by their inner wisdom. I serve as the translator of the soul's truth, midwife of the divine's miracles or healings, and facilitator of God's loving grace.

You just finished writing a book that's due out in March of 2005 titled "Oz Power". What is the book is about and what is its primary message?

The book is entitled Oz Power: How to Click Your Heals and Take Total Charge of Your Life. In it I use the fairy-tale of the "Wizard of Oz" as a metaphor for our own human experience. By following

Dorothy through her challenge-filled journey through Oz and by demonstrating how she, inch-by-inch, owned her empowerment, I show how each of us shares those same challenges, invitations and possibilities. Then I show people how to take charge of themselves and their lives in the same way as Dorothy.

I move the readers from the time of their birth into their child-hood, then through their experience of schooling, adolescence, adulthood and finally sagehood, demonstrating all the possible ways to live this human experience powerfully. So, John, the book is about (1) our vast human possibilities, (2) the great capacity each of us has to step into the innate power that is our birthright; and (3) how to use that power strongly and wisely to achieve our life purposes.

We hear the term "enlightenment" bantered around so much now days. How would you define enlightenment and why does there seem to be so much confusion about it? Is there a difference between "enlightenment" and "awakening"?

Well, first I'd like to answer the middle question about the confusion. I think the confusion is often a by-product of the very nature of the human experience, John. What I mean is that, while the bigger truth of life is that we are all one, the immediate illusionary experience for almost everyone is that we are all individuals, all different, all unique. While individuality is indeed an illusion or dream, it's a quite compelling one.

So the dream-like state of life is very much built upon the assumption of individual differences with each person having an individual personality, individual orientations, preferences, etc. In that scenario, the path to and experience of enlightenment is going to appear a little different for one person than it is for another. Also, people will be drawn to different definitions or nuances in relation to the word "enlightenment", "awakening," "self-realization," "nirvana," or even the word "inner-peace."

As I shift to the question of "what is enlightenment?", John, I'll share with you my personal experience of enlightenment. And I do so with tenderness and sensitivity to many people, because, again, the path to that wondrous state is internally unique to each person. So I don't want this description of my own experience to take anything away from the validity of anyone else's experience.

To me, enlightenment is an experience of and identification with the divine—that quality of the divine that is uncluttered, non-complex, simplicity-centered, without description, and with only the experience of essence. To say that another way, to me being enlightened simply means "living in and as the Light," that is, that Light of life which is the divine. This light is not one that pulsates and moves as energy or as definable thought, of course, but is that light that simply shines in the center of the Self, in the center of life.

So for me, John, in my unity with all life, I feel like I "sit" in the middle of, in the center of, in the shining essence of all Life. Indeed, I feel identified with all Life and actually experience myself as that all-ness of Life. To me, God's essence and every aspect of Life are one and the same, even if they seem or look different to many people. In short, everything is God, and I'm privileged to experience it as such. To me, it feels like I'm daily tasting the central Truth of existence.

This brings up the next topic I would like to address. There seems to be a lot of discussion about the apparent divide between the spiritual and the material, heaven and earth, nirvana and samsara. In many instances, people who identify themselves as "spiritual" have a hard time relating fully to the world. Historically they have used various means of disassociating themselves from the world through certain kinds of meditations and practices that in some sense marginalize or trivialize worldly, material, bodily existence, and tend to get stuck in absolutism. On the other hand, another part of society remains essentially narcissistic, and nihilistic about material life and, they have lost their connection with the vast spiritual context that holds, and is greater than or transcends material existence. Help us understand what there is to know about the dynamics involved in all of this, and how a more holistic perspective can be realized?

Well first of all John, I want to say I am really impressed with not just the way you have asked that question, but the visionary perspective that you have outlined in putting the question together. I think you have really captured the two extremes that many people live in.

What's fascinating to me is that we as a human family have developed a great loyalty not only to duality, but to our moral value judgments about duality. Thus, people who are strongly materially oriented often develop loyalties to that material world in a way that excludes its spiritual quality.

Likewise, many people who are very spiritually oriented do the same thing in terms of excluding the material. Such an approach creates a divide, an automatic barrier to the full experience not only of life but of enlightenment. It's a bit ironic because being enlightened means that we absolutely live in the center of all life in a way that includes all life. To separate ourselves from any aspect of living automatically precludes a state of enlightenment.

For example, John, I lead mentoring groups in "Spiritual and Human Mastery" where I take those two aspects of this seemingly dualistic world, the spiritual and the human, and help those in the groups learn how to embrace, feel one with, and live masterfully in both the spiritual world and the human or material world.

To me, any distinction between the spiritual and material, the human and the divine, heaven and earth, or body and spirit makes no sense. It ignores the deeper truth that the human and the divine are all one, we're all one, everything is all one. Also, it perpetuates a belief, and it's only a belief, that there's a difference between what's spiritual and what's human and, therefore, invites us to experience what is basically a lie.

To me the lie of the human experience, and I use the term with great sensitivity, is that we are separated, that we are disconnected from the divine, or from each other, or from our own Self. And that's simply not true. It's a mind-set, a belief. It's an assumption that most of us as human beings have adhered to, but believing it takes nothing away from the bigger truth that we are all one. Everything we define as God is in every blade of grass and in every cell of every human being. It's in every thought that every one of us has, it's in every breath of air. So God is, as I sometimes crudely say it, in our toe-nail as much as in our heart or on that proverbial throne in heaven.

This brings us the next topic I want explore. Because there seems to be a split between the spiritual and the material, a lot of seekers have struggled with "awakening" and "enlightenment" to dissolve and resolve this split for years or possibly decades. Many people have mostly experienced a series of major disappointments along the way leading to a feeling of hopelessness. Help us understand that particular anomaly, that malaise, and what can be done to help that situation along.

It's a perfect question, John. First of all I believe that the disappointment comes from the fact that well-meaning, spiritually-oriented, enlightenment-directed people are trying so hard to live out deeply-embedded assumptions they probably don't even know are there. For example, the assumption that to be spiritual one should get beyond the "human stuff." They live out that assumption either by ignoring, denying, or sometimes actively healing their human stuff as a way of getting rid of it. Often, people's motivation in healing is to have that human aspect of themselves go away so they can hang out in a more "pure space." So the set of assumptions I am referring to is a set of beliefs that there is something about the human state that we should be graduating from rather than dealing with, leaving behind rather than embracing. And I've seen how that assumption sets people up for a lot of pain because in truth what is human is Divine. So if we're trying to leave what's human behind, we're trying to leave behind the very Divine that we're searching for and it becomes an impossible juxtaposition of opposites.

What can people do? They can affirm, "I choose to take every aspect of life and self, no matter what it is, and call myself to the truth that it is God. I call myself to embrace it, live it, experience it, know it, feel it, and be in intimate relationship with it in whatever way my soul/truth moves me to. This is my path to God." This is a powerful affirmation, whether that something happens to be a life-long pain, an unresolved conflict, an intimacy issue, or an aspect of life that the person has judgment about. In other words, until someone who is on a path toward enlightenment can look at ALL facets of life and somehow embrace them and find peace with them—not just cognitively, intellectually and philosophically, but also experientially, emotionally and energetically— that person is just going to live in the very frustration that you are talking about.

Another way of saying this, John, is that we show up to and have an intimate relationship with whatever is on our plate. One of the beautiful things about "Life" is that it always brings to us exactly what our soul invites, and gives us precisely what we need at every moment to further that experience of enlightenment-oriented unity. To me, John, life is already a God-centered, soul-directed, beautiful experience. Everything that happens is the dance of life, and that is where we find God. So if there is a war that is bothering me—in that event is where I can find God. What I would call myself to is to embrace that experience with every bit of feeling I have, every bit of consciousness I have, every bit of soul I have, and say, "O.K. God's here somewhere, and God's inviting me in some way to the fullest possible experience of Self, in and through this experience."

As wonderful as this approach is, John, many spiritually-oriented people have a very hard time with it, because they hold such severe judgments about whatever they define as negative, evil, bad or wrong. So many try to reach a point of an enlightened state through holding tightly to and riding the horse of those negative judgments about life, and it is simply an impossibility. Indeed, the bigger truth from an enlightenment perspective is there is no such thing as evil, bad or wrong. So, I mainly invite people to a reality-based embrace of what's on their plate, so that they can expand their mind-set, let go of every judgment, and be totally open to Divine Grace.

This brings me to the next subject. You've recently begun conducting three-day meetings with four small groups of 25 to 30 students over a period of several months. What's been the result of these meetings, and what have you and the students learned in the process?

I call these experiences "mentoring groups." They're for people who feel a soul-level calling to spiritual and human mastery, either in their overall lives or in their healing approaches. In these groups we explore the true nature of Life—that God's Essence or Being is the only true Reality—then re-experience every aspect of the "human" condition (our light, our energy, our consciousness) as intimate ways of expressing the Divine. These groups are very experiential and are strongly centered around receiving the divine workings of Grace.

When I say Grace, John, I mean the level of miracle-oriented activity that happens not primarily from our own human efforts but from our own human "letting-go." So we learn how to "let go and let God" in ways that are beyond what we have done before. Then, we experience a state of awe as we are filled with the gifts and loving interventions of Grace.

This is the point where I should define the term Grace a bit, John. Grace to me is that expression of the all-loving, unconditionally embracing, endlessly giving, caring quality of God. I often compare it to the unconditionally loving mother who wants nothing more than to keep giving and giving to her children in ways that allow those children to receive everything necessary for their fulfillment and joy. So what happens in these meetings is that Grace just infuses itself into us, thereby allowing us to move into next levels or larger "skin," if you will, of the divine/human selves that we are.

Wonderful! Just to broaden it out a bit, you mentioned previously that in the last few months you have been moving forward with forming a spiritual community. Please share with us what your vision and purpose for this community is and how you see it developing and unfolding?

My vision, John, is that there are on earth at this time more and more people who are not only spiritually-oriented, but are here with a purpose of blessing, loving and impacting other human beings, and the world itself, in a very strong way. I've felt powerfully moved, along with my wife Donna who's very much an equal partner with me in this, to form a community of those who feel called to live at a deep soul-level—that is, to live in an inner space of love, truth and inspiration—form their lives around that soulful center, and then express that soulful living meaningfully in the world.

So, this community is a supportive resource for anyone who is looking for (a) a family of like-spirited people, and (b) tangible help and experiences to further his or her own soulful living. Again, let me underline, John, that "soulful living" implies living in the deepest Truth—the truth that "all there is is God"—and experiencing that sacred Truth in every aspect of human living. To support that purpose, this community offers seminars, retreats, mentoring groups, teleconferences, and journeys to the world's sacred sites. All of these experiences help each person to open more fully to the miracles of God's Grace, be filled with Life's enormous blessings, and live in soulful union with all Life.

I'd like to express the nature of our community another way, John, if it's okay. I feel that at this time God is calling our human family to take the next steps in waking up from the illusion or dream that we've created. I believe that our Creative Source is reaching into this special dream world of ours and is lovingly inviting as many people as will respond to the bigger Truth—the truth that what is God is also us ... that the Divine courses through our veins, moves through our bodies, enlivens our energies, and is a daily part of our lives. We have a grand opportunity to awaken to this liberating Truth and fortunately are privy to a unique and generous Divine spark that can support us in this shared awakening. That spark I call Grace. And this community is very much here as a transmitting station and receiver for that Grace. For these reasons, John, you can see why the spirit of our community is centered around the words "Soul" and "Grace."

Again, the name of the community is ...?
The Center for Soulful Living.

Is the community something where people would live together or is this is a gathering where they can continue to tap into deeper soulful aspects of themselves where they live now?
At this point, John, it's very much the latter. We have no plans or vision about it being a physically centered community with buildings, etc. That may be an option in the future if God moves us in that direction, but at this point a physical or geographic center is not at all our focus. Our intention and practice now, as you mentioned in your question, is to invite people to join together in shared events and experiences. At this time I travel regularly to most major cities in the country to lead seminars. We're also developing regional retreats. I'm currently leading four year-long mentoring groups. And we're starting a system of monthly conference calls, etc., where people can come together without being limited to a physical location or building.

If a person wants to find an authentic spiritual teacher or a spiritual community, what should they be looking for, and what would the most life-supporting relationship to such a teacher or community be like?
It's a very important question, John. I deeply believe the answer springs mostly from the inspiration and truth that lives in each person. Because of the uniqueness of each individual, every person will be looking for something different, both in a teacher and in a community.

Having expressed and honored that principle, allow me to make a couple of generalizations from my own life experiences about ideal teachers. First, I believe that most spiritually oriented people would do well to look for a teacher whose teachings, dynamics and personality resonate at their soul level as "right." For example, does the seeker's soul say "This teacher is truly 'right' for me"? In other words, it's important to look to that internal tuning fork, to one's own inner truth—and listen carefully to its wisdom and guidance.

A second theme that I think is important, especially for persons who are looking for personal empowerment as a part of their spiritual mastery, is to look for a teacher who is for the most part not demanding total loyalty to himself or herself. For example, John, I've seen many Western-oriented persons become totally submissive to a guru, in an historically Eastern-style manner, totally giving away their own power or authority to that teacher. While this approach is certainly theoretically sound, especially in Eastern systems, it so often doesn't work, simply because the Western-oriented person frequently needs a different approach. Many of these well-meaning followers have truly lost themselves and have to spend a fair amount of time re-finding themselves and their identity after they've left the guru behind. So it's important for spiritual seekers to take responsibility for choosing a teacher whose style is consistent with their own.

When it comes to choosing a spiritual community, John, I think most people would do well to seek a community that will help them stretch. While many spiritual communities give and reinforce a sense of belonging and security—I sometimes call these "feel-good" communities—a person oriented toward enlightenment, awakening or self-realization shouldn't be looking for too much comfort. After all, the path toward enlightenment and mastery is one where a person is always stretching, expanding, letting go of "smaller skin" or older boundaries and is opening up to life's next bigger invitations. The acid test of a helpful spiritual community is not that it will give us a sense of security and comfort, but that it will help us grow, stretch and expand.

You used the word "mastery". There are some people who would say that "mastery" is something one gains over time by doing certain practices, meditations or activities either spiritually or materially. On the other hand, there is that aspect of life that is already "mastering every-thing." Some people would say that it's not gaining mastery, it's being mastered by something that is over, above and beyond themselves so they can fully express what that is within their own lives and within the human context of being in this world. Would you help us under-stand a little more about that?

It's a wonderful question, John, and I'm delighted to respond to it. Of course, both the up and down side of the word "mastery" is that it can be interpreted from so many different angles. It can mean totally different things to different people depending on their personal per-spective. So in that sense it's probably a great word because it can mean all of the above. (Laughter). Yet, because of our built-in set of differences, it behooves each person who feels called to masterful liv-ing to look reflectively at the question, "What does mastery mean for me?" and proceed from the nature of the internal answer.

I'd like to make a generalization here, John, keeping in mind the fact that any generalization usually has millions of exceptions. Here it is. It seems to me that most people on a spiritual path go through two stages in their spiritual growth: the first is more doing- and practice-oriented and the second is more non-doing or "being" oriented. For most people the first stage usually lasts a long time, often decades, while the second stage need not take so long. For whatever reason, most of us take a long time to come to the awareness that there's little to no cause-effect relationship between our practices and our ultimate spiritual growth, that is, that we really don't have to center our growth around those practices. Those practices—meditation, yoga, healings, etc.—can be beneficial in many ways but our ultimate spiritual and human freedom is not dependent upon them.

I sometimes crudely express to people that these practices make for great entertainment. They entertain the mind; they give us the feel-ing that "Oh, good, we're participating", we're co-creating, we're doing something special to set the stage so God can enter onto that stage and take us over. But the truth is, they're mostly fillers of time and space—meaningful and entertaining fillers, but fillers nonetheless.

Once each person discovers this fact, he or she is free to put less emphasis on "doing" and more focus on "letting go and letting God". And once that person chooses to quit trying so hard and then lets go, that bigger Divine Presence simply takes over, does the bulk of the work, and leads the person into freedom, unity and ultimately—if it is truly that person's calling—enlightenment.

When I say that the Divine Presence "takes over," John, I mean that this bigger force guides us, moves us, inspires us and, if you will, masters us. We feel so swept up into that bigger force that our identity becomes one with that bigger force and we gradually (or all at once) lose our sense of separateness from God and Life.

Let's apply these words to the state of enlightenment, John. When one gets closer and closer to that experience called enlightenment or unity, we realize that no doing, no practice, no effort, no behavior, no attitude, no decision makes any difference. So perhaps the purest approach we can take to enlightenment is (step one) to "let go and let God," open ourselves to awakening whenever awakening wants to happen, and (step two) let go of any anxiety, worry or concern about whether it will or won't happen. Just assume it will, whether it happens tomorrow, next week or thirty years from now. And in the meantime, (step three) continue to show up to whatever is on the plate of our lives, embracing it from the level of our soulful truth and inspiration. And finally (steps one and four) just stay in that state of letting go, spiritual abandon and infinite expectation which simply calls us to be at peace as much as possible.

Of course, many people can't or won't "let go;" they choose not to—often because they don't feel deserving, are holding on to feelings of shame or guilt, or simply define that they're not ready. These people tend to stay more oriented toward practices, etc. When I meet this group of people, I try to support them in their practices, while helping them experience as much divine love, grace and intervention as they can digest. In this way, filled with more of God's love, they can later begin to take steps toward a more intimate relationship with God, and maybe feel more worthy to be totally loved, and finally "let go" and let God do the work.

I think you've answered the next question which is: Is it possible to hasten the experience of liberation by doing various spiritual practices, prayers, meditations, psychological or emotional clearings, or is it mere folly to think that we can do anything at all about it at all?

You know, John, the bigger truth is that it is mere folly or illusion to use spiritual practices to "further" or "hasten" liberation. It simply can't be done. Yet, in a sense, we almost can't fault anyone for loyalty to practices and devotions, behaviors, decisions, healings, etc.— because we live in a world where one of our underlying illusions and beliefs is about the value of hard work. In America, for example, we're historically very much about individuality and hard work—those two values are the human foundations of this particular country.

It's like if I don't do anything or work hard at it, nothing's going to change.

Yes, that's exactly the mind-set of many people. In fact, we've built societies on the foundation of that particular mind-set. On the one hand, John, it's an understandable mind-set; on the other hand, in terms of how the Divine works and in terms of the larger Truth of Life, there's absolutely no validity to it. As you know, Life has its own rhythm and unique style, and works according to an infinite design that has little or nothing to do with human efforting, trying, desires, needs, etc. And of course what's difficult for many people is that, when they are really dedicated (should I say addicted?) to their desires, efforts, practices, etc. they simply can't grasp that it's okay to let go.

In the spiritual arena, a large number of traditional and non-traditional interpretive maps have arisen in the form of Christianity, Buddhism, Hinduism, Islam, various New Age Paradigms, post-modern integral approaches and so on. To various degrees and depths, these interpretive maps color or frame the taste of awakening experiences, enlightenment experiences, finding God, seeing God, being one with God, and so on which are not easily conveyed or translated. It seems then that how enlightenment gets translated is as important as the experience itself.
Given the increasing number of interpretive maps, is there a way to embody "enlightenment" without falling into the malaise of it being perceived as only a collection of relative truths based on one's individual experience, and the interpretive maps that are employed? Or is there a basic truth, presence or essence that transcends all relative truths and how does it relate to the infinite numbers of interpretations, translations and maps?

I love your question, John. It gets to the heart of the question of the many paths to enlightenment and the frustration of a lot of people who so genuinely approach enlightenment and wind up getting confused by all of these paths and maps.

I deeply believe, John, that there is an essential state of enlightenment. Or, to say it another way, that there is a unified experience of the infinite that is central, integrated, non-complex and unifying—and everyone who is called to enlightenment can have this simplicity-centered state. After all, it's Essence and Essence subsumes every seeming difference into itself. It is above and beyond the limitations of the different paths that you have talked about.

However, most people on their way to that simplified state, as they're expanding into their bigger Self, and opening to that essential experience of the Divine, will be taking paths that are more individuated, more culturally and religiously customized, and more tailor-made to their individual differences. It appears that for the first many steps toward enlightenment, people will have to walk through that relativity-centered maze—because they still believe that individual differences are reality. Then at some point we all enter that unified field where God is God, Essence is Essence, Truth is Truth and we're all One.

My sense for persons in these initial stages is that they need to take significant responsibility for choosing their path. To use an analogy, John, it's like going through a grocery store and picking this type of food and bypassing another one, based on a deep inner knowing of what food that person's body is calling for. The same thing is true with our paths to enlightenment. It's a matter of reaching out for that particular cultural, religious, spiritual or philosophical approach that feels right and saying "no" to others that don't feel right, basing our decisions on a deep soul-level knowing about what is best and right for us.

The value of this approach, I believe, is that the person is more and more listening to the soul's internal tuning fork, that inner knowing about what is right, and begins to trust his or her inner knowing. Then, when the time is right for that person simply to "let go and let God," the foundation for that leap into Grace has been internally set.

This is why I've so dedicated my life to helping people listen to, connect with and deeply bond with their soul, their inner truth and inspiration. It's at that level—where our deepest wisdom resides—that we can know what's appropriate, perfect, helpful, genuine and truthful for us.

Bill, what would you like to leave us with that would sum up the primary message of your teaching?

There is this beautiful, enormous Divine "All" that is an intimate part of each human being, indeed of all life. Every cell in us vibrates with the Divine. Our every energy moves with the power and the passion of the Divine. Every thought in our mind expresses the creative juices of the Divine. Our bodies embody and manifest not just the wonder of the earth, but also the love of God as that love speaks in every pulsing of our heart.

Every facet of every human being is Divine in its essence and therefore, Divine in its human expression. So my message to our human family is this: God is in your every thought, feeling, intuition, vision, knowing and aspect of life. And if we but dare to call ourselves to that truth, we can have an experience of heaven on earth—because we'll be able to see our earthly world through the loving, non-judgmental eyes of God. We can know the Divine not just as an abstract or other-worldly creator, but also as an intimate, internally centered and a powerfully expressive earthly and human force. What a way to live life!

So, in short, everything is God . . . infinite and Divine, without exception. And all that we define as the qualities of God—qualities such as love, power, creativity, light, etc.—are in every little particle and sub-particle of the human experience. Again, how wondrous to call ourselves to that truth and invite ourselves to the experience and celebration of that God that lives everywhere! Here's the point at which each person can make the ultimate choice: to perceive life as an invitation to live in this pure Truth; to embrace life as a dance with God in and through every experience; and to see the beauty of God in every person, circumstance and event. These possibilities are so achievable and all we need do is say "yes" to them in our lives.

I've found, John, that when we can define the human experience as God, when we can live the human experience as Divine, and when we can celebrate the human experience as an expression of the infinite, then (a) miracles begin to happen in abundance, (b) inner peace builds an unending reservoir within us, (c) we find a deeper happiness than ever before, and (d) well, it's just a really cool way to live life.

Bill, thank you for your time and wisdom. We wish you all the best with your new book and your on-going teaching endeavors.

Thank you, John. This time with you has been a true pleasure and privilege. At a deep level this interview has allowed me to celebrate your beauty, the beauty of everyone who will read these words and the beauty of life. So I thank you and the reader for this beautiful celebration. It seems fitting to close by saying, "It's been Divine."

DAVID CIUSSI

D avid Ciussi is a spiritual teacher who lives and works in France. I discovered him through my good friend Doris Lajoie. Doris and I have been "dharma buddies" since the late 1970s, sharing the ups and downs of spiritual evolution, watching our children grow up, and vacationing together throughout North America. Doris, who is French Canadian, had the good fortune of meeting David several years ago when David was teaching in Quebec. He was immediately taken with David's clarity, spiritual presence and impeccable approach to liberation. Because David's first language is French, I asked Doris to interview him and then translate the interview into English. The interview took place in Bromont, Quebec, in September 1999. I think that you will find that the joy of David Ciussi transcends all languages.

Doris Lajoie writes:

The first time I heard David speak he said, "How can I explain something that is so simple?" Such is the dilemma facing David and others who have been graced with the experience of awakening to the Self. How does one describe the indescribable, speak the unspeakable that is truly beyond words? And all of the fuss, as David tells us, is about something that is closer than words, thoughts, even breath. It is present in each and every "Here and Now" moment of our existence.

David lives in Nice, France, where he teaches human resources as part of the Engineering faculty of Nice University. He is married, has two children and loves to climb mountains. He has recently written a book, *Rêve D'éveil (A Dream of Awakening)* and holds workshops in France and in Quebec, Canada.

David is a soft spoken man who laughs probably more than he speaks. And when he speaks, he moves in mysterious ways. Like a child discovering the magic and the power of words, David constantly re-invents language so as to liberate and to express poetically the silence of the Now from the enclaves of words. [Translator's note: it is unfortunate that David's wit and humor expressed in his word-creations and word-plays cannot be adequately translated from French. What a "pun-ishment!" This is why we offer you the original French text along with the English translation.]

This is the first formal interview David has done. He reluctantly agreed to let his words be recorded, but not before adding a "listener beware" caveat—"The Truth is not contained in words but in the silence between them, the silence of the ever-present Now."

The first answer in the interview came out as a long deep laugh and the rest followed as easily as a mountain stream follows its course to the sea, cooling and nourishing everything in its path.

ᏩᏨᏩ

David, in a few words, what does "being awakened," mean?

[Laughter] It means to sleep well. [More laughter] To enjoy the sleep of the just. It means to sleep in peace, being peaceful, consciously being, "I do not know, I am not this." To be pure presence.

Will you share with us the spiritual path that finally brought you to this state of awakening of the Self, to your permanent state of enlightenment?

Since I was a child I've always had a passion for self-discovery. Like all the children of the world I felt a calling, a desire, nostalgia. This desire nourished all aspects of my life. I was like someone who, being passionately in love with life, could not be satisfied with just "thinking life." I wanted to touch life, to taste life.

This is very much like when we are in love, when we fall in love. Our whole life is focused on the Beloved. She becomes a devouring passion that demands and holds all our attention. Only the Beloved exists. To be in her gaze, to touch her, to hold her hand, to feel her delicious touch, to smell her perfume, to hear her voice. This was my spiritual path. It was the search for my Self as I progressively discovered how much life has always loved me, how much I am in fact, the Beloved.

However, I often got lost on this path. Sometimes I had peak experiences where it seemed I was walking hand in hand with God. I was with my Beloved and nothing else mattered: no doubts, no guilt, no suffering, no judgment. I was who I was, at one with my Self. There was no distance from my Self, no differences. It was a unifying Self. And then, not yet being ready to accept this totality of life, I fell from these mountain peaks and again found myself identifying with the suffering of the world.

Being very, very stubborn and very determined, I began yet another ascent of the inner mountain, of a higher plateau of the Self. But as I was not completely ready, as I had not discovered and faced all my lies, and all my beliefs, well, again I fell. And so on and so forth, a succession of summits and valleys, of successful climbs and doomed failures, have made up my journey. Surely God took pity on this boy, this young man, this father, this married man, and Grace finally allowed access to reach the summit of all summits.

How has awakening changed your day-to-day life, especially the relationship with family and friends?

Nothing has changed and everything has changed. Nothing, for I am still a man. I still have the same body and these human shortcomings. Yet everything has changed, for I have become honest, impeccable, a man of integrity. It is such an inexplicable changeover. It is very difficult to speak of the inexplicable, of the ineffable.

As far as my wife is concerned, awakening has shown me how to serve her better, to be more attentive to her needs and to regard her as the most precious object in the world. Before awakening I was too caught up with my spiritual progression. I was too busy taking care of my appearances and myself. Now the fiancée is always a fiancée. She is not my wife but my fiancée and our relationship is very pure. I see her "a-new" every day, as I am "a-new," continuously being born to the world. Being born continually, I become "at-one" with life.

The same thing happens with my children and with my friends. No room is left for David who was always in want, in need. There is no more room to serve this individual. From now on David, the little child, is here to serve others.

Every time I meet someone I am moved by this fire, this urgency. How can I show this person what he already is? What can I do to help him remember the small innocent child he used to be? How can I help him re-discover his own freedom? This is my soft, light and tranquil obsession that I follow with determination. Everyone can taste this freedom for themselves.

We all want to live in this lightness of being and with the innocence of children, yet many obstacles in life prevent us from doing so. What must we do to discover freedom and to be free from the fears of the past and the worries and uncertainties of the future?

What must be done is to immediately stop being a victim and to stop becoming victims. The path to freedom is for brave men and women who have integrity. Freedom comes to good people. A courageous man is a strong man who faces the challenges of life without hiding behind non-action.

Thinking impedes action. Of course we can and should think and plan for the future and we can certainly remember and learn from the past. This is no problem. But it is absurd to use the past in order to justify non-action or to perceive the future as full of difficulties.

When I was young, if I had the thought "there, over there on top of that mountain . . . no, no, I can't go there, I'm too afraid." Then immediately courage came and the question became "how can you be afraid if you've never climbed this mountain?" This got me going and I went to see if I was truly afraid. I soon realized that there are imaginary fears, those that are born even before beginning to climb a mountain. This is the fear of being afraid and this is worthless. However, fear arising out of a real life situation is legitimate and wholesome. This is a just emotion, a survival instinct, for if there are no guardrails on the mountain we could fall in the abyss.

In my life I have thus learned to face reality, to transform it if need be, and to be wary of imaginary fears. There are real fears and imagined ones. This is the old story of the rope thought to be a snake.

You have said, "The mystery of life is not a problem to be solved but a reality that must be experienced." Facing reality when we are troubled and worried is not always easy. How can one face Truth?

We must use reality as it is, in each and every situation and event, in every relationship so as to grow and discover that the "other" is, in fact, a solution. The "other" in life is really opportunities urging us to re-discover our solutions. It is important to face life's real problems and not imaginary ones. We must learn to single out which is which, or else we will live in a utopia and will be kept prisoner of this utopia.

In A Dream of Awakening *you have written: "Awakening does not bring anything new: it liberates. It does not bring security or comfort … awakening is a perpetual birth." Yet many if not most people believe that awakening is a permanent ecstatic state full of bliss. Your words are rather alarming. Can you clarify these points?*

[Laughter] Security does not exist. [Laughter] There, are you reassured? [More laughter] Now that we know that security no longer exists we will not try to find it. Awakening frees us from illusions and we are left with reality. Gradually we discover that reality is what it's all about. Reality is about being alive, existing. It is the thought that thinks, "Ah, I exist". Reality is being amazed to be living and to be able to experience life. Like small children always in awe of colors, a rose, a mother's touch, a songbird, playing outdoors. This is reality! This sense of wonder, this sense of awe is what satisfies us totally and truly fills our hearts.

The sense of wonder of the Now – of the present moment – this is truly what life is all about. This is your teaching, is it not? You don't really teach a philosophy or a psychology. Even in your workshops you don't really answer questions. You seem to prefer sharing your experience of the "immediate Now" with the course participants. What are some of the techniques that you use?

They are techniques of the "Now." I like to feel the sense of wonder and I love to share it and surprise people. I have discovered that I can, everybody can, be born again in each and every instant. This is true fact and not a fairy tale. To be in a state of awe and wonder, to surprise oneself, to be alive, these are concrete actions that must be done in order to discover our freedom.

Every person must follow this path by himself; I am not here to offer gifts. I am here to remind you that you are here and that is your present, your gift. I am here to redirect your attention to the heart of the Now so that you may have a taste of the living present, the gift of life.

So in my workshops I try wholeheartedly with all my soul and with my limited abilities to make you taste what I taste, hear what I hear, touch what I touch, feel what I feel.

I try to do this without bringing in new beliefs and abstractions or knowledge that will comfort your mind and caress your ideals. I am here to "friction," to bring unease to your ideals so that something practical can arise. Intellectual knowledge only provides analysis, separation, self-distance-non-self which implies that I must seek what I am not. I find that this mechanism for the justification of separation has no sense. Therefore the only thing I'm interested in is to teach you practical things.

Being conscious is a concrete action. Everything in life is practical. If you're thirsty, you drink, you want to go somewhere, you walk, you want to learn how to ride a bicycle, you have to act, you want to eat, you must do an action. Everything is practical. A workshop that is not practical but solely theoretical would imply that you cannot live the fullness of the present, here and now. Such a teaching would postpone awakening for another time, another place. What I try to do in the workshops is to share the "taste" of the Now. Only this taste, the taste of the present, the taste of the Now. What if this Now was the only path, and if this Now was truly all that was?

So "now" what is there to do?

[Laughter] Well, you can keep asking questions. [More laughter]

Ok, so for the fun of it let's continue. You often allude to the playfulness of life and to the fact that unfortunately we tend to take our beliefs a little too seriously. However, since childhood we have been handed down beliefs from our parents, our teachers, church and society. Some of these beliefs are good and some seem destructive. How can we deal with these beliefs so that we may awaken and become, in your words, a warrior of the present?

Beliefs are like old clothing that we must throw away. When I was a child I believed in Santa Claus. When the reality of life made me realize that Santa didn't exist I was disappointed. I blamed my father and mother for this tragedy. So you see we must discover and renounce these old beliefs, these old clothes and allow our selves to be only in the emotion of the Now, in the desire of the moment and in the truth of the present moment. Vigilance, discrimination and lucidity are needed so that we don't get caught up in badly written life-scenarios. Since childhood we have been shown how to censure our emotions, how not to be ourselves in the present moment. We have been conditioned to behave according to appearances. It is now necessary to get rid of these old clothes. This has to be done not for the sake of rejecting society, but in order to check if these beliefs are keeping us away from freedom. These are necessary steps for self-discovery, to realize here and now one's own reality and one's own freedom.

Beliefs that are guilt-laden, that constantly bring self-judgment and false comfort . . . all these beliefs must be well examined. We must transform beliefs into action, into acts of freedom. We must become "one-who-acts." Old beliefs that support non-action have to be beheaded by warriors of the present.

A warrior of the present is one who is established in the art of peace. Established in the art of peace, he knows how to cultivate the art of honesty. He knows how to be in action for he is "action itself." To accomplish this he is vigilant and precise, for he has been able to behead all the beliefs and untruths that were not "here and now". He is established in "when I see, I see, when I think, I think." He does not confuse these two points of view.

Vigilant, he is impeccable, and in an impeccable manner he keeps his hand on the pommel of his sword ready to jump into action. However, he does not use his sword to go to war and to designate others as enemies, such as his wife, children, the world, bankers, even wars. He only uses the sword of vigilance to restore the real relationship between his Self, pure consciousness and his small self, victim of the world. Doing this, established in his unity, in his impeccability, he does not allow the birth of conflicts to arise. By disallowing inner conflicts he does not encourage war with the circumstances of life. He is what he is, established in a beneficent quietude, attentive, serving life, being "action itself." He is a warrior who uses his sword to heal, not to kill. He uses his sword to heal the relationship between his Self and his imagined separate self.

Established in such a beneficent quietude, how can parents deal with the emotions and perpetual changes in their children, especially in regard to teenagers?

Parents must learn to be truthful. One can only be true to one's Self in the "Now." Trouble arises when parents aren't true in their immediate relationships. They must convey to their children that it's ok to have emotions, to react to each other in the moment, but only with the anger or the joy of the moment. One must not give the impression that we can hold these emotions indefinitely. If parents do not teach by example, children can not have reference points.

Parents must cultivate the art of wonder at being alive, and they must learn from their children, who stand in awe at butterflies, blades of grass, tiny worms inching their way on the pavement, flying insects. Parents must go to their children's playground. Being in this special relationship with the world, they will become as children. To cultivate the art of wonder, of being alive, to cultivate an immediate relationship with emotions, to encourage action and playfulness, to play with children, to touch and caress them, for children need to be acknowledged.

Discipline is also needed. Children have to learn about limitations or else they will constantly protest about what is not happening "Now." We must not allow children to lock themselves up in a mood that will justify non-action. It is better to avoid that world where lazy people would rather sulk than move to action.

Parents must teach their children that the only truth is in the Now. They must nourish them with the softness of what they truly are. They must help them express their emotions. How can a child learn to express himself if a man cannot tell his wife, "Today I noticed you put on a new dress, I like your hair this way? You know, I'm happy to be your husband and to return home. I love your presence and I enjoy being with you." Parents must learn to talk to each other, to mutually nourish themselves in a way that is constructive, permanent, dynamic and creative. Relationships never end, they keep growing in each and every second.

If parents don't express their love for each other, if they only show the other facet of married life, that is, "I'm tired, why did you do this or that, you should have done this or that," then children will do the same, blame and protest all the time. This does not imply that parents should never quarrel, for this would be absurd, as children need to learn valuable defense mechanisms.

What I am saying is that parents must learn to be true and to never forget to nourish their relationship. Society spends most of its time unfortunately destroying relationships. The number of failed marriages is a proof that life is not nourished. A child must be fed, not only with food of the earth, but with food of life, and this they learn by their parents' relationships. A child must be nourished by the art of wonder, the art of respect and the art of a true relationship with reality.

Is facing reality the same as facing the mystery of life?

[Laughter] Let us preserve the mystery. Let us not desecrate the mystery of life. Let us be consciously "I am not, I do not know."

David, if there is truly nothing to learn in life except being completely in the "Now," then what is the value of meeting an awakened man?

Man is such an adept in the art of creating concepts, in the art of self-illusion and in the art of tricking himself. He creates increasingly sophisticated levels of reasoning to justify and protect his points of view, opinions and beliefs—all anchors to his small self. He has even conceptualized consciousness as being outside of consciousness. This is how beliefs become articulated and fixed. We come to believe that paradise exists over there, in heaven, and thus cannot be found here, in the Now. We have come to believe that God is elsewhere. This is absurd. To meet an awakened man is to take the risk of finally meeting your Self, stripped of masks, appearances, personal beliefs and identifications.

Fundamentally I do not have the power to transform reality and the world. I am not the creator of this world. I am more like a ray of sunshine or like a son to his father. I know I am my father's son; I am not the Father as the ray of sunshine knows it is not the sun. God creates and man dreams, thus does the masterpiece become. God writes the book of life, reality. I can but read my pure existence by being conscious that I am here now. Thus God and man walk hand in hand. Together they write the history, they share "His" story of the eternal relationship, the eternal alliance, the eternal love. Only God creates. I only know that I am his cherished child and because I know this, as I hold God's hand, I am being active in the here and now. This is the only way to honor my relationship with God and with the world.

What I, David, can do is help you rediscover the sense of wonder that is already in you. I can only give you a glimpse, a taste so as to urge you to taste your own freedom. All that is needed is already here now in this moment and only for this moment. In this Now, time stands still. It is but a measure of infinity where the child within is saying yes to life.

Contact Information:

France: David and Nelly Ciussi
46, boul. de Cimiez
Nice, 06000 France
Internet: www.davidciussi.net

Canada: Doris and Anne Lajoie
100 Le Geai Bleu est
Shefford, QC J2M1R2
CanadaE-Mail: aalajoie@videotron.ca

Note: David's book, *Rêve D'éveil* as well as video and audio cassettes are available in French at the above addresses.

Entrevue avec David Ciussi
Le 16 septembre 1999
Bromont (Québec)
Accordée à Doris Lajoie

Doris Lajoie :
David Ciussi est né en 1946. Il est marié et père de deux enfants. Cet ancien ingénieur, créateur d'entreprise et sculpteur, vit à Nice. Après la réalisation de sa nature véritable, David est resté trois années dans le silence. Pendant cette période, il a écrit "Rêve d'éveil". Depuis, il donne des conférences et anime des ateliers en France et au Canada.

David, en quelques mots, " être éveillé "ça veut dire quoi ?
[Rires] C'est de bien dormir. [Rires] C'est de dormir dans le sommeil du juste. C'est de dormir en paix, étant paisible, entrant consciemment dans " je ne sais pas", "je ne suis pas." Être présence pure.

Veux-tu nous parler de ton cheminement spirituel qui a finalement abouti à cet état d'éveil à soi-même, à ton état d'éveil permanent ?
Depuis que je suis tout petit, j'ai toujours été passionné par la découverte de ce que j'étais. Au fond de moi comme tous les petits enfants du monde, il y avait une nostalgie, un appel, un désir. Ce désir nourrissait tous les aspects de ma vie. J'étais comme quelqu'un qui était passionnément amoureux de la vie mais qui ne se contentait pas de la penser. Je voulais toucher la vie, je voulais goûter la vie. C'est comme quand on est amoureux, quand on "tombe en amour" comme vous dites au Québec. Tout ce qu'on est se focalise dans cette recherche—une passion dévorante, une qualité d'attention, une persévérance. Seule la fiancée existe, seul se plonger dans ce regard existe, seulement pouvoir la toucher, mettre la main dans sa main, sentir ce délicieux contact, sentir son parfum, entendre sa voix. C'est ça mon cheminement spirituel. C'était d'être à la recherche de moi et de découvrir progressivement combien la vie m'a aimé, combien je suis aimé.

Dans ce cheminement je me suis souvent égaré; parfois j'ai découvert certains sommets où il me semblait que là Dieu me prenait dans ses mains, où j'étais avec ma fiancée et que rien d'autre n'existait: aucun doute, aucune culpabilité, aucune souffrance, aucun jugement.

J'étais ce que j'étais, unifié à moi. C'était un moi qui n'avait pas de distance, c'était un moi où n'existait pas la différence, c'était un moi qui unissait tout. Et puis, n'étant pas prêt encore à recevoir la totalité de la vie, je suis tombé de cette montagne et je me suis identifié à toutes les souffrances du monde. La vie ne m'a pas épargné, je n'ai pas été un privilégié et là, avec une très très grande obstination, avec détermination, je suis reparti à l'assaut d'une nouvelle montagne de moi- même, d'un nouveau sommet de moi-même. Certainement Dieu a dû prendre pitié de ce gamin, de ce jeune homme, de ce papa, de cet homme marié, et Il a permis à ce que de nouveau, j'accède à un nouveau sommet. Et comme je n'étais pas encore prêt, je n'avais pas encore découvert tous mes mensonges, toutes mes croyances, eh! bien, de nouveau je suis retombé. Et ainsi de suite, une succession de sommets, une succession de verticalités, d'altitudes, une succession d'échecs ont jalonné ma vie.

Comment l'éveil a-t-il changé ton quotidien, plus particulièrement ta relation avec ta famille, tes amis, tes collègues ?

Cela n'a rien changé et cela a tout changé. Rien parce ce que je suis toujours un homme. J'ai toujours le même corps, j'ai toujours des défauts qu'on peut interpréter comme humains. Cela a tout changé parce que je suis devenu intègre, honnête, impeccable. C'est un bouleversement tellement inexplicable; il est très difficile de parler de l'inexplicable, de ce qui ne se commande pas. Au sein de la relation avec ma femme, l'éveil m'a appris à la servir davantage, à être attentif davantage à elle et de la considérer comme le bien le plus précieux du monde. Avant, j'étais trop occupé à regarder ma progression spirituelle et à m'occuper de moi et de mes apparences. Maintenant la fiancée est toujours fiancée; ce n'est plus ma femme, c'est ma fiancée et ma relation avec elle est une relation de virginité. Je la vois nouvelle et je suis nouveau, naissant au monde. Naissant, j'entre en naissance. La même chose avec mes enfants, la même chose avec mes amis. Aucune place n'est réservée à ce petit David qui revendiquait trop a titre personnel. Il n'y a plus de place pour le servir ce petit. Maintenant le petit David, le tout petit enfant est là pour servir les autres. À chaque fois que je rencontre quelqu'un, je suis animé de la même flamme, de la même urgence. Comment vais-je pouvoir lui transmettre ce qu'il est déjà ? Comment vais-je faire pour qu'il redevienne ce petit enfant innocent qu'il était ? Comment vais-je faire pour qu'il retrouve sa propre liberté ? C'est une obsession mais qui n'est pas lourde. C'est une obsession de communiquer pour que chacun d'entre nous puisse goûter cette qualité de liberté.

Nous voulons tous vivre avec la légèreté d'être et avec l'innocence des enfants mais les fardeaux de la vie nous en empêchent. Que faut-il faire afin de se libérer de ces fardeaux, de ces peurs du passé, de ces angoisses et des incertitudes du futur ?

Ce qu'il faut faire, c'est d'arrêter d'être victime et de construire sa victime. La conquête de la liberté est réservée aux hommes et aux femmes intègres, aux gens courageux. Elle est réservée aux hommes généreux. Un homme courageux est un homme qui est fort et qui fait face à tous les défis de la vie où il ne se cache pas derrière la non-action. Penser freine l'action. On peut penser pour agir en introduisant le futur, l'imaginaire ou en gardant le passé, ceci n'est pas un problème mais se servir du passé pour justifier la non-action ou se servir du futur en prétendant qu'il y a une difficulté de l'action est une absurdité.

Quand j'étais tout petit, si la pensée me venait : "Tiens là-bas, là-bas, tout en haut sur la montagne, oh! là, là, non, non, je ne vais pas y aller, j'ai trop peur." Immédiatement en moi c'est levé le courage et la question était : "Comment peux-tu savoir si tu as peur puisque tu n'y es pas monté ?" Alors je me mettais en marche et j'allais voir en haut. J'allais voir si j'avais peur ou pas. Je m'apercevais à ce moment là qu'il y a les peurs du réel qu'il est nécessaire de garder sinon, s'il n'y a pas de garde-fou en haut de la montagne, on va se jeter dans le vide. Donc, il y a une qualité de peur qui est naturelle. Par contre, la peur de la peur, celle qui était imaginaire avant que je fasse l'action de monter sur la montagne, celle-là est inutile. Dans la vie, j'ai appris à faire face au réel, à le transformer et à combattre l'imaginaire. On ne peut pas agir avec un mirage. On ne peut pas manger l'ombre de la pomme. Si on a faim, on mange la pomme.

Tu as écrit : "Le mystère de la vie n'est pas un problème à résoudre mais une réalité à expérimenter." Faire face au réel quand nous sommes troublés, angoissés, ce n'est pas toujours facile. Comment affronter le vrai ?

On se sert du réel, de ce qui est, de chaque situation, de chaque événement, de chaque relation pour grandir et pour découvrir que l'autre est une solution. L'autre peut être un homme, une femme, l'autre peut être une situation géographique, ça peut être une voiture qui tombe en panne, ça peut être un obstacle dans la nature, ça peut être un orage, ça peut être le soleil, tout ce qui est autre n'est qu'un prétexte à ce que je redécouvre ma solution. Il est important de faire face aux problèmes réels, pas aux problèmes imaginaires et de bien discriminer les deux, sinon, on est toujours dans une utopie, on sera toujours dans une utopie de la gestion de nos problèmes.

Dans ton livre "Rêve d'éveil" tu as écrit : "L'éveil n'apporte rien en plus : il délivre. Il ne donne ni la sécurité ni le confort. . . l'éveil est une naissance perpétuelle." Mais tu sais, pour tous ces gens qui croient que l'éveil est un état perpétuel d'extase et de félicité, tes propos sont plutôt alarmants. Peux-tu nous éclairer sur ces points ?

[Rires] La sécurité, ça n'existe pas.[Rires] Te voilà rassuré [Rires]. Puisque, à partir de maintenant ça n'existe pas, alors on ne va plus aller chercher ce qui n'existe pas. L'éveil délivre des illusions et ne laisse place qu'au réel. Et progressivement, on va découvrir que le réel ce n'est pas rien. Le réel, c'est de pouvoir exister, c'est qu'une pensée puisse penser "Ah! j'existe" et ça, ce n'est pas rien, c'est d'être étonné d'être en vie et de pouvoir faire l'expérience de la vie. Ah! Tu sens, c'est un petit ah!, comme quand on était des petits enfants, quand on s'étonnait de voir une couleur, de voir une rose, de toucher sa maman, d'entendre le cri d'un oiseau, de parcourir les alentours de la maison et là, cette espèce d'émerveillement, d'étonnement d'être à la vie, est quelque chose qui nous satisfait totalement et qui nous remplit le cœur.

L'émerveillement du moment présen,t c'est ça la vie. C'est ça ton enseignement plus ou moins. Tu ne sembles pas enseigner une philosophie ou une psychologie. Même dans tes ateliers, tu ne réponds pas aux questions. Tu préfères plutôt partager avec les participants cette expérience du "ah! de la vie." Quelles sont les techniques utilisées dans tes ateliers ?

Ce sont les techniques de l'instant. J'aime entrer en émerveillance. J'aime m'étonner. J'ai découvert que je pouvais faire le geste de m'étonner, j'ai découvert que je pouvais être nouveau et que le monde pouvait être nouveau dans chaque instant. Ceci est un acte concret. Ceci n'est pas une fable. S'étonner, s'émerveiller, entrer en existence, ce sont des actes concrets qu'un homme doit pratiquer pour redécouvrir sa propre liberté. C'est un cheminement qu'un homme doit faire seul. Je ne suis pas là pour vous faire des cadeaux. Je suis là pour vous rappeler que vous êtes là et que ça c'est un cadeau. Je suis là pour vous ramener au cœur de votre présent pour que vous goûtiez que vous êtes le présent vivant, le présent de la vie.

Alors dans les ateliers, peut-être avec une certaine maladresse, j'essaie de tout mon cœur, de toute mon âme, de vous faire goûter à ce que je goûte, de vous faire entendre ce que j'entends, de vous faire toucher ce que je touche, de vous faire sentir ce que je sens. Ceci, non pas en vous "embarquant," comme vous dites au Québec, dans des croyances supplémentaires, des abstractions, dans de la connaissance qui va faire du bien au mental, qui va caresser l'idéal. Moi je suis plutôt là pour vous frictionner l'idéal pour que ça soit quelque chose de pratique. Tout ce qui est connaissance intellectuelle permet d'entretenir l'analyse, la séparation, moi distance non moi. Moi, je dois chercher ce que lui doit vivre. Ce mécanisme de la justification de la séparation est inconcevable. C'est pour ça que la seule chose qui m'intéresse c'est de vous apprendre des choses pratiques.

L'acte de conscience est un acte concret. Tout dans la vie est concrétude. Vous avez soif, vous faites un geste pour boire; vous voulez vous déplacer, vous marcher; vous voulez apprendre à rouler à bicyclette vous faites un acte; vous voulez manger vous faites un acte. Tout est pratique. Un partage qui ne serait pas pratique et qui ne serait que théorique, qui justifierait que vous ne pouvez pas vivre ici, maintenant, serait un enseignement qui entretiendrait l'âge d'or, un âge plus tard, plus loin, une autre fois. Ce que j'essaie de partager c'est le goût de l'instant. Seulement ce goût là, "présent," "présent," "maintenant," "maintenant." Et si c'était la seule voie "maintenant "et si tout était là "maintenant "?

Et maintenant, comme le dit la chanson : "Et maintenant que vais-je faire"?

[Rires] Bien continue à poser des questions. [Rires]

Pour le jeu nous allons continuer. Tu parles souvent du jeu, le jeu des croyances qu'on prend un peu trop au sérieux. Dès notre enfance nous recevons des croyances de nos parents, nos professeurs, le clergé, la société. Il y a des bonnes croyances et des croyances destructives. Qu'est-ce qu'on fait avec toutes ces croyances afin de s'éveiller à soi-même et faire de nous un guerrier du présent ?

Les croyances sont de vieux vêtements dont il faut se débarrasser à tout prix. Dès mon enfance, j'ai cru au Père Noël. Lorsque la réalité de la vie m'a fait découvrir que le Père Noël n'existait pas, j'ai été très déçu. J'en ai voulu à mon père, à ma mère, et j'ai vécu ça comme un drame. Donc, il va falloir voir et dénoncer ces croyances, ces vieux vêtements et s'autoriser à être seulement dans l'émotion de l'instant, dans le désir de l'instant, dans la croyance saine du seul moment présent. Vigilance, discrimination, lucidité doivent être les qualités qui nous permettent de voir lorsqu'on embarque dans des scénarios trop mal écrits. Dès notre enfance, on nous a appris à censurer nos émotions, on nous a appris à ne plus être vrai dans l'instant. On nous a conditionnés à être par rapport aux apparences. Il sera nécessaire de démonter ces vieilles peaux, d'enlever ces vieux vêtements. Pas pour rejeter tout ce que la société a fait jusqu'à maintenant mais seulement pour voir que ces croyances ne doivent pas entraver ma liberté. Ce ne sont que des étapes nécessaires pour la découverte de je suis, de maintenant, de ma propre liberté et de ma propre réalité.

Les croyances qui me culpabilisent, les croyances qui font que je me juge continuellement, les croyances qui me confortent dans ce que je ne dois pas, toutes ces croyances là doivent être examiner avec lucidité. Il faut transformer ces croyances en une action, en un agir de la liberté. On va devenir "agissant." Les croyances qui justifient la non-action seront décapitées par les "guerriers du présent." Un guerrier du présent, c'est celui qui est établi dans l'art de la paix. Celui qui est établi dans l'art de la paix, sait cultiver l'art de l'honnêteté, il sait être dans l'action, il est "l'agi." Pour cela, il est vigilant, précis, et il a su décapiter la tête de toutes les croyances et de tout ce qui n'était pas vrai dans l'instant ici, maintenant. Il est établi dans "quand je vois je vois, quand je pense je pense." Il ne mélange pas ces deux plans. Vigilant, il est dans le geste de l'impeccabilité et le geste de l'impeccabilité, c'est de garder la main sur le pommeau de son sabre. Il ne se sert pas de son sabre pour partir en guerre, pour désigner les autres comme étant des ennemis : ma femme, mes enfants, le monde, les banquiers, les guerres. Il se sert de son sabre pour restaurer la relation entre lui et lui. Entre lui, victime du monde et lui, victime des autres. En faisant cela, établi dans son unité, dans son impeccabilité, il ne permet pas aux conflits de naître entre lui et lui. Ne mettant, ne permettant pas aux conflits de naître, il ne nourrit pas la guerre de la relation avec les circonstances et les autres. Il est ce qu'il est, établi dans une quiétude bienfaisante, attentif, servant la vie, étant "agi." C'est un guerrier qui se sert de son sabre pour guérir, non pas pour tuer. Il se sert de son sabre pour guérir sa relation entre lui et lui et toute supposée séparation.

Établi dans une quiétude bienfaisante, comment un parent doit-il faire face aux émotions, aux changements perpétuels chez ses enfants et particulièrement chez l'adolescent ?

Les parents doivent apprendre à être vrai. Être vrai, c'est maintenant. Le malheur commence maintenant si les parents ne sont pas vrais maintenant dans leur relation entre eux. Ils doivent transmettre qu'il est juste d'avoir des émotions, qu'il est juste d'avoir des réactions mais ceci étant seulement que l'émotion de l'instant et la réaction de l'instant, la colère de l'instant et la joie de l'instant. Il ne faut pas faire naître chez l'enfant qu'il existe une potentialité à bouder, à stocker son émotion ou à garder cette insatisfaction permanente. Si les parents ne montrent pas l'exemple, les enfants n'auront pas ces références. Être vrai. Être vrai seulement pour cet instant là.

Les parents doivent cultiver l'art de l'étonnement d'être et de se laisser enseigner par les enfants qui vont s'étonner du papillon qui passe, du brin d'herbe, du petit ver de terre qui traverse la rue, d'une mouche qui vole. Les parents vont devoir aller à l'école des enfants. En étant dans cette qualité de relation, ils vont redevenir eux-mêmes des enfants. Cultiver l'art de l'étonnement d'être. Cultiver la relation immédiate avec les émotions. Cultiver l'action et entretenir les jeux. Jouer avec les enfants, les toucher, les caresser. Les enfants ont besoin d'être reconnus. Une discipline est aussi nécessaire. Il faudra leur montrer quelles sont les limites, autrement, ce n'est pas leur rendre service que de ne pas leur montrer les limites de la revendication qui ne serait pas l'émotion de l'instant. Permettre à un enfant de s'enfermer dans une humeur, c'est lui permettre d'entrer dans un monde de non-action. Là, on entre dans le monde des fainéants qui préfèrent bouder l'action plutôt que d'être dans l'action. Les parents doivent nourrir les enfants pour la seule vérité qu'est l'instant présent. Ils doivent nourrir les enfants de leur délicatesse de ce qu'ils sont. Ils doivent leur transmettre à exprimer leurs émotions. Si un papa n'arrive pas à dire à sa femme : "Tu sais, aujourd'hui j'ai remarqué que tu as changé de robe et que tu es coiffée comme ça. Tu sais, je suis content d'être ton mari, tu sais, j'aime rentrer à la maison. Tu sais, j'aime ta présence, j'aime ta compagnie." Les parents doivent arriver à se dire entre eux, à se nourrir entre eux d'une façon constructive, permanente, dynamique, créatrice. La relation ne s'arrête jamais; elle se construit chaque seconde. Si les parents ne font pas voir ça aux enfants, s'ils ne montrent que la face opposée c'est-à-dire : je suis fatigué, pourquoi tu as fait ceci, pourquoi tu as fait cela, il faudrait que tu fasses ceci, il faudrait que tu fasses cela. Les enfants apprennent par mimétisme à reproduire ce genre de revendication. Ceci ne veut pas dire qu'il faut que les parents ne se disputent pas du tout, ce serait absurde parce que les enfants n'auraient pas les repères pour savoir se défendre. Ceci veut dire que les parents doivent apprendre à être vrais, mais ne pas oublier de nourrir. La société passe son temps, actuellement, à détruire. Le nombre de mariages détruits est la preuve que la vie n'est pas nourrie. Un enfant doit être nourri, non seulement de la nourriture terrestre mais de la nourriture du vivant, de l'exemple que les parents doivent donner entre eux. Une enfant doit être nourri de l'art de l'étonnement, de l'art du respect, de l'art de la relation avec le réel.

Faire face au réel, est-ce faire face au mystère ?
[Rires] Préservons le mystère, ne soyons pas des profanateurs de mystères. Entrons consciemment en "je ne suis pas", "je ne sais pas".

David, rencontrer un éveillé, s'il n'y a rien à comprendre, qu'est-ce que ça donne ?
L'homme est tellement habile dans l'art de créer des concepts, dans l'art de s'illusionner, dans l'art de tricher avec lui-même. Il arrive à des niveaux de raisonnement de plus en plus sophistiqués pour garder ses points de vue, ses opinions, ses croyances, ses ancrages. Il

arrive même à conceptualiser que la conscience est en dehors de la conscience. C'est comme ça que les croyances s'articulent, se fixent. On arrive à nous faire croire à nous-mêmes que le paradis existe dans le paradis. Ca veut dire que ce n'est pas ici. On arrive à nous faire croire que Dieu, c'est un ailleurs. C'est absurde. Rencontrer un éveillé, c'est prendre le risque de vous rencontrer, vous rencontrer au-delà de vos masques, de vos apparences, de vos propres croyances, de vos propres identifications. Fondamentalement, je n'ai aucun pouvoir pour transformer le réel, pour transformer le monde. Je ne suis pas le créateur du monde. Je suis comme un rayon de soleil ou comme un fils envers son père. Je sais que je suis le fils de mon papa. Moi je ne suis pas papa. Je suis ce rayon de soleil seulement, je ne suis pas le soleil. Dieu crée, l'homme rêve, ainsi l'œuvre s'accomplit. Dieu écrit la vie, le réel. Moi je lis mon existence pure, ma conscience d'être personnellement là. Ainsi l'homme et Dieu sont main dans la main. Ensemble ils écrivent l'histoire, ils se racontent l'histoire de la relation éternelle, de l'alliance éternelle, de l'amour éternel. Dieu seul crée. Je sais seulement que je suis son enfant chéri et c'est parce que je le sais et que je sais donner la main à Dieu que je sais faire l'acte de "maintenant," que j'honore ma relation et que j'honore mon humanité. Je ne peux que vous faire redécouvrir la présence à l'émerveillement qui est déjà en vous. Je ne peux que seulement vous donner le goût pour que vous goûtiez à votre liberté. Tout est déjà là maintenant seulement pour cet instant. Seulement pour cet instant—là où le temps est la mesure de l'éternité, où l'enfant est relié au vivant.

ELIZABETH KLARICH

While researching various teachers, I stumbled upon an exquisitely beautiful yoga and meditation center in Costa Rica called Pura Vida. The facility sits on a twelve-acre mountainside estate surrounded by a stunning tropical atmosphere, laden with butterflies and colorful birds. It's a wonderful space to simply relax and be tranquility itself. Fortuitously Elizabeth Klarich was offering a yoga retreat at Pura Vida at the same time my wife Sylvia was consulting with Colorado State University's International Clean Air Conference in San José. The timing was perfect.

Clutching a crumpled piece of paper with directions in Spanish, I hopped into a San José taxi in search of Pura Vida. It was night so the streets all looked alike. To make things more challenging I was hopelessly illiterate in Spanish and the driver knew about ten words in English. We did a lot of hand waving, pointing and laughing. As the taxi bumped through the streets toward Pura Vida I wondered what it must have been like to get there without any road at all. A similar experience no doubt. We finally arrived at Pura Vida and two large iron gates swung open revealing an Eden-like enclave where Elizabeth and her students were housed. The taxi driver and I exchanged good-byes as if we'd known each other from childhood and shifted on to our next adventure, his with yet another itinerant tourist devoid of language skills and directions, mine interviewing a yoga adept.

Elizabeth has been a yoga instructor for twenty-four years. Her depth and breadth in this discipline are exemplary. She has a rare quality of heart and body awareness that unfolds very naturally as a wonderful vehicle of selfless giving. Working out of Billings, Montana, Elizabeth is well suited to our definition of an "emerging spiritual teacher." Being with Elizabeth is like going to a remote town outside the buzz of a big city and finding a castle in the wheat fields. Have you heard of Pella, Iowa? In the middle of a vast expanse of America's heartland is a pristine little town full of tulips in the spring (they have a tulip festival each year), perfect lawns, scrumptious bakeries, and cleanly scrubbed kids. Like this, Elizabeth is a brightly colored tulip sprouting in the vastness of the universe for all of us to enjoy being with.

ॐ ॐ ॐ

We are very pleased to be visiting with Elizabeth Kalrich, who is an "Intuitive Yoga" instructor and has been teaching yoga for twenty-four years. Our meeting is being held at a beautiful facility in Alajuela, Costa Rica, where Elizabeth and a number of other yoga and spiritual teachers offer courses and retreats. Elizabeth, thank you for spending time with us this evening.

Thank you.

Where did you grow up and what impact has it had on your life?

I was born and raised in Kansas City along with three sisters and six brothers. So I was made aware at a young age of the inevitability of pain and suffering in life. My parents, devout Catholics with a strong work ethic, struggled to make ends meet. My external environment, as is always the case, could not give me the peace, love and joy that I craved. Exploring the "inner environment" for the Divine qualities that I sought began in early childhood and impacted my choice to begin the study of yoga when I was a teenager. As a very young child I was blessed with the intuitive guidance to discover techniques for deepening self-realization. One practice that I found myself doing was to gaze into my own eyes in the mirror to look for unconditional love. I found it there, discovering the phenomenon that "the eyes are the windows of the soul."

Did you spontaneously come upon this practice or was it something that you read, heard about or got from some source outside of yourself?
It was a spontaneous discovery. I had not read or heard about it.

Were your parents very religious people? Did they actually go to church and have a formal practice of religion?
Very much so.

Did you find anything in their religion that connected with what you knew to be true about yourself?
What I found in the particular branch of "churchianity" that my parents practiced and raised me in as well as other organized denominations I explored, was emptiness and unanswered questions. That gave me more motivation to find fulfillment within myself and to be rooted in inner spirituality. Organized religions did not hold the truth that I was looking for, so my desire to seek and find the peace and love that I was looking for turned more intensely inward.

You're using the term "emptiness" in a different way than the Buddhists would refer to as "emptiness," aren't you?
The "emptiness" I speak of is positive in that it served to pull me toward deeper inner seeking in order to find the fulfillment of feeling connected, loved, at peace, in joy and with purpose.

While growing up, do you recall any "awakening" experiences that really deepened the recognition of your spiritual nature?

Oh yes! Awakening experiences are happenings that expand my mind and open my heart. As a child, and to this day, I have the experience of "seeing through" concrete objects, as if they were transparent. This lifts my awareness to a place of "knowing" that physical objects are simply "energy" in frozen form. I've always had the innate desire to look for and see the good in all. I've always been fascinated by the exploration of life. I've always been blessed with the ability to see the light within the darkness. I am a sensitive and idealistic person, so any level of violence from disrespect to overt abuse felt anguishing. Turning inward to find peace and truth gave me the clarity to see that violence is rooted in fear and in the ego's desire to control.

Violence often disguises itself in self-righteousness and in a myriad of addictions, so it gets justified, leaving offenders tangled in the sticky web of denial. Violence and fear are not always blatant. They can wear a variety of costumes including greediness, authoritarianism, possessiveness, jealousy, arrogance, sycophancy, criticism, gossip, judgment, perfectionism, rejection, depression, moodiness, polluting, yelling at or scolding another in a harsh or attacking way, and complaining. Fear-based noxious habits manifest in varying levels of intensity, from low to high. The low-grade levels of harmful attitudes and behavior are harder to see and accept. They are the last to be weeded out of a person's garden of behavior traits. Unless the roots of violence are pulled, they perpetuate and recycle.

Healing my wounded heart has required that I face my fears and embrace my suffering so that ego could no longer hold me hostage in the claws of violence and illusion of separation. From my perspective, demons of the past are inherent opportunities for "awakening experiences." Courage, trust, and love are necessary for one to move through fear, pain, shame, and anger into a place of acceptance and deepened compassion. The bigger picture is that each person needs to do the hard soul work of healing personal wounds in order to release the past, purify body-mind, open the heart, experience wholeness, and ultimately serve mankind, and thus help raise the consciousness of the planet.

How do you define the term "Yoga," and what brought you to this particular path?

To define yoga as "union" is simple and easy. When I share this definition with students through participation in a guided meditation of inner body and breath awareness, the result is that a sense of being connected and whole (united) is experienced. In this way, words and definitions expand into meaningful inner knowing through a transformative body-mind-breath experience.

Intuitively, I was drawn to this path as a child, exploring my inner body, breath and mind. I would watch my breath and "play" with various ways of controlling it. I would watch my thoughts and feelings as if I was an outside observer, and feel the energy in my body as it moved in and through me. I loved to stretch and hold my body in a variety of positions just for the pure joy of feeling how it shifted my energy. None of this was taught to me. I just did it because I was "drawn" to inner exploration.

When I was a young teenager, my sister exposed me to Kundalini Yoga. Upon taking my first yoga class at the age of seventeen (at Phoenix College), I realized that I had been practicing techniques like these already, and was delighted to find that what I was doing had a name: yoga! Other people were doing it also and there were places to share it! I knew right then and there that I would be a yoga teacher, and would devote my life to being a student of yoga. The level of peace, bliss, joy, upliftment, and contentment I experienced in that first class left me with no doubt that I had found my path, and I gave up all other pursuits in my life to study yoga.

Why is the type of yoga that you teach called "Intuitive Yoga"? How does it differ from other forms of yoga such as kundalini yoga, iyengar yoga, asthanga yoga?

All types of yoga that you mentioned, and many others that you did not, have specific techniques and forms to be performed by everyone in a "follow the leader" manner. Some approaches to yoga determine exactly which poses to perform, the order in which they should be practiced, the length of time to hold each pose, specific instructions on how to hold every body part in each pose including repetitious patterns of exercising postures, and directing every person in the class to do exactly the same thing. This allows little or no variation to accommodate the differences in people. The practice of hatha yoga increases strength and flexibility, yet lends itself toward greater ego-identification with attachment to accomplishments in the poses.

In contrast, practicing "Intuitive Yoga" increases strength and flexibility through releasing attachment to ego identification. "Intuitive Yoga" is living in each present moment completely. It is letting go of the past and allowing the future to take care of itself. "Intuitive Yoga" begins with exploring the inner body to discover how each person feels, what each student needs, where tension is held, and then how to effectively release blocked energy. "Intuitive Yoga" is rooted in acceptance and respect for the individuality of each person, and is a conscious process of self-exploration. It is a personal and freeing approach to practicing yoga rather than a specified system dictated by outside authority. It is a practice of awareness and exploration that enhances self-trust. It is nurturing to body-mind, heart and soul.

Doing yoga in this way develops intuitive faculties. Albert Einstein said, "the only really valuable thing is intuition." The science and art of yoga continues to evolve, and practicing yoga in an intuitive way encourages this evolution by serving to expand consciousness rather than advocating the conformity and rigidity of identifying with a specific path or method.

Conforming to established methods develops discipline and security, yet ultimately can be stifling and contracting to soul growth. "Intuitive Yoga" is creative and enjoyable, comforting and calming. It is practicing the presence of peace, thus deepening contentment. The more we dwell in our center of peace, the more we experience the power of peace in our lives. In the twenty-four years that I have taught classes, no two classes have ever been the same. The starting point of each class is an inquiry into the special needs and requests of the participants, and proceeds by encouraging the individuals to put their developing intuition and body awareness to use at all times! Intuitive yoga is the opposite of "one-size-fits-all" yoga. I would never advocate "no pain, no gain" or physically nudge a student beyond their intuitively determined edge.

Some spiritual teachers have said that one cannot practice "unity" because we are always already in unity presently. Others claim that striving and practice is necessary. Is there such a thing as "effortless realization"?

Words get in the way here. "Effort" takes on different connotations for people, depending on the needs, the level of awareness, and the place of consciousness that a person is experiencing. For one person, perhaps it takes effort to choose, and do that which honors self and others. For someone else, perhaps letting go of effort—surrendering—is necessary for realizing peace and unity. For me, there are times when I need to exert effort so that I can focus my energy toward the light of acceptance, clarity, forgiveness, and gratitude. Inherent in the process of consciously focusing my energy is the process of surrender: letting go of expectations, desires, the need to control, judgments, resentments and fears. As spiritual beings in a human experience, we live in a world of duality, so we will face the obstacle of unreliability until we are anchored in the Divine.

Ego is required in order to move in the direction of transcending ego. Most people will find it necessary to put effort into being reliable and true, yet at the same time, will need to let go of trying so they can fully "be" in the present moment awareness where peace and unity are found.

When the famous Indian saint Ramakrisna was asked to become anyone's guru, he always replied, "Satchitananda or absolute bliss consciousness is the one and only guru." Can you comment on this statement?

"Absolute bliss consciousness is the one and only guru." This statement rings true for me. As I hear you say this, the energy of these words feels good in my heart, body, mind. The one true center of bliss peace, joy and love which is within each one of us is truly the guru. However, just as I would want and need a great teacher and guide before I attempted to climb Mount Everest, I believe in the efficacy of true spiritual guides in showing the way and providing techniques to assist in the spiritual quest. Personally, Paramahansa Yogananda's teachings and his techniques, including Kriya Yoga, together with my practice of intuitive yoga serve to put me in touch with the guru within.

Elizabeth, how would you define the term "enlightenment"?

Enlightenment is; in Light always. It is freedom from the vrittis (whirls) of thought/emotion; freedom from the illusion of separation. I have been blessed with "glimpses" of enlightenment, dwelling there, then losing full consciousness again. Oh, how I long to be anchored there, in the Divine, in that peace, love, light, joy, bliss, indescribable infinity of ever-new joy! It's there within me, always, and within all beings. We only need to improve our knowing and consciously practice our awareness of "enlightenment" as our essence. Our minds and egos get in the way of seeing our true essence. Our birthright is to go home, know truth, be in peace and love eternally.

Do you think "enlightenment" could be one's essential realization even though thoughts and emotions arise?

Enlightenment is our true essence and reality. All else is an illusion, a dream, not real. Enlightenment is absolute bliss; seeing the dream world of maya (the illusion of physical form) as if it were a movie on the screen of life. Enlightenment is being in complete peace and clearly seeing beyond or through the dream world that seems real to us when we are under the spell of maya.

Why do you think there remains such confusion in these times about enlightenment?

Because we are in an age that is evolving in the right direction yet still quite a long way from an age when enlightened human beings will be plentiful on the planet. As more human beings become enlightened, there will be a "rippling effect," so the confusion will start to melt away. This planet is serving as a laboratory for soul evolution and it is presently hosting a large number of works-in-progress in a very useful and functional way. A lot of confusion exists because many seekers don't want to accept that this trip to enlightenment is a long-haul journey.

Do you think there is such a thing as "personal enlightenment" where an individual becomes completely "fulfilled," or is it only possible from an "impersonal" perspective which goes beyond the "personal"? Is there anything to gain or lose by becoming enlightened?

Jesus, Buddha, Krishna, Yogananda, and many other individuals have reached "enlightenment." Since our essence is Divine, the only thing to lose is our ego attachment to the illusion that we are separate.

Do you think there is anything to gain?
Ever-new bliss and freedom from suffering.
Personal enlightenment for some would mean that they "own" enlightenment, that they "gain" enlightenment for themselves. Impersonal enlightenment would mean that there would be nothing to gain and there would be nothing to lose.

The great ones who are Self-realized, or "enlightened," are One with All, and live for the purpose of helping all souls to find the light of peace and love within themselves and within all of life. There is a preservation of individuality according to my spiritual teachers even though this seems paradoxical in some respects to the notion of being united with the One. Paradoxes seem to be the rule rather than the exception when it comes to such spiritual matters. Perhaps enlightenment is both personal and impersonal just as our relationship to God can be.

Who are some of the most influential spiritual teachers that you have encountered?

My most influential spiritual teacher is Paramahansa Yogananda and his lineage of teachers. The Buddha is a strong influence in my life. Saint Francis of Assisi has been a strong connection for me all of my life. His "Peace Prayer" has been my silent mantra (prayer) for many years. I am instantly blessed when I silently pray, "Lord, make me an instrument of Thy peace; where there is hatred, let me sow love; where there is injury, pardon; where there is doubt, faith; where there is despair, hope; where there is darkness, light; and where there is sadness, joy. Oh Divine Master, grant that I may not so much seek to be consoled as to console; to be understood as to understand; to be loved as to love; for it is in giving that we receive. It is in pardoning that we are pardoned, and it is in dying that we are born to eternal life."

Also the great souls of Mahatma Gandhi, Walt Whitman—I often think of his quote: "Every moment of light and dark is a miracle." Also Ralph Waldo Emerson and Henry David Thoreau have inspired me tremendously. *The Quiet Mind* by White Eagle is a wonderful pocket-sized book filled with messages of inspiration. When I open this book to any page, I find something to uplift my spirit. For example, White Eagle says, "Apply love to your problem. Love is the great solvent of all difficulties, all problems, all misunderstandings. Apply love, by your inner attitude towards any human problem. Put aside the reasoning mind. Let divine love operate in you. Give from your inner self God's love, and you will be surprised to find that every problem will be solved; every knot loosened."

What about any particular yoga teachers who deeply effected you?

Paramahansa Yoganandaji, who taught yoga, has strongly effected my spiritual growth. Many of his inspirational sayings are favorite mantras for me. "Live each present moment completely, and the future will take care of itself. Fully enjoy the wonder and beauty of each instant. Practice the presence of peace. The more you do that the more you will feel the presence of that power in your life! Calmness is the living breath of Divine immorality within you. Be actively calm and calmly active. You are the master of the moments of your life." I share these sayings in my classes frequently, and I have silently repeated these powerful words over and again in my mind so that I feel their inspiration in my heart and their effect on my life.

Is there anyone who is currently alive, or who is a contemporary that has been an important influence?

Sri Kryananda, also known as Donald Walters, has had a strong influence on me. He lived with Yogananda, and shares Yogananda's teachings along with his own life experiences and thoughts on yoga. Daya Mata, who presently leads the Self-Realization Fellowship—Yogananda's organization—and is a pure light in the world. Also Sri Eknath Easwaran who wrote "The Supreme Ambition" and "Your Life is Your Message." He founded the Blue Mountain Center of Meditation in Tomales, California. He just recently died. He was an incredibly inspiring spiritual teacher. Gary Zukav is inspirational; his book *The Seat of Soul* is great! Joan Borysenko is wonderful! She wrote *Minding the Body, Mending the Mind, Pocketful of Miracles* and many other great books.

Deepak Chopra, Jon Kabat-Zinn, Richard Carlson and Wayne Dyer are also uplifting mentors. Georg Feuerstein, founder of the Indian Academy of Yoga, and Co-Director of the Yoga Research Center at Durham University, is a tremendously dedicated teacher. My husband and I subscribe to "The Science of Mind" magazine which is also great food for the soul. I've recently read *The Power of Now* by Eckhart Tolle. I'm very inspired by his powerful consciousness-raising message! Mother Teresa's life has been awe-inspiring, as is the Dalai Lama's. There are many inspiring souls in our world that are uplifting the collective consciousness of humankind, and I'm grateful to them for sharing their gifts.

Have you spent any time with Kriyananda?

I've met him and spent some time with him, and have heard him speak several times over the past twenty-four years. He's always uplifting and enjoyable. I've spent time in the community that he started— Ananda—in Northern California. I've studied with Valerie and Santosh O'Hara, participating in their yoga teacher-training program. Valerie wrote, *The Fitness Option* and *Wellness at Work*. I hold them in high regard as personal mentors who have deeply influenced my life's work. I am eternally thankful to them for how they've blessed my life in many ways.

Some controversy has arisen around Kriyananda and the community of Ananda. Do you have any information about that or what is going on there?

I see Ananda and Self-Realization Fellowship both in a positive light and I have watched their controversy as if two of my family members were at odds and feuding. It has been unsettling at times but I know that both spread Yogananda's teachings in a significant way. I am chagrined by the personal attacks on Kriyananda because his service to Yogananda and the legions of seekers is remarkable. I have been impressed with the way the Ananda community has seen the spiritual blessings behind this darkest of clouds, which has threatened their very existence.

Historically there's either been a predominance of female energy or a predominance of male energy. How would the fusion or balance of these two energies best come about in the world today?

Rooting ourselves in reverence will deepen our respect for all of life in its many aspects. We can then teach tolerance and celebrate diversity, thus finding balance. Many great yogis start to manifest even physically a balance of male and female characteristics. The widespread practice of yoga would indeed be the best way to accomplish the fusion and balancing.

A famous spiritual teacher once said, "the sole purpose and goal for human life is to cultivate love. The most pure, passionate, intimate love—to be the very incarnation of Divine Love." How does yoga work to bring this about?

Those words are music to my heart! That quote describes my purpose for living. Living for love is my reason for teaching in a personal, intimate way and with a deep passion for sharing the joy and freedom of intuitive yoga. My path of mothering [Elizabeth has a daughter named Carissa Shanti] has been devotional (bhakti). I want to nurture the pure love that is the essence of this child that has blessed my life. Bhakti Yoga is the path of devotion. Karma Yoga is the path of action, without desire for the fruits of our work. Raja Yoga is the practice of bhakti, karma, jnana (wisdom, knowledge), plus meditation. Practicing hatha yoga for the purpose of nurturing our body, mind and soul is doing yoga with and for heart expansion. Sharing yoga with others, especially when we meet people where they're at, and are willing to serve their needs in a caring way, opens the heart and deepens our compassion. In classes, during savasana, we focus on the peace of our breath waves, the light of loving energy in our beating hearts, the wisdom of truth in our uplifted eyes (gazing through the brow point—the spiritual eye), and the joy of gratitude in our smiles.

How does a person choose which spiritual path is best for them?

Learn trust in oneself. Take time to be quiet and listen within to that one clear voice of intuition. Listen to and follow the soft inner guidance rather than being influenced by the noisy external distractions of the crowd that relinquishes personal empowerment to an outer authority. If the mind is active and resists quieting, then practice silent repetition of a Holy Name or a hallowed phrase or a memorized inspirational message. Then be quiet and feel the effects within.

Look to others who are on a heart-centered path for spiritual companionship, mutual inspiration and support rather than for identity, answers, or power. Find joy in helping others. Draw inspiration from writings by and about the world's great spiritual figures and from the scriptures of all religions. Trust that the guru is within, and the best spiritual path for each person is found within. "Know thyself" and "to thine own Self be true!"

Some spiritual teachers indicate that true spiritual liberation is beyond opposites, including good and evil, and it's not possible to evaluate such persons based on their outward behavior. What's your take on this perspective?

Are you basically asking, does good and evil exist, or.....?

There are some teachers who have had "great awakenings" even to the level of being self-confessed realizers, or they have been recognized by other individuals as being a "realizer." And yet when it comes to their outward behavior, sometimes it winds up being completely contradictory to what "normal" moral and ethical behavior would tend to dictate. What's your take on that? There are a lot of people who have a difficult time sorting all of this out for themselves as it relates to spiritual teachers who do things that have been characterized as "Crazy Wisdom."

Living in the moment with deep, well-established inner roots empowers us to live with discrimination and intuition which then guides us. When we are anchored within our own being and practicing the presence of peace, we are able to see clearly when our own ego and the ego of others gets in the way of pure intentions based on love. Self-reflection is essential. Are we walking our talk? Are our actions consistent with our values? If so, then we can clearly see those who are living truth and those who are ego-oriented. Although strange behavior has been attributed to some apparently very advanced incarnations, I am intuitively drawn to those high souls who live their life—like Yogananda—extolling the value of common sense and exuding kindness.

Can you speak of identifying with the body versus not identifying with the body in the state of spiritual liberation?

The body is the vehicle and serves to transport us into Self-Realization. We are more than our body mind. Our completeness contains our body-mind. Our bodies are gifts of life, temples of Divinity through which we can love, serve, and remember our essence, our origin, which is peace.

I'd like to go back a bit and talk about something we discussed before the interview. You mentioned that you have been doing some work in hospitals. Can you share with us what your experience has been, and what it's meant to you in terms of your own spiritual growth?

Working in a hospital as well as in other settings, I teach yoga, stress-reduction, relaxation and meditation. I am also involved with my golden retriever in the canine volunteer program. These venues for helping others have served to deepen my compassion, expand my mind and humble my ego.

Rather than focusing on yoga forms, techniques and systems, which can be the normal approach at centers specifically designed to offer yoga, I have consistently put myself into a situation where I must adapt to a variety of environments along with the people that I meet there. In these arenas, I encounter people who are not typically on the bandwagon of doing yoga because it's the cool thing to do now.

I frequently serve a population of people who don't even realize that yoga has something to offer them! I thrive on the challenge of moving through fears people have about yoga and self-exploration! A little fun-loving kindness works wonders! I also enjoy the challenging serious student who wants to be told just what to do, how to do it, and who wants to "get it right"—attain perfection as pictured in the respected models of hatha yoga. I've mentored several students and have learned volumes doing that. I learn so much from everyone, and I am ever growing and changing.

The tools that I give people to play with are enjoyable, user-friendly, and easily adapted to their personal life-style. Within a common ground of people from all walks of life, I have developed the capacity for understanding how to relate to a wide range of people, and meet them in their comfort zone rather than trying to teach to them or instruct them to do what I think is best or right. I just enjoy the colorful mandala of people, and delight in the solitude, which is necessary to live intuitively. I find joy in serving others. I only want to love, serve, and share joy and peace. If anything that I do is helpful to them, then I am grateful.

What is your dog's name?
Raja.

That's Indian for "royal" isn't it?
Yes! Raja, my wonderful pet-assistant is a one hundred-pound "Royal King of Love and Joy." His presence makes people smile, even when they are very ill. He has such radiant joy for life and love for people. He brought laughter to a young girl who was dying of cancer, and tears of gratitude to her mother who said that her daughter hadn't smiled or laughed for months! The patients feel so uplifted when he visits them! This is the formless yoga of love and the present moment of bliss.

It is amazing how an animal can give such unconditional love and act as a catalyst for bringing about that human love and the human heart in its fullness.
Truly! Pure love just for the sake of love, in all its radiant joy—this is what Raja and my animals can bring about. Moments like these are "glimpses" of enlightenment!

What are some of the most important lessons that you've learned from working with students during the last twenty-four years?
Wow! Where do I begin? I've learned so much from working with students, being married for nearly twenty years and being a mother. I've learned to respect, revere, and honor myself, others, and all of life. Through humbleness I can effectively serve others, get out of the way and just "let it happen." Procrastination feeds worry and hurry, thus blocking creativity. Eliminating procrastination and hurry opens a pathway to calmness. It keeps things simple. Experiencing betrayal is a manifestation of growing pains. Roses are beautiful and also have thorns. Accepting both with equanimity leads to serenity.

Devotion and loyalty are the most powerful healthy pesticides. Practicing loving kindness deepens devotion. Loyalty is a rare quality and is to be treasured. And relaxation is a pathway to releasing fear and pain. Gratitude is a pathway to contentment that has power! "Ah" and "Om" are my favorite sounds.

However, human beings are ever unreliable. Until we are completely anchored in the Divine we all make mistakes. All mistakes are forgivable. Through the power of forgiveness, surrender is possible and through surrender we know freedom. To request permission before touching, that conscious touch is healing; that listening is magical! Listening with ears, eyes, touch and heart is magical, miraculous!

It's also to sing with joy and to recreate in nature! To do so is to glean something from every path of yoga, all religions and all life experiences. It is to create a space especially for meditation. It's to just look upward; to meditate before making a decision or doing a job; to explore the splendor of discovering ways to make action a moving meditation. It is to be mindful, to be grounded and firmly rooted within my body and into Mother Earth. It's to see that patience is powerful and beautiful; that waiting is a gift, an opportunity to meditate. It's to have fun, laugh and enjoy the wonder of beauty, of life. It gives me the ability to help people tap into and utilize the power of breath and posture with movement as well as stillness, and to develop mental focus in order to relax, energize and even help heal from addictions, body aches, and emotional stress. It's a recognition that being service-full is not about pleasing everyone all of the time.

I've learned to accept compliments and gifts with graciousness, to generously give with detachment. Attachment to the need to serve and help others causes suffering. Inner contentment is more awesome and everlasting than the fleeting happiness of accomplishment. See life as holy now! Contemplating on any one of these truths deepens inner "knowing." It's a recognition that "All is One."

If someone were genuinely interested in studying with a spiritual teacher, what should they look for, and what would be the most appropriate attitude to take as a student?
What I look for in a teacher is purity of intention, reverence, respect for people and for all of life. I look for simple kindness, sincerity and compassion. I want a teacher who creates a safe and caring environment. I look for humbleness and groundedness. I want a teacher who nurtures and uplifts my spirit. As a student, the most appropriate atti-

tude to take is one of knowing that the one true guru is within. When looking to another person for learning, I keep solidly anchored in my own inner guru. I explore what needs I have and how I can ask this other person to help me meet those needs.

If you could give one bit of advice to someone truly focused on realizing spiritual liberation in this lifetime, what would it be?

Love yourself, love others, be respectful. That includes being humble, forgiving, nurturing, practicing the presence of peace in each moment. When life gives you a lemon, make lemonade. Cultivate an attitude of gratitude. Spend time alone. Spend time in nature. Enjoy music! Learn and practice the techniques that work for you to be centered and rooted within. Find a spiritual guide who can teach you specific techniques for working with the inner-energies. Kriya yoga is a powerful technique along this line and can hasten one's evolution immensely! Explore being an objective observer of your thoughts, feelings and inner body. Practice slow, deep, complete "retention breathing" as a pathway to settling into your core of calmness. Practice silent repetition of a mantra whenever the mind is idle or agitated. Stimulate, loosen, and lengten the spine; live in your spine, and even shake your body daily! Take breath breaks hourly; inhale fully, then hold the breath in and feel the fullness. Exhale with an "ah" (aum) sound. Be heart centered with your touch. When you lose connection with your inner being and find yourself riding a wave of thought-emotion that pulls you away from your center of peace, return back to your center as soon as you realize you've disconnected from your roots. Be willing to die, surrender. When someone says, "Have a good day," think make a good day! And encourage others to do the same! As Yogananda says, "Be a smile millionaire!" Live for love; love life!

Elizabeth, tell us about your current teaching schedule, and what you hope to be doing in the future. Do you have anything that's scheduled beyond this particular retreat?

I'm very content living in the moment so it's challenging for me to plan and organize for future events. I've found that life unfolds for me and things simply fall into place when I just let go and allow things to be. I teach several classes each week at a local hospital (St. Vincent's), the YMCA, a Racquet Club, and the Adult Education Center.

Twice a month, I tape two half-hour yoga programs for our local community television, which air three mornings and one evening every week. I teach occasional classes in businesses, at schools, senior centers, and the local Cancer Center. I teach yoga to the high school tennis team and help coach the girls' team that my daughter is on. I'm beginning to offer five-to six-day retreats in Red Lodge, Montana; a beautiful mountain setting where we can combine yoga with outdoor recreational activities such as hiking, biking, site-seeing (near and in Yellowstone Park), tennis, golf, and just having fun in one of the most spectacular areas of our country. I've done weekend retreats in Red Lodge for the past several years and will offer my first five-day retreat in August, 2000. For the first time, I am offering a retreat in Tulum, Mexico in January, 2001 and Hawaii in March, 2001. My husband of nearly twenty years has recently retired from high school teaching and would like to help support me in doing more retreats. Putting retreats together requires a lot of planning and organizing, so I'm taking it slow and doing it on a very small scale.

It sounds like now that your husband's retired, he can take on some of those responsibilities?

We hope so! He's teaching part-time at a local college (Montana State University-Billings), and still coaches the high school tennis team that our daughter is on. She's a junior this year. We're taking one step at a time, and will just see how it all unfolds. Life is full and life is good no matter what direction it takes us.

Elizabeth, thank you very much for spending time with us. We hope to meet again in the near future and best wishes with your teaching work.

Thank you John! Best wishes to you also with your book and your life's work!

Contact information:
Elizabeth Klarich
937 N. 24th St.
Billings, MT 59101-0837
E-Mail: intuityoga@aol.com

ECKHART TOLLE

I was first introduced to Eckhart Tolle at the "Gathering 2000", a two-day event in San Diego hosted by Inner Directions. A number of spiritual teachers were invited to make presentations: Ram Das, Lama Surya Das, Adyashanti, Rabbi Shapiro, Byron Katie, Krishna Das, Robin Rabbin, Eckhart Tolle, and others. Five hundred people attended, and everyone seemed to enjoy the event immensely. It turned out to be a relatively light affair sprinkled with lots of humor and laughter which blended beautifully with the weighty topics of enlightenment and liberation.

Eckhart Tolle was scheduled to do his presentation close to the end of the second day. On the stage were two chairs. One chair was over-sized, stuffed and inviting. All of the previous presenters used it. The other chair was a plain, straight-backed wooden model positioned for guests. Eckhart came out and sat in the wooden chair.

Eckhart's presentation lasted for approximately ninety minutes. His delivery was soft and clear. He adeptly articulated main points about "The Presence," the "Pain Body" and other terms referred to in his book, *The Power of Now*. He has an English/German accent and possesses a delightfully droll sense of humor. Eckhart was incredibly insightful as he took us through the mechanism of the mind and presented "the Now" in such a way that it became self-evident. When he finished speaking, the audience literally leapt out of their seats and applauded wildly. The audience's response seemed to arise not from what he said, but from his simple presence of Being. He was clearly an example of someone living in "The Now" and people immediately recognized it. It seemed as if the entire Gathering met in "The Now," and it was awesome. Afterward, Eckhart went outside the meeting hall and autographed his book. Long lines of attendees made their way toward him. He hugged them all. Many had tears of joy in their eyes.

When I arrived at the Gathering I wasn't sure who I wanted to interview. I had heard others ecstatically talk about Eckhart and his teachings, so I made arrangements to interview him the day after his presentation. After hearing him speak, I immediately bought his book, returned to my room and started formulating questions.

The hotel I was staying in was very close to where Eckhart had rented a room. I found myself at his hotel a bit early so I strolled along the shimmering shoreline for a few minutes reflecting on what he shared with us the day before. The simplicity and profundity of "The Now" was still lively in my awareness.

I interviewed Eckhart for nearly two hours. When we finished, I knew I had found someone who was exactly the kind of spiritual teacher I wanted to share with you. He is not well-known, yet exudes a tangible spiritual presence that is genuine, powerful and easily recognizable by many people. I must have said, "Wow!" to myself a dozen times a day for weeks after the interview when I put my attention on Eckhart and his teaching. Please welcome Eckhart into your life and through the "Power of Now" tap directly into your own essence.

This morning we are speaking with Eckhart Tolle. As a note of intro-duction, can you share with us where you grew up and how it impacted your outlook on life?

Yes. I was born in Germany, where I lived for the first thirteen years of my life. At age thirteen I moved to Spain to live with my father, who had gone to live there, and I spent the rest of my teenage years in Spain. So that became the second culture in which I lived. The second language for me became Spanish. At nineteen I moved to Eng-land. For most of my adult life until about five or six years ago, I lived in England. So the fact of having lived in two or three different cul-tural environments perhaps was important because I was not condi-tioned by just one particular culture. People who have lived exclusively in one culture, part of their mental conditioning is the cul-tural collective conditioning of that country. It probably helped to live in more than one country, so that the conditioning was not so deep. One became more aware of the surrounding culture without being totally identified with it.

Another interesting fact is that at the age of thirteen I refused to go to school any longer. It was an inner impossibility for me to go to school. I was not a rebellious child at all, but I simply refused to go to school. The environment was so hostile. I simply refused, and so between thirteen and twenty-two or twenty-three I had no formal education. When I went to live with my father in Spain—my father was a very unconventional person, which is wonderful—he asked me, "Do you want to go to school here?" I was thirteen. I said, of course, "No, I don't." And he said, "O.K. then don't go to school. Do what you like; read, study languages, you can go to language classes." And that's what I did. I pursued my own particular interests. I read some litera-ture. I was very interested in astronomy. I read books that I wanted to read. Of course I learned Spanish fairly quickly. I went to English lan-guage classes. I liked languages and studied some French. And I spent a lot of time just being with myself, free of the external pressures of the environment or the culture. So that was very important.

It was only later in England at age twenty-two or twenty-three that I became interested in intellectual matters. My mind became more and more active. I was seeking some kind of answer through the intellect, through philosophy, psychology, and literature. And I believed that the answer was to be found in the intellect and philosophy. So that is when I started getting qualifications in preparatory evening classes that I needed to get into the university in England. That was my free choice and there was no internal compulsion behind it, nor external compulsion.

Did you study philosophy then or ...?

As a subsidiary subject, but it was mostly literature and languages that I later studied in the university. So the fact about my childhood is that schooling stopped at thirteen. There was this space of freedom between thirteen and the rest of my teen-age years. [Chuckle]

Interesting. Do you recall having any spiritual experiences as a child that created or brought about the "longing" to know yourself?

Well, my childhood was not a happy one. Spain perhaps was relatively more happy than Germany, the first thirteen years. There was a lot of conflict in my home environment, as many people find, of course. Even as a child I could already feel what later would become periods of intense depression—I could already feel the beginnings of that. That certainly was not a "spiritual experience" but somehow it can be a prelude to it. Even as a child I would sometimes think, "How can I eliminate myself from this world?" "How can I commit suicide?" and was working out possibilities of how to do it. [Laughter] Schooling was also so unpleasant for me. As a very young child I didn't have the strength to say "No" to it. Basically life was not happy as a child. There was no "spiritual experience," as such, except—yes, there was: although we lived in a fairly big city, I had a deep intimacy with nature. I remember getting on my bike and going beyond the outskirts of the city and looking around the world of nature, having just left behind the miserable world of school. And I remember the thought going through my head, "This will always be here, this will always be here." Nothing—just that—and looking. [Chuckle]

Did you actually do any work after you had finished school?

Yes. My first job was at seventeen. I was a tourist guide. [Chuckle] We were living in Southern Spain where many tourists came. It happened naturally. So that was my first job there. And later when I moved to England, somehow, although I did not have qualifications, I was offered a job to teach German and Spanish in a language school which I did for over three years. [Chuckle]

One more event about "spiritual experiences." When we were in Spain, I was about fifteen when a German woman came to visit us and then was going to return to Germany. She said, "Can I leave a few things with you?" She left some books with us. There were five books that were written by a German Mystic, early twentieth-century writer, not very well-known abroad. His spiritual name is Bo Yin Ra. I started reading these books. The text was written in almost Biblical style, pointing towards mystical experience. And I responded very deeply to those books. And I felt later that these books were left there for a purpose. I even copied parts of those books. They created an "opening" into that dimension. A year later she came back, and my father said to her, "So you left some books with us." And she said, "No, I didn't leave any books; I don't remember." She didn't want him to remember that she had even left any books with us. [Laughter] So I still have some of these books at home, and I value them greatly.

Could you briefly share with us the main experiences you had that led you to become a spiritual teacher? You have a recently published book titled, The Power of Now: a Guide to Spiritual Enlightenment. *In your book, you mentioned a very profound experience, or a "shift" that took place.*

Yes. I was about twenty-nine, and had gone through years of depression and anxiety. I had even achieved some successes, like graduating with the highest mark at London University. Then an offer came for a Cambridge scholarship to do research. But the whole motivating power behind my academic success was fear and unhappiness.

It all changed one night when I woke up in the middle of the night. The fear, anxiety and heaviness of depression were becoming so intense, it was almost unbearable. And it is hard to describe that "state" where the world is felt to be so alien, just looking at a physical environment like a room. Everything was totally alien and almost hostile. I later saw a book written by Jean-Paul Sartre called *Nausea*. That was the state that I was in, nausea of the world. [Chuckle] And the thought came into my head, "I can't live with myself any longer." That thought kept repeating itself again and again.

And then suddenly there was a "standing back" from the thought and looking at that thought, at the structure of that thought, " If I cannot live with myself, who is that self that I cannot live with? Who am I? Am I one—or two?" And I saw that I was "two." There was an "I," and there was a self. And the self was deeply unhappy, the miserable self. And the burden of that I could not live with. At that moment, a dis-identification happened. "I" consciousness withdrew from its identification with the self, the mind-made fictitious entity, the unhappy "little me" and its story. And the fictitious entity collapsed completely in that moment, just as if a plug had been pulled out of an inflatable toy. What remained was a single sense of presence or "Beingness," which is pure consciousness prior to identification with form—the eternal I AM. I didn't know all of that at the time, of course. It just happened, and for a long time there was no understanding of what had happened.

As the self collapsed, there was still a moment of intense fear— after all, it was the death of "me." I felt like being sucked into a hole. But a voice from within said, "Resist nothing." So I let go. It was almost like I was being sucked into a void, not an external void, but a void within. And then fear disappeared and there was nothing that I remember after that except waking up in the morning in a state of total and complete "newness."

I woke up in a state of incredible inner peace, bliss in fact. With my eyes still closed, I heard the sound of a bird and realized how precious that was. And then I opened my eyes and saw the sunlight coming through the curtains and felt: There is far more to that than we realize. It felt like love coming through the curtains. And then as I walked around the old familiar objects in the room I realized I had never really seen them before. It was as if I had just been born into this world; a state of wonder. And then I went for a walk in the city. I was still in London. Everything was miraculous, deeply peaceful. Even the traffic. [Chuckle]

I knew something incredible had happened, although I didn't understand it. I even started writing down in a diary, "Something incredible has happened. I just want to write this down," I said, "in case it leaves me again or I lose it." And only later did I realize that my thought processes after waking up that morning had been reduced by about eighty to ninety percent. So a lot of the time I was walking around in a state of inner stillness, and perceiving the world through inner stillness.

And that is the peace, the deep peace that comes when there is no longer anybody commenting on sense perceptions or anything that happens. No labeling, no need to interpret what is happening, it just is as it is and it is fine. [Laughter] There was no longer a "me" entity, a "little me" that lives in resistance to what is.

After that transformation happened, I could not have said anything about it. "Something happened. I am totally at peace. I don't know what it means." That is all I could have said. And it took years before there was some "understanding." And it took more years before it evolved into a "spiritual teaching." That took time. The basic state is the same as then, but the external manifestation of the state as a teaching and the power of a teaching, that took time. It had to mature. So when I talk about it now to some extent, I add something to it. When I talk about the "original experience" something is added to it that I didn't know then.

You mentioned that after a profound realization had occurred you read spiritual texts and spent time with various teachers. Can you share what writings and teachers had the greatest effect on you in further realizing what had been revealed to you?

Yes. The texts I came in contact with—first I picked up a copy of the New Testament almost by accident, maybe half a year, a year after it happened, and reading the words of Jesus and feeling the essence and power behind those words. And I immediately understood at a deeper level the meaning of those words. I knew intuitively with absolute certainty that certain statements attributed to Jesus were added later, because they did not "emanate" from that place, that state of consciousness, because I knew that place, I know that place. But when a statement emanates from that "place," there is recognition. And when it does not, no matter how clever or intelligent it may sound, it lacks that essence and it does not have that power. In other words, it does not emanate from the stillness. So that was an incredible realization, just reading and understanding "beyond mind" the deeper meaning of those words.

Then came the Bhagavad Gita. I also had an immediate, deep understanding of and an incredible love for such a divine work. The Tao Te Ching; also an immediate understanding. And often knowing, "Oh, that's not a correct translation." I knew the translator had misunderstood, and knew what the real meaning was although I do not know any Chinese. So I immediately had access to the essence of those texts. Then I also started reading on Buddhism and immediately understood the essence of Buddhism. I saw the simplicity of the original teaching of the Buddha compared to the complexity of subsequent additions, philosophy, all the baggage that over the centuries accumulated around Buddhism, and saw the essence of the original teaching. I have a great love for the teaching of the Buddha, a teaching of such power and sublime simplicity. I even spent time in Buddhist monasteries. During my time in England there were already several Buddhist monasteries.

I met and listened to some teachers that helped me understand my own state. In the beginning there was a Buddhist monk, Achan Sumedo, abbot of two or three monasteries in England. He's a Western-born Buddhist.

And in London I spent some time with Barry Long. I also understood things more deeply, simply through listening and having some conversations with him. And there were other teachers who were just as meaningful whom I never met in person that I feel a very strong connection to. One is [J.] Krishnamurti, and another is Ramana Maharshi. I feel a deep link. And I feel actually that the work I do is a coming together of the teaching "stream," if you want to call it that, of Krishnamurti and Ramana Maharshi. They seem very, very dissimilar, but I feel that in my teaching the two merge into one. It is the heart of Ramana Maharshi, and Krishnamurti's ability to see the false, as such and point out how it works. So Krishnamurti and Ramana Maharshi, I love them deeply. I feel completely at One with them. And it is a continuation of the teaching.

You mentioned that you have been a spiritual teacher for ten years now?

It is very hard to tell when I started to be a spiritual teacher. There was a time when occasionally somebody would come and ask me questions. One could say at that point I became a spiritual teacher, although the term did not occur to me then.

For awhile I thought I was a "healer." It was a few years after the transformation happened. Occasionally people would come to me. I was sitting with a woman one day and she was telling me her story and I was in a state of listening, a state of bliss as I was listening to the drama of her story, and suddenly she stopped talking and said, "Oh, you are doing healing." She felt something and she called it "healing." And so at that time I did not understand completely what was going on, and thought, "Oh, so I am a healer." For a while then, people called me a healer. [Laughter] And when I saw the limitations of that term, I dropped that. [Laughter] And later on, somebody called me a "spiritual teacher" once, and that must have been the beginning. [Laughter]

How long did it take after the "shift" to integrate what was revealed?
Many years. About ten years. And "spiritual teacher" of course is not an identity. "Spiritual teacher" is a function. Somebody comes, the teaching happens. Somebody leaves, there's no spiritual teacher left. If I thought it was my identity to be a spiritual teacher, that would be a delusion. It's not an identity. It's simply a function in this world. I have been very happy being nobody for many years after the transition. And I was nobody even in the eyes of the world, really. I had not achieved any worldly success. Now, there is a book, and the groups are getting bigger and bigger. And people think I am "somebody."

How do you deal with that?
Well, I smile. I still know I am "nobody." [Laughter] Even though all these "projections" come that I am "special." And for many teachers that is a challenge, to be bombarded with projections of "specialness." And even teachers who have already gone very deeply sometimes fall back into illusion. The impact of projections that they receive from all their followers or disciples is so strong that after a while the delusion of "specialness" returns. And that is often the beginning of the end of the power of the teaching that comes through. They may then still teach from "memory," but when the "specialness"

returns, that is the end of spiritual power coming through. Any idea of "specialness." And I have seen it with spiritual teachers.

Yes, many times it has happened. What have you recognized in individuals who have come to you—and I don't know if you would refer to them as "students"—and in yourself that would lead you to believe that your realization is "true" and that it can be realized by others?

The certainty is complete. There is no need for confirmation from any external source. The realization of peace is so deep that even if I met the Buddha and the Buddha said you are wrong, I would say, "Oh, isn't that interesting, even the Buddha can be wrong." [Laughter] So there is just no question about it. And I have seen it in so many situations when there would have been reaction in a "normal state of consciousness"—challenging situations. It never goes away. It's always there. The intensity of that peace or stillness, that can vary, but it's always there.

It often becomes more intense when there is an external challenge, if something goes wrong or there is a great loss externally. And then the stillness and peace becomes extremely intense and deepens. And that is the opposite of what usually would happen in the normal state of consciousness, when loss occurs or something goes wrong, so to speak. Agitation, upset, fear arises. Reactivity arises. "Little me" gets stronger. So this is the opposite.

I noticed it the first time I was watching a film not long after the transformation. It was a science-fiction film, and one scene showed the annihilation of Japan, the whole country going up in flames. And I was sitting in the cinema, feeling the bliss deepening and deepening, until there was only That. Then the mind came in and said, "How strange! How can you feel so blissful when you're watching disaster?" And out of that, a realization developed into what would later become part of my teaching. That is, whenever a great loss of any kind occurs to anybody, loss of whatever kind, disaster, something goes drastically wrong, death, for some people that has been their spiritual breakthrough.

Loss is very painful, because any kind of loss leaves a hole in the fabric of one's existence. A person dies, or something you had identified with completely is gone. Your home goes up in flames. There is extreme pain at first. But whenever a form dissolves, which is called "death," what remains is an opening into emptiness. Where the form once was, there's a hole into emptiness. And if it's not resisted, if you don't turn away from it you'll find that the formless—you could say God—shines through that hole where there was a form that died.

Maybe that is why the Buddhists spend so much time practicing in the graveyard?

Yes, that is right. I'm talking about this now in connection with my inner state, which is always the same although the intensity varies. And it intensifies through any loss or disaster. Has this knowledge become part of the teaching? Yes, because often people come to me because they are in great pain, because of some recent or imminent loss. They may be faced with death. They may have just lost a loved one, or lost their position. It's often at that point that life becomes too unbearable, and then there is "seeking," "spiritual seeking." So I point out that if you surrender into the loss, see what comes through that hole. It's the winds of grace that blow through that hole.

It's interesting. When I first read about your "awakening," I was reminded of St. John of the Cross and the "Dark Night of the Soul." It seems like you have gone through something very similar. But what I heard you say yesterday at the Gathering (2000) is that it really isn't necessary.

No.

The "Dark Night of the Soul" seems to be one way that some individuals have managed to have a "shift" in their consciousness. I hear you saying that there is another way. What I have experienced with other spiritual teachers is that almost to the person, they have gone through a similar shift. There has been a "dark night of the soul" and then the "shift" takes place. I have yet to find someone who has done it the other way, who has actually been able to have that realization and not go through "the abyss," and has been able to help other individuals realize that it is not absolutely necessary.

Yes. One could say that everybody in this world has a spiritual teacher. For most people, their losses and disasters represent the teacher; their suffering is the teacher. And if they stay with that teacher long enough, eventually it will take them to freedom. Maybe not in this lifetime. So everybody has a spiritual teacher. But a "spiritual teaching" in the narrow sense of the word is there to save time and suffering. Without it you would get there anyway, but it saves time.

And every spiritual teaching points to the possibility of the end of suffering—Now. It is true that most teachers have had to go through the "Dark Night of the Soul," although for one or two it was very, very quick. Ramana Maharshi had one brief death experience. For J. Krishnamurti, it happened when his brother died. He [Krishnamurti] wasn't "free" yet when they discovered him. There was great potential in him. But he really became "free" after the death of his brother.

Humankind as a whole has been through such vast suffering that one could almost say that every human has suffered enough now. No further suffering is necessary. And it is now possible as spiritual teachings are coming through with greater intensity, perhaps greater than ever before, that many humans will be able to break through without any further need for suffering. Otherwise I would not be teaching. The very essence of the teaching is the message, "You have suffered enough." The Buddha said it. "I teach suffering, and the end of suffering," which means, "I show you how suffering arises," which is an important realization—I talked about that yesterday—and how you can be free of that. So that is the very purpose of spiritual teaching. Jesus says the same, "the Kingdom of Heaven is here, Now" accessible to you here and Now.

In your book, you mentioned that "enlightenment is simply our natural state of "felt" oneness with Being and a state of "feeling-realization." Is enlightenment based on feeling rather than thinking? Help us understand who feels it and where it is felt.

Yes, well it is certainly closer to feeling than thinking. There is no word to describe the state of connectedness with Being. I am putting together two words in the book: feeling and realization hyphenated. Because there is not a correct word that I can use. Language doesn't have a word for that. So I can only use something that gets relatively close but that's not it either. Realization sounds a little bit as if it were a "mental" thing. "Oh, I know." Feeling sounds as if it were an "emotion." But it is not an emotion. And it is not a mental recognition of anything. Perhaps the word that is closest to it is the realization of still-ness, which is when the mental noise that we call thinking, subsides. There is a gap in the stream of thought, but there is absolutely no loss of consciousness. In that "gap" there is full and intense consciousness, but it has not taken on form.

Every thought in consciousness has been born into form, a tem-porary form and then it dies and goes onto another form. You could say the whole world is consciousness having taken birth as form, man-ifesting as form temporarily, and then dying, which means dissolving as form. What always remains is the "essence" of all that exists—con-sciousness itself.

Now, when a form dies, I pointed out earlier it is an external loss; it's a great opportunity for the formless, pure consciousness to be rec-ognized. The same happens when a thought-stream comes to an end. Thought dies. And suddenly that which is beyond thought—you may call it pure consciousness—is realized as deep stillness.

Now the question you may ask, and perhaps have asked, is, "Who realizes the stillness?" If there is no longer the personal entity there, who is it that becomes enlightened? [Laughter] One could say, of course, nobody becomes "enlightened," because it is the dissolving of the illusion of a separate "me," which is not anybody's achievement, or anybody's success. It looks as if there were a human being becom-ing enlightened, but that is an external appearance. What is really happening is that consciousness has withdrawn from its identifica-tion with form, and realizes its own nature. It is a "Self-realization" of consciousness. Therefore it is a cosmic event. What looks like a human being, a person, becoming free of suffering and entering a state of deep peace—from an external viewpoint—in reality is a cos-mic event. Please remember that all language is limited, so these are just little "pointers."

Consciousness is withdrawing from the game of form. For mil-lions of years, as long as the world has been in existence, conscious-ness has been engaged in the play of form, of becoming the "dance" of phenomenal universe, "Lila." And then consciousness becomes tired of the game. [Chuckle]

It needs a rest.

Yes. But having lost itself, that was part of the game. Having lost itself in form, after having lost itself in form, it knows itself fully for the first time. Don't take anything I say too literally. They are just little pointers, because no one can explain the universe through making "sounds" or thoughts. So it is far too vast to be explained. I'm not explaining the universe. These are just tiny hints. It is beyond words, beyond thought. What I am saying could almost be treated as a poem, an approximation, just an approximation to the Truth.

What is "enlightenment," and why does there seem to be so much confusion about it in these times?

Well, the confusion arises because so many people write about it without knowing it directly. One can become an expert on it without knowing it directly. Because an expert means you know a lot "about" something, but you do not necessarily know "it." Confusion arises there.

What is enlightenment? Again, it is so vast not any one definition would do it justice. It would be a tiny aspect of it. And you can look at it from so many perspectives, this one, that one, that one. And every time it looks as if it were different.

Another reason why it can be confusing is you reach one person's definition of enlightenment, he or she is looking from "this" perspective. And then you read somebody else's, and they are looking from that perspective. There's the ancient old Indian story of blind men describing an elephant, one touching the trunk, another a leg, the tail, and so on. [Laughter]

The confusion arises in trying to understand through the mind what enlightenment is. That is impossible. Any description is only a signpost. So the mind can only go a certain way, and then the signpost has to be left behind. And the mind gets attached to a signpost, which is a teaching or description, a concept. And then confusion arises because then it sees another signpost and says, "Oh, maybe that is the true one." It becomes defensive, identifies with "this one" and says that's me.

So, to the question, "What is enlightenment?" one could say simply, it is when there is no longer any identification with thinking. When there is no longer self-identification with thought processes and self-seeking through thinking. Then the compulsive nature of thinking ceases. Then gaps arise in the mind-stream. That means the unconditioned consciousness arises and is realized as stillness or presence. There is nobody there who "realizes." It is realized. It realizes itself. [Chuckle]

In your book you also mention the "observing presence." Is it possible to practice being the observer to the point of recognizing it as your natural state or condition?

Yes. The beginning of spiritual awakening is the realization that "I am not my thoughts," and "I am not my emotions." So there arises the ability suddenly to observe what the mind is doing, to observe thought processes, to become aware of repetitive thought patterns without being trapped in them, without being completely "in them." So there is a "standing back." It is the ability to observe what the mind is doing, and the ability also to observe an emotion. I define "emotion" as the body's reaction to what the mind is doing. The ability to "watch" that without being identified. That means your whole sense of identity shifts from being the thought or the emotion to being the "observing presence."

And then you can observe a reaction, a mental or emotional reaction. Anger arises. The anger may still be there. But there is the observing "presence" which is the alertness in the background that watches the anger. So there is no longer a "self" in it. The ability to observe thought already is the arising of stillness. Because it is from that dimension that thought is observed.

And then the observer becomes stronger. And what is being witnessed has less heaviness to it, less momentum. So at first you are witnessing. Then you become aware of the witness itself, the power that lies in the witnessing, the power of stillness, the power of consciousness. And then you know that as yourself. You are That.

If you dwell in that continuously, it means you are free of the world of form. Until that happens you are imprisoned in physical and mental formations. You are trapped in thinking. You are trapped in emotions. You are a fictitious self trapped in form. The true self is beyond form and to know that is liberation.

I want to get into what is traditionally referred to as "Cosmic Consciousness," where the Self, unshakable silence or Beingness is separate from activity. There appears to be a maturity that takes place beyond "Cosmic Consciousness" where an awakening occurs to the reality that no separation between the Self and the world really exists. Adyashanti, who also spoke at the Gathering (2000) yesterday mentioned something about this "maturity" when he got into the three statements, "the world is illusion," "Brahman is real," and "the world is Brahman." It appears a "maturation time" is required, but in some sense no time is necessary. How does this come about?

Well, certain sages made the statement, in India, especially, "the world is unreal," and of course when people read it, it becomes a belief, and they repeat the belief, and then they argue with others who say, "No, no it is real, can't you see it is real?" Those who made the statement originally and where it came from—I know exactly why they said it. Because I feel exactly the same.

The way I experience the world, it's like a surface phenomenon. There's such vastness of Being, the stillness is so all-encompassing. It fills almost everything, it fills the whole space and yet it is empty. And anything that happens, events, or phenomena in people, are like ripples on the surface of Being. That's how I perceive. And ripples, they come and go. They are not all that real. No ripple or wave has any separate existence from the whole. It just looks for a moment as if the wave or ripple was a separate entity. But it isn't.

So the whole phenomenal world to me is like a ripple on the surface of Being. And in that sense I could say, although I never say it as such, "the world is unreal"—unreal relative to what I know to be true, what I feel, what I experience. Experience is not the right word, because it implies time. So it is to be rooted in that timeless state of consciousness, because it's only in the phenomenal world where time arises. And there is what looks like an entity, a "person," that exists simultaneously as form in time, and yet is the formless. So there is a paradox coming in whenever one realizes. As form you are still in time. As the formless you are beyond time. So the formless, the unmanifested, shines through you when you have realized the formless. It shines through the form into this world. It's like God shining through. The form becomes transparent.

You see this in anybody who has "realized," the absence of personality or ego. There may be certain traits of behavior, but they are not ego. It is the absence of needing to be somebody. And then it can take time as it did in my case, for this to become a teaching. Ramana Maharshi also went completely into the formless, into Being, and didn't even speak anymore, and didn't feed himself anymore. And then time passed on the "external," not within—he was rooted in the timeless. But on the external, time passed and as things changed, he started eating and feeding himself again. He started interacting with people. He started to speak again. And then the teaching arose out of that. Time was needed for that to happen.

So there is a role for "time" to act as "grist for the mill," which allows for that union between the unmanifest and manifest to come about?

Yes. There is always a paradox when one talks about time in the context of "spirituality." There's a question that is sometimes asked, "Do I need time to become enlightened?" Because it does seem like that. And the answer is yes and no. The answer I would give to that contains a paradox. And I say, yes, you need time until you realize that you don't need time anymore. [Laughter] So the truth here, it is only through paradox that this truth can be expressed. And to do away with paradox would limit it.

How do you define the term "ego?" Is it possible to have any remains of an ego and be perfectly enlightened?

Ego means self-identification with thinking, to be trapped in thought, which means to have a mental image of "me" based on thought and emotions. So ego is there in the absence of a witnessing presence. There's the unobserved mind and the unobserved mind is the ego. As the witness comes in, ego still operates. It has a momentum that is still there, but a different dimension of consciousness has come in. The question whether somebody can be enlightened . . .

Yes, is it possible to be perfectly enlightened and have any remains of an ego?

Well, perhaps not perfectly enlightened, but there can be remains of ego still there, because I have seen it in teachers. I have seen the ego return in some teachers. So the ego can go into almost a "coma," [Laughter] and then wake up out of its coma perhaps due to the projections, ego-projections that the teacher is bombarded with. As the teacher is there, more people appear and gather around the teacher. And they (those who gather around them) all have their own ego-projections. They make the teacher very "special." And specialness is always ego, whether special in my misery or special because I am the greatest, the ego doesn't really mind. [Chuckle] So perhaps in those teachers the ego was not completely gone. It just had been reduced to an extremely weak state, but then gained strength again.

Ramakrishna refers to a "provisional ego," where there is a very thin line between that which is real and that which exists in time/space which allows some sort of presence in the world. I think he said something like fifteen out of sixteen particles are not there in an ego form, but it's that one-sixteenth of a particle left over that is able to interact with those who are still in possession of an ego.

Yes, that's good.

Some spiritual teachers advocate spiritual practices and others reject them as a waste of time. What's your perspective on this?

There may be a place for spiritual practice. The difficulty with spiritual practice is again that most practices give you "time." They are based on time and on becoming, or "getting good at" something. In the end every practice will have to be left behind. No practice can take you to liberation. That is important to know. It can be a little step that is useful until you realize you don't need it anymore, because after a certain point it becomes a hindrance.

Now if a teacher gives you a practice, he or she would perhaps point out when you don't need it anymore or you realize yourself when you don't need it anymore. No technique can take you there. That is the important thing.

Personally, I don't teach practices as such. The power of the teaching is sufficient without needing to go for any practice. Although some people when I speak of awareness of the "inner body," call it a technique. I would not call it a technique because it is too simple for that. When the oak tree feels its roots in the earth, its connectedness with the earth, it is not practicing a technique. That is its natural state, to feel that connectedness. So I would not call "feeling the inner body" a technique.

Surrendering to "what is" or "the Now" seems to be an important aspect of your teaching. Is there a distinction between "surrendering to what is," and the use of the popular cliche, "go with the flow of life, where ever it takes us"?

Surrendering only refers to this moment, whatever "is" at this moment—to accept unconditionally and fully whatever arises at this moment. "Going with the flow" is a more general term. For some people it is an excuse for not taking action and it refers usually to one's life situation. Let's say you are in a particular job and that is the flow, you stay in it.

Surrender is only in reference to Now. So "going with the flow" is not necessarily true surrender and may lead to passivity, lethargy and inaction. Surrender to the Now is something very different because it only concerns accepting the reality of this moment. Whatever action is needed will then rise out of that state of complete acceptance. The most powerful state for a human to be in is the state of embracing completely the reality of what is—Now. It is to say "Yes" to life, which is now and always now. There is a vast power in that "Yes," that state of inner non-resistance to what is. Action arises out of that if it's needed, as a spontaneous response to the situation.

So surrender to Now never leads to inaction because it only concerns the reality of this moment and perhaps action is needed. In the book I give the example of being stuck in the mud. So you wouldn't say, "O.K., I surrender to this and I'm going to stay here." It simply means, "it is;" there is a recognition of "it is" and to saying yes to "it is." And there's much greater power now that arises that will move through you and manifest as action if it is needed than there could ever be in the state of saying, "no" to "what is"—and then perhaps taking action that is always contaminated with negativity. Whenever you say "no" and then action arises because you are fighting "what is," that is karmic action in Eastern terms, and it leads to further suffering because it arises out of suffering, which is the non-acceptance of "what is"—suffering. Action arising out of suffering is contaminated with suffering and causes further suffering, and that is karma. Action that arises out of a state of "acceptance" is totally free of karma. And there is a vast difference.

In the Bhagavad Gita it says in Sanskrit "Yogastha Kuru Karmani," which translated means "Established in Being, perform action." I think this is what you are referring to.
Yes that's exactly what it is.

By becoming a "watcher," which is a term that you use, or "observer," are we to dis-identify with the world in order to become free of it all, of its pain and suffering? This may be interpreted as escapism in some fashion.
"Watching" is mainly an internal process. You are watching whatever arises within, a reaction, an emotion, a thought. Or sometimes it will manifest already as behavior, and then you watch the behavior. It refers simply to being aware of whatever arises within and being a "witness." There is no further attempt to achieve any state when you are the watcher. You are not the watcher in order to become detached from the world. There is no further aim.

Being the watcher is an end in itself. It is not a means to an end. If it were a means, you would be saying, " I need to get to the state of being detached from the world," and you would be creating a future state to be achieved. You would become unhappy because you would realize you are not yet detached from the world. You would project an image of a "perfect self," detached from the world, and you would want to get there. You would not be there. Continuous conflict would arise.

It would then be an agenda coming from the ego, wanting to be separate, wanting to be special?
Yes. And so it is the acceptance of "what is" that is part of the "watching." You can't watch completely without at the same time accepting completely.

I point out with reference to acceptance, that if you can accept whatever arises externally as a situation, or an event, or a person, then there is no reactivity, no negativity. Life becomes very, very simple.

If you cannot accept "what is," some reaction will arise as an emotion, a judgement, an inner saying "no." But even here, you can now practice "Level Two" of acceptance. If you missed the first opportunity, which is to accept what arises externally, if you missed that and some reaction came up, then you can still watch the reaction. So your second opportunity of surrender is simply surrender to what arises within you, the emotion, the reaction. Watch that and accept that. "There's anger here." Accept the anger. Of course, the anger arose because you couldn't accept something that was "out there," i.e., "This shouldn't be happening, life shouldn't be like that." But that was an unconscious reaction, so you missed that one. So now accept the inner. If you can't accept the outer, accept the inner. [Chuckle]

It's the benevolence of Truth! [Laughter]
Yes. One man called it Plan A and Plan B. [Laughter] And then he asked, "Well, if there is Plan A and Plan B, is there a Plan C in case you miss B?" And I said, "well yes, Plan C is enjoy the suffering." [Laughter]

You mentioned in your book that women are closer to enlightenment than men, yet historically there seem to have been more men than women who have been recognized as enlightened beings.
Yes, that seems to be the case, although I suspect that there have been enlightened women who remained almost completely unknown because they lived in patriarchal societies where women had inferior status.

In many traditions, such as Buddhism, women seem to have become gradually more and more excluded. What seems to have happened is that the male teachers saw that any gain in consciousness women achieved—the arising of presence—tended to be lost again at the time of menses. As I explain in the book, the collective female pain-body becomes activated at that time and tends to pull women into unconsciousness. And so the teachers said, "Well, all a woman can hope for is to be reborn as a man in the next lifetime. Because obviously it was not working."

But there is far greater consciousness coming in now, and especially through women. The very thing that was the obstacle—the collective female pain-body and the fact of menses—can now help bring about the awakening of consciousness in women. Perhaps the ancient alchemists already saw that possibility, because in alchemy a comparison is drawn between a base metal being transmuted into gold, and the action of the menses.

So this is why I talk in the book about how to bring "presence" into that time when women would usually be pulled into unconsciousness and identification with the pain-body—to become very alert at that time even before it is likely to happen—very alert, very present and begin to watch the whole movement and stay present when this powerful movement of collective female pain-body comes in. And stay present throughout, because the pain-body can be a great teacher for "presence." I say use that time and bring "presence" into it.

And I can see already that there are always more women than men coming to consciousness groups. Sometimes it is seventy percent women. And I can see how consciousness is now emerging very rapidly through women. Also because they are more in touch with the body. That helps.

And the feeling level.

Yes, because underneath the feelings is the stillness. So all you need to go is a little bit deeper. If you are stuck in the "head," then you first have to go down into the emotions. It's not easy to get out of the "head."

It's another step, then.

Yes.

How would men go about creating an opportunity like that in the pain-body? Maybe their favorite football team is losing and they can drop into it every time their team is not doing well? [Laughter]

Both men and women have "pain-bodies." Both men and women are identified with the mind. But the emphasis for women is to work with the pain-body. The emphasis for men is to work with identification with mind and thinking. The other always comes in also. These are just the respective focal points.

If time is an illusion, as you mentioned in your book, then does this mean that nothing real has ever happened within the realm of time?

Yes.

Is this a correct interpretation?

That depends on how we use the word "real." All the world of phenomena—every phenomenon in this world, whatever it may be, any event, anything that exists, its existence is fleeting. Everything that happens in time is very fleeting. Yesterday you were at the conference—that's gone. Where is it now? You came in through this door an hour ago—that's gone. If you could see this room, if you could see a speeded-up film of what is going to happen to all the objects in this room over a period of time, say two or three thousand years—when condensed into one minute, you would see it becoming dust, crumbling to dust and then nothing. Gone.

So the whole world is moving continuously into nothingness. It comes out of nothingness. It moves back into nothingness. It's a fleeting [swishing noise]—gone. If you are rooted in no-form—the formless which is timeless, birthless, deathless, eternal, the stillness out of which everything comes—from there the whole world is quite unreal. But it is very real if you do not know that dimension; the world of birth and death is all there is. It holds great promise, because it promises you fulfillment at some point. At the same time it is a threatening place. So you are trapped in the world of form, torn between desire and fear.

What would enlightened relationships look like as compared with the usual psycho-social circumstances we see today?

The need for drama is gone. The need for conflict is gone. It's important to realize that the "little me," the egoic entity needs conflict. So as long as that operates, no relationship is free of conflict and drama. The pain-body loves drama because it feeds on pain. As I explain in the book, pain-bodies are dormant for a period of time, but they cannot remain dormant forever because they need to feed on the experience of pain.

So the pain-body rises up into the mind and feeds on your thinking. It becomes aligned with it. The pain-body is old pain, human pain, partly collective—partly personal. It lives in you. Even if you accept every moment as "it is" and so create no further pain, you will still be faced with the pain that has accumulated from the past. That is the pain-body and it will periodically come up and attempt to feed on your mind—negative thinking, destructive thinking. And it will attempt to feed on somebody else's reaction. And that happens in almost every intimate relationship. Pain-bodies periodically become active and that is the need for drama and conflict in a relationship. Because the pain-body loves it. And then it feeds on the other person's reaction. It pushes the right buttons and feeds on reaction.

When the pain-body is no longer there, i.e., it has been transmuted by bringing "presence" into it, the very life-energy that was trapped in the pain-body becomes now freed. The very pain that was there turns into presence. It is like a fire. Consciousness transmutes everything into itself. Then there is no need for drama. There is no need for conflict. Love can then flower in the relationship as a continuous state.

In some spiritual teachings it is said that the Self, Being or Truth unfolds Itself to Itself by Itself. Is it possible then to hasten the process of liberation by "doing" anything, or is it just folly to think that by "watching" our mind as a function of "doing"—it will happen quicker?

There is no "doing." You can't really get there by "doing" anything. But can you speed it up? Yes. The need for time disappears when you realize the significance of embracing this moment as it is. You are not "doing" anything. You are simply allowing this moment to be. That speeds it up because then you don't need time anymore. It speeds it up so much that the whole need for time is gone. [Chuckle]

You mentioned in your book that "transformation is through the body, not away from it." Does that imply that the formless makes itself known through the form of the body, which by its nature is constantly changing and not ultimately real?

That's right. Within every illusion there must be something real, because even the illusion could not exist without some reality somewhere, which then turns out to be consciousness itself appearing as the body. So look for the real that is concealed within that fleeting phenomenon we call "body." And to go beyond the appearance of consciousness, you can simply feel the inner-body as emanating presence within you, and so go beyond the form of body, to its formless essence.

Is the inner body the unmanifest aspect of the body?

Yes. That is the doorway. You go through the body. The doorway into the unmanifested is through the inner-body.

How would you like to be seen as a spiritual teacher and what is the proper relationship to you for a student?

I have no view on that. Every moment is simply as it is. People come. When I interact with people I am a spiritual teacher. When they leave me, the very moment somebody leaves, I'm no longer a spiritual teacher because that is only a temporary function. Somebody comes, the teaching happens. So I don't see myself as a teacher. Being a teacher is not an identity, but a function. I would never see myself as a teacher, so I have no view of how I would want to be seen. Because it's only a temporary function.

The moment I am alone in the room, there's no spiritual teacher left. It only arises when somebody comes. So beyond that there is nobody. There's no spiritual teacher.

When you assume the role as a spiritual teacher and someone comes to you for guidance, how would one best approach you to maximize the opportunity for full realization?

Whenever anybody comes, I completely accept the way they are. If there's unconsciousness of any kind, pain-bodies, people come with pain-bodies. I cannot say that they should be this way or that way. They are as they are at that moment, and I completely accept the way they are as they sit there in front of me. That's the way they are. There's complete acceptance. I never say, "When you come to me you should behave like that or do that." Just be there and that is enough. Everything else arises out of that deep sense of acceptance, which is "presence." Whatever needs to happen in the teaching situation then happens. There is no further need for anybody to try to do something or be somebody or behave in a certain way.

If students decide that they would like to start bowing to you and wash your feet or do those kinds of activities with you, would you be accepting of that?

Well, it has happened. Some Indian people came to see me and did that. And I accepted that because it's so normal for them. It's part of their culture. And also one or two Western people who spent many years in India have done that. But so far no other Western person has done it, except those who have had a very, very strong association with India.

Or maybe with Christianity, because it is part of that tradition also. So it could happen in a Western sense?
Yes.

And you would be O.K. with that?
It's impossible to say until it happens.

O.K. [Laughter]
I have sent people away sometimes when I feel there is an excessive attachment. I have sent people away who I feel need to spend a period of time away so that an excessive attachment is not formed to the form of the teacher. So that happens. But I don't have any kind of mental framework on it. It all happens spontaneously.

There is a particular form of spiritual teaching called "crazy wisdom." It sometimes manifests as a difference between what someone says and their actions. Sometimes "crazy wisdom" teachers use it as a teaching technique or method. Zen teachers use a stick, which appears to be physically abusive, but it may not be. Other teachers use sexuality in a "different" form where it would be with more than one woman, or it might be with someone outside of a marriage. Can you help us understand what this is about and how it fits or doesn't fit with your teaching?
Well, on the one hand, the mind may have a certain image of how a spiritual teacher should behave, but that may not have very much to do with reality. So to have certain expectations of how a teacher should behave and then find that the teacher's behavior does not conform to those expectations, that can often happen. And then either the student would leave or would have to re-examine expectations or become aware of their mental expectation of how a teacher "should" behave. Those expectations are almost certainly wrong, because they come from mind and from ego.

On the other hand, it can happen that certain spiritual teachers, when ego reasserts itself, that they abuse their position. And usually you will find that there comes a discrepancy between what they say they are and what they do. And when that's discovered it has nothing to do with a mental expectation of how a teacher should behave. You're simply watching whether there is a discrepancy between the teaching, or what the teacher says, and the behavior of the teacher. For example, the teacher might say, "I've been celibate for my whole life, for the past thirty years." And then somebody discovers the teacher in bed with someone. [Chuckle] There you have a discrepancy in the teaching and the teacher's actions.

And I know certain people may have the expectation, the mental image, that a spiritual teacher must be celibate. That of course is not the case. Although I have been celibate for several years, I have never said that celibacy is the way. I have never said that. I've never said that I'm going to be celibate for the rest of my life. I may be. I may not be. It makes no difference to the teaching. But if I said, "Celibacy is the way," and then turn around and not be, that's where the delusion starts and the deception begins to creep in which has to do with ego. So simply to watch out for that—a teacher could have relationships with women or men or whatever. But if there's no discrepancy between that and the teaching, then that's how it is.

Sometimes it's very difficult to identify a genuine spiritual teacher. What should a person look for? It could be that the teacher is really breaking boundaries and moving in an unorthodox manner into the boundless. On the other hand, there could be extreme deception. There have been examples in the past where a teacher has said, "I am not what I teach," and they teach in a crazy fashion. In the same manner they might give a "teaching lesson" that appears to have nothing to do with who they are in their essence. What perspective should be employed by those who are faced with this challenge?

People feel naturally drawn to certain teachers. Even that is not necessarily the best indication that that teacher is right because there may be—the ego may feel drawn to a very big ego in a teacher, or to the glamour associated with a big ego in a teacher. But if that is the case, there would be no point in saying to this person, "don't go there," because that is what's happening.

So any teacher you are drawn to is ultimately the right teacher, even if it is the wrong teacher. If you are drawn to a teacher with a big ego, that's because there is a lot of ego in you, and that ego feels bigger in the presence and association with the bigger ego and in that, feels bigger itself. And then the bigger the ego gets, the more suffering will appear. And that will be the teaching and the teacher. So in some way you could say any teacher you feel drawn to is the right teacher for you at that time, even if the teacher is wrong.

What is the single most important summary statement you can make for those interested in realizing liberation in this lifetime?

Liberation means the end of seeking, the end of time. Do you believe that you need more time to get there? That's the perpetuation of the illusion. You don't need any more time when you allow this moment to be as it is. The only difference between you and the master is that the master lives in complete alignment with what is. The Now is welcomed instead of resisted. Allowing this moment to be as it is, that's the key. If you are not ready for this act of surrender, then that's fine too. You need more time and you need more suffering that's inseparable from time. And eventually you will reach that point anyway. Eventually you will realize that liberation does not require time. Liberation is from time. Or realize it Now and you are free Now.

A delusional aspect that might jump into this situation is when someone says to themselves, "I don't realize liberation in this moment, so I need more time to 'create' more suffering which will speed things along." This may simply be an egoic activity which takes the form of self-flagellation.

Yes. Well, that's been done in the past within the context of religions, Medieval Christianity. Sometimes also in Hinduism they practice that. It doesn't work because it is an ego-induced activity. And that kind of suffering actually strengthens the ego. Because the ego gains strength; it's created it. There's enough suffering in anybody's life. It's quite enough. You don't need to create it, because that would be strengthening of the ego.

Your teachings are gaining quite a bit of popularity these days. Do you see yourself getting involved with more travel to different places and possibly setting up a main center or location for your teaching?

Yes. If a center happens—I will not go out and create a center. But if it comes into being naturally and spontaneously, then that may be a good thing.

It's something you would accept?

Yes. And the traveling, also. There's already a lot of traveling and maybe some more to come. But I will always have periods when I don't travel and allow some time for writing.

Aside from book sales, how do you support yourself and your teachings? Do you charge at public meetings or for personal counseling sessions?

Yes, there is a charge for meetings and groups. And I rarely do counseling sessions these days. It's mostly group work.

Eckhart, thank you very much for your time. It's been great talking with you today. And I'm looking forward to getting with you again in the future.

O.K. Thank you. Thank you.

Publications:

The Power of Now: A Guide to Spiritual Enlightenment. Namaste Publishing, 1997.

Contact information:

Eckhart Tolle c/o Namaste Publishing, Inc.
P.O. Box 62084
Vancouver, B.C.
Canada V6J 1Z1
Website: www.eckharttolle.com
www.namastepublishing.com

MIRA

I first met Mira (now referred to as Ganga) in Boulder, Colorado, during the summer of 1999. Mira's given name is Geneviéve Decoux. As a young Belgian girl living in Africa, her childhood experiences helped shape a spiritual journey which eventually took her to India. While having tea in December, 1968, at the Lakshmi Hotel in Hardwar, she had an unexpected rendezvous with H.W.L Poonja (a renouned Indian spiritual teacher affectionately known as 'Papaji') and became his devotee. Papaji renamed her "Meera" (alternatively spelled "Mira"). We chose to use the spelling "Mira" to avoid confusion with "Mother Meera", another female spiritual teacher from India who resides in Germany.

Mira was one of the first Westerners to meet and spend time with Papaji during the late 1960's. Eventually Papaji and Mira became husband and wife and had a child together. For a comprehensive biography on Papaji which includes further details of their life together, please refer to an exceptional three-volume set of books titled, *Nothing Ever Happened* by David Godman, Avadhuta Foundation, 1998.

While visiting Boulder, Mira offered a number of public satsangs ("meetings in truth"). I was delighted by her softness, laughter and deep strength of Being. She radiates a spontaneous joy and ease that melts the hearts of those who spend time with her. Mira clearly reflects the essence passed on to her by Papaji's grace.

Mira currently resides in Europe and Australia. She also holds meetings in the U.S. and other parts of the world.

ॐ ॐ ॐ

Mira, thank you for spending time to speak with us this morning. As a note of introduction, would you please share with us where you grew up and some of your childhood experiences?

Yes. As a child I grew up in Africa. I was born in Belgium. A month later I went to Africa where my father was employed as a court judge. Also, on the side of my mother's family, my grandparents were coffee planters, so we had quite a generation already in Africa, in the Belgium Congo. I spent my childhood up to age thirteen there. It was just paradise. I was in nature. I knew what laughter was; dance, happiness, and we were very free in our movements. So it was a beautiful childhood.

My mother is an artist, so in the house there was always an atmosphere of something else, something which was not visible that could be touched by art, so I started to paint, like her. My father was more the rational side, but very beautiful background.

Of course when [Belgium Congo] independence came in 1960, we had to go back to Belgium. From one day to another I was put in an apartment, in serious school, in a grey-weather country, and I really had that deep profound feeling that I lost paradise, and my search started more consciously, because through art I was already very passionate to find something else. But then this was quite a dramatic question: What is life? Why are we here? Where did we come from? These were the three questions I saw in a painting of Gauguin. That struck me.

How old were you when that happened?

Thirteen.

You were just barely a teenager.

Yes. I thought art was the only way. I didn't know more than that. So I really deeply started to paint with more passion, thinking that through that I would find something. So years passed in this very hidden search. I was quite secret about it. Otherwise on the outside I was a quite happy and easy child.

So then I went to the university. I became totally rebellious from one day to another. It was freedom. The year was 1966. Freedom was in the air; hippie time, beatnik time. It was what we called it.

Where did you attend university?

In Brussels. I studied the history of art and archeology. There I started to be very rebellious as all the students were, but with this determination that I had to find something else. I was totally unhappy. So I started to try some drugs, some sex, enjoyments, art, whatever was presented, and I was never satisfied. I was more depressed, because each time I tried something it was not "there" for me. I was twenty at the time and remember having to pass examinations in philosophy. I read a line of Socrates, "Know Yourself." It really jumped into my heart directly. "It's That, that I am searching for," I said to myself.

So Socrates was your first teacher?

Yes, totally. I really saw that's what I was searching for, and I didn't know my self. So on the spot I wanted to find a living Socrates. Three days later I was on the road to find a living Socrates. I didn't find them in Greece nor in Belgium, so I said to myself, "well, a living Buddha then," and I went to India.

How old were you when you went to India?

Twenty. I left my studies. I completed only two years instead of four—to search.

Do you recall any childhood experiences of spirituality; something beyond the mind, or something that transcended your thinking as a child?

Yes. I was not aware of it, but I had known ecstatic happiness, that is for sure. With nature, I felt totally in harmony, and ecstatically happy. I think it was my first main experience.

Was your family at all spiritually inclined? Did they study in any particular traditional religious fashion?

My mother read a lot. She started with the Heart Sutra of the Buddha. So it was beating in the house. I saw books and art. A lot of it was art. And alchemy, all of those esoteric things.

Were there other important spiritual events that led you to Papaji or other teachers that were available at the time?

There was nothing else in that sense. It was all very depressing. I was totally not at peace. At some point I had to leave, find something else, some solution or I wanted to die. I remember I had one mystical experience of absolute cosmic love when I came back from Africa. Because I came to know the religion (Christianity) when I went to school, and heard about Jesus, I had this experience of loving him. And that's all. Otherwise I had a very secret search.

What was the greatest influence for you in continuing to pursue spiritual activities, knowing that you'd run into dead ends?

I think it was to have known the inner sense and purity in life. It was not someone particularly.

Can you say a few words about Papaji and what your spiritual relationship was like with him?

Sure.

When did you meet him?

When I went to India, I stayed three months there, asking questions of a few yogis. There I started to meditate, to learn meditations. Also at some point I was confused because everyone was giving a different way to meditate. So I just felt to leave everyone and assimilate by myself and see. Three months later, Master, I call him Master [H.W.L Poonja, affectionately known as Poonjaji], came to me, to help me. At our first meeting, I just got a glimpse of deep recognition of what I always knew. When I just looked, after having been quiet for awhile, I just thought, "Oh, it's so simple; everything was as it is. And it was just perfect." So then I recognized him as my Master, yes. Later on, my first relation to him from my side—

because I don't think he ever said that he had a master/disciple relationship—was as a disciple with the Master. So that was the priority of all of my life with him. And due to destiny—though I don't use this word, but it's quite understandable—we developed adult relations like man and wife. He became the father of my child. But somehow I always felt this was the fulfillment of very old connections, just a burning of what has to be burnt. But the background was Master. That was very clear.

What was the most important aspect about Papaji that initially attracted you to him, and enhanced the desire to stay close to his teachings?

He was so obviously the embodiment of emptiness.

You recognized that in him?

At first when I got that big glimpse. It was because emptiness was in front of me that it could happen.

What kind of experience did that elicit in you in recognizing that emptiness? How did it affect you as a person?

Oh, from this desperation I became totally fulfilled, and in natural ecstasy with life from one minute to another. And I never came back to my previous tendencies of mind. So it was a total metamorphosis; yes, a new life.

The concept of enlightenment seems to have taken on many meanings in these times. Can you share with us what your insight is regarding enlightenment, and what it might mean in relationship to other terms like emptiness or shunyata?

First of all, as you say, enlightenment is a concept, so now knowing this we can speak. You want a description. You can say that when you are totally in complete fullness the search is totally fulfilled. You don't even need to know what "it is" because you are "it," you see? When there is not a single inch of anxiety about anything, that could be called fulfillment of life, of one's search. And also what strikes me is to have realized what is "the present." For me this is an incredible realization. Just to have realized what "present" means. I never could guess that we live all the time in past or future. I was not guessing it.

And that makes all the difference, because then each aspect of existence is aliveness itself, you see.

What do you feel are the most essential elements of Papuji and Ramana Maharshi's teachings?

To "keep quiet." And you can understand that in many ways, but at some point you will really know deeply what it means to keep quiet. It is not to nourish the slightest movement of the mind. That is their absolute greatness.

Some say that through silence alone one can realize enlightenment. Others say it's through action alone. Can you help us sort this out?

You have to make a tremendous decision, "I want to be free," you see. And then once you do it, and I know this "doership" and "action" and "doing" is what many teachers might not agree with, but since you are a seeker you are still in "doing" things. So it's your tremendous determination to be free. So it's an action, because you have to drop everything else. So through that action, silence can unfold.

So it is through action, through an intention or a strong desire to be free that sets the stage for that silence to really make itself known?

You know it's different for everyone. That's why there is no teaching. For me I know it was through this very strong determination. But maybe some other cases are different. You know, there are no rules.

Ramana Maharshi said at one point in time, "That which is not present in deep dreamless sleep is not real." Can you help us understand the meaning of this statement?

Yes. You know, "to be," just "to be" which is our nature, doesn't depend on any "states," and doesn't belong to any "states." So, when you sleep in a deep sleep state, if you realize your Self you are awareness itself, and "states" are just playing on you like waves in the ocean. So in deep sleep, the world disappears. Even our talk about reality disappears. Even satsang (a spiritual meeting) and "no teaching" disappears. So all of this is unreal. What's real is just what is left, and we may indicate it by the words "awareness itself."

So that awareness is actually coinciding with that deep dreamless sleep. It's the awareness of awareness itself that's there. Even underlying all of the waking, dreaming and sleeping states or relative states of consciousness or awareness?

Yes. It is here, each instant, whether there is a world or not or somebody sleeping or not. Yes, sure.

Is there anything beyond that? If through self-inquiry we begin to realize a constant condition of witnessing all states of waking, dreaming and sleeping, is there anything beyond this realization, and how would it come about?

You know, when you want to realize, the big thing is to be awareness itself, who you are. Once you are "who you are," those questions don't arise anymore. And to try to define exactly what it is doesn't occur, unless you have maybe a mind with a philosophical tendency. So in my case, what I see is that the vastness is endless. I remember that I call it awareness itself, otherwise I don't even remember what it can be. But it's just "what it is."

Remembering it would take it into the past, wouldn't it?

Yes. So of course in satsang we have to take words to speak. According to the background we take it. But otherwise, today it would be really very hard if I had to remove all what I knew as an indicator. I really wonder what I'd say! [Laughter]

So it's not something that you can conceptualize in the mind, or contain within the mind. It's something beyond that?

It's absolutely something beyond that. That's why one is blown up when they truly see themselves. There is no sign in behavior. On the contrary. They are completely free. So there's no reference point, not even a philosophical one.

If someone were interested in a genuine spiritual teaching or teacher, what are the most important things to consider? If you were a student and were looking for some teacher or teaching, what should you be watching for, what are the important things to make sure you're on a pure path?

That there is no issue of mind, that there is no pride, and then opening the heart near the teacher to see if something is opening up. Otherwise go to the next teacher.

So what I hear you saying is that it's important to also approach a teacher as a student with an open heart so you can receive what is being given to you. That's part of the intention you mentioned before in having that strong desire for enlightenment?

Yes, a burning desire for enlightenment, and then you will meet the proper one. That I believe, because it was my experience. I had no address, no name, and somehow he even came to me. So that burning desire will bring what you need.

It's been said that enlightenment is beyond even good and evil, right and wrong, and that self-realized individuals aren't even accountable to God. In our daily lives, what's the best way to deal with decisions that we must make, or in dealing with destructive tendencies in others who want to cause wars and death, and extreme suffering—which appears to be very wrong?

You see that's why it's so urgent to realize one's Self. So realize your Self, and that silence takes care of everything. This means sometimes it's not understandable how it takes care, but that full surrender will make things as it is to be. I profoundly see that. Because mind gives limited solutions in right and wrong. It's limited, you see.

So we allow that silence to be our guide?

Oh yes. Let it invade our lives and then it is very contagious.

Is there any free will then, once we've made the surrender to silence?

It doesn't look like it.

How do we hold ourselves and others accountable for actions that take place?

You see, once you solve the problem of the search, it is not in our hands. Some people can still fight, in politics for example. Each one has their function. And they will do it totally because they are carried away by another force which will make them act this way or that way.

And for some people their function is to teach, for some people it is to keep quiet, unknowingly, yet they are absolutely useful to the world. We don't know. It's quite mysterious. But surely, the realized one is carried by Beingness itself. They bring war, they bring peace. Who knows? It's a cosmic game, you know.

If all is God's will and some unscrupulous people use this as an excuse to do very bad things, how are they held accountable for their actions?

They are absolutely unreliable. You have to be absolutely immaculate, you see, to say that all is God's will. Otherwise they will destroy more.

So with regard to the person who says " It's God's Will that I'm doing this," we have to observe exactly what the results of the actions are?

Absolutely. One has to see from where the actions come. It's so easy to speak and, as you said, to justify behavior. I don't speak of those people, that is for sure.

When Papaji says "Nothing ever happened," what did he mean? It appears to us that there's an infinite display of "happenings" constantly churning before our eyes and swirling in the universe. Can you help us with this?

This is ultimate realization, when you ultimately see that only Beingness exists. And Beingness exists means—I would love to say "nothing ever happens"—yet you can express it also so that all which looks like "happening" is included in it. It doesn't reject anything. It is just "as it is," as it ever was, as it will ever be. So in that vastness, nothing ever happened, you know, nothing being the context underlying time. Nothingness itself is not in time. So the realization is That. It is That which is the background of everything.

So at that level, nothing has ever really happened. Nothing changes, it's immovable?

Absolutely, and yet one ought not to land on this concept of immovability. Everything is included.

So the movable and immovable form some kind of seamless continuum or oneness. The Tibetans refer to it as "One Taste."

I prefer "non-separation" of anything. Because the concept of "oneness" also can be misunderstood, you see.

Oneness as separated from the rest. That's a problem also, isn't it?
Oh, language is quite something! [Laughter]

What's the importance of having thoughts?
Why not? Some people say because of thoughts you have at some point to search from where they come. All is included. Everything is possible. That's it!

So there's no problem with thoughts, then?
That is no problem. There is a problem when there is an "owner" of thoughts. When there is a "doer." That's the only problem. All the rest is not a problem.

So if you identify with your thoughts. . . .?
Then there is some direction, and then you are lost.

You get lost in the process of thinking and thoughts then?
Absolutely. Because it comes from the background of ownership, of somebody who has got the thought.

If you could give one piece of guidance to individuals very interested in realizing freedom in this lifetime, what would it be?
I would just keep quiet myself.

So it's that silence, the unspeakable?
Totally.

During this last year you have begun to hold public meetings or satsangs in Europe and the U.S. How did this come about?
Oh, yes, it was very simple. You know, when my Master left his body, I was just left by myself. At some point in November [1998], somebody came from Lucknow [India] with the ashes [of the Master] to share with everyone. So I was called in Amsterdam. I was with eight people at a friend's place taking tea. There was a psychiatrist from

Romania who lived in Amsterdam who was there too, but we didn't speak. When I went back to Brussels, she [the psychiatrist] phoned me to get to know my life, so she came to Brussels. After a few hours being together she asked me, "will you give satsang?" I said yes. And then only I realized what I said. But I didn't take it back. She took her agenda and the wave took me. [Laughter] It's a real wave. I'm just carried away by the wave which may last or not. It's not in my hands. My life totally changed in that sense. I really feel I'm carried away by a force. It happens this way. It may disappear, and it doesn't matter too, you know. But it's very beautiful. Very beautiful.

Yes, it appears to be very lovely. Do you have any plans to continue teaching in the near future? Do you have some satsangs arranged in the U.S. and Europe?
Well, it looks like the schedule has formed fast, and yes somehow I can say I'm booked for a while. But you know, who knows? I will not continue the schedule if really that force doesn't carry me any more. That's totally open.

Are you planning to go back to Europe after being here in Boulder?
My normal place is Europe. I go back to Belgium only a few days a month, otherwise I go from town to town. And sometimes I will again come to the States if the demand is there. Like that it happens.

Thank you so much for spending this time with us. Possibly we can meet again and continue our dialogue into the Truth.
I thank you. Thank you for sharing that. Namaste.

HOWARD BADHAND

I first heard about Howard Badhand from a writer friend who lives in Boulder, Colorado. She mentioned that each year Howard was invited to the Naropa Institute in Boulder to do an interpretation of the I Ching for the coming year. As I looked further into Howard's background I discovered an intriguing blend of the spiritual and material. Howard is a Native American from the Lakota Tribe who attended both Dartmouth and Harvard. He is a recognized I Ching expert, and has a strong affinity for Taoism. He mentioned to me that over the years he has become a reluctant shaman although he is asked occasionally to perform various Indian rites and rituals. Prior to our interview, he said with a big laugh, "I've done so many sweat lodges I don't think there's any more sweat in me!"

I phoned Howard several times at his home to arrange for an interview. We finally connected and he gave me directions to his house. Sandra Kyle, a dear friend and fellow writer from New Zealand, was visiting during the time of the interview, so we thought it would be a good adventure to tour the Santa Fe/Taos area while visiting Howard.

An amusing event happened along the way. Upon our arrival in Santa Fe, we became easily overwhelmed by the abundance of incredible art, churches and shops. We suddenly realized that the time for Howard's interview was approaching. We located the street name Howard gave us, but mysteriously his exact house address was no where to be found. After what seemed an eternity of driving up and down the same street, we spotted an office building and dashed in to find help. A kind person armed with a map discovered that we were looking for Howard—in the wrong town! He lived in Taos, not Santa Fe. Infirmity strikes in mysterious ways.

I called Howard right away and told him what happened. We had a good laugh. When we finally met up the next day in Taos I said, "Howard, how are we doing? We're exactly twenty-four hours late for our interview!" He laughed and said something like, "I had a soccer game with the kids anyway, so it all worked out." Sandra sat in on the interview. Howard served us tea at the kitchen table with wires and microphones strung everywhere. Howard's kids were watching television in the adjacent family room. We had intermittent teenage visitors foraging through the refrigerator. Finally things settled down a bit and we launched into the interview.

Howard has a warm, amicable personality and a great sense of humor. We could tell right away only the tip of the "story-telling" iceberg was going to be penetrated in our short dialogue. As the interview unfolded, it became crystal clear that my white, middle-class upbringing was never going to fathom what it was like to be a Lakota Souix raised on a reservation. What came from Howard was a rich feeling of being grounded in the Earth. There was a palpable sensitivity to "the moment" as he weaved his way through the questions. His presence was one of simplicity and candor that smoothed off any rough edges to life.

Howard's answering machine message says in closing, "and whatever you do, do it well, and pray for peace." So be it.

ၭ ၭ ၭ

Howard, thank you very much for spending time to speak with us this evening. As a note of introduction, can you please share with us where you grew up and how it's impacted your perspective on life?

Before I was in my teens I grew up on the Rosebud Reservation, Rosebud, South Dakota, as a Lakota. I was with my own people until I was about sixteen. Then I went away to prep school in Massachusetts. When I left the Reservation in 1965 I moved to the Northeast for about twelve, thirteen years. Then I moved back out West to Denver. Now I'm here in Taos. [Chuckle]

When you went back East to study, was there a particular academic discipline you were interested in?

I think everyone has ideas when they're growing up of getting off the Reservation and going back to help the people. And there's no specific way you can do that. It's the dream most kids who I grew up with were given. I think the idea was to get us off the Reservation first and then worry about whether we would make it or not. So in that context I didn't really have a specific idea or agenda to do anything other than I was supposed to go out and make it [in the world] and go back and help.

Human realities really generate some greater realities that say, "Once you get out of the nest you really can't go back." So my whole experience of having left the Reservation was that it probably separated me more from my people than really helped. Even though my good fortune is that I grew up in a family of "singers," and so we know a lot of the sacred traditional music. And so being "Song-Holders" and "Song-Makers" they also tend to become like the "Healers" and the "Holy People." So my connection to "the people" was more not from the academic or material side as it was, and still is, a much greater spiritual role that I seem to have fallen into over the years. But there's no specific agenda as to how I was supposed to go back and help.

Did you have an opportunity to continue "singing" when you were back East? How did you maintain your skill in that area and keep those traditions burning?

I ran into a lot of Anglo kids who were very interested in the music. I taught them how to sing and got them involved in the music and actually had a group up there called "Hilltop Singers" and "Red

Leaf East" because my family's singing tradition is called "Red Leaf," from the "Red Leaf" community located on the Western side of the Rosebud Reservation. But teaching these kids, I used to bring them back out to the reservation during the summer and during the dances or pow-wows. And that generated a lot of racial upheaval but [Laughter] it worked. [more laughter]

Racial upheaval from the Indian side or from. . . .
    Yes. [Laughter]

Do you recall any spiritual or deeply insightful experiences you had as a child growing up on the Reservation as you were taught the songs and dances?
    When you're growing up in that reality and you're given a world view that looks at the "spiritual world" being co-existent with the "organic world"…you know I often run into people who tell me they have these "visions" and they have these great "spiritual emergences." You know when you grow up in that context it's practically the same. So living is the same as having your "spiritual experience." And as much as we do our ceremonies, one of the key terms is we do these things to live. So as a practical way of growing up, "dreams" and "seeing things" were an accepted part of reality, if you will. And so growing up I didn't have the distinction of, "this is different than the spiritual side."
    Probably the greatest spiritual experience I had was learning how to operate as an alter boy in the Roman Catholic Church. But I didn't call it "spiritual," I called it "religious." It was learning the rules.

Was Catholicism a part of your family, then?
    It was part of my grandmother's upbringing. She used to get me to go to church every Sunday and every first Friday. I used to be an alter boy for one of the priests, and he said, "If you make it to the first Fridays nine months in a row, you're guaranteed a gate into heaven." So I did that really quickly so I could mess off the rest of my life. [Laughter] But I call that a "religious experience." It's a matter of learning the rules about the Catholic ritual and things of that nature. And because the Lakota people are so into ritual and ceremony, one of the easiest ways for them to use the Catholic format or liturgy was the

whole ritual process.

I think when you grow up with a cosmology that really looks at reality as that which you have to do all the time, these rituals only convey what opportunities you have to get people together.

I want to revisit your schooling. Prior to our interview we discussed your higher education background. After finishing prep school you attended various universities. Can you tell us about that experience?

I went to Dartmouth College only because I happened to be in a summer program. I was making a transition between public school and a private college prep school through a program called "ABC," administered out of Boston. So I spent the summer on the campus at Dartmouth College. And I liked it so much I decided to go back. The other thing I went back for was to change the whole institutional view toward Indians because it was supposed to be an "Indian School."

One of Dartmouth's mandates was to be an Indian school?

Yes. And so when I went back there as a student, I made sure they got an Indian Program. They probably have one of the best in the country now. But it was only by charter that they had to do it. Without the charter it would have been an uphill battle. [Chuckle].

How would you characterize the kind of work you're doing now spiritually?

I find so many people drawn to what they call "spiritual work," and if they live a good life they're being "spiritual." O.K.? If you want to look at what I do to make a living, that's a practical, organic way of being in the world. I do a lot of "readings" of "The Book of Change" (The I Ching) because over the years somehow I've become a master of that whole process. Amongst my own people I lead "Sun Dances" and ceremonies, "Night Ceremonies." There are seven major rituals our people do. And I help in that area. But you know, as a "practical way of living" you do the things necessary to unite people to achieve common purpose. I look at "spiritual work" as just plainly living.

Were there any parallels between the "Book of Change" and the Native American culture that you came from?

I think in any traditional culture in the world, when it looks at nature and its manifestations, you're going to arrive at the same truths. All that the Taoist's did in constructing the "Book of Change" was to develop a system that kind of took a photo snapshot, if you will, of events and the unfoldment of natural law. Lakota people do that through ritual and ceremony. It's like getting in touch with the same kind of trends and patterns of the natural process. And when you take a look at the natural process in this way you can see its trends and patterns. You can see its past, you can see its present, and you can certainly see where it's going as it's future goes.

If you want to look at spiritual work, it is the practical idea of living and has nothing to do with religion. Religion is really man's efforts, attempts, if you will, to "talk to God" or what they perceive as the "higher order" or "mind" or whatever. And they become organizations of order and sometimes disorder. Spiritual life is really looking at the natural process of your daily living, waking up, breathing. It's trying to make decisions that balance out not only all your energies but your whole mode of seeing the world. And so I make a huge distinction between those—"religions" and "spiritual work." And by doing the process of what I call "the Tao," we see the Tao and Lakota philosophy are incredibly similar. We have different words for the same thing basically. Perhaps the distinction between the two cosmologies is that the Taoist view I call "scientific" because people actually sat and watched nature for 5,000 years and wrote about it. In Lakota it's called a "visionary process" because you're more into your dreams and your symbols and your view of what the world shows. But the foundation for them being of natural order, is the same.

How did you get introduced to the principles of Taoism?

Mainly by study and also because I ran into *The Book of Change* in the Minneapolis airport back in the late 1960's. I was actually intrigued by astrology and I was walking into the Occult section trying to figure out what my future was. And I was pretty blitzed, too, because I hated flying in airplanes then. You might say that my thinking was very free. Maybe not clear at the time, but very free. And I happened to pass by this book that I say, "called my name." [Chuckle] So I picked it up and opened the page and was reading and it was very appropriate and relevant to what I was going through. The cashier checked me out. I put it on the shelf at home and didn't open it for another two years until I attended Dartmouth College.

From then on *The Book of Change* has been a constant companion and study. Getting into *The Book of Change* is really getting into what I call the laboratory of life, the laboratory of the universe. The sages developed a very, very intriguing model to see how the world operates and see how it's going to operate. So having memorized the text, I soon had people calling me to talk about it in person. I had people asking me to do readings for them. And so that evolved quite naturally and that's what I do predominantly these days to make a living. I'm trying to get out of the "shaman business" altogether. I doesn't seem to work. [Laughter]

When you mention the "shaman business" what are you referring to?
When you become a leader of ceremonies and ritual in amongst your people, you're considered either "holy people" or those who hold the traditions of your people. In that, others start to attribute all kinds of power to you. And they start calling you a "medicine man," a "shaman," a "spiritual leader." If anything you become a spiritual leader and all those other titles as simply titles. There are so many different visions and dreams people have within the tradition where they become adept at what their dream or vision is. And to coin them under the term "medicine man" or "spiritual leader"—I guess that's O.K., but that still doesn't define the specific work. So I make a lot of jokes about "getting out of the shaman business." Because the "shaman business" is a business right now in the sense that there are so many people out there trying to express their power, competing against other shamans as to who's better and who's not. When I tease about it and joke about it that's what I mean. I want to get out of that competition business. It's not spiritual work.

Sure. That's interesting because it seems there's a lot of ego involved in that, and possibly personal or spiritual agendas that don't have anything to do with the truth, and understanding the truth of life.
I think that's what they get drawn by, however when people search for a spiritual path. It's like experiencing yourself as God. And

there are dangerous elements in that. You do have quotes that "the greatest force is within you" because you're the image of it. But it doesn't mean that you are the absolute, or whatever that is. As human beings, just by waking up every morning you realize there's a commonality of life amongst people but it's a "common person." You find balance in life that expresses the spirit appropriately according to who you are. But to look for absolutes I think it's a fruitless search. For people who get caught up in that, it becomes a very dangerous mechanism for power or perceived power.

Being a Taoist and being a Lakota you know, power to me—all it means is the capacity to correct your mistakes and having the capacity to love. Those are the only two things that are given as a human being to make what your life is worth and what it's about. Everything else are "tools" in relation to tools. So if you're living in the world you just learn to find your right tools to accomplish the things you set out to do.

I read recently where a person posted on his office wall: " I have not promised to make you feel better, I have promised to make you feel more." As we develop a broader vision into reality, are people becoming more blissful and happy, or are all the emotions, even the painful ones, simply getting more intense? Is it absolutely necessary that they get very intense before they can be dissipated?

You know, being a Taoist and also being a Lakota leader in ritual and ceremony, one of the most beneficial things you can do for yourself is learn how to lay your emotions aside. Because your emotions and your feelings do not convey reality. They generate a passion, they generate a desire. And desire and passion are the worst things you can use on the spiritual path because you're always trying to make something that "you" want happen. And that doesn't often coincide with "what is." So, being from that order of thinking, I would say that people's emotions and passions are getting more intense. I would agree with that statement, because everyone's trying to achieve a sense of power about "self" in the sense of "wanting," wanting to be God if you will. How do you want to be something when you are already that?— that is the view I have. [Chuckle]

As a Taoist and as Lakota leader who really works with the whole process of emotion and passion and how you put those things aside, I would say that people's feelings and their passions are getting more intense, and they're going to pay the consequences for that. That's what I see happening.

What spiritual teachers have had the greatest impact on you in terms of living a more holistic life, and helping others to do so?

I think the study of the "Book of Change" which is called the "I Ching," that alone has really generated a lot of truth in my life in the sense of—you know a book cannot direct you or give you something other than the tools. The others behind you gave you that intention to look at truth and look for the processes of truth. And the study of that alone has opened me up incredibly. And it's called a "sage" for that reason—opening up incredible contemplation about life and it's processes. In that unfolding, I've learned what life truly is. And so I'm free to do great things and bad things all at the same time, and enjoying the hell out of it actually. [Laughter]

But in terms of the "ritual process," my own uncles and my own family really generated a lot of challenge for me to look at our own people, look at reality, how they created, how they take part in it and how they're moved by it. And those were my uncles. The very first teacher I had actually took me on what is called a "vision quest." And his name was Adam Boreo. He was on the Rosebud Reservation. And after him was a fellow named Raymond Hands Horses. People just taught me the ritual process and the do's and don'ts of the ritual process. And then after him was a fellow named Jim Dubrey—very incredibly gifted and adept person spiritually. You'd never know it because he had a foul mouth most of the time. [Chuckle] He was incredibly gifted in seeing reality and how you could work with that reality. You know what people see as "reality" is not always so. And through him I was able to see that. It was very encouraging.

And then after him I worked a lot with my own biological uncle. His name was Percy Badhand. He passed away about two years ago. And like I said, some of the Roman Catholic priests that I was alter boy for. It's not that they taught me "spiritual truths" so much as some of them were simply genuine. And some of them aren't genuine, but in learning that you learn a little bit about humanity. I would say that I cherish some of the experiences I had with some of the Roman

Catholic priests that I knew. Meeting people around the world at different levels in their development have been great teachers as well. While there's not one that sticks out, I would say that those people I mentioned were very, very beneficial to me. And even studying the life of Jesus is important. He was a Taoist. I think the Christians have made him into something that he's not. But on the other hand I think they're on their way to finding out. [Laughter]

Other than the I Ching or Book of Changes, do you have any particular kind of practice or meditation or spiritual techniques or means of prayer that you currently practice?

That to me gets into "religious practice."

I see.

As a Taoist to get up and say, "Hi God, thank you for the day" is important enough. Or "Hello Spirit" or whatever you want to do. To me the true expression of spirit is when you go out and live your life. And live it in a way that balances your goodness with your capacity to see illusion and delusion. To me those are—whatever you do to enjoy that day is your "practice."

Ritually there are certain things we have to do, like in the Sweat Lodge we have to do the formalities; load the pipe and go through the motions, go through the do's and don'ts, always going clockwise in a circle. When you pray together everyone has a chance to pray openly, and so you follow those forms. But that's "religious practice." I do them when I'm called to lead a ceremonial purification lodge or a night ceremony or whatever, but those rituals are really designed to unify minds that tend to get distracted. And so applied to my personal life, do I get up and go around the bed four times, put on my shoes a certain way—no. [Laughter] Whatever is spontaneously important to do that day to enjoy it is my practice.

A famous Buddhist Master once said that, "There is nothing which can be attained. This is not idle talk, it is the truth. You have always been one with the Buddha, so do not pretend you can attain to this oneness by various practices. If at this very moment, you could convince yourselves of its unattainability, being certain indeed that nothing at all can ever be attained, you would already be Bodhi-minded. Hard is the feeling of this saying! It is to teach you to refrain from seeking Buddhahood, since any search is doomed to failure." On the other hand there's the biblical statement, "Seek and ye shall find." Can you help us with understanding the meaning of the word "seeking" in each of these cases, and how it fits into the context of what we could term "liberation" from those fetters that tend to hold us from that?

You know, if you look at, for instance, the Jewish history and the whole Christian history, and the whole process of "attainment," it is based on order, hierarchy. And that's one of the primary difficulties that spread all over the Roman Empire. It kind of incorporated the whole Christian tradition into their cosmology, an empire; making God the king, the emperor if you will. That's a very powerful historical foundation for people to follow which gives that kind of order. Those same "movements" of empires that used the Christian faith really have difficulty with people whose purpose is "self-development," not a governmental development. And so you see an anomaly between those two worlds, or thoughts.

To Jesus is attributed the whole idea of "Seek and ye shall find." The point of that whole statement, to me (if it came from Jesus!), is that if you truly seek the truth, you don't have to go anywhere else, because you are an ordinary example of it. And that's what Christ really teaches, if you look at the foundations, not the dogmas, not the liturgies. But the whole process of seeking truth—if you seek outwardly you're doomed to failure. If you seek inwardly and realize that you are an expression of everything you're seeking all the time, then you've accomplished your purpose. That's the same for Christ, Buddha, everyone else who's ever taught, who became a great teacher. This is the very "foundation-expression" of what you are. If you constantly seek this truth outside of yourself, you're always separate from the very foundation of your own life, and it's going to cause you problems.

Many of the great teachers who were rejected, even killed, by their own people, they stepped outside of that search—even Jesus. When you start to defend a principle in a "form" as the truth, you're going to endanger your life. To me some of the greatest teachers were not known by many people because they simply expressed what the creation gave to them to express. And their greatness was manifested in the teachings they left behind. But anytime you step outside of that expression of your own Being, as that divine purpose, and it becomes a political game, you'll leave your name in history, and you may find fanatics to follow you along the way, but you're endangering life and its duration. This came about because he (Jesus) stepped outside of that expression.

The concept of enlightenment seems to have taken on many definitions in these times. What does the term "enlightenment" mean to you?

The term "enlightenment" is just for the first time to see everything clearly, in a proper relation and in your relation to it. We say that you shouldn't "seek it," because it's a very brief moment in your life, maybe a second, maybe three minutes, whatever. But if you're in constant search of it, again you begin to seek outside of yourself because you're looking for that one moment of insight, that one "Aha" moment.

For those on the path who have had "enlightenment," it's just one of those things that happens. It's like waking up. Once you wake up, you have a lot of work to do. Any given day you go to sleep, and regenerate and regain your energies. You wake up the next morning and all that you've done is opened your eyes to the light again so you can participate in relationship. And you still have a lot of work to do. So "enlightenment" is one of those very brief moments that will happen if you really do experience clarity and you experience your relationship to the world. But it's a very brief momentary process. And it's not worth the search if you understand it. [Laughter]

Some say that through silence alone one can realize peace or deep liberation. Others say it's through action alone. How can we cut through this dichotomy?

In my world there's no dichotomy between those two statements. By setting aside emotion you get to a "still mind." You do attain tranquility. I think when people think of "peace," they mistake it for "tranquility." Peace is a very dynamic development, a stage of being. It's when all the forces are in motion and you can create reality out of it. If you sit in meditation and you calm and still the mind, you've brought yourself to a state of "tranquility." To live organically and purposefully in life you have to take the other part of your life as that "waking up" process. You have to relate to other people, otherwise you may as well go and be apathetic and waste away. But the process of living is a relationship, and how you use your tools. So how you experience "peace" is by action in harmony with the demand of the time.

You mentioned the word "tools." Can you give us some examples of what those tools might be?

All things that are related to all other things within the world serve a purpose to each other. That is a tool. Some don't relate so they're not tools in relationship to each other, but they're still tools. Human beings in relation to each other are related by tools, how we benefit each other, how we help each other out. Anything above that is undefinable, unknowable, and unnamable. So that hasn't happened yet. But the moment we experience it, it's just a tool. The form in which we experience it has to be a tool. But you only use the tools for purposes within relationship.

A famous Indian saint named Ramana Maharshi said, "That which is not present in deep dreamless sleep is not real." Can you shed some light on the meaning of this statement?

I agree. The reality that you experience as a divine being is also a being who has responsibility in the world of form and relationship. If that truth doesn't exist even while you're sleeping, then it's not truth. It's part of your illusion, it's part of your delusion of how things should be and/or shouldn't be. And so if your divine truth is the same at all levels of your being, it should even exist in sleep. You still have access to it because you are That. The waking process for human beings is important because then we think we experience and we "see." But our reality in sleep should be the same—that we are living, that we are breathing. We're just regenerating. So if that truth doesn't exist there, then it's an illusion.

It doesn't exist at all.

Right.

What's your favorite analogy or metaphor in nature that best points to what the Truth is about it, and how it can be most effectively realized? Do you have a story to express or relate this?

I've always liked the one that comes from the Bible, and it's also very consistent within the worldviews of natural order. That's the term, "I Am, I Was, and Ever Will Be." This truth of spirit, this truth of divine principle preceded us, is with us now and will continue in spite of us. It's the metaphor to me that signifies that your present moment, if you're in touch with it—you're eternal. If you carry on for whatever levels of development that you attain as a human being, then that becomes everlasting. And so that term, "I Am, I Was, and Ever Will Be." It's very powerful.

Why do you think there remains so such confusion about the integration of nature and spirit in these times?

Well, because people are looking for what I call "the Pop Pills," pop-psychologies and pop-spiritual means. It doesn't take a lot of work to know that you are divine Being. You just have to get rid of the mess that got there before you realize that truth. If you're constantly after separating spirit from nature, it's again that "search." You'll keep failing because what you're not accepting is that nature is simply an expression of spirit in all of its various forms, all of its thousands of ways of expression. So nature comes after spirit to show its expression. Our attempt to integrate that is an anomaly. It's already within you. So why would you want to try to find it "out there" in nature so to speak? In saying that we are nature, we are the very thing we keep defining as separate from us. It's especially true in the Western world. We are already That.

What are the most important aspects to consider for someone sincerely interested in a genuine spiritual teaching or teacher?

To me spiritual development is really the process and work of your own efforts to get to the truth of your own divine nature. If you don't know how, then you seek somebody who's at least been on the path and experienced it. All they can teach you is to get rid of the junk. They can't give you something that you have already. And if you buy into that, then you have a real relational issue to work out. And it will probably show up that way.

If you are seeking a teacher, and you are seeking because you don't know something, you have admitted to yourself that you don't know something, a know-how, or whatever. It takes putting your emotions and desires and things aside. If you don't know how to do that, a teacher is helpful. If you take the attitude that it's simply going to arrive, you're going to sit the rest of your life. For some, it may, for some it may not.

If you go out and seek a teacher simply because you want the right tools to do something, you'll know who that teacher is, male or female. I'm not one of those people who says we go out and seek students. There's a whole tradition in the Tao where teachers are to go out and try to find leaders, kings, emperors, to try to teach for the purpose of helping the people, because some of those emperors and kings weren't that great. That was the only time that teachers went out and tried to find a way to teach through government because they understood the human nature behind things. But in nine out of ten cases, you as a seeker should identify what you don't know and look around and look at the people who do know.

It's a relationship. You ask because you don't know how to do something. And that person should be able to help. But the moment you've done the work, it's still your journey. And you either achieve enlightenment or attainment or whatever, but the teacher is only helpful for those purposes. They can't give that thing to you that you already have.

It's been said by some very well known spiritual teachers that enlightenment is beyond even good and evil, right and wrong, and that true realized individuals aren't even accountable to God. In our daily lives, what's the best way to deal with moral decisions that we must make, or in dealing with destructive tendencies in others who want to cause wars and death, and extreme suffering—which appear to most people to be very wrong?

First of all we have to accept that there are always, and always will be, people who are contrary to the truth of God. And whether you agree with it or not, they're going to exist and they're going to kill people, they're going to cause wars. If you're truly wanting to help peace in the world, you've got to find it in yourself. If you do that, then worry about the other stuff.

Most people do it backwards. They want to go and fix the world because they think they can do it better and end up causing the same wars. My view—and that's why we say self-development is such a critical factor in the spiritual process—is, "Why worry about peace in the world until you really find it in yourself first?" And if you find it, then go share it, and you'll have a lot more people at peace because of it. But you know, for one to have the illusion that we're going to be rid of all of these people who are evil and who cause destruction, war, and death—that's an illusion. They'll always be there, because there will always be the lower parts of the human experience; they'll always exist.

A person who gets into power who doesn't have a good spiritual foundation is going to be corrupted by it. You see it over and over. And you'll always see it over and over. As long as you give each individual the opportunity to express that Divine nature within one's life, then you're going to have a greater chance. Our view within the Lakota world is, "If there's one person who achieves peace in the world, there's a chance." If everybody loses it, however, then this world truly doesn't have a chance. But that can't happen either. That's one of the great "chews" of life. [Laughter]

If all is God's will, as some spiritual teachings would have us believe, and some unscrupulous people use this as an excuse to do very bad things, where would accountability for their actions most appropriately reside?

Well, you can break it down to simple cause and effect. If you as a human being decide to go out and hurt somebody, and you continue to do so, you're setting yourself up to be hurt by the very same process. It's the whole idea, "live by the sword, you die by the sword." Simple cause and effect says that if you do enough of these things it's bound to catch up with you. Just the numbers, you know, logic, statistics. If you do something long enough you'll accomplish your purpose because to go and hurt people, to cause death, is causing death and destruction for your own path. And it will catch up with you.

So even in the name of God's will, some people will say, "Well it's all God's will and therefore whatever happens is that will rather than . . . "

I think any person who holds that God controls the world is going to justify their actions that way. When you have a spiritual viewpoint that looks at the truth of things exactly how they are, God doesn't control the world. God gives an opportunity to get to that peace and goodness which means personal responsibility.

But so many of the natural worldviews don't have this idea that God controls the world. I don't. [Chuckle] I believe God expresses through nature. The very people who are using this creative expression from God are justifying their actions by God's will, but God's will is that you "live" and that you can love and do good. That's the will of God. And the will of God is goodness. But beyond that, every person who's living, who's done something evil to someone else, has used the very same gift from God for that purpose. And that's their use of that free will, their responsibility to do so. But each path carries different consequences. Look at the stories of Stalin. He didn't die a very loved individual. And very few people were by his side when he went. But that man killed millions of people. It caught up with him. He didn't leave something behind that endured. So in his world, whether we call it God's will or not, he was justifying his actions.

Historically, there seems to be either a patriarchal or matriarchal dominance. The patriarchal either ignores or idealizes the matriarchal, and the matriarchal seems to be rooted too deeply in the world, in nature. Can there be a fusion of these two great principles, and if so, how would it best come about?

I think that true peace in human experience cannot happen until that fusion actually takes place. Because peace is the unification of the spiritual and material forces in such a way that life is enhanced. It's given greater opportunity and development. That's true peace. We're not talking about tranquility here, we're talking about peace. And until those two are separated (tranquility and peace) in the worldview of humanity, peace won't be here. The whole reality of human-kind is progressing forward in time, at least at the practical level. And it happens because of the fusion of male and female energies. If you and I didn't make love as human beings, we wouldn't have children. Well that's a holy act at its most basic level. If we don't have the ways and means to support its duration, that is, loving in a good way, then we won't experience true peace in the world. That's where most people forget. We develop more difficulty around that whole action. At the same time we are moving toward the Godly act that it is. We develop life out of it. So the whole foundation of that experience has to be that unity between the male and female in order for the human race to progress and endure.

You know, we go in cycles. There will be long times where we do attain that peace and there will be long times where we really mess it up. But that's the human cycle. As we're approaching "the end-times" we're approaching a lot of change in paradigms. That makes the opportunity to unite the male and female even stronger. Whether we do it or not is left up to every individual. But again, in order for that truth and experience to take place, it has to happen within each individual if greater numbers are going to experience it. That's where the personal journey becomes very critical.

Is there some particular dominant principle that you feel can bring that fusion about today?

I think it is understanding your Divine nature. The truth of the male/female exists within each individual whether you are male or female.

So it goes beyond gender then. . . .

It goes beyond gender. It's a force of life, a force of the universe.

You mentioned "the end-time." How is that defined?

"End time" just means complete shifts in paradigm. I'm not a doomsday person. We can get into some pretty big messes, war-wise and computer-wise and things like that, but I don't see an end to the world coming.

Not any time soon.

No. We have some terrible weapons and I think we can really mess up the order of life a little bit but I don't think we can stop it.

And by the time we do get "kicked off the planet," we'll have enough knowledge to go other places. There's still a chance. [Laughter]

If you could give one piece of guidance to individuals very interested in realizing freedom in this lifetime, what would it be?

As glib as it might sound, "learn to be your Self," without the rules of society, without the rules of religions. Look for the creation within yourself, and give expression to it. Why? Because you are doing that unconsciously now. But if you become conscious of it, you'll understand the true creative capacity you have. And if you do that, you have to remember, only you do it. And then you're free to go share it. If you want to find teachers to help you to that end, be careful. But if you find a teacher, then use the tools that you have to remove the stuff that blocks it. Because that's the most a teacher can give you. You really shouldn't seek what you already have.

You have been teaching Taoism and the integration with nature for quite some time now. What's the most important thing that you have learned from this experience?

I believe that the search for truth always gets back to the search for Self, in that the Self is an expression of these very things that we always seem to be looking for outside of ourselves. If anything, studying Taoism has taught me that two peoples from different parts of the world (Taoists and Lakotas) arrived at the same conclusions in different ways. What that showed me is that this Truth, and whatever is "Truth" as the foundation of life, is just the expression that we are. Everything else we've developed around these truths is called religion. We find do's and don'ts. If I bow three or four times I'm going to get a blessing. It's somewhat of an illusion. If you want to be nice and be appreciative and do that, that's great. But that does not guarantee a blessing. Now if you didn't do the "bow down" three times, and you just experienced your life in relation to the creation for what you are, that blessing is always there. That's the kind of truths I think I found just from the study of the Tao; finding that expression of yourself. It becomes very critical. Because if you don't express that yourself, you'll be forever failing at your search. You're not accepting the truth of who you are.

You mentioned earlier before the interview that you had met with the Aborigines in Australia more than once. Did you also see that this insight was available through them in your interaction and your relationship with them at that time? A commonality of spirit we could say?

A holy person is really not someone who has gained power and influence in the world. A holy person is one who simply and easily expresses that principal of truth that's called divine through their actions in relation to others. And when you see that amongst truly holy and simple people, then you know they've touched it. And it does not relate to the search for knowledge, it doesn't relate to the "practice." It's just that every individual who's ever experienced "That," and is willing to share it with the world is a very divine individual. They're just expressing their divinity.

You mentioned "through their actions." Sometimes it is the case that their actions don't appear on the surface to be completely ethical. Sometimes it may give the impression that it's actually hurtful or it creates more difficulty and confusion than less in a person's life. Yet at some level it might be fundamentally nurturing to the person. I think this is one of the most difficult things for people who are looking at situations that have occurred around spiritual teachings. For instance, Jesus was a pretty rebellious guy. He did a lot of things that were very unacceptable. And of course there are a number of other historical examples that we have. How does a person sort through the maze of actions to determine whether or not it has integrity?

To me if a person has not truly, truly done something evil, has done something immoral, they can get away with their actions. Immorality is breaking the rules of order. Doing evil is perverting life. The good teachers who might have been seen as rebellious and who may even have seemed to have done "immoral" things, if you look at their actions in relation to evil, have they done evil? And if you can answer "no," then this person has probably really innocuously benefited their environment. But to me the term "ethics" is important because if you're a teacher, you're going to do some things that really do shake up people's lives. As long as you don't do "evil" and cause harm intentionally, then the teaching will gain duration.

All they're doing is getting the person to use their own strengths to get that same expression that you are conveying, if you will. But you have to be careful in the area of "ethics" and "morality" because "morality" is very rigid. That's what most people defend. "Ethics" is more looking at the demand of a given time and having to do what that demand calls for. And if you do that as a teacher or even as a common individual, and some bad things happen "morally" to somebody but you haven't done "evil" and life hasn't been perverted, then the benefit is still possible, and probably will find expression. That's the best way I can answer that.

Howard, thank you for spending time with us.
Enjoy your journey.

Contact information:

Howard Badhand
5803 NDCBU
Taos, NM 87571

BYRON KATIE

Byron Katie is one of the most intriguing and endearing spiritual teachers I have encountered. She's called Byron by some, Katie by others, and Kate by her husband. Katie's "awakening" is an archetypal story of Phoenix rising from the depths of hell. As a former drug- and alcohol-addicted housewife and businesswoman, she was propelled into the depths of acute suffering to the point of contemplating suicide more than once. In the midst of this incredible torment something astounding happened. Katie puts it this way:

"One morning as I awoke on the floor in an attic of a halfway house, I opened my eyes, and I saw without concepts, without thoughts or any internal story. A foot appeared, along with a cockroach crawling over it. My next perception was that of laughter—it just poured out of me, and it wasn't mine. The laughter was coming from Awareness. It had just manifested as an entire universe. This was the birth of awareness; seeing itself as everything, surrounded in the vast sea of its own laughter."

From Katie's "awakening," "The Work" was spontaneously born. "The Work" is a unique process of self-inquiry. It creates an opening for a person to discover for oneself the reality of any belief or issue. When issues or beliefs are seen for what they are in truth, the power of pure awareness flows forth like a river of light eliminating the darkness of illusion. "The Work" is a simple, yet very effective process that is suited for anyone. As issues arise she asks you to apply the following questions:

Question 1: Is it true?

Question 2: Can I really know it's true?

Question 3: How do I react when I think this thought?

     a: Do I see a reason to drop this thought? (And she's not asking you to drop it.)

     b. Do I see a reason that is not stressful to keep this thought?

Question 4: How or 'who" would I be without this thought?

Following the inquiry into these four questions is an all-important "Turn-Around" activity. The "Turn Around" gives you an opportunity to inquire into your own statements regarding issues that seem "outside" of yourself and turn them "inside" for further inquiry. Unfortunately there's not enough space to spell out the full details of "The Work" here. We encourage you to explore the written materials referenced at the end of the interview and to contact her directly.

A comprehensive story of Katie's spiritual awakening and further details about "The Work" are captured beautifully in a book titled, *A Cry in the Desert: The Awakening of Byron Katie* by Christin Lore Weber.

I interviewed Katie in Salt Lake City where she was offering a public weekend meeting at a downtown hotel. Hundreds of people were in attendance. Katie only accepts donations and does not charge for her meetings.

Katie does "the Work" one-on one with volunteers who come forward with issues or beliefs. Everyone in the audience clearly benefits from each participant's issues because they are also typically our own. Wonderful realizations into the truth frequently washed over the participants with the same kind of laughter Katie experienced when she "awakened." There were also buckets of tears streaming down faces full of joy and relief. It's a great blessing to know Katie and experience the wonderful work she is doing. "The Work of Byron Katie" operates as a non-profit educational system. It is not affiliated with any religion, sect or therapy. The Work Foundation is located in Manhattan Beach, California. Katie also resides in southern California.

As Katie and I sat drinking tea together overlooking the city, I realized just how lovely it was to simply be in the moment with her.

❧ ❧ ❧

Katie, thank you very much for taking time to speak with us today.
Welcome.

A publications about your work mentions you were propelled into a deep spiritual experience at the age of forty-three. Can you help us understand what this experience was, how it might have come about at this point in your life and what lasting changes it brought with it?
Well I was lying on the floor, opened my eyes and could see everything clearly. "IT" was not an "I", yet "IT" was born into existence. "IT" was born. It was as though "IT" was an embryo, yet fully mature, and yet the concepts "that is what is born" and the thoughts "It's born as That" were present. And at the same time there was a knowing that there was zero validity to anything that appeared which was only "thought."

Only attachment to thought prior to investigation could leave the appearance of a world—the mirage or residue of believing thought is valid. And it might appear like, "I want my husband to pick up his socks." And it was not true. It's only thought manifested "real" opposing reality of "what is". I could see that nothing was true. I could see that everything was backward. "My husband should pick up his socks, my husband should not pick up his socks—how do I know? He doesn't." Thoughts were not matching reality.

So I could see that prior to thought there was peace; non-existence. I use the word peace, no-thing prior to the appearance of the thought. And then thought equals world is "birth"; the beginning—now, now. It was as though a volcano had erupted or an earthquake had happened. And it was the body as "all" apparently born. So that is the "Third Question" in the inquiry that I bring. And the "Fourth" [question] and the "First" [question] and the "Second" [question]; just the noticings and the turn-around to that instant noticing and the laughter, the laughter that comes with or as awareness. If it's anything, it's born as laughter. So how has it effected what you call my life then? It's just "Itself." It's a love affair with Itself and it is everything. Everything is Itself, everything; what you see. Everyone; every breath; every sip of tea.

It seems that most highly regarded spiritual figures have gone through a monumental internal crisis before truth is revealed. Does the "dark night of the soul" or extreme angst need to be passed through?
No.

So it's not a requirement?
It's not a requirement. I bring this "inquiry" so others can skip that pain part. You could say my birth is the "inquiry." And everyone who works with this "inquiry" is finding freedom. And I don't know about freedom over...people talk about long-term. Because I don't know about time. I have no reference for it. I just say, "Can you be happy now?" and inquiry brings that. And it's for everyone, not just for "spiritual" people." It's for everyone. Children love this "Work." They'll say, "Why didn't someone tell me? It's so simple!" It's the end of confusion. Confusion is the only suffering. Inquiry is the end of ignorance, confusion and chaos.

There must have been a huge amount of confusion though in your life prior to this experience?
Only that. Only confusion. What a poor innocent woman.

That is what I was referring to as the "dark night of the soul".
Yes, and rightfully so. It was "dark." There was no way out. It was a tunnel that only went deeper. It seemed infinite and suicide was my prayer.

So in actually penetrating the "dark night of the soul", did you feel like you got to the bottom? Was there a hopeless, no-way out, no-exit situation that actually occurred to you in that moment?

No. I was simply asleep on the floor and the eyes opened. I was a human being asleep on the floor. So it's difficult to answer the way you've phrased the question and where I can go with it is… it (the pain) went so deep that when it went beyond what was bearable, the shift took place because pain is never more than what we can bear. It's all a concept. When it goes past human endurance, that particular person, that particular human's threshold of pain, it has to shift because the mind cannot develop a concept beyond its own experience and that's when the shift takes place. It has no past story to reference. So it could be someone stubbing her toe, experiencing the same threshold of "unbearable pain" as one in deep depression for many years such as I. Pain is pain. The pain comes after you stub your toe, not immediately when you stub your toe. Concepts have to kick in for the pain to kick in.

Was there a conscious intention on your part to penetrate beyond that which you could understand with the mind?

Yes, suicide, death. I thought I had to die of the body to be released.

So that was your choice?

I didn't know I had a choice. I didn't have a teacher to teach me such things as, "You can find freedom and stay alive in the body." Any teacher I would see would be someone in a…well, I couldn't imagine what it would be. I know that one night, I (because I was so paranoid it had to be night), got into my automobile and [being] agoraphobic it was very difficult to leave the house. I went to a box outside a church. I remembered they had brochures. And I drove to the church and grabbed some brochures and came back to the house. I remained in my house for days trying to understand any one sentence of what they were talking about. I could not grasp it. And clearly now I see every religion is valid. Every way is valid. I had one. I had a very deep profound belief in, "My husband should pick up his socks." That was my religion. My children…"I want my children to understand me." That was my religion. And I was into it and devout.

Prior to the extraordinary experience that you had, do you recall any interest in understanding or living the truth? Did your parents or your home environment have any impact on your interest in sacred or spiritual life?

No. I just wanted the pain to stop. That was what I was seeking. I wanted the pain to stop. But I thought you had to die to have that. I didn't know it could be found anywhere else. No one told me there was another way. I was totally ignorant. I would watch television and see these religious people and I just couldn't understand. I could see it moved them, but I could not comprehend. They just looked ridiculous to me. So when I look ridiculous to people, I understand and I do not expect people to understand, ever.

Some famous spiritual masters have said that there's nothing to seek since we are always already free and can know the truth as it is in the "Eternal Now." That is, the truth will never happen based on some future event nor does it have its basis in past patterns. It can only be realized in an instant just as it happened to you with the cockroach. It's the constant seeking in dilemma for what is already here in the "Eternal Now" that prevents us from having this revelation. On the other hand there are thousands of years of traditions suggesting that spiritual practices, meditations, prayers and various psychological, emotional, spiritual inquiry techniques need to be employed which is epitomized by the Biblical statement, "Seek and ye shall find." How can we best sort this out?

Well, my way is very simple. What I'm hearing from what you've just spoken is that there are many ways for all of us and they're all effective for this one, or this one, or this one, whichever way is natural for them. For me "seeking" means finding a tea bag if I want tea. Or it comes to me to call my daughter or one of my sons. I seek the telephone. It's just absolute reality; mind and body in absolute sync. It's a beautiful thing; living poetry. It's just doing the thing it knows to do itself. I have no religion and just continue to give and give and give. It's where you really "get." And it's as simple as saying, "yes" to the center of you. And here we are. What is better than that? What is better than reality without illusion of past or future?

So it's really staying in that "Eternal Now"?

Well you may as well, here you are. A cup of tea in hand, a couple of microphones. This is it! It doesn't get any better or any worse than this "Now."

Is there any process to reach that? Is there something in the future that will bring this about or is it in the "Now," it's always been in the "Now" and it's the recognition that if we continue to push things into the future we're never going to "reach" it?

Yes, well we cannot reach it. We have already arrived always. We cannot push things into the future because the future is nothing more than a concept. If I have the thought, "I would rather be walking in the mountains with Dean this morning" then I'm totally, mentally out of the room in a fantasy. I'm missing sitting here with you now and absolutely insane, "pretending" to be where the body is–faking life, really. It's a wonderful daydream and assures that I miss what's "real." So that's where "inquiry" comes in you know. "I need to be with Dean." Is it true? Well what's the reality of it? No! I'm sitting here. I'm not walking with Dean in the mountains. I don't see me even asking him, or I don't see me walking up the hill to find him. What do I get for holding the belief, "I don't want to walk with Dean and I'm sitting here with you"? I miss life, the way it really is. And who would I be without it? Present here with you. "I need to walk with Dean" turned-around, "I don't need to walk with Dean." Obviously!

So I call this inquiry "check-mate." It brings people to reality, sanity; people who want it—now. But people who want to seek a future that can only come "now"...I mean even when they find it, it turns out to be "now." That's not my way. "The future" was my way for forty years (planning for a future). But I just drink tea with my friends now.

We do only three things: we sit, stand, or lay horizontal. That's about it. But the story we tell as we're doing it, that's confusion. Inquire of that and be present—or not.

I think you probably answered this question, but let's try again. Maybe there will be a different angle. What is "The Work"? You mentioned that "The Work" in a sense "collapses time and space that it thought exists." How does this come about and what is the role of "the four questions" in bringing this about?

The awareness of what's real, of reality. The first question is: "Is it true?" And in case you missed that one or if it could apply easier for people, "Can you really know that it is true?" And "How do you react when you resort or attach to the story that you're in - to the belief, to the concept, to the thought, to the story you're experiencing in the moment? And then the fourth one is, "Who would you be without your story?" And then the turn-around. Simple, just simple. Some people will just entertain one of those questions and it changes their lives.

What is reality or truth and how do you find it best conveyed and realized by others?

Truth is what each person perceives it to be. And inquiry can give them how to realize what it really is. Reality for me? It is what it is and I am a lover of reality. I am a lover of "what is." It's too good to miss. So again sitting here with you and Christie and Diane, that's everything, that's real, all I can see. Whether I like it or not has nothing to do with it. It's still everything. So when I can see that, it's over. Not only do I like it; it's everything revealed. We could say it's the total accumulation of a lifetime, everything, every breath for this "Now," and am I going to throw it away by attaching to a concept of a past or future? This is reality. So reality . . . I hear teachers say, or people who say teachers say . . . reality . . . they hold it in a lofty sense, like a spiritual sense. What "I Am" is so prior to that; it can't be spoken. I'm not going to attempt to expose myself for what I truly am. I am already revealed. I love "what is." It's my Self. I'm swimming in my Self. And it's a love affair. I'm full. I'm all of it. Everything.

You use the term "I-I" in "The Work". What does this mean?

Everything is "I-I", "I-I." But see reality, "One," is itself pure, and the "other" is its mirror image, a world that I refer to as "a story." So by "pure" I mean "stands alone," no story and that's what "I am." And then you tell a story or a story appears within "I" and we have the mirror image of itself. Everything is as it is and it's beautiful. There is nothing terrible. Terrible is not real or possible; it's just an illusion.

And what a wonderful trip the sight of Self. Everyone loves their own movie once they understand it's not real.

Do you see any difficulties that arise with teachings of "non-duality"?
Do I see any difficulties in it? No. I wouldn't use the word "difficulty." But on "non-duality" it's to me a religion like any other. It's a story and that is beyond people's evolution sometimes. And it's a whole thing of theories—until it's realized. When it's realized it's no longer a theory. I see people teaching "the religion of non-duality" from pulpits. And it's a wonderful thing, and I see it's just one more religion. Until it's realized it's religion.

Some people refer to it as "the talking school."
"The talking school," yes, "the talking school." Don't you just love what is?

Before it's realized it's just another grasping onto concepts, presumptions....
Exactly.

You stated in a marvelous book recently written on your teaching called "Losing the Moon" that, "there is no evil and there never will be."
Yes, that is my experience.

On the other hand we see people apparently inflicting astounding pain and suffering on others. How can we get past this dichotomy?
Well, is it true that anyone can inflict pain on you? How is that possible? Someone slaps you across the face, you tell the story of what that is or means and you inflict pain on "you." This can last a lifetime and a slap lasts a second or less or the sting less than a lifetime. Who is the more merciful, the slapper or the slapped? Who would you be without your story? Who would you be without the story? Where's the pain now? What do you get for attaching to the belief that "they inflicted pain on you?" An enemy? You know? Without inquiry the enemy lurks inside of you. It's very painful. If someone slaps me across the face, I understand. I am my problem and I am my solution. It all begins and ends with me.

When I go into prisons, where there are murderers, rapists, men who have incested children, all of the stories that go with high security prisons, the first thing I do when I walk into the room, after I get their eyes (and I don't begin until I get their eyes), is thank them for giving their entire lives to teach my children why not to do the crime, why not to harm another human, why not to steal, kill, rape. They are the true teachers that would sacrifice their life for my children's sake, for my friends. That they are "good" and there's nothing they can do about that. Preachers sit in their pulpits telling our children, telling adults why they should not do the crime and it does not penetrate the way the true teacher penetrates by their living sacrifice and example. There are no accidents. Every teacher is chosen. No one has ever done anything but good. And a story uninvestigated would keep us from the awareness of that.

And each time we step into "higher" awareness through inquiry, our actions shift and there's nothing we can do about that. It's done for us. Ignorance follows ignorance—our own. In the ignorance of my attaching to these concepts that are so dense, my life reflects that. And as "Inquiry" enlightens, that "free life" has to follow the life as a mirror of our attachment to beliefs. The world has to heal when a person realizes or becomes aware. And then the one "behind" does the crime and you're spared, and on and on because everything has equal value; no mistake. It's nature; it's like a wave coming in. It never changes. But once you're free, you're free—now. And "inquiry" is the medicine that takes us to realization, the penetration, to vibration. It's everything. It's the end of ignorance, the end of confusion for people who have an interest or are tired of the pain of losing the war.

At some point does "The Work" begin to go about its business naturally or spontaneously within one's self, or is there always a choice of either turning away from it or toward it in any given moment?

I would say when people do "inquiry" for awhile it wakes that mechanism up inside and I don't have any other experience with people than that. I have experience with thousands and thousands of people and once it's practiced it begins to "undo" and all the knots begin to untie. They begin to pop loose and it's such fun, such fun. And there's nothing else to do. It's entering "apparent reality" from another polarity. It ceases to be "negative." I would say once we begin "inquiry," the opposite polarity is stepped into, and it's infinite just as the painful way seemed to be. And again what fun a horror movie can become.

I don't care if people are enlightened or not, I don't even care what that means. You know I hear that term a lot applied to me. I have no caring. It appears to separate me from others. It's very misleading. I am potent as the appearance of a human, a friend; less potent as a "higher than you" holy one. That is so far reaching. To investigate that and be aware of that, that "he's not going to or he is going to pick up his socks"—or not. It is what it is. It happens or not. But just to be aware that I want him to put his socks where he puts them, that's the bottom line.

So what I hear you saying is that there is no "personal" enlightenment. There's no "I" or there's no "someone" who becomes enlightened?

Yes. No dream of where or what.

But there is "enlightenment" in terms of enlightenment for its own sake?

Yes. What people call everyday living. If you think there's a problem you're confused. "Inquire" and set yourself free. Not that it's a great big huge overall thing, but just "this—Now." And it flows across the board in all of life, just to undo "one." It's like a stack of dominoes or a stack of cards. It just falls.

A famous Indian saint once said, "That which is not present in deep dreamless sleep is not real." From this statement can you help us understand what he was referring to as "real" as distinguished from what is not "real"?

There was just nothing. That which is not present, well nothing. Of course it's not real, it's nothing. Some of these things are so silly. They're just so simple. Can you hear it, that which is nothing? That's the end of that. How can it be discussed past that point?

It's unspeakable beyond that point?

Yes. It's nothing but the statement of "It's nothing." That's all.

I think what he was referring to is that there's pure consciousness that underlies all of the relative states of waking, dreaming and sleeping which is always already present and will always be there. That is "real." The things that are layered upon that come about afterwards, and therefore are always changing in that "unreal" realm.

Yes and good and absolutely so. And now everyone can seek to find that. You see where I am coming from? These types of philosophies only give people a lot of hope, a future, time, space, and one more religion.

Yes, more "talking school."

Yes. And good that it is spoken. It is what it is.

You mentioned humor. Where does humor fit in to realizing and living the truth and how do you see it manifesting in "The Work"? Is it beyond irony?

I'd say definitely irony and beyond. For me to attach to the story, "I want my husband to pick up his socks," I mean that is the cosmic joke. He doesn't do that. His job is to drop his socks where he drops them. For me to think, "He should pick them up, I need him to pick them up" anything like that, there is the joke. There's the irony. And it is. "I want my daughter to hear me." Well that's a joke. But I'm talking really, really a joke. When these things started coming to me for the first time, appearing for the first time, oh my gosh. The laughter was unceasing. And I learned not to laugh. So when people experienced the same story (learning not to laugh means I got used to it) that this is what is, arising, appearing now, the story. But now when people say, "I want my daughter to hear me," "I want my son to understand," the laughter doesn't come pouring out. It lives as an internal lightness, a huge power—it's own real strength, and appears as understanding and gratitude. It just understands.

When you say your service is a "totally selfish act, it's the ultimate ego-trip" what do you mean?

Well to sit here with you is much fun for me. You just sit with a tree. I'm the benefactor of "your" experience as you to walk or breathe. Where am I not the benefactor? Where am I not the one experiencing everything? You just think you are "you". What can be outside of me? All the outside is my inside. Where am I not the bene- factor? Your breath behooves me.

Is there anyone "there"? Is there anyone "separate"?
No.

Therefore the ego must be gone?
Yes. And I could say it's "pure ego." Pure ego, Self-love. What is more egoic than self-love—all of self—the whole "world" without conditions? What is more all consuming than that? It's what all greed is about, "I." And when it's understood, it's very sweet, very humorous. I-All.

So when you say "self-love" you're not really referring to someone who's separate as an "ego" who's experiencing "self-love" of the ego. It's love of that which is....
Everything.

You have an interesting way of expressing yourself. Sometimes you say, "It speaks" rather than "I speak" and it must be referring to what we just discussed. Can you help us get more clarification on this?
Well, the first three years I might say to my husband, "She thinks she wants a drink of water now." And it was the only way "I-not-per- sonal" could communicate. "She" this or that, or "It thinks it needs to step outside now." And then the reaction....I could see the alienation from my very own self that we call a human, another human. And when I saw fear in their eyes, it would shift. When I saw that, it would put me up or down, on pedestals, then it would shift until it found an ordinary language. There began a "maturity" about it. It becomes extremely hidden and more aware. It becomes ordinary as its thought- less goal; ordinary, not more not less, just integrating with all that we refer to as the world; and unseen, unseen—that's its sweet place. And its communication is always Self-love revealed. It looks ordinary, the same. And until even communication matches that, it's not done. It's like a child learning the vibration of what is most natural in its center.

You mentioned that you experience "myself on my knees to myself."
This seems to imply that there are two elements involved which are
separate from each other; someone who is doing the bowing and that
which is being bowed to. On the other hand you say, "it's joined to."
Isn't everything always already "joined" to begin with, and the concept
of "joining" brings up the question, "How can there be a joining when
there's never been separation?" Yet it seems that in some sense it's pos-
sible to bow to one's self. It's like a wave bowing to the ocean, and in
turn the ocean bows to the wave, yet knowing in truth that bowing is
just bowing in reverence, in gratitude to its essence.

Exactly so. Exactly so. The things I say I will meet the "cause," the
questioner. I will meet them where they are. I don't care if it's lofty or
appears as egoic. I could care less about the effect of how I'm seen or
portrayed. I am going to meet the person where they are. There's no
"I" or "self" to bow down. Just to meet always. And this bowing, you
know the way you read the words, "bowing at its own self to its own
self," ah, always, only it's not a "down on the floor" thing, it's just
every moment. It's a "being," a gratitude, an awareness. And you put
it into words and it always . . . you won't go out to meet the questioner but it will always remove its essence apparently through a
communication. And also communication is everything. There's only
communication . . . how is it meeting itself? And everything is itself
without alienation or effect of separation.

You said in the book, "Losing the Moon," "I have come to flow as a mir-
ror-image, no more no less." What happens as a result of this activity?

Everything but only everything. Everything and it's good. Everything and it's good. It's itself. How could it be less? Totally. Totally.
Totally. Self-love revealed to itself as itself can't be described. True
beauty can't be described.

You've also mentioned that "people are their own salvation." What's
the role of a teacher or facilitator of the truth, then? Is it preventing
people from becoming self-deluded and thinking that they've "saved
themselves" by pulling themselves up by their own bootstraps, or is
there more to it?

We all know already the same thing they need to hear, and to directly "teach" is to hear what you need to learn coming at you. You say only what you need to hear, that's all. That's why I love "inquiry." It takes the apparent "other" back to their own solutions, knowledge, their own realization. If someone says something and I say something perceived as impressive, again lofty, then they are hearing "my realization;" it's a second generation realization. Then we have another religion. And we have one more "feel good" that backfires. But to "know" everything, to be the wisdom and to sit with itself, to meet their story with less than that, for people to realize themselves—they must meet me without barriers.

So why would I teach or how could I? I'm not a fool. "Inquiry," you're own realization. It's the only thing valuable. You can appear as wise, you can collect many students, you know, and "How are you doing?" "How are you doing?" But to give inquiry—to realize for yourself is everything. There's no interest in a student coming to be with you when you are…well, what I can say is, I have no interest. So when asked I say "yes" and show up to give four questions. The rest is none of my business. I've met my commitment. Who would say "no" to their own invitation?

If "there's nothing we can do or not do what we do until we simply don't do it anymore" and if changes occur but we "didn't change anything because it is what it is," then it seems we are not the "doer" of anything in our lives because we change nothing and nothing changes. There seems to be an absence of "personal responsibility" for what happens, sort of like a predestined existence or "everything is God's will." Can you help us with this?

There's a place when you "realize," and that's through "inquiry" in my experience. But in that place where you are free of "Who would I be without my story?"—in that awareness the decision is already made, and "I am the apparent doer" is not deluded, it is clean, it is "itself doing it and it realizes and sees that it is good." But in the place of wanting, needing, in that place of time, of future, in the absorbed, in the attachment of any concept, the idea of a change, in that you think decision is required and that you are the only one who is doing it. And that's the big difference. It's very painful. So I say to "turn left," the worst that can happen is a concept. To "turn right" the worst that can happen is a concept. And not to make a decision, the worst that can happen is a concept. It's (a concept) the only thing that has ever happened. So to understand is to be free and in that, you're unlimited as a "doer" because you are "The Doer." Turning left is IT. There was no other choice; all else was the illusion, the story around it. " I decided to turn left," for example. But it is itself as the "doing." Choiceless. Choiceless.

Is that what's meant by "nothing ever happens"? You also said that nothing exists. It's just not going to happen. It's all an illusion. It never did exist. It doesn't exist. There's no way it can exist. It's all a reflection of a concept attached to inside.
    Exactly.

If this means that the world and cosmos disappear, how does this come about and what replaces it, if anything?
    It doesn't disappear. It doesn't exist to disappear.

What replaces it if anything?
    Nothing. Nothing.

How does this differ from absolute nihilism then?
    What is nihilism?

Nihilism means that everything is destroyed.
    Well that's why people fear "inquiry." You lose the world as you have known it to be. You lose your world. But what is left is "Itself Seeing Itself Revealed" and that's the "I-I," "Itself Seeing Itself." The real can't appear as real. [Laughter]

So it's an elimination of the illusory existence, we might say, and it is then able to "see" clearly what "reality" is by the elimination of that? Some people would say, "Well if everything is going to disappear then I might as well commit suicide. There's no reason for my existence."
    Well that's just one more concept. I would say to that person, "Can you really know that that's true?" That's definitely not my experience. There's nothing more exciting than "Me." I'm It! But I understand now "I." "I" understand now, myself appearing—and not. You

see people can get these words down and . . . if they're confused they would be suicidal, depressed, etc. What I say is: what is—is good. So if you're not in a position to see it that way, welcome to inquiry. Welcome to life without depression.

You said, "the great cosmic joke here was "I—I AM GOD—this thing's done. No identification. Fully realized. It's known Itself. It's finished."
Well you can hear the "I AM GOD" as identification. [Laughter] And it's as close to speaking it as I would speak. What fascinates me about *Losing the Moon* which is where you got some of this is I was invited to Lone Pine by students and teachers of non-duality. They asked me specific questions from that point, from that space. And I can only answer them from that space. I am just amazed at how far reaching this "losing the moon" is going. Because without inquiry it becomes just one more religion when it's heard or read. And my interest is the main body, everybody without exception, not for special groups. And there are words for it like "mainstream." Without inquiring it can be heard as just another religion. And that's my experience. I can only answer what I'm asked. I am love meeting myself without any conditions.

There's a finished quality to the revelation of "what is." Yet on the other hand it seems to go on forever. . . .
Well it can only go on forever if you are attached to the illusion or story of a past, and the stories, a future. So when you investigate your "stories" as many of my friends do, and lose the illusion of "a past," "you" lose your future. And what does that leave? Reality. It's what is really so simple that mind cannot comprehend it and that's what I love. Until a person steps into investigation, they are not privy to such clarity. And in that we could almost say it's "earned." We are responsible for the sweet dream now.

And when people go into inquiry to answer . . . I worked with a woman on her thighs in Israel. She was the cutest! And she could not do the investigation because she was attached to the concept and therefore the fear that if she answered truly and went too deep into it, she'd end up with "fat thighs."[Laughter] And when inquiry works with questions around the body, people rarely trust to get that honest and that is as it should be.

And the truth is we would rather have (as in this example) "thin thighs" than take the risk of freedom from the illusion of control, you see! And we all have something, "thighs" with her and "money" with another or "relationship" with another. But you know I love being with these people. They want freedom and they cry and they beg and they come. And when you get down to their "sacred cow" what I call "their religion"—"I want my husband to pick up his socks," "I want my thighs to be thin," when you get to their "religion" these devotees of thirty and forty years have no interest in freedom. Zero. Their true "religion" has been attacked. And they're the only one left to attack. I simply say, "Sweetheart, can you really know that it is true?" And you'd be amazed how these people of "devotion" run. [Laughter] That's why I love to ask when someone sits with me, "Do you really want to know the truth?"

Why do you think there remains such confusion about "enlightenment teachings" in these times?

So many unenlightened teachers teaching it! I prefer to offer the simpler gift of inquiry. And everything serves equally.

If someone is sincerely interested in a genuine spiritual teaching or teacher, what do you feel the most important things are to consider?

For me it would be to sit with someone I call "friend." Ultimately it is to sit with yourself and ask four questions and turn it around. All the answers are waiting inside to be met. Just ask. You are the only book to read.

In our daily lives what's the best way to deal with simple right and wrong decisions that we must make, or in dealing with complex destructive tendencies in others who want to cause wars and death, and extreme suffering—which appear to most people to be very wrong?

I would really go into it on paper. And I would judge them. I would judge them very harshly. And with each sentence I would do the "inquiry" and turn it around and see how easy it would be to live it myself. That's the end of the outside world as we know it. And it puts us in a position that we have so radically put them in mentally and it leaves us to live it. And there again I say, "How are you doing?"

Can I live what I expect them to live? Well, that's a life's work and it keeps me out of their business. And I say that when I get it down, then I'll teach and preach.

So it's really being ruthlessly focused on "what is" and not allowing anything else to really intercede into that inquiry of "what is" in one's life?
  Yes, just deal with your own. And when you get it down, come talk to us. When you learn how to change, then you come teach it.

What is "The Divine," if by definition "the Divine" cannot stand apart from anything? If this is true then is there anything we can say or do that is not "Divine"?
  What is "the Divine"? Everything. And any concept you would attach to it that says that anything is less than that, investigate. Because in that moment without investigation, you are the experience of confusion. There's only good. I call that "the last story." There's only good. You can play with the zero's there. Only God, only good. Anything that would argue with that, investigate, because you're arguing with your own nature, your very own Self.

What do you feel is the most appropriate way to hold ourselves and others accountable for our lives and what happens in the world?
  Oh my! I would be insane to hold anyone accountable for how I live in the world, or how anyone else lives in the world. I just hold myself. I'm the one. Investigate. It is always already being done.

That's our business.
  Yes. Say it again.

What do you feel is the most appropriate way to hold ourselves and others accountable in life and what happens in the world?
  I don't have a world to judge. "How do I hold the world?" As totally innocent, totally innocent like children. So good. So good. There are no words for that. So good. You are so good. And any place you lose awareness of that is pure ignorance. Investigation is the end of ignorance.

If all is God's will, as some spiritual teachings believe, and some unscrupulous people use this as an excuse to do very bad things, how would they be most appropriately held accountable for their actions?

They hold it with every breath. That is the accounting. If you're not comfortable, investigate. The "books" are within you. The accounting is within you. If you're not free, investigate. Write it down. What I say is, "Judge your neighbor, write it down, ask four questions and turn it around." "Judge yourself and write it down, ask four questions and turn it around." The accounting is the experience you're holding inside of you every moment...if it's not very, very comfortable, if it's not really liking it, get your debits and credits straight and welcome to "The Work" of Byron Katie.

If you could leave us with a brief summary statement for those seriously interested in living the truth, what would it be?

You have always been living your truth. If you want Self-realization, "judge your neighbor, write it down [Laughter] ask four questions and turn it around." Until you love yourself and your neighbor as yourself, your work's not done. And when you love yourself half of it is done and the other half is the gift that meets it. You will love us because we remain always your projection, a mirror image of your own thinking.

Katie, you've been offering "The Work" for several years now. Literally thousands of people have participated in workshops and events. Can you share with us what "The Work" has meant to you and others who have participated in it, and your future plans for the Work Foundation?

[Laughter] There aren't any. Yes, there is, it seems. If someone calls our toll-free number, orders the "little book" through the web, it is to simply be there to get it out within 24 hours at no charge, or simply pick up the phone and forward the "little book" without charge.

Thanks very much, Katie. It's been fun!

Thank you, John. Good being with you this morning.

Publications:
Books by Byron Katie are available through The Work Foundation and retail bookstores:
Loving What Is, Byron Katie
I Need Your Love: Is That True? Byron Katie

Contact information:
Byron Katie International
520 Washington Blvd. Box #821
Marina Del Rey, CA 90292-5442
Tel 1-800-98KATIE (52843) (US Only)
Tel 1-815-220-1392
Fax 1-815-220-8738
www.thework.com

TIMOTHEE ROI DIERS

Timothee Roi Diers is a wonderful example of someone who walks in silence and yet is dynamically engaged in the world. While being with Timothee one gets a deep sense of contentment, peace, sensitivity, and love. He is soft-spoken and gentle yet exudes a noticeable physical and spiritual strength. His eyes are crystal clear and engaging. When one is with Timothee, there is a feeling of being drawn into the presence of this moment, and no where else.

I interviewed Timothee during the summer of 1999 at his modest home in Logan, Utah. At the time of the interview, he was working as a crew-supervisor for the forest service and was called out for firefighting duty periodically. One evening while we were enjoying a scrumptious dinner Timothee prepared, he mentioned a time when he found himself trapped in a death-defying fire. As soon as I heard this story, I knew I had to share it with you—it is included at the end of the interwiew. Observe what happens to your relationship with death as you reflect on this amazing event.

Timothee is a rare combination of artist, firefighter and spiritual guide. He consciously lives a very simple existence free of typical materialistic trappings. He is very humble about his spiritual prowess and is quite low-keyed about assuming the role of a "spiritual teacher." In this sense, Timothee is approachable and easy to be with. Timothee recently moved to Billinudgel, Australia, which is close to Byron Bay. He lives at a beautiful retreat site called Madhuban. Timothee holds periodic public meetings in Australia and the States.

ॐ ॐ ॐ

Timothee, thank you very much for spending time to speak with us today. As a note of introduction, can you please share with us where you grew up and how it's impacted your perspective on life?

I grew up on a family farm in Minnesota. It was there in this environment that I had my first experiences with what I consider spirituality. I didn't connect with institutions or religions when I was young. It was primarily through the cycles of birth and death; with the animals, with the crops, with the weather. The first memory I remember was of holding a small bird dying in my hands, and watching this bird with open eyes, warm body, shift into glazed over eyes, and a cold body; and as a little boy being thrown into the mystery of birth and death. This happened continuously on the farm. The whole mystery of it was so intriguing, of embracing that every day.

But growing up on a farm in the middle of the United States did not have much room for outside influences in terms of other things that were happening around the world. And after around seven or eight years old I would sometimes become withdrawn and sad because there was an inner ache which asked to be explored and discovered, but I did not have any influences to awaken this. So a lot of my youth was spent alone in the woods, walking, exploring nature and not socializing much. I didn't do well in school. I felt I was in a vacuum except I had a tie to the earth which I have never lost.

You have brothers and sisters?

Yes. I have three brothers.

How did they react to your approach to life? Did you have much inter-action with them, or were you pretty much off on your own?

Since my older brother and I are close in age we spent a lot of time together as younger brothers do. And we were outdoors all summer long, riding bicycles down a dirt road to the beach every day. There were lakes everywhere. We would play along the creeks in the woods with the neighbor children. The older I got the more I realized how differently I felt and saw life.

Was your family spiritually inclined when you were growing up? Did they practice any form of religion or spiritual practice?

My parents were very religious. I grew up in a Protestant religion and went to church every week. My parents loved their children and they were very nurturing. But I was coming from someplace different. Their formula for happiness didn't work for me and my heart rebelled against it. The place that I was going did not have a map. When I was young there was an unbroken connection with life. After rainstorms when I would ride my bicycle on the back roads, I would always be getting off at little puddles to pull drowning bugs from the water. It was an obsession. There was a stock tank behind the barn where the cows would drink. If I'd go back to do chores, I could spend a long time pulling all of the insects out of the water. And I still find myself doing similar activities. My mother once told me that when I was a small boy I would not let her kill flies in the house, which annoyed her quite a bit.

Do you remember anything that triggered a very strong desire to know the truth? Was there any specific situation other than the 'bird event' that you didn't understand, or was there a lingering mystery to it?

There were daily events on the farm because life and death happens every moment. The harvest, the planting of the crops in the spring, and animals dying and being born. I remember sitting by a mother pig in the barn, in one of the dark rooms where the livestock would go to sleep. She was taking her last breaths, and I was just sitting there with her. I feel the raw energy around birth and death. I have always been drawn to be around those two events because the superficiality of life is so stripped away. Morality, ethics, everything falls away.

One event in my early twenties also became a landmark. I was living alone in a cabin in the mountains of Idaho where I was packing horses. And it arose that I had to find out if there was a God, not a God of books and tradition, but a living God capable of communicating with me. There was a Christian church I became interested in and I began taking some missionary lessons. I had to know if God existed, or it wasn't worth living anymore. It was in the spring, and I took these missionary lessons, and had these manifestations happening. One time I woke up from a nap and there was an evil spirit hovering over my body. The mind was so powerful to create these energies.

This duality was created by the memorized knowledge that I was learning, with God on the good side and Satan on the evil side. I prayed constantly to know whether this church was true. Then one evening I came back to the cabin after the last lesson. It was a clear spring evening and the stars blazed above me as I walked home. The [church] lessons were at my landlord's cabin which was about a fifteen minute walk. I came into my cabin, sat at the kitchen table and there was—I am always at a loss to describe this—there was no sense of me as an individual. Everything disappeared and consciousness remained, infused with infinity. I do not know how long this lasted in terms of conventional time. It could have been less than a second or two hours. Then suddenly there was a shift back into time with the mind again functioning as before. And this mind said, as I had memorized from the missionaries, that this was the Holy Ghost and that their church was true.

Years later, in India, I read parts of the book *Talks with Ramana Maharshi* and someone asked him a question about a similar event. What I remember Ramana Maharshi answering was that events may arise in our lives which become a catalyst for this opening. And the first thoughts that arise immediately after the opening will be ones which will define the experience. We have this profound opening and then we spend a lot of time defining, comparing, trying to get back to it again.

You mentioned Ramana Maharshi. What spiritual teachers have had the greatest impact on you in terms of living a more holistic life and helping others to do so, whether currently alive or not?

To lead up to this answer I want to describe what happened in this church. From the morning I was baptized in an outdoor hot springs, I started to die within, because the curiosity and the openness for Truth was now being replaced with other people's experience with Truth, whether it was direct or indirect. And it did not relate to mine. I was asked to now memorize what God is, why we are here, how we should live our life, and what happens after we die. This happens to all of us, whether it comes from a religion, a politician, a parent or teacher. I even see this happening within some Satsangs (meetings), within the philosophy of non-dualism. It is memorization, perhaps not of Christ but of Ramana Maharshi or Sri Poonjaji. This is why any teaching can become prison, replacing one for another.

After nearly a decade of confusion and deep reflection, I finally came up with three decisions. I was studying sculpture in Arizona and living in a trailer miles from town. My whole world was crushing down at that point. This was probably back in about 1987. And the three decisions were: 1) I would stay in this religious institution and be miserable; 2) I would end my life; 3) I wouldn't care what happened after this body died. And I went to a little library that was at a community college where I was studying, pulled out a book, opened the page and it said, 'Life is like a river, flow, and when you come to a rock don't push it over, but flow around it.' Take the path of least resistance. It was a simple book on Taoism. I let out a great sigh of relief. That marked the beginning of my interest in the East.

Sometimes the patterns and repetitions in our lives interfere with our vitality and inner joy. As a child, most of us opened our eyes in the morning to excitement and the possibilities of a new day. But as we get older we begin to repeat body and mental patterns and we arrive at an inauthentic life. This was occurring to me at this time with the "Western perspective." So I knew I needed something to break that pattern of repetition and recognizing symbols. My first contacts were through Buddhist teachers like Thich Nhat Hanh. I found a little book of his called *Being Peace* or something like that. And then I bought Suzuki Roshi's classic book,which later brought me to the San Francisco Zen Center. After reading about the Buddha, an intense desire arose: I had to know if there was a living person, somewhere in the world who actually lived and realized what the Buddha said, and if so I had to find that Master. Then I would know that the Buddha's words were not just another philosophy thought up by inspired minds. From this desire arose another desire, which soon took me on a 3 year journey around the world to see for myself if it was true. This journey ended in India in 1990 upon meeting Sri Poonjaji (H.W.L Poonja).

Another interesting event occurred. During the fall of 1988, I visited my younger brother in Ames, Iowa who was working on a doctorate degree in plant genetics. This agricultural university had a bookstore. As I walked through it one day, I saw a photo in a book that went into my entire Being. Though I did not understand anything within the pages, I knew the book was mine. This was the year that Shambhala Books first published *The Spiritual Teachings of Ramana Maharshi.* The cover had a classic sepia photo of Ramana. During the next two years I kept this book so I could see the photo wherever I lived. Two years later it would be through this photo that Sri Poonjaji and I would meet.

In December of 1988, I flew to the Zen Center in San Francisco and got my first teaching of meditation practice. Once a week for an hour I met with Paul Haller, the head meditation instructor. It was through my interaction with him that I began to see the absurdities of my beliefs. He was my first mentor. Later I lived at Green Gulch Zen Farm and Tassajara. The following spring I participated in a retreat with Thich Nhat Hanh at Mount Madonna Center. I also stayed at a Christian hermitage near Big Sur, California. I mainly went to meet Brother David Steindl-Rast. We had corresponded for a couple of months and I felt a deep love for him as a friend and because of his interest in the East. I was very focused on the archetype of the Monk and wanted to explore that.

One afternoon just before I left the hermitage, Brother David and I took a walk along a dirt road that switched backed up to the center. The Pacific Ocean stretched out to the west, which made it spectacular. You have this immense ocean in front of you. At some point I asked Brother David, "Do you believe that Christ rose from the dead?" Brother David stopped, and from what I can remember he said, "As a historical fact there was a man named Jesus that was born in Palestine about the time the Bible says. It's also documented that he performed extraordinary events, and that this man named Jesus was crucified on the cross. But whether he rose from the dead? It is not relevant!

Because if one's relationship with Jesus is on the 'Historical Christ' then you have missed his teaching. His whole message was that 'you' wake up from the dead here and now."

After these meetings, I went back to the Zen Center and there I spoke to a man who had recently participated in a three-month retreat at the Insight Meditation Society (IMS) in Barre, Massachusetts. This is a Buddhist center from the Vipassana tradition coming out of Burma and Thailand. That was the longest retreat I knew of in the world. I applied and got accepted. In the fall, I flew to IMS. My teachers were Joseph Goldstein and Carol Wilson. There were four or five teachers for the three month retreat, but we were personally assigned a couple of teachers that we would be meeting with every four to six days for a ten minute interview. Other than that it was complete silence. I remember the week before going into silence that it felt like I was going into the eye of a hurricane. I had no idea what would happen. Three months of meditation!

After this retreat I stayed on as a long term yogi, which meant I had my own tiny room and could participate with the many teachers that came to teach. By spring I had stopped practicing any meditation 'technique' and was beginning to understand the words in the book I had on Ramana Maharshi. Then one week Sharda Rogell and Christopher Titmuss came from England to give a retreat. I was still considering monastic life and requested a ten minute interview with Sharda to ask about this. On the appointed time I walked into her room and upon entering I noticed a table with a small picture of an Indian man. Suddenly, upon seeing that photo, there was an explosion in my Heart and I knew this was my last teacher. I asked who this man was. She told me that she had just returned from India where she had been with him and his name was Sri Poonjaji. I asked her what he taught since I was now going to India to meet him, and she said he was a 'Self Realized' devotee of Ramana Maharshi. It was then that I realized that Ramana had come for me. Immediately I wrote to Sri Poonjaji in Haridwar asking to meet him and within a short period I had in my hands the most powerful letter ever written to me, and an invitation to come to India.

You mentioned Zen practice. What is your impression or insight about the popularization of meditation or meditation techniques as a means to gain a deeper sense of reality or enlightenment? How do you see it now that you have gone into that experience and have had other experiences since then?

If one is looking for a conditioned peaceful life, then those practices have benefits. If we are stressed out and we use a meditation practice, whether it is on the breath or whether it's on a mantra, we may have a feeling of relaxation since the scattered attention has now been placed on an object of focus. But it's conditioned, because one needs an object to hold the attention on, and to create an object you need the mind. After the three-month retreat had ended I was surprised to find that there were people who had repeated this retreat many, many times. And I thought, "How could that be? How many times does it take to be on a retreat with that intensity before one reaches the so-called goal of enlightenment?" Self-realization is beyond any practice, otherwise it's conditioned.

This goes along with what a famous Buddhist Master once said in the statement: 'There is nothing which can be attained is not idle talk: it is the truth. You have always been one with the Buddha, so do not pretend you can attain to this oneness by various practices. If at this very moment, you could convince yourselves of its unattainability, being certain indeed that nothing at all can ever be attained, you would already be Bodhi-minded. Hard is the feeling of this saying! It is to teach you to refrain from seeking Buddhahood, since any search is doomed to failure." On the other hand however, there's the biblical statement, 'Seek and ye shall find.' Can you help us understand the meaning of the word 'seeking' in each of these cases, and how it fits into the context of no intention, or no effort in realizing liberation?

I cannot find anyone that can do any seeking. Who is it that is even separate to search? I can speak to people about looking for a teacher, looking for a practice, investigating, observing the mind, but at some point one will find there are absurdities in even these. Is there anyone who chooses self-realization? How can intention even come to play? To have intention one starts with the idea that 'I am bound'. It's the same with choice. It starts with the idea that 'I am not free', therefore I'm choosing something that would be better for me, which is in the field of time because I project that somewhere along the road in the future, that by doing something, by investigating, that I will be liberated. And since self-realization is beyond time, those ideas are completely irrelevant. All it can do is fatigue us, so at some point we give up all those ideas that we are separate from the Divine. Call it surrender or grace.

In our dreams at night we can practice meditation, focus on the breath, and we can practice self-inquiry. What is the difference from that and doing it here? When we wake up in the morning and realize it was all a dream, then we realize the futility of doing all that practice. Isn't it possible that in this waking state we may also be doing the same?

It might be a little bit difficult for people to understand what you just said: that there really is nothing to do and there is nowhere to go because we're already in that enlightened condition. Most people simply don't have that realization. They can't cognize that, or they don't realize that in their own daily lives. Can you help us with this?

Life will show this to you. The resistance that one has will finally become fatigued. If an "enlightened" individual and a "non-enlightened" individual both moved their hands, would the energy that moved one be more 'divine' than the other? Truth does not discriminate. Nothing is excluded.

Even untruth?

Both are creations of the mind. There isn't anything we can say or do or feel that's outside of divinity.

It's like saying that something that's part of the ocean is separate from H_2O?

Yes.

And yet the mind is part of that also. It's just that it's in a limited form we could say?

Thoughts, suffering, non-suffering, non-thought, they're all contained within it. There is nowhere you can go to escape truth, to go outside of Beingness. The only way one can seem to do it is to create a story that says "I am not complete." Sometimes I use the analogy of the sun. If the sun is burning, one can look on the outside perimeter and see little flames moving out and coming back in. Now, is that flame separate from the sun? Of course not. It is the sun. The only way that flame can say it's separate is to make a story out of it, and identify with the form, with the height, and with the movement of the flame moving back and forth. It is the same principle with the waves on the ocean. The only way the flame cannot be the sun is through a dream, to say, "I am not that." Now what can that flame do to be the sun again? Well, really nothing. It just drops away. Nothing's even changed. It's always been the sun.

So it's the identification with the flame or with the wave that is causing the forgetfulness of the H_2O, or the essence of the fire itself?

Do not even reject the identification, since in doing so one enters truth and untruth, right and wrong. You are not in control of your life, not even in creating and dropping the story. There is an intelligence beyond the mind.

There seems to be a lot of confusion and many definitions in these times about the term "enlightenment." What does 'enlightenment' mean to you?

Every teacher and every student will have a different definition of enlightenment or self-realization. There cannot be a concise definition because it's beyond words. Words are only metaphors of something. There are certain words that can symbolize it. In India they say, "I am That," or "Isness." What does that mean? It is absurd in the West. But those are some words that can come close. If I say 'God', then that has so many definitions and mental images. So sometimes one can say 'Is-ness' or 'That' and be instrumental. What do I feel it is? Well it's certainly not anything that happens. It's not in time so there's really no enlightenment. Enlightenment is not a verb and it is not a movement. Without using the memory how can you know that you have gone anywhere?

Some say that through silence alone one can realize enlightenment. Others say it's through action alone. How can we cut through this dichotomy?

Allow everyone to follow their own path. What difference can action or non-action have on your essence? In a sense none of them are relevant. Certain personalities are more inclined to do physical work and service, which in India is called the path of Karma yoga or in Buddhism it is sometimes expressed through the Bodhisattva teachings. I believe the Bodhisattva vow states that one should not become enlightened until the whole world does so. This may be a beautiful idea but it is mixed with intention and postponement. That is why I ask people to tell me something about themselves that they have not memorized from a book, a teacher, or any other source. Because all these teachings are indirect information memorized. Your essence will not be touched whether you sit or move.

The famous Indian saint Ramana Maharshi once said, "That which is not present in deep dreamless sleep is not real." Can you shed some light on the meaning of this statement?
    In the waking state and in the dream state there is a constant illusion of movement, and with our identification with this there is a dissatisfaction which results in restlessness. And yet, even though each state seems very different from one another, there remains something untouched, which some may say is awareness or consciousness. This is the only thing in one's life that is constant and unchanging. But beware not to memorize this or it becomes another philosophy.
In sleeping, it appears that there is a separation between witnessing the world and directly participating in it. Is there anything beyond this realization?
    Please explain that to me again.

We have relative states of consciousness or awareness which are waking, dreaming and sleeping. And we also have the witnessing state of consciousness or awareness itself which appears to be separate from the world and yet directly participating in it. There's a separation between relative states of consciousness and the absolute state of awareness itself. Is there anything beyond this realization of that separation, and if so, how would it come about? If there is non-separation in unity, how does that come about between the relative states of awareness (waking, dreaming, sleeping) and awareness itself if there is no separation?

So the apparent feeling of the relative truth and the witness being separate from that?

Yes, as being a constant "awareness." The relative states of conscious-ness are constantly changing. That which is "awareness" itself is never-changing. There appears to be a separation between the two because they cannot possibly be 'unified' if one is non-changing and the other is constantly changing. Is there something beyond that realization, that dichotomy between the two?

The witness itself is unchanging. There is only the appearance that phenomena shifts and changes, because we use the memory to compare and contrast. The mind is no more than images or sounds that appear to be happening in the present. And in that moment of memory we may say "something happened" twenty years ago or five seconds ago. Yet neither is true. There is no time in the "Now" because the past and future are only projections. And if this is so, then does anything change or happen?

What I speak of is very, very simple. I find that when we spend a lot of time and energy investigating the different "states" it becomes philosophical. I'm not interested in any "state." There is only this moment and if what one wants is absolute peace then it cannot be dependent on anything, not even investigation, not even thinking there are different "states." "States" have to do with hierarchy. I have no interest whether people see auras or have "spiritual experiences." Investigating chakras has nothing to do with unconditional peace.

People can spend their whole lifetime under practices and inves-tigation. And peace itself is immediate and simple. It's the idea that spirituality is complex that gives people the illusion that it's difficult. If we are complete already, then why do we have to know anything about the dream state or any waking state? I'm not really even inter-ested in speaking about any of those things. Other people have done an excellent job in doing that.

What's your favorite analogy, metaphor, aphorism or story that best points to what enlightenment or the Truth is and how it is realized?

I would like to relate a story of when I was in India with Sri Poon-jaji that summarizes the projection of suffering and the immediacy and accessibility of the love which remains unchanged within us. I was in India for about 3 weeks, and one day in Satsang an energy ripped through my being like an electrical circuit blowing out and I lost consciousness. I was taken back to the Chowdry Hotel where I was staying. From this blow to the body it became weak and it no longer had the strength to resist illness. That night I came down with acute dysentery. Day after day it became worse until I finally lost the desire to live. Because of my weakness I did not go to Satsang and even so, I had the feeling that I no longer needed Master (Sri Poonjaji), that I could do everything alone. But it was coming from an egotistical viewpoint.

One night, Sharda Rogell and Murray Feldman came to my room for a visit. Each evening my friends would come over and tell me what happened in Satsang and bring electrolytes for me to drink, to keep some strength up. They said, "We don't believe you have surrendered to Master. You speak about having it all yourself, that you can do it by yourself, but the joy and happiness is missing in your life. Perhaps you have not completely surrendered to Master." After they left I then realized the truth of what they said. All through the night, I cried out to Master "Please come to my room, please come and help me, save me!" If one could imagine one's whole life as being a long and dynamic river, then being in Lucknow with this Master was meeting with the ocean. Nothing else had any meaning. For me he was the incarnation of the Divine.

The next morning a friend came in and said, "Master is coming to your room tomorrow morning!" I was ecstatic. It was as if Christ was coming to my house, literally. So in anticipation of that, the next morning, Sunday morning, I got out of bed early. I was still very weak but I cleaned the room and brought some chairs next to my bed. Around ten o'clock there was a knock on the door. I opened the door and there was Master with Sharda, Murray, Yamuna, and Ron who was from England. Papaji entered the room and immediately started to look around, making comments like, "Oh, what a nice room Timothee has here." He continued in this way without speaking directly to me or making eye contact. They then sat down in the chairs by the bed without acknowledging me. Because of this behavior my anxiety was heightened. I felt he could immediately stand up and leave the room, and in my state of illness I might never see him again. In desperation

I began to plead with him. "Master," I said, "tell me what love is. I don't have love. I need love. Please show me." He shifted his attention around, avoiding me. No eye contact. Again he said, "Oh look, Timothee has a fan up there, and over there is the bathroom." Then finally he turned and said, "Murray, Timothee isn't getting better. Tomorrow I would like you to make arrangements to bring him on the train to Delhi where my daughter lives, and he can then fly back to the U.S. There is no reason for him to stay." I was completely shocked. Here was my teacher, my Divine teacher sending me away, not even asking me. And knowing this, Sri Poonjaji for the first time turned to me, made eye contact, and said, "Are you going to stay or are you going to go?" And I said, "Master, I am going to stay!"

Suddenly, without warning, he turned on me like a raging thunderstorm coming from nowhere. The words, the energy, and the glance were from a source I had never experienced before in my life. I had read about the wrath of God and could never understand how this energy could be useful. And now, in this moment, I was in its fierce fire like being under the sun with a powerful magnifying lens. His words were knives into my ego. He said, "How dare you be in my presence! You call yourself spiritual? You're nothing but shit on the floor! There are other people here more worthy than you! How dare you be here now in my presence!" And on and on he went. I went completely numb. And then one thought arose, "When Master leaves, I will kill myself." I could not imagine how I could continue to live after this humiliation by my Master. Murray told me later that he had not seen this level of wrath before, and that he too had the same thought that I would kill myself after this. It was that intense.

Then a miracle arose. A tiny spot in my body began to vibrate and it quickly spread. Finally my whole body trembled, shaking uncontrollably. In a flash the mind and the ego shattered. I dropped to the floor and hugged his feet. Tears flooded out. At that moment Sri Poonjaji completely shifted from a thunderstorm to blue sky. And Master said, "How can you ask for love? You're like a fish in the ocean gasping for water. All that is needed is to open your mouth. You are love itself, can't you see? Sometimes a Master has to slap their students. Get well, we love you, come back to Satsang." So in that split second, I went from wanting to commit suicide to complete bliss.

What happened? What happened there? In this story you will find all the keys to self-realization.

That was a great story about Poonjaji. If someone were truly sincere about finding a genuine spiritual teaching or teacher, what are the most important things to consider?

First, decide what one wants in a teacher. If that happens to be unconditional peace, then allow yourself to be chosen of a teacher that expresses that peace. Of course a teacher may provoke and bring up issues that are uncomfortable, but there has to be an overriding factor of silence and peace if that is what one is looking for.

I might say there are two functions of a teacher: to be a mirror, because if they are not a mirror, you're going to go into a situation with a dependency that may not end. You may leave one dependency and go into another. That teacher must be a mirror if you're looking for silence and peace, of which you are already. All they can do is mirror it back to you. And then, most importantly, break that mirror. This is called liberation. Use honesty and sincerity, and it will take you exactly where you need to go. The perfect teacher cannot refuse to chose you, whether it be a tree, a cloud, or an "enlightened sage."

And finally, you will know if your love for the Master is unconditional by whether you need to think about her or him to radiate love. Can you love the Master without the mind, without thinking? Because if you need that image, then you are still bound. I find that if people grieve when their Master leaves the body it is often because they had not completely married the Master into their Hearts. They are still objectifying their teacher which is a dependency to receive something from them. That is why the mirror must be broken, or the grieving person will then again look for a new teacher.

It's been said by some very well known spiritual teachers that enlightenment is beyond even good and evil, right and wrong, and that self-realized individuals aren't even accountable to God. In our daily lives, what's the best way to deal with right and wrong decisions that we must make, or in dealing with destructive tendencies in others who want to cause wars and death, and extreme suffering—which appear to most people to be very wrong?

If we believe that we are accountable to God, then we are still behaving in a parent/child relationship, and we know the shortcomings of that. Why does one concern their life with right and wrong decisions? Why is it that no one can agree with what right is? It is arrogant to claim that we even control our lives. We create in our mind a whole lifetime of plans and expectations without realizing that all of this is dependent on the heart whose beat continues or finally stops independent of anything one thinks.

What do you feel is the most appropriate way to hold ourselves and others accountable for actions that occur?

If we live our lives completely based on ethics and morality, right and wrong, good and evil then the world will continue as it is. For thousands of years we have had people of distinction who have lived and died proclaiming that their way of conduct is the only means that can bring peace and well being to humanity. And where have we gotten to? Stress, instability, crime, competition, environmental destruction, and overpopulation now exist on a level never known before on a global scale. There is a widely held feeling among scientists and those who closely watch changes in human and planetary life that we only have twenty or thirty years left. Either we make a huge shift, or civilization will end as we know it. So what, may I ask, is the result of these thousands of years living by ethics and morality? A lot of wars with some people having more than others. Many of us live in convenience at the expense of other people living in poverty.

So I ask, can one live a life without any belief at all? Because ethics and morality are just beliefs we've memorized. When we wake up in the middle of the night without a thought, are we a Christian, are we a Buddhist, are we a follower of anyone? Can we live a life without being anything? Can we live a life trusting that whatever it is that allows the heart to beat and the breath to move will also take care of this "event" we call our life?

If all is God's will as some spiritual teachings believe, and some unscrupulous people use this as an excuse to do very bad things, how should they most appropriately be held accountable for their actions?

I have no idea. I have no belief that there's any God outside of us that will hold anyone accountable. All of those people who are committing these acts are living in belief systems. Many of these people are outcasts of the mainstream belief system and then create an opposing belief system. These are individuals that we want removed because they cannot behave in a way that allows us to live the way we want. And this life may, in fact, be one that is contributing to the final collapse of life on earth.

Historically there seems to be either a patriarchal or matriarchal dominance. The patriarchal either over focuses on the transcendental aspect of life leaving the world as something separate from reality, and the matriarchal seems to have rooted her too deeply in the world, in nature, de-emphasizing the transcendental. What would a radical fusion of the two appear as, and how would it best come about?

Well it would only be relevant within a philosophical system. Those are only separations and dichotomies that occur within beliefs and thoughts. One can put one's hand in the dirt, or reach it into the air and it hasn't changed anything. The only thing that may seem to occur is within the belief system. Those that herald these philosophies tell us we have to find a path, that this is better than that. And then we have to read the appropriate books, listen to more CD's and go to more teachers. It's all complexity. At some place we have to say, enough is enough. What's going to be important when we are on our death bed and we are taking our last breath? How will anything that we have ever memorized be relevant to anything at that point? Everything we've ever done in our life will have no meaning, especially if we do not remember anything. Then who are we?

You have begun holding periodic Satsangs in parts of the U.S and Australia. Can you share with us what the meaning of Satsang is, and how you present it to participants?

More and more I even avoid this word because it is becoming overused and is advocating a philosophy of non-dualism. Satsangs are becoming an institution where even the questions and answers are predictable and rehearsed. The word Satsang originally refers to emptiness, without any reference. So many Satsangs today have photos of their teachers and are always referring to sources outside themselves as if to justify that what they say is valid. Teachers are creating careers for themselves out of this association to a teacher. The whole belief of lineage is coming out of the mind. There is no lineage or tradition in Being. And if one would challenge me that Ramana Maharshi and Sri Poonjaji advocated otherwise then they must have been with someone other than who I was with. When I was with Sri Poonjaji in 1990 he never allowed any association with him. That was his uniqueness and power, to simply be. Now with the passing of his body, he is becoming an institution and people are canonizing his words, when in fact, he was always contradicting himself. He was not interested in a new philosophy or teaching.

With this said, what can I then express in these meetings? It has been many months since I have met with people in a formal way. Perhaps I am waiting. When one cuts the links to all landmarks then the sun will arise spontaneously and without effort. If I have anything to share it would be these words: Hold onto nothing. Love never separates. Everything will come to completion. At some moment, even now, you will forget the individual trees swaying in the wind, for love cannot see distinctions.

Timothee, again thank you very much for spending this time with us today. We are very grateful for the opportunity to explore these important topics with you and hope to have the opportunity to do it again in the near future.

You're welcome. I look forward to this meeting. Thank you.

FIRE STORY

Timothee, you have worked as a fire fighter off and on for the last couple of decades. Most recently you have been working and living in Utah. You mentioned in our prior conversations that you had an extraordinary experience when you were fighting a very ferocious fire. Can you share this experience with us?

Yes, I would love to. The last couple of decades as you said, I have worked seasonally for the United States Forest Service, supervising trail crews in the back country. But also doing a fair amount of wildland fire fighting. In 1995 I was a supervisor on a "hot shot" crew in

Logan, Utah. The crew was comprised of twenty people highly trained in wild fire fighting in the Western U.S. It was a very wet spring, which created a lot of green vegetation.

By August when the vegetation started to dry out, there was an enormous amount of dry fuel available to burn throughout the western states. There was a period of heavy lightning activity that would roll across central Utah every evening and start fires. And with all the fuel available it was explosive and very dangerous. Because of these "flashy fuels," which include brush, high grass and small juniper trees, a fire can race much faster than people can run if there is a strong wind. With a change of wind direction, they can find themselves trapped.

We were on a large fire that was one or two hours west of Salt Lake City in somewhat of a mountain range. It started to spread down lower into a valley. We were there several days and often would get helicoptered into the more dangerous sections of the fire. There were several crews working on the fire. We weren't able to get a handle on it. So we went some miles ahead of the fire to a small dirt road. We did what is called "back-firing." That means we get ahead of the fire's direction, sometimes a mile or two and burn off fuel from a safe point like a road. If the direction of the wind blows correct, the new fire will burn a large black strip before the "main fire" gets to it so it will stop, or the new fire will burn up into the "main fire" itself.

We back-burned all day long, maybe fourteen miles along the road, walking and burning with drip-torches and fusee's, torching off all of the fuel along the way. It was a long day, and we were breathing lots of smoke. It was getting toward evening. In the late afternoon, fires generally lie down because the humidity comes up. The wind tends to slow down and the temperature goes down because the sun is setting.

This particular day we were all very tired because of the smoke and walking great distances. Everything was working well. The wind was going back into the road so that we could do a clean burn-out without getting trapped. I was in the "Holding Crew," breathing a lot of smoke, keeping the fire from crossing the road behind the main "burners." The "burners" were walking along with drip-torches setting a line of fire. The foreman of our crew came to me and asked if I wanted to join the burning crew. I agreed and quickly went up and joined seven other people.

I started to shoot off some pin-flares. I was the last person on the 'Burning Crew.' We were setting an enormous amount of fuel on fire. Everything was fine because the wind was going back into the road. I was about a hundred or two hundred feet into the interior, in the grass and brush, burning out a strip. The rest of the burners were ahead of me. Everything is O.K. as long as the wind goes back into the road and if the 'burners' stay close together. If for some reason something happens, like the wind direction changes, under normal procedure I could run ahead of the front burners and get back to the road safely.

We all let our guards down because it was getting toward the end of the day. We weren't watching the weather very closely. At one point the wind was going into the road, which was a safe place, but within a very short period of time, the wind turned. I remember the column of smoke. Instead of going over the road, which allowed me to be safely interior, it went straight up, and then suddenly it came directly into me.

Now I had fire all the way behind me because we had just finished burning along the road, and I had fire ahead of me to the front burners. We were really stretched out. We had too much space between us. To get ahead of the front burner, back to the road, was a long distance. The wind came back and flames started to pick up and move towards me. The only option was to find a way back to the road through the fire, or get around the front burner. But everything happened too quick. The front person was too far ahead. At first, I thought I was going to make it back to the road because I had been in other situations over many years that were close but I always felt I could get back safely. But within a few seconds, all of a sudden the wall of fire closed in, all the way back. It was too far to run, and it started to race towards me, faster than I could run. I ran like a rabbit, attempting to get away from the flame front, but couldn't do it.

I remember fear running through my body, trying to find a way back to the road, and knowing I absolutely could not. People back on the road got on the radio (we carry hand held two-way radios) and said, "Timothee, get back to the road! You have thirty-foot flames racing toward you!" That's how intense it was because I had just torched off a lot of high fuel, a lot of tall brush that was burning extremely hot and with towering flames.

I tried burning out where I was, which is what we are taught—to burn out a patch so it stays cool enough to get burned over. But everything happened too suddenly; too quick to get a fire shelter out to escape the heat, too quick to burn out. So after trying to outrun the fire, which was now exploding towards me, I knew that I wasn't going to make it out. I got on the radio and said, "I'm trapped. It's over." At that point I knew I wasn't going to make it through. The body was going to die. I remember being surprised because I'd been through so much fire before, even in huge timber fires, and always had a way out. Now on this grass and brush fire, it would be the end of my life.

At this point there was still a great deal of fear in the body, fear for my life. Suddenly I totally accepted my death, which I had never done in my life, and I turned and faced the fire as it was roaring toward me with thirty-foot flames. It came in front and circled around me. Within a few seconds I would be burned alive.

I stood there, motionless, facing my death, and when I accepted that fear with an absolute acceptance of death, all fear left. There was complete silence, everything went quiet, and for a brief moment all this madness and intensity stopped. It was like a vision, a chance to look into the Heart of immortality. I then faced the wall of fire as it was about to burn over me, and at that point of surrendering, the flame length lowered down in one particular spot. Intuitively without thinking I covered my head with my hands—and ran directly into the fire. In most circumstances with this type of heat coming from this fuel-type, you would be burned alive. In fact many people die in these types of fires. But what happened after I entered the fire, I have no memory of.

I then found myself standing with fire all around me in a blackened spot large enough to escape the intense heat. I waited for perhaps thirty minutes until the area cooled off enough so that I was able to make my way back to the road, back to the rest of the crew. It was very miraculous, a living miracle in a way. In fact for the next several days I felt I had died, and everything was a dream.

The next year I was in a session with Janet Bishop Sinclair, a healer, and the vision came back through me again. I realized that what I feared most was what I loved most. I had wanted to lay down in the fire and be consumed. It was a shamanistic death. I allowed myself to be finally consumed by the fire. Then the image of the Phoenix arose and I realized it was a very powerful symbol, the symbol of the resurrection from death. From the death of the ego arises pure consciousness.

JAMES STEINBERG

D uring this last year, I have had the privilege of spending time with James Steinberg. I was introduced to his writing while inquiring into various spiritual subjects. I always came away impressed with how much hard work went into his books. James is a long-time devotee of Avatar Adi Da Samraj and expert on the subject of guru-devotee relationship, particularly as it relates to the West. He is a public speaker on the subject throughout the U.S. and in Europe.

When I first started writing this book, I considered the title, "Dialogues with Emerging Spiritual Teachers and Extraordinary Students." It was a mouthful. I view James as an extraordinary student because of his lengthy, one-pointed devotion to a dynamic spiritual teacher who is still alive. However, being an extraordinary student does not detract from his ability to teach and convey a spiritual teaching in its essence. He certainly teaches us very important lessons about the significance of being a devoted student—lessons about patience, steadiness and perseverance.

I met with James in Marin County, California, at a beautiful house owned by some devotees of Adi Da Samraj. James had just driven into Marin from the San Francisco airport, having completed a visit to some mid-west universities. James is in his late 40s and lives close to Adi Da's sanctuary. He makes his living as a researcher (often indexing books for publishers), writer and lecturer but the majority of his time is spent in the service of Adi Da.

As we weaved our way through the interview, there was always a feeling of uncommon enthusiasm and energy surrounding James. His spirit beams forth from decades of surrender, devotion and service. Some technical terms that are native to Adi Da's teaching were referred to. If they still seem vague after reading about them, please refer to Adi Da's website or to some of his books for further information.

᪥ ᪥ ᪥

This afternoon we are speaking with James Steinberg, a long time devotee of the spiritual teacher Avatar Adi Da Samraj. James, thank you for taking time to meet with us.

My pleasure.

Please tell us how long you have been formally involved with Adi Da's Teaching, and then give us a snapshot of a typical day as a devotee.

O.K. I became involved with him in 1973 at the age of twenty-one. And so it's twenty-six years now. It's a very full life of practice. Practice begins with morning meditation. Generally, if you can rise at five o'clock that's considered best, from five to six-thirty at my level of practice. Depending on someone's maturity they do more or less meditation, reaching a maximum of about an hour and a half in the morning. And then after that we do a ceremony of worship. It's called a puja, the Hindu term for it; Ruchira Avatara Guru Puja. We use Adi Da's picture, which serves as the focus of communion with him. It takes about an hour. It's a very beautiful ceremony; waving of lights and chanting, singing, and a lot of recitations of Adi Da's Teachings. That takes you to about seven-thirty—six-thirty, seven-thirty. And at that point people go back to their bedrooms and study a little bit. We also do morning calisthenics and then have breakfast.

Do you practice hatha yoga exercises?
In the morning we do more vigorous exercises in order to get the heart rate up; a more aerobic type of exercise in the morning. Later on into the evening we do more relaxing, stretching yoga exercises.

So there's physical practice as well as a non-physical spiritual practice in this tradition?
Absolutely. Adi Da stresses that the body itself is to be enlightened, and that the body itself is the vehicle for enlightenment. So there's a practice fully throughout all this, a "conscious process" or "devotion" but also of conductivity; moving the energy through your body, being very aware of the energies in the body, and learning mastery of those energies to free up energy and attention for practice itself. When people have finished their morning routine, they either go off and work in the world, or if they work for the community they do their service until lunch. Then they wind up activities at the end of the day. Now if someone is living on one of the sanctuaries or in an ashram, at the end of the day there's another ceremony that's done called an "arti." Arti means "roar." It's called that because what you do at the beginning of an arti is make a lot of noise in the sacred place— the arti site.

How do you go about doing that?
Beating on drums and bells. Someone takes a bell and runs through the whole ashram calling everyone to the arti. It ends the day. You've transitioned from your work day back into your devotional day, because the evening is generally dedicated to some sort of devotional activity, some sort of study activity. It's a weekly schedule in the evening. One night we get together and we study Adi Da's teaching together. On another night we gather together and consider our practice with intimate friends of ours. Another night we'll actually do some sort of special service together. If you have an intimate relationship, another night is set aside. If you're not in an intimate relationship, it's spent with your friends. So that's the evening schedule.
We also have in the evening schedule one night where we get

together with our parish, which is a group generally the size of twenty-five or thirty or so. Its kind of very human sized so you know everybody pretty well. And we get together and discuss issues that relate more to our cooperative life with one another. It usually gets over around nine o'clock. Then we meditate again. So the day starts with meditation and ends with meditation. And when you're a beginner you start with just ten, fifteen minutes of meditation and work up to my stage of practice to about an hour in the evening.

Is meditation typically done by yourself or in a group?

It's best if you can do it with others, because if you can meditate with others it serves your own meditation.

How does that work?

Well, if you're there with others the intensity of their practice and the intensity of your practice communicates with one another. It helps you to focus, helps you to stay with it. When there are fifteen, twenty or thirty people meditating together, then it's much easier to get into it. A bell is rung at the end of meditation. Sometimes, either right before the arti or before we go to bed, we will also do yoga. And then in the evening we also write a diary. It's a "practice diary" in which we write about what our practice has been like, what the quality is like. So that's our daily schedule.

The weekly schedule is Monday through Friday. And on Saturday's it's usually a day when we try to do more extended service, some service project. I live around the Mountain of Attention which is our sanctuary in Northern California. It's about a 1,200 acre sanctuary. People in Lake County very often go over to the Mountain of Attention and do service. A lot of it can be "bodily service," raking, or just caring for the place itself.

Sunday is our "Guruvara Day" or our day of the Guru. It's a retreat day. One day a week is dedicated to that. We do an extra meditation on that day, we listen to presentations of the teaching. If there is a video tape of Adi Da that's come, we will watch that. If there's a sacred arts performance done by devotees we'll watch that. It's a day that we don't do business, not do our normal thing, and actually drop out of those discussions. Sometimes we have a silent day. Then seven times a year we have a celebration weekend. We'll celebrate Adi Da's birthday.

During the holiday season, we call it Donavira Mela, or the Feast of the Hero of Giving is what we call it in our "way." This is very often where larger groups get together. If you're in Chicago everyone will come in from Michigan and Ohio. Large numbers will get together at this special time. It has an extra energy when everybody's together. It's much more celebratory. Once a year you are asked to have an extended retreat of seven to ten days. And anytime a devotee can, at various times Adi Da allows devotees to come into his company for a more extended retreat. I've gone on both three-week and five-week retreats in his company. Those are very special times.

You mentioned a parish. There's been some indication that this is the creation of a new religion. How does it differ in its approach from other religions in the past?

Adi Da, even though his own practice included study with Hindu teachers, and he attended a Christian Seminary, he has no formal affiliation with any tradition. The Way of the Heart, or Adidam, as it's named, is based on his own realization. And so our practices were not designed because they were something that was traditional that we needed to do to maintain the tradition. Instead they were designed to actually fit the question, "What are the spiritual needs?" and "What really serves one's practice in this time, in this place?"

I worked with Adi Da for example on the creation of our Ceremonies of Worship. He sent me out and I studied with American Indians, Hindu Pujari's [teachers of ceremonies]. I received training by people who did "puja" [an East Indian ceremony] with other teachers. I would come back to Adi Da with this knowledge and he would say, "Yes, but what was it about? What's the essence of it? What about it did you like?" And then "How would we adapt it to our Way?" We don't have to be encumbered by any of the things in the past. Some of it is just historical baggage. We can simply adapt it to this time and this place.

When we started to do many of our practices, devotees were a little concerned because they practiced let's say with a Christian background and sat through Masses that were boring or didn't attract them. And there wasn't so much spirituality perhaps in the ceremonies they attended.

It was more ritualistic, then?

Some were. And so at first it took us some time to really get beyond that and realize that "real ritual," "real practice" of all kinds, when you actually are making contact with the Divine, is full and wonderful.

What are some of the key elements of surrender to Adi Da as your spiritual master?

The first and most key element is recognizing "him," understanding who he is. For me, when I first came to him I had been reading his teaching. I had some appreciation of him. Only over time did my recognition grow where I realized that he was a genuine God-Man, a "Realizer." And what that means or implies to me is that he's transcended his ego. In other words, he's not operating on the same basis of identification with the separate self, but is set free. And because of that, he's a perfect conduit for the transmission of the Divine. And that's the basis upon which I have a relationship with him.

Relationship involves devotion, devotion to the truth or reality. For me Adi Da has shown me or revealed to me what the Divine is. He provides a focus then for my practice. It's not simply a teaching but it's actually a relationship with him; a relationship that's based on literal transmission of spiritual blessing or spiritual energy. As years have gone on in our community it's become more and more established in that. All the other practices have actually become subsumed in our devotion to him.

James, Adi Da has written twenty-three books.

At least.

And has indicated that his Teaching is now complete.

Oh, the twenty-three source books. Right.

What's the essential import of Adi Da's teaching in the world today, and how is it different from other spiritual teachings past and present?

My understanding of Adi Da's teaching is that it is a complete and full revelation of the entire process leading to God-Realization. He gives a beautiful map of consciousness called the "Seven Stages of Life." And it's a revelation of all that is necessary to progress and mature through all of those stages of life and to realize the full divine enlightenment, the "Seventh Stage" of life. What he teaches, he says, his devotees can also realize. In other words it's not his exclusive realization. He has come to teach that realization to all.

What he says about it is that it is a "new revelation." In other words, no one has ever fully taught this complete Seventh Stage realization. My own background has been working with him on the "Great Tradition." I was his librarian for many years, which meant not simply that I took care of the books, but I worked with him, with his work relative to the "Great Tradition." The "Great Tradition" is his term for all of the various sub-traditions of Buddhism, Hinduism, and Christianity as traditions. The "Great Tradition" is a term that he uses to refer to all of them together. And he has done as he's felt it was necessary to do in this time and place.

We're confronted with everything. You go into a spiritual bookstore and you can find Sufism,Taoism, everything. And how do you make sense out of it all? In his teaching he has one book called *The Basket of Tolerance*, which is specifically oriented to his work relative to the various traditions, to try to give a map or a discriminatory tool so you can make sense of it. And so he has all the practices and processes of all of the various traditions. He's shown their "place" and where they fit into the schema of the "Seven Stages of Life." So that then when you practice, "Well O.K. now I'm at a practice which is very akin to this teaching and this tradition, and now I'm doing something that you could say is very much like 'this one.'" And because of that, he's assumed a role as the "Master of the Great Tradition," the entire tradition itself coming at this time. You couldn't have done it a couple of hundred years ago. All of the books would have been very hard to get together. A lot of the traditions have only now come out.

I assume he had you do research into specific traditions in order to locate information that he was interested in articulating that related to his own teaching?

Absolutely. My particular mission in all of this was to get everything to him that could possibly represent a real spiritual teaching way. Anything and everything. I felt that if I didn't bring something to him, then he wouldn't see it and that would be tremendously unfortunate. Because here you have a Divine Realizer willing to make the sacrifice to look through all of this stuff, and to make sense of it for us. And so I got him absolutely everything.

I was in the Bay Area, which was an excellent place to do it. But I also traveled. I went to bookstores all over the U.S.; went to India and went through not only the regular bookstores but used bookstores; went to ashrams, wrote to ashrams, Buddhist ashrams, Hindu ashrams, and Christian monasteries, and got all of the publications I could. There were also books relative to what you might call "religious and spiritual things." He also wanted to see everything on diet, a healthy diet; everything relative to sexuality – how sexuality was lived by spiritual practitioners. It included other things he was interested in like books on human anatomy, so that people could know what the mechanism is. And the whole process was like filling out the picture; the structure he already knew. The "Seven Stages" were there. But he wanted something that would represent the entire structure. He wanted Fifth Stage books and Sixth Stage books, in other words, so that every part of the structure was filled out.

In mentioning the "Stages," you're talking about the Seven Stages that he has identified in the process of enlightenment?

Right. Body, emotion, mind are the first Three Stages. The Fourth Stage is about devotion, or an allowing of the "Descent of the Divine." The Fifth Stage is about higher yogic processes or the "Ascending Current," and then ultimately, ascending to the "Ajna Door" and then the whole brain core.

The "Ajna Door" meaning . . . .

The "Third Eye." Just as the opening point, the entry point into the higher brain mysticism.

Adi Da's teaching is that all mysticism is founded in the body, and if there's an experience, you can locate the place in the body where the experience arose, ending in Nirvikalpa Samadhi or the highest samadhi of the Fifth Stage, which is the full ascent. And then the Sixth Stage is the domain of sages or consciousness, what's called the "Witness Position."

Are those specific levels of consciousness associated with the body?

They are associated with what you could call "the causal body," which has its point of association with the physical body and the "heart on the right." The Seventh Stage of Life, in terms of this esoteric anatomy, is "Amritanadi," which starts in the "heart on the right," (the right side of the chest) and ends at the "sahashrar" going through an S-shaped curve through the head. I've spent my life studying this and it's nowhere else described, that actual structure of the Seventh Stage and the S-shaped curve. I spent a great deal of my life looking at all of these books and comparing Adi Da's teaching with them and trying to find similarities. I can tell you that his teaching as I've seen it is absolutely unique and extraordinarily profound. It represents a new revelation, a unique revelation of truth.

Help us understand something. I read a quote of Adi Da's, and we're going to have to find the right context in relationship to what you just shared with us. He says, "No process high or low in any plane of manifestation is Truth itself or leads to Truth itself." Yet there seems to be a very technical set of processes and practices that are part of his teaching?

From the beginning Adi Da invites people to self-transcending communion with him: self-surrendering, self-forgetting, self-transcending communion with him. Or to go beyond this grip, this ego. He talks about how the ego is not so much a "thing" as an activity. And he describes that we're "pinching ourselves," we're assuming this separation. So from the very beginning he has always criticized seeking, always criticized the search. He used to say early on, "I would rather beat you with a stick than give you a mantra." In other words, he doesn't go for the spiritual materialism of a "search." It's from the disposition of liberation, from the disposition then of "already communing with Him," already knowing that That is the true state, that you are truly free and you're simply making the contraction moment to moment on top of that. If you're choosing to do that, from that viewpoint he says, "Come to me when you're already happy." He says, come to me when you're ready to drop the search, when you have this understanding with me, when you've studied my teaching, and you know your search has to come to an end. But just to know that doesn't mean your search is over. And so then there's the process and all the practices. But each of the practices are done from that disposition. It's done from the disposition of already communing, not done from the disposition of a search.

So there has to be some level of "realization," then, that you are always already happy and that you have had some kind of experiential basis for that realization before you can actually understand the context or the disposition of the practice?

Adi Da calls it "Liberation with a small 'l.'" And it's even in this process I described earlier of "recognition," of recognizing him. In a moment of truly recognizing him, the Divine as the Divine, you have a moment of happiness, a moment of intuition, a moment when it all falls away.

Who recognizes that?

You as you truly are.

So it's not an intellectual recognition, then, or some emotional recognition? It's coming from a much deeper level?

Heart opening.

"Heart" meaning…?

The deepest place.

Is it beyond the body or within the body?

It's associated with the body through the processes I described before. But it's not simply the physical body. It's also associated concretely with the body at the heart on the right and so forth.

So there's a physical location for this revelation that comes from being with him?

A bodily location. He calls it sometimes "the shock of God." And everybody has moments of that. Every body has a moment. I remember a moment when I was ten or eleven years old and I was in my parents' house. And I walked to the light switch. On my way to turn on the light I felt the mystery. I felt some sort of divinity or presence or reality or something. I just stood there saying, "There's something more going on here." It's just not everything I've been told by my Mom and Dad, by science and all that kind of stuff. And that's the same intuition that when you read Adi Da's teaching, there are the words, but there's something communicated, a Siddhi, a presence, a blessing through the words. Sometimes people feel that when they see his photographs. Some people find it when they hear him laughing. It cuts through everything. And there's a moment of freedom in that. And that's the basis upon which we meditate. That's the basis upon which we do the practices. That's the basis upon which we continue to study.

Do you feel that when you had that experience at age thirteen that it was the beginning of the "search" for you spiritually? Was your family a religious family?

My parents were very good people but I wouldn't call them "religious." They weren't.

They weren't practicing any particular traditional religion?

It was a Jewish family. But I never went to a day of synagogue in my life. It was mostly cultural.

That triggered something in you, then, as you grew older. Did you have a feeling maybe at a deep level that there was something missing?

Yes. [Laughter] Moments like that occurred often. Many moments like that. And everyone gets those moments. Adi Da said, "The Saints make their entire lives on this." As soon as they have a moment like that, then they dedicate their lives to it. With me it was a slower process where I'd have some of those moments. There was also another kind of sensitivity. Adi Da speaks of two sensitivities. One sensitivity is to that happiness, that freedom. The other sensitivity was to my suffering. And I realized even in high school that it wasn't really working. And I looked ahead and I didn't see how it was going to work. In other words, I was raised in a middle-class family and I never wanted for food or shelter. But I was wondering, "What's real happiness about?" Because this doesn't seem like it's it. I was a very smart kid. And my parents really liked that. But I saw pretty soon it wasn't making me happy.

I finally went off to Harvard and checked all of my professors. It didn't seem like the mind itself was making them happy. My parents had always taught me that money was not going to in itself make me happy. So that was a gift that they gave me. There are many billionaires and millionaires who aren't happy at all, but they have as much money as they need. All of those kinds of things were pretty active in me fairly early, so I was a "searcher."

How did you actually meet Adi Da? What was the initial meeting with him like and how did that come about?

Starting in high school I was already looking for something. I already knew that just going on and getting a career and doing this and that was not going to be enough for me. I already had a sense that there was this great "reality" and I had an acute sense of my own suffering. And so I checked out different things. I didn't have too much available to me. My parents didn't provide anything really spiritual. So in high school I was reading Carl Jung, Herman Hesse, Jack Kerouak, and the Beat Generation. It looked like maybe there was something a little more open there.

When I got a little older and started off to college I got more involved with some spiritual things. I got into food like macrobiotics and raw foods and tried all of those things. They made my body feel this way or that way but they weren't really "spiritual" all together. And finally I ended up working at a spiritual bookstore in Boston, a Tao bookstore. It was there I was exposed to a lot of different things. This was in the late 60's and early 70's. A lot of spiritual teachers were coming through. So I went and saw Chogyam Trungpa. I'd been raised Jewish, so I got involved with Hassidic Judaism, the Lubavitcher sect in Brooklyn, and met the Lubavitcher and tried to see if that would work for me. I got involved with a little Sufism with a teacher named Sufi Sam.

That's a great name! [Laughter]

Yes. And I could go on and on and name all of the different teachers of all the different traditions. But I didn't really find anything that "stuck." I appreciated and valued what it was, but when it came to the point of, "Do you want to take your initiation? Do you want to go onto the next step and really formally practice this?" I couldn't make my movement.

When I first saw Adi Da's books, I actually saw an advertisement for *The Knee of Listening* while I was working in the bookstore. I was in the back room filing away all of the things that were sent in the mail. We were sent an advertisement for the book. This shows that my own recognition of him only grew over time, because the first time I saw the picture of Adi Da, what went through my head was, I'd lived in Los Angeles and grown up there. "Those people in Los Angeles, they'll believe anybody's a guru! [Laughter] Look at this guy, he's got white skin! He can't be a guru! He's wearing sunglasses. He can't be a guru!" My idea of a real spiritual teacher was probably an Easterner.

I didn't order the books. My friend ordered the *Knee of Listening*. One of the other guys in the store said, "We should get this book." So it finally came in. A guy came into the bookstore and he said, "I've been out to Franklin Jones' (Adi Da's) ashram and this is a 'real person.'" He told me, "Swami Muktananda said that Adi Da is the most powerful man in America." Now that was interesting to me. He got my attention.

You were impressed because it came from an Indian guru who was respectable and had already established some sort of reputation in the West?

Yes. Because I had a Swami Muktananda section, he was a real person. Whereas I didn't know who this "Franklin Jones" was at that time.

That was his name in the beginning of his teaching, Franklin Jones?

Yes, Franklin Jones.

Franklin Jones went through a few other iterations of his name as his teaching evolved or changed over time?

Every time he went through an extraordinarily profound process within himself, he was in effect a different person. Then he took a different name which is done for example in the sanyasin tradition in India. When you become a sanyasin you burn all your possessions, and then you take on a new name. It's like the starting of a new life. He's had this occur several times in his life.

How do we explain the fact that in a sense his realization was complete, but yet there was something more that was added over time?

There have been many processes as he's gone on. He describes that the Seventh Stage of Life (in realization) which occurs at the beginning of the "Seventh Stage of Life," as having four stages to it. And he in his own life has been progressing through those stages. And as he has (progressed), not only has his teaching work changed, but also his (spiritual) "transmission" has changed. In the earlier days he much more reflected and embraced our tendencies, in order to teach us. He became like us in order to teach us out of it. And he told us from the beginning, as years went on, that over time he would withdraw from that and simply bless and transmit. And you could see the progression of his life as a teacher has been that way. There have been dramatic moments in it. The most dramatic was in 1986 when he had what he calls his "Divine Emergence." At that point it was a more full "dropping away" of some of those earlier functions and simply assuming more of a blessing disposition.

He actually went through some kind of "death experience" at that point, didn't he?

He had experienced a deep submission to his devotees by 1986 when this occurred, a full, total and complete submission to them. He had done everything he possibly could. And at that point there was almost revulsion because he saw that it still wasn't effective. He said spontaneously the body was given up. And he said for a few moments there was a yogic swoon in which doctors present thought he was dead. But then that passed and when he re-emerged, which he calls his "Divine Emergence," certain functions he'd done earlier in terms of the way that he taught, and identification and reflection to others, just fell away.

It was almost as if he had been "re-born," in a way?

Like a re-birth. And all of us who had been with him for all of those years, at that point I had already been with him for thirteen years . . . when I saw him again, he looked different. He looked like a new person; the same in many ways but many differences, too.

So his form had changed in some way, his physical form?

His physical form and the quality of his blessing and transmission.

Adi Da said, "What I do is not the way that I am, but the Way that I Teach." In traditional spiritual ways of thinking, a teacher's words and actions typically must coincide, otherwise there is some form of hypocrisy. How can we sort this out?

Well, let me tell you the story of that, because I was involved. In his early years, Adi Da taught relative to all sorts of things that were very direct. He got off his chair and came down into the congregation.

And we had all sorts of questions and concerns about all manner of things, particularly where we were at in the process. We were into money, food and sex. We were Westerners who had been brought up in a very secular culture. And so he did that with us. He basically showed us in life, "What about sex?" "What about food?" "What about money?" He played with us. A lot of the stories from those days, we called them "lilas," "the teaching stories," which he did with us were tremendous gifts in which he would say to us, "O.K, what should we do about sexuality? What about this celibacy thing? What about this promiscuity thing?" And then, based on our consideration we would do it. We would all decide, "Well, we're going to try that."

So it was a very experimental period of time?
It was very experimental.

Trying to figure out what worked?
But he was always teaching in the midst of it. In other words, he didn't simply teach us by saying, "This is what you should do." He taught us by saying, "O.K. let's try it." And then we'd try it and he'd say, "So what was that like? Did that serve your practice? Was that something that really has to do with our 'impulse' and why we're together in the first place?" Because it was always totally in the context of our spiritual practice, that was what it was always about. And so when he would do those things with us, he already knew. He already was enlightened. He already was free, but he did those things with us in order to teach. That's why he says, "What I do is not simply who I am but the Way that I Teach" – it is for our sake. So he said, "I had to become more like you than you are," because you're full of all sorts of inhibitions and "shut-downs" and this and that. This was in order to provide the lessons, which at the end of that period of time really coincided most dramatically in 1986 with the "Divine Emergence" we talked about earlier.

At the end of that time there was tremendous "instruction" relative to all of those things. And not just instruction that was "textbook instruction," but instruction in life. We tried every kind of diet. We tried all sorts of different sexual this's and that's. We tried every kind of arrangement relative to living. We tried this way of living and that way of living. And we saw, "Well, what served our practice the most?" "What made the most sense?" At the beginning all of the men and the women were together all the time. Then we separated the sexes. There were times when we had the ladies wear veils and button up their sleeves. And there were times when we had none of those prohibitions whatsoever. And, "What did it feel like?" "Why do you think these people that do it, do that?" "What was that about?" And not simply talking about it, but we did it! We saw it!

It was based on direct experience in other words. And in order for that to really unfold at a deep level, he felt like he had to sort of step out into the community with it. He knew the script already. He was sort of directing the "play." But at some point in time he felt in order for it to really be effective he needed to get out of his "director's chair" and go directly onto the stage?

Exactly. Beautiful way of saying it.

And to work with those individuals to get the "parts" right in order for the play to really unfold in truth?

It was tremendous submission on his part. And basically he had no reservations because his enlightenment was so firm he knew he had nothing to lose by it. And it's what they have called in traditions "Crazy Wisdom" sometimes; it's spontaneous. But now "Crazy Wisdom" is a mis-used term even these days. Now people have rules for what a Crazy Wisdom teacher is supposed to do and not supposed to do based on some tradition of Crazy Wisdom. It wasn't based on any tradition of Crazy Wisdom or anything else. It was based on his direct, compassionate regard and service to those who came to him. What he did was what we wanted him and needed him to do to serve us.

Now that particular sentence ("What I do is not the way that I am, but the Way that I Teach") that you referred to, comes because in 1975 a Hindu swami, Swami Chidmayananda wrote a letter to Adi Da which I received because he doesn't receive the mail directly. I opened the letter and it said, "Please desist. Don't teach this way. It's too wild. It's too crazy. Go back to the traditional ways, please." And Adi Da wrote an essay in response to it. He said, if you think that who I am in my realization is all this kind of....this is my teaching. This is my instruction. And he says even in that essay, "It will only be that way for a time." He always told us, "I'll do this for you for a while until you get the point."

And then we'll move on to something else at a different level of practice or different consideration of the truth?
In order to enter into the considerations with Adi Da we all made an agreement that when the truth was revealed at the end of that consideration, we would abide by it. We were all full participants in it. And it was always fully discussed. It was never him just saying, "Do this." It was like "O.K., based on our wisdom, what about it?" And then he would say, "Do this."

Within a spiritual context, there are difficult circumstances that arise particularly as it unfolds in a Crazy Wisdom direction. What's the most appropriate way to hold ourselves and others accountable for the results of actions that might occur in a Crazy Wisdom environment?
What are you driving at?

It seems that there are some things that may be so culturally different from what normally takes place in a typical Western cultural context that it might appear abusive. Or it may seem extremely radical.
For instance?

In some situations that have happened in the past twenty-five, thirty years there have been sexual abuses in some communities. There have been reported physical abuses. Zen roshis in some instances beat people with sticks. How can we help individuals sort this out so they can understand that there is a genuine teaching actually taking place underneath all of this? Shouldn't there be some accountability for the individuals who are teaching in this manner and for students participating within this context?
Well it was always understood that you're asking about the whole guru-devotee relationship and the basis of it in spiritual authority.

And I want to go more in depth into that in a few minutes.
In a book I wrote on the guru-devotee relationship, *Love of the God-Man*, I have a chapter called "Spiritual Qualifications." And in the traditions the way that they dealt with such issues is that there were

always very extensive lists of what was necessary to be a true guru and what was necessary to be a true disciple as well. The guru was enjoined not to take a disciple unless the disciple was truly qualified. Nor was a devotee to come to the guru unless the guru was truly qualified. This is not a new subject brought up by those who are worried about cults and all those phenomena. This was the basis of the traditions. It was always understood that you didn't just randomly pop in on a teacher. That you were tested before he would accept you. Nor would you go to a teacher unless you truly trusted who he was.

Regarding the actions of a teacher, what's understood is, many of the actions of the great teachers can't be understood unless you have the same realization as theirs. In other words, if they are operating from a higher vantage point, then it's very difficult for you to understand their actions because you are not similarly at that vantage point. Yet on the other hand there is always testing that has to occur. When I came to Adi Da I tested him very, very much. I had a Western background. And I was brought up with a very scientific mind. And I tested everything to see if it was true or not. Ultimately the basis of authority of a spiritual master is his realization or her realization because they are spiritual teachers as well. And what the devotee must come to a clear certainty about before he or she becomes a devotee of any master is that there is that realization on the master's part. It's only in that context that you allow or give permission to the master to act freely.

Where do we draw the line in that act of freedom? Once that trust is given, is there carte blanche, anything goes? What's happened in the past is there have been abuses and difficulty in recognizing a person's realization. They may have great Shakipat or spiritual energy that emanates through their body and draws people into that realm of experience. Students feel very blissful, happy and so on. On the other hand, there have been terrible abuses that have accompanied great spiritual power. How does a person know, based on past experience or investigation of a teacher where to draw that line?

Well, there are false teachers. There are charlatans. There are people that basically are teaching under false premises. And the devotee always has to reserve the right to say "no." Anytime. You may be with a guru for a long period of time, but you have to reserve the right. If there are any actions that you see that you don't understand, it is your right to question, and to discuss with others, and to say "no" if you're asked to do something.

These days I do a lot of speaking and talking on the guru-devotee relationship and the big question I get...it's the undercurrent ever since 1978 is, "If your guru asks you to take Kool-Aid or to kill yourself, going back to Jonestown, would you do it?" When Adi Da talked about this when the question was put to him to discuss the whole matter, he laughed and said, "I wish my devotees did everything I asked them to do. They don't do everything I ask them to do when I ask them to meditate and eat a good diet. Why would they do everything if I asked them to kill themselves?" So it's kind of a false issue, but the point that needs to be made in this area is that you must . . . spiritual life is not about the abandonment of responsibility. Spiritual life is about engendering in yourself more and more responsibility. It's not about becoming some blind-faith believer who now just follows whatever is told. It's a matter of more and more personal responsibility for everything in your life. And so anytime a teacher asks you, it's always a test, it's a test to see. And you've come to a teacher obviously because you believe the teacher has a realization that you value and can teach you something about that. So you want to say "yes" to him and you obviously value that he has wisdom to give you. But in any particular circumstance there always has to be reserved the right to say "no."

If you can't say "no" your "yes" doesn't really mean anything. Your "yes" is then just cultic following. It's just very childish. So there's a whole childish thing that needs to be gone beyond, but also an adolescent thing. The West tends to be more fixed in adolescence right now, in which they want to throw the baby out with the bath water. There have been some teachers who have done some things that were wrong, unethical, a dis-service to people, some of whom have been very dramatic and gross. Then somehow people feel like, well, then the whole idea of any spiritual instruction or any spiritual teacher should just be thrown out.

And possibly the process of guru-devotee type-relationships in spiritual development?

Of course that's not true at all. Any serious spiritual tradition will say in general that the master is not only useful, but for esoteric or high realization, necessary. You wouldn't think about it if you were trying to be a world-class gymnast. You wouldn't think about just trying to prepare on your own. You wouldn't think about trying to be a great pianist or a baseball pitcher without a pitching coach. When it comes to spirituality somehow we feel like, "Well, I'll just do it on my own."

You mentioned the book Love of the God Man *which you wrote a few years ago. Can you share with us some details of the book, where the idea came from to write it, and in writing it how it affected your own spiritual practice?*

Adi Da asked me to write it. And the reason he asked me to write it is because the West so poorly understands the idea of having a spiritual teacher. When you really look at it, the only one that's really kind of known by people was Jesus of Nazareth. And there really isn't too much written about him. As far as what my intent with the book was...what I wanted to do was to give people a glimpse of what it actually is like to be a devotee of a master, and the incredible grace and blessing that that is, the advantage that it is. And I felt that that voice was not out there. There are lots of voices from a scholarly and critical point of view, but there aren't so many voices of devotees, particularly in a Western context.

Someone like myself, who grew up in the 1950's and 60's in Los Angeles, who had no spiritual background whatsoever, and then becoming involved with a teacher from a very early age, I felt I had a very important story to tell about the incredible benefits, and how it was that all the instruction I'd been given was completely useful.

I've come to understand, and maybe we'll get into this more later, but I've come to understand that I've been served just as much by Adi Da's kick in my rear end as I have by his kiss and his hug; that I needed both of them. And I came to trust him enough based on real inspection over years and years and years. I came to trust him enough to allow him to give me those "kicks" and to more and more be grateful for them. It's like when a Zen master hits you with a stick, you bow down and say, "Thank you. I was falling asleep." It's the same when Adi Da gives you a lesson... "Thank you. I needed to understand something about that." And even though for a moment it smarts, the rest of your life you're freed of something.

I'd like to go into some other things that are addressed in Adi Da's teaching. It's been said by many spiritual teachers that "mind creates the uni-

verse." *How does this come about and what are they referring to?*"

The world is a psycho-physical place. Everybody's experience is different. And ultimately we need to define "the mind." But there is a teaching, a spiritual teaching in which basically this realm is understood to be completely fluid and created simply by the type of consciousness you have. It's a type of world that's created. And one of the big questions in the traditions is, "What does the guru see? What does the realizer see when he looks out?" He sees a world that's completely different. He looks out and says, "I hold up my hand, and I see the hand and I see the space around the hand. But in both cases I see God, I see the Divine. I see the hand is God, I see the space is God." Depending on our point of view, we create a different world. One who is totally locked into the scientific point of view or locked into what's called "scientism" sees simply a very gross world. Those who are shamans and mystics see a world full of spirit, full of all sorts of things happening. And so in that sense you can say that the world we create, that we see, is created by "mind," a point of view.

So in a sense for as many individuals as there are, there is a "world" that has been created by them that is different in every case?

Right. And when you come into someone like Adi Da's company, they describe coming into a realizer's company as a "revelation." Because what he'll do when you come into his company is, he brings you into a whole other reality which you truly realize is your own deepest reality, your own deepest intuition, but he's in it all the time. Whereas you get a glimpse of that world when you're in his company. He talks about "The Divine Domain." You could think it was a heaven. But he talks about when this world is truly seen as the divine, then this becomes the divine domain. This very place. This very moment becomes "The Divine Domain."

It's not someplace else.

No. But it's not this world as we're seeing it now either. It's outshined with "Brightness." The word that he's always used from his childhood is "The Bright" to refer to the fact that this real condition, this truth, this reality, this divinity is "bright," is full, is radiant. He refers to "Radiant Transcendental Consciousness." It's not simply consciousness, it's consciousness as brightness, as fullness, as radiance. It's tangible with ecstasy.

Another common statement that's been bantered about is "there is only One Mind." What does this mean? Does this mean that when we are in that pure consciousness or that "brightness" that only "One Mind" exists?

Everything else falls away. Mind is used in the Buddhist traditions as another metaphor for "reality" or "truth" or "consciousness." It's the way that Western scholars have translated Buddhist teachings. So they'll talk about "the mind," they'll talk about "the transmission of the mind" outside the dharma in the Zen tradition. And what they're trying to refer to there is this consciousness itself, or reality itself or truth itself.

So obviously this is different from the thinking mind. . . .

Absolutely. It's the substratum in which all arises. There are many intuitions of this "one divine reality." The Buddhists don't like to use "divine." Buddha made a decision early on not to use the word "divine" because he felt that it "objectified" truth or reality and made it an "object apart." And therefore as a teaching mechanism he referred to "the unborn condition."

And that is the "one mind" that they're referring to, then, that unborn, unchanging. . . .

Yes, it's an intuition of that. And sometimes in some traditions they'll exclude the radiant aspect of it. So when they describe that "one mind" it seems almost like a... one word that was used early on was "the void." Emptiness. And so it then tends to cut away the happiness and the ecstasy part. And Adi Da has made it very plain to us that in realization it's greater than one would have hoped for, not less. It's full, bright, radiant and happy.

So it sounds like it excludes nothing. There's nothing excluded from That?

Nothing's excluded from that, but its not simply a synthesis of everything. It's a whole different condition in which everything exists, not simply everything all put together in one heap.

To know anything about awareness seems to demand almost an impossible reflexive act like trying to see one's own eye. How can the knower best be known and how is it brought about in Adi Da's teaching?

Well, that's why its been said in all the traditions that the best thing one can do for one's spiritual practice is to come into the company of a realizer. They asked that of Ramana Maharshi who apparently didn't have a guru, and he said, "Yes, I did. The mountain (Arunachala) was my guru." But for most of us, the most potent form is in a human being. Swami Vivekananda said, "If you're a cockroach you need a cockroach guru; if you're a bull you need a bull guru, but a human being, when a human being looks in the eyes of another human being, there's communicated that Divinity." And in relationship to a true teacher, that being "drawn" into that "Divine Condition," of what you were referring to here as "knower" is a moment-to-moment process if one presumes a relationship to the realizer. That's why it's a relationship. It's to be lived 24 hours a day. And every moment in which you actually enter into that relationship, there's a reflection. And then as you grow and surrender more and more of your faculties and grow in your point of view, then the guru is first present in a body. And then the guru becomes spirit. And then the guru is understood as consciousness. And then the guru is understood to be the divine reality itself, no different than you.

What is Adi Da referring to when he says that truth is the "Only-by-Me Revealed and Given Wisdom Way." Or that he is the "One and Only and Self-Evidently Divine Reality and Truth."

Here he's speaking ecstatically about his divine realization. We tend to think because of some of our Western tendencies and even some of the ways we've heard spirituality that we can somehow find the truth within us. The truth is only found when we transcend ourselves. When we transcend ourselves, yes there is that divinity as us, but it's in our own self-transcendence. The way that's revealed most effectively is in the company of a realizer who reveals that, who's in that condition and then draws you into that condition, in communion with that and in self-surrender in communion with that. Then it is revealed by him, given by him.

When he says, "Only by Me" does that mean that there's no one else who's doing it?

What he means by "Only by Me" is you can't do it with your ego.

The "Me" is not his ego either, then?

No.

He's referring to his "Divine Condition"?

His divine revelation as the divine person. He says that obviously he's been present before. But he says this particular incarnation, he's present in the fullest form, uniquely full form. And because of that, he says it transcends time and space and that it will eternally be available. That's his promise to his devotees; to all of us that he will eternally be available in that relationship.

What is Adi Da saying when he refers to himself as "a Divine Self-Emergence and Avatar who supercedes all other spiritual teachers, past, present and future." In what light does this put other teachers or teachings? Doesn't this in some way relegate everything that has come before to a lesser or inferior position?

Well, it's not really so much a matter of inferior or superior. That's judgmental language that we add to it. And we're very quick to do that. Adi Da's not judgmental in that way. He has tremendous respect and value for all spiritual teachers. And there have obviously been great realizers in the past. He's simply pointing to the unique revelation that he's bringing and saying that what he's bringing now is a new revelation which does fully and completely finish the whole process. In other words he brings the full and entire teaching. And previous to this, the revelations were not as full as the revelation he's bringing now. But it's not a judgment or a put-down. And he's simply stating it as a fact of what he's understood and what he's seen in himself. For myself, I don't claim to be a knower relative to these matters, but I can say that what I've seen in his company I haven't seen elsewhere. And that's not any criticism of anyone else, because I have great respect and value for many different . . . I mean I've spent my life studying the many different traditions. But in terms of Adi Da, he's proclaiming his availability as that full, total and unique revelation.

Adi Da also refers to "The Perfect Practice." What does he mean by this term?

The "Perfect Practice" is a technical term that he uses for your practice when you've entered into the Sixth Stage of Life. What that means in simplest terms is when you're ready to begin the "Perfect Practice" you no longer are distracted or feel that truth lies in any kind of experience whether the experience be of the body-mind or subtle experiences. You've had enough of those experiences to know they are not the point, that truth is beyond those. And you enter into, therefore, the domain of not simply being attached to all of those experiences high or low, but you can "witness" them.

So the experiences really do take place, but they're not really received by something that is less than that pure consciousness itself?

The experiences occur but you're not identified with them. They're not the point. What becomes the point then . . . at that point energy and attention is freed up when you begin the "Perfect Practice." It's freed up to actually witness what's happening rather than to be identified with those experiences.

So, who's witnessing what? Is it consciousness witnessing itself?

Ultimately, and of course I'm not a realizer of this… I'm not in this stage of practice yet, so I'm simply speaking to you from what I understand of his teaching. But there are different stages to that "Perfect Practice." At first there's enough free attention to witness and to be free as attention to witness.

Witnessing means free as attention itself, without any obstruction or attachments. . . .

To phenomena high or low. And what is seen then finally is as all arises, what's finally become aware of is that the principle contraction itself is the illusion of relatedness. It's not your attachment to any experience high or low, but your attachment even to your self as someone who's experiencing anything, even as attention itself. In other words attention itself is a witness, the contraction that is attention. He refers to it as "the causal knot." And in that understanding of that illusion of relatedness, that truly there is not "self" and "other."

Then there is awareness of the feeling of Being itself.

Is that feeling coming from Being, coming from itself?
It's coming from itself, but the teacher in this sense magnifies your awareness or your capacity to recognize that.

So in that sense is consciousness unfolding itself to itself?
In that sense you could say, well, always that consciousness is unfolding itself.

But there's recognition of that?
There's a recognition of this root contraction of the causal knot in the heart on the right, which is located in the heart on the right. And the feeling of Being that is prior to that. And you then can rest as that feeling of Being.

Beyond the knot?
Beyond the causal knot.

What happens to the knot then? Does it dissolve, dissipate, and therefore is recognized for what it is?
It's recognized for what it is, and there's no longer identification with it. Being able to rest stably in that feeling of Being, there's a samadhi of "Jnana Samadhi," in which you simply abide as that blissful consciousness, that feeling of Being – fully. But there's still a subtle tension in that in which all else is seen to be different from that. When that's undone, that's the awakening into the "Seventh Stage of Life" in which the "eyes open." Adi Da describes the "eyes open" in which all phenomena are seen or recognized tacitly as the transparent and non-binding modification of the One reality.

But even though it is modified, it remains the One reality itself?
Instantly recognized.

Instantly recognized as That also?
Right.
So in that sense, nirvana and samsara are the same?
They truly are.

And that's the realization then?
Yes. From that point of view. Prior to that, to say nirvana and samsara are the same is just philosophical talk.

So that is enlightenment?
That's divine enlightenment. He calls it "Divine Self-Realization."

There have been so many definitions bantered around in these times about what enlightenment is. What does it mean in Adi Da's teaching, the "Seventh Stage"?
Adi Da uses very technical terms for it because, as you say, depending on tradition you'll find a different definition of enlightenment. Adi Da's definition of enlightenment is this transcendence of the causal knot, this bodiless feeling of Being, and this recognition which is that of everything arising. There is no withdrawal, no contraction whatsoever into consciousness apart from phenomena. Consciousness and phenomena are seen as one, instant divine reality. The simplest way he describes it is that there's "Only God."

There is "Only God"?
There is "Only God."

Where does that leave us with the classic free will and determinism then? If everything is God's will, sometimes there have been those people who would take a statement like that and abuse it. They might say, well if I do this, then it's just simply God's will no matter what I do. How do we approach that?
In enlightenment, that question doesn't arise any more. Prior to enlightenment that's an important question. And what's always been understood traditionally is that's where you basically use the guidance of your master. That's why the master is so important. Because once you enter into these higher stages of life, ordinary ethics fall away. The ordinary ethical decisions don't hold in this divine realization. But to talk about that prior to divine realization, we're mixing the two different states.
It's simply an intellectual exercise then?
And for someone to presume that they have no ethical standards

prior to realization, is a conceit. It's the same thing as trying to say that nirvana and samsara are the same as a "talking school."

And not realize it?
And not realize it.

I would like to go further into the topic of the guru-devotee relationship. Are there any other spiritual teachings that demonstrate a close affinity to Adi Da's? He refers to it as "Ishta Guru Bhakti Yoga." Where do those terms come from?

The basis of the guru-devotee relationship is you become what you meditate on. If you meditate on T.V. you become "T.V.-mind." If you meditate on sports, you become a jock. Whatever you put your attention on, you tend to become more and more like that. People who are afficionados of anything, they tend to take on the same characteristics. So what's always been enjoined in the traditions is "meditate on the divine." And meditate on the divine through the form of the guru. In terms of others having lived this guru-devotee relationship, yes. Many traditions have. Adi Da points to his own lineage which involved Rudi, Swami Muktananda, Swami Nityananda, and ultimately the Divine Goddess herself who appeared in subtle form and led his sadhana (spiritual practice). He said that the whole tradition is full of this same kind of guru-devotee relationship in which it's understood that the principle means is the contemplation, blessing and transmission of the guru through meditating on the guru. To meditate on an ordinary man or woman is simply cultic.

You could be a movie star or it could be a sports figure or it could be a politician. And you could read all sorts of books about them and all you're going to realize is their particular qualities. Why you meditate and contemplate and live the guru-devotee relationship with your guru is because you understand your guru is realized as one who has transcended the ego. And in terms of that relationship the practice of meditating on the guru through what Adi Da calls "Ishta Guru Bhakti Yoga"…Ishta means "chosen"…what it means is you want to be with your guru.

It's not simply that you are born a Christian and therefore Jesus Is That. You chose Jesus. You chose your guru. You chose your guru because you've recognized your guru. [That's] why it's called a "yoga."

Yoga" means "union." And the practice is about wanting to become like the guru.

And if you don't think your guru has a great realization and want to become like your guru not in terms of his personal characteristics but in terms of his realization, then you probably shouldn't be a devotee of that guru. When you see a guru, in my experience, when I've come into Adi Da's company, I've seen the most extraordinary, incredible revelation of divinity and love. It's the foundation of my life; it is that revelation that I've seen in his company. It's what I can tell you is love, is what I've experienced from his eyes because he's so fully awake and aware and alive. What I can tell you I know is the God, is what I've seen in his eyes because I have no other experience that's more powerful than that, of the revelation of divinity. And so that is the realization that I want, that I desire. That's my urge to that. And that's what the basis of this "Ishta Guru Bhakti Yoga" is.

How would people interested in approaching this teaching best do so?

First thing is to study his books. Very often the most common way that people feel Adi Da and get connected to him is they realize that his teaching is true. And they read his books and say, "My gosh." Something clicks for them at a deep level. This is what I've been looking for. I've been looking for somebody. I was always . . . who knows about this place? What am I doing here? What's it about? I was always looking for somebody who could tell me, who could teach me about those kinds of questions. Yes of course I had good teachers in my colleges and universities on this and that. But who knows relative to the deep things?" The first thing is to study that teaching. And does it resonate with you? How do you feel when you read it?

After you've done that, then talk to some of the devotees. Talk to people that have seen him. Talk to people that have seen him a lot and ask them, "What is this Way about?" Use their experience. Come to some of the places, like Adi Da's established sanctuaries; and there are centers. Go to some of those places and, what do you feel when you're there? And it's always a Heart matter. It's not simply an intellectual matter, but use your mind, truly use your mind. But also use more than your mind. What's often said is that you really need to have the desire. You know, the guru comes when they are needed, the guru will appear when you really need him or her. And with Adi Da, the people who come to him are the people that are ready for the "real thing." He teaches the "real process." He gets down to it with us all. If you really want to be divinely realized, if you really want to realize this ecstatic and complete happiness, then he'll tell you what to do.

So the people that come to Adi Da are serious, they're serious about the matter; not somber, it's not negative in that sense. But he calls it a hard school. He says, "a happy way of life but a hard school." It's hard because it requires real work to transcend the ego. He says it can be done in one lifetime. It's not a matter of having to go lifetime after lifetime. You can realize the same condition he's in, in one lifetime. He says it requires a lot of you in that lifetime.

All of you I would say.

Absolutely. [Laughter] Ultimately it requires everything. In that sense, it's called the most heroic thing that a man or woman can do because it's not just part of you, i.e., I won't worry about dying at this moment. You have to look at every little piece and let it go. But the reason that's so wonderful is you realize each of those pieces is your suffering.

If you could share one crucial bit of insight with individuals very interested in realizing freedom in this lifetime, what would it be?

Interesting question. The thing that I tell people is that there is a real way, there is a real teacher. You were never taught that. We grow up not really knowing that there's anything different than the kinds of opportunities we're given. There is a genuine teacher and there is a real way and it requires that you really be looking for truth, for real happiness. And it requires that you be sensitive to your suffering. If you think somehow that anything that you're going to do can make you radiantly happy, you're going to do that thing. But when you realize that none of the ordinary paths make one happy, then that's what Adi Da calls the "Lesson of Life."

It's a hard lesson.

Hard lesson.

But if someone is interested in true happiness, then that lesson must be swallowed and seen in the context of the whole?

Truly everybody is interested. I'm convinced that underneath the shells that we all have, everybody is very aware that living in this world, this isn't heaven. And everyone has this urge to happiness. A lot of people have given up. A lot of people feel like, "Well, I'll just make do, I'll do the best." A lot of people are distracting themselves from this dis-ease, this feeling of suffering. But if somebody will take a hard look they'll see that it's not really working. And then the good news, the happy gospel is that there is a real teacher here who offers a relationship. And not only can you grow, you can also realize mightily depending upon your own impulse and your own practice.

What are some current activities that are being carried out by yourself and others in the community to advance Adi Da's teaching?

As always we're publishing his teaching. He's now put his teaching into a form so that it can continue after his death with these twenty-three books. And we're also trying to do a mission whereby he can truly become known by people.

I was at Xavier University doing a little lecture, and was telling this class about Adi Da, that he was a God-Man, that I felt he was the God-Man that everyone had been waiting for. In all the traditions they talk about a God-Man coming at a particular time when mankind is in difficult straits and looking for help. And I said I firmly believe he was that one and he was alive today. And wouldn't it be profoundly interesting to you to know that Jesus of Nazareth, or Gautama the Buddha or Mohammed or some great teacher, prophet or realizer was alive today and you could go and be in his company? And as I was talking about this a lady shouted out, "Why didn't anyone tell me until now?" [Laughter] And I feel like part of what our work is now is finally, after all this period of time, to really tell people who it is that has appeared, and who it is that those of us who have been with him have had the opportunity to see. And let people know so they can use him. He's going to be sixty this year. Let people know that they can use the remainder of his life. They have the opportunity that it is for a God-Being like this to be on the planet.

That's interesting. Did you also get the typical cynicism when it comes to making a proclamation that there is someone who is available now who is a true God-Man? Did you see that happen or was there a genuine peaking of interest in those folks to really pursue it a little bit further and take another look at it?

When I'm able to really communicate who Adi Da is, people always want to go a little bit further. But I'll get a question which is, "How do you know?"

Yes. By what standard? This is the question that I hear often. By what standard can you make the proclamation that this in fact is true or that this teaching is "perfect"?

And it's a good question, because I don't want to sound like a Christian Fundamentalist who just says believe in Jesus; "I'm telling you Jesus is the one so you should just believe in him" and that's it. It's not that message. I simply say based on "my own," being in his company, studying his teaching, being around him, that it's become true to me. And it's true as an intuition. There's no test that one can take or a litmus test that proves it because it transcends all of those kinds of qualities. But it's more certain to me than my own mind is. Because I watch my own mind. I know from day to day my mind can be in all sorts of different places. But I know my certainty about Adi Da, and what I've seen in his company is deeper than that, because even in his company I've seen the flittering of my mind. And I've seen the nature of my mind in his company. So the basis upon which I can say that he's the "Promised God-Man" is through my twenty-six years of testing him and reading spiritual books and being in his company.

And there is an invitation, I would assume, for other people to also test and to approach this teaching in a very discriminative way?

You must. You must. And the teaching is ultimately self-authenticating. The ultimate bottom-line test is that you do it and it works. And you see it in your own life. I often say, if you don't practice it isn't going to work. You have to do it. And you can dip your toe in and then you can dip your whole foot in. And always at a certain point when you've come to that certainty there's a "holy jumping off place" in which you basically say, "O.K. I'll give it a try." But life is full of that all the time.

It's available in every moment. You start simply by running, and at a certain point jump right off the edge.

Exactly. And at some point if you don't open you can't receive. At some point the reason that devotion and surrender is so necessary in the guru-devotee relationship is if you don't devote yourself and open yourself, whatever it is that you're holding onto is going to prevent you from receiving. And therefore they describe it that the teacher is like an ocean. But you go to the teacher with only a thimble, you go to the ocean with only a thimble, you're only going to get that much water. It's the capacity to be able to surrender. You'll see devotees doing all sorts of surrender at the guru's feet that would revolt a lot of Westerners. But that's done not because they're lowering themselves by bowing to another ego. It's in their recognition of the guru as the divine and recognition that in that openness is how they can receive the most.

Would we sum up what we've talked about so far—the essence of spiritual life?

The essence of spiritual life is to abide in communion with the divine, to abide in communion with happiness through self-transcendence. If you try to do that abstractly, then you can delude yourself and it can be pretty fruitless. You can be really good at it one day and the next day, who knows? To be mastered, to have a master and to allow that master to master you makes that process real.

James, thank you very much for sharing your insights with us today. We're very grateful for the opportunity to explore your life and Adi Da's teaching with you.

My pleasure.

Publications:

Love of the God Man: A Comprehensive Guide to the Traditional and Time-Honored Guru-Devotee Relationship, the Supreme Means of God-Realization, As Fully Revealed for the First Time by Adi Da Samraj. Dawn Horse Press, Clearlake, CA 1990.

Divine Distraction: A Guide to the Guru-Devotee Relationship. Dawn Horse Press, Clearlake, CA 1991.

Avadhoots, Mad Lamas, and Fools: The Crazy Wisdom Tradition. The Dawn Horse Press, Clearlake, CA 1982

Contact information:

James Steinberg
10336 Loch Lomond Rd., Ste 106
Middletown, CA 95461
E-Mail: JamesSteinberg@adidam.org
Web Site for Adi Da's Teaching: www.adidam.org

HANUMAN DAS

After the interview with Howard Badhand, we stopped by the
Neem Karoli Baba Ashram in Taos, New Mexico. My good
friend Rick Frires who has close ties with Ram Das and
Neem Karoli Baba's teaching said the ashram was a wonderful refuge
and a must place to visit. It was a beautiful Sunday morning when we
arrived. The ashram facilities were unpretentious and well main-
tained, surrounded by splendid landscaping. Volunteers were busily
preparing a scrumptious free meal served every Sunday for anyone
who wanted to participate. Usually sixty to seventy people attended
each week. As I stepped into the kitchen, I was immediately struck by
the joy and happiness that abounded. There was a tremendous feeling
of selfless-giving and service.

I introduced myself to Hanuman Das, the ashram manager who had been there off and on for fourteen years. I didn't have any plans to interview anyone during the rest of the trip, but that suddenly changed as soon as I met Hanuman. His gaze was filled with light and softness. There was a deep presence of devotion and love that was undeniable. I had to probe into it. I had hoped to find a Westerner closely aligned with the Hindu tradition to interview. Here he was.

Despite Hanuman's self-proclamation of not being a "spiritual teacher" per se, he clearly embodies the form of his name which means "Servant of Hanuman." Hanuman represents the consummate servant of God in the Hindu tradition. Because of his deep devotion to Hanuman, his spirit is received in a very direct fashion.

As I interviewed Hanuman, I was reminded in a powerful yet sweet way how important it is to be active in service to others. When Maharaj-ji (Neem Karoli Baba's devotional name) said to unconditionally "feed everyone, love everyone, serve everyone, remember God, and tell the Truth," he was pointing to the full expression of our own Heart.

After the interview, we went to the meditation hall where there was a wonderful statue of Hanuman and beautiful Maharij-ji artifacts brought from India. We sat in silence for about half and hour feeling the warmth of Being as it permeated the hall. At one point I looked around the room. There were several brass bells of various sizes hanging from the ceiling. The smallest bell was very slightly swaying even though it appeared there was nothing moving it. Fascinating. An hour later, we attended a celebratory ceremony called an "arti" which was performed by Hanuman Das. There was chanting in Sanskrit, singing, ringing bells, waving oil lamps, and upbeat clapping.

After the arti, we paid our final respects to Hanuman Das, and began our journey back to Colorado. As we drove through the enchanting landscape, we were greeted by long moments of silent reflection on the exquisite nature of unbounded love.

ॐ ॐ ॐ

Today we are speaking with Hanuman Das at the Neem Karoli Baba Ashram in Taos, New Mexico. Thank you for being with us today.
You're welcome.

As a note of introduction, please share with us where you grew up and how it has impacted your perspective on life?
I didn't actually grow up in any one place. My Dad was in the Air Force. I was born in California. When I was about six weeks old we moved to England. The next six years we moved all around Europe. Then we returned to the U.S. Basically the impact on my growing up wasn't so much influenced by the place, but by the fact that we moved around so often. I had a broader view of the world, possibly at a younger age than most people would have had. I became very adapted to change and different places. Also one of the main things that I came out of it with, is that it wasn't so important where I lived, but the fact that I had a lot of love in my family regardless of where I lived.

Do you recall any spiritual insights as a child?
There are several things. As a very young child, around four to six years old, when I would go to bed at night, I would have these visions or visitations—I don't know how to describe it exactly. I was in a way more open to something else going on than what is hardcore reality. Consequently, throughout my life, I have continued to look for that feeling and that vision that is beyond the material reality. I still carry that feeling with me and always looked to see what was "behind" the material forms that I would see.

Was your family spiritually inclined? Did they practice any particular form of religion or spiritual practice?
My father was raised a Catholic and so his children were. My parents were not very "religious," but they were spiritual. I would say in this sense my parents values were better than most people that I come across these days, and my mother's whole spiritual thing was just to love her kids. Love was the basic spiritual reality in my life as a child.

Can you give us a brief synopsis of who Neem Karoli Baba was, what he taught, and how he has spiritually impacted seekers in the West? He is also referred to affectionately as Maharaj-ji.

Neem Karoli Baba was an Indian saint who was well known in Northern India, and for most of his life, there was no fixed place he could be found by his devotees. In his later years, the devotees built several ashrams, making it easier for them to find him. Even as a young man he was known as a very high spiritual being and attracted devotees everywhere he went. His basic teaching is that "It is all One," and to "Feed everyone, love everyone, serve everyone, remember God, and tell the truth." These simple teachings, if taken literally and without qualification, are, in my opinion, all one needs to know how to live in an enlightened way and have a positive influence on the world around them.

When did Westerners start going to Maharaj-ji and recognizing who he was?

I think it was probably in the mid-sixties when the first Westerners became aware of Neem Karoli Baba. He left his body in 1973 so it was a very short period of time Westerners were going to him. Due to Richard Alpert (Ram Das), his teachings were put out in the West very quickly through the book, *Be Here Now*. After that book came out, quite a few Westerners went to India to find Him. Unfortunately they only had a few years before he left his body.

Your name is Hanuman Das. Hanuman occurs as a major figure in Hindu mythology. Historically what does Hanuman represent and how did you wind up with his name?

Hanuman is one of the major figures in the epic scripture from India called the Ramayana or the Sri Ramcharit Manas. Hanuman is an incarnation of Shiva. Shiva decided to incarnate as a monkey so he could serve Vishnu who was incarnated as Ram, and is an incarnation of Vishnu. The Ramayana is about Ram's life and is basically a template for a life of duty and devotion. In the story Hanuman met Ram, recognized Him to be an incarnation of Lord Vishnu and became his servant and devotee. One of Hanuman's most important aspects is that he is the "perfect servant" of God. He can think of nothing else except Lord Ram and therefore everything he does is in service to his Lord. Because everything else he does is in service to his Lord, there is nothing that he can't do. Everything is possible such as jumping across an ocean or lifting a mountain. As a monkey, he couldn't normally do that, but as a servant to God, he can do anything.

In the Ramayana, how did Hanuman relate to Ram (Rama) and Sita, and what happened between them and their relationship with Hanuman?

Ram was the son of the king of one of the greatest domains in India at the time. When he was about to be crowned as the successor to his father one of his stepmothers called in a boon from her husband the King saying, "Wait a minute, you said you would give me anything I wanted. Well, I want my son Bharat to be King and not Ram. I want Ram banished to the forest for fourteen years." Ram was banished with his wife Sita and his other brother Lakshmana to the forest. They roamed the forest for approximately twelve years during which Sita was kidnapped by Ravana who was the demon-king of Sri Lanka. While Ram was looking for his wife Sita, he met Hanuman. Hanuman recognized him as Lord Vishnu and became his servant. Ram sent him off to find Sita his wife.

Because of Hanuman's devotion to Ram he was able to follow the path of Ravana and jump across the ocean to Sri Lanka and find Sita in a grove and bring her a message from her husband that he was on his way there to rescue her. There were many great heroic feats Hanuman accomplished. He had his tail set on fire by the demons and with that fire he burned a whole city down and left it in ruins. He returned to take Ram to his wife. When they, plus the Monkey and Bear armies, arrived in Sri Lanka, a tremendous battle ensued. In the battle, Hanuman defeated many of the demons. During the battle, Lakshmana, Ram's brother was killed. Ram and the army were devastated. There was only one herb on a mountain many thousands of miles away that could revive Lakshmana. Hanuman went to the mountain to find the herb. When he arrived, Ravana with his magic powers had made every herb look the same. Hanuman couldn't tell one herb from another. He then uprooted the whole mountain and brought it back to the battlefield. There, a doctor found the right herb and Lakshmana was brought back to life. Ravana was defeated. Sita was rescued and Ram was restored to his Kingdom. Hanuman continued to serve Ram through the rest of Ram's life. Hanuman was given the boon by both Sita and Ram of eternal life. Hindu's believe he is still alive and available. One of his names means "reliever of suffering," and his devotees call on him when they are in need. Even Lord Ram dropped his body and is no longer available in the same way Hanuman is. Hanuman is the only one of the Hindu pantheon of Gods that has an eternal "form" on earth.

And how did you wind up with your name Hanuman Das? Was it given to you by someone?

My name was given to me by a "Ma" in India who is one of Neem Karoli Baba's greatest devotees. Her name is Siddhi Ma. About a year and a half before I became caretaker of the Ashram, I went to India. I met Siddhi Ma at Maharaj-ji's Ashram there. She had me spend time with a Hanuman priest to learn the Hanuman puja. It was during that time she gave me the name Hanuman Das. After I returned from India, I returned to Taos and began serving in the Ashram and taking care of Hanuman. Hanuman Das means "Servant of Hanuman." I suppose Siddhi Ma had an inkling of what I'd be doing with my life.

So you've been heading up the ashram here for fifteen years now?

I came to the Ashram in 1987 and I've been here ever since, except for two years when I went to India from 1994 to 1996.

You mentioned some pantheistic elements of Hinduism. Many Monists have difficulty with this for various reasons. What's the proper perspective in viewing Krishna, Rama, Vishnu, Hanuman and other spiritual figures as various forms or manifestations of God?

That's exactly what they are. In the Hindu tradition there are many, many aspects of the "One God." In the Vedas it says that there is one inseparable being that encompasses the entire creation. God is One and everything in the universe is contained within that One. Unfortunately the mind cannot comprehend all of who God is. Thus, in the Hindu tradition, all the different aspects of God,Brahma, Vishnu and Shiva, are the three of the main aspects that most people know about. God as the Creator is called Brahma, God as the preserver is called Vishnu, and God as the destroyer is called Shiva. All these forms and names are just so the mind can have a way to understand the infinite nature of the One.

There is a strong relationship between Ram and Hanuman. What is that manifestation or form of energy that's manifested as him?

Hanuman, as I said before, is an incarnation of Shiva, and Shiva is the formless absolute. Shiva as the formless absolute had the idea, "What would it be like to be a devotee?" that is, to actually experience the bliss of being the "Lover of the Beloved." That is when Hanuman, in his foresight, saw that Vishnu was going to take "form" as a man on earth. Shiva decided to take the form of a monkey and serve Vishnu so he could experience the bliss of devotion.

Can you share with us the main mission of the Neem Karoli Baba Ashram here in Taos?

It is a difficult thing for me to really define. In the beginning there was no actual "mission statement," you might say, for the Ashram. It originated as a place for Neem Karoli Baba's devotees to gather. Over the last twenty years it has developed into what it is now. In my opinion, it has become a sanctuary and refuge for everyone whether they have anything to do with Hinduism or being devotee's of Hanuman or Neem Karoli Baba. Many people come here and find an uplifting "spiritual vibe" that gives them a feeling of refuge from the world. The main thing that we do at the Ashram is try to follow His teachings which are: "Love everyone, serve everyone, and remember God." Consequently a lot of time is spent here cooking and feeding people.

What is a typical day like for you around the ashram? What time do you get up and what do you do? How does your day unfold?

On a typical day I usually get up between 5:30 and 6AM. At 6:30 the ashram is actually opened. And then at 7AM we do an "arti celebration" which takes about 35-40 minutes.

What does the word "arti" mean?

"Arti" is a very traditional Hindu ceremony where you make several different offerings to God, being fire, cloth, incense, water, food and flowers. All of those offerings are made during the celebration. The fire is offered in a little lamp that you wave, and at the same time we sing a song of praise to the guru and the other gods that are represented in the temple room.

How is it different from what is called a "Puja"?

It is a "Puja." Puja is kind of a generic term for any religious celebration or ritual that you do in the Hindu tradition.

After you've completed the arti, what do you do?

Chai is made and there is a daily routine of cleaning. It's a daily ritual here, to make Chai every morning and every afternoon.

Your Chai is excellent by the way! [Laughter]

So I make Chai and there's the daily routine of cleaning. And then it's just people coming. On a typical day I would say maybe 20-30 people stop in. Sometimes they don't need any interaction with anyone, and other times I spend a lot of time with them either having "satsang" which is a form of "dharmic talk" or counseling. You never know what a day will bring or who it will bring.

Do you typically have a lunch period?

Not every day. If there are guests actually staying in the ashram then we make lunch and dinner. If the guestrooms are empty then it's kind of—I'll cook for myself or whoever happens to be here, but it's not the same as when there's someone actually staying in the ashram. And in the evening we do another "arti" celebration. And then we close the Temple at 10PM. From 6:30AM to 10PM the doors are open and people come and go as they like. The grounds are beautiful so a lot of times people come just to spend time in the outdoors and on the grounds and never even walk inside the ashram building.

Can you tell us what happens on Sundays? Sunday seems to be a little bit of a different day.

On Sunday's typically I start cooking a meal at about eight in the morning which is usually to serve anywhere from a hundred-fifty to two hundred people. So that's the main activity in the kitchen anyway. And then at 11AM we sing eleven Hanuman Cheleesa's which is a forty-verse song in praise of Hanuman which ends with a shortened version of our "arti" after which we serve the food (also referred to as prasad or food that has been blessed) to the people attending.

Who usually comes to the meal?

Everybody's welcome to come. I would say probably about sixty to seventy percent of the people who have the meal are not actually, and don't consider themselves to be, "devotees" here. But they enjoy the food and they enjoy the space. Since there was no qualifications when Maharaji said, "Feed everyone" he didn't say "Feed people that love Hanuman" or that "know me," he just said "Feed everyone." So everybody's welcome. We try to remember that and serve everyone that comes.

Do you find that there are many homeless people or people who don't normally have a significant income that might stop in?

I would say the majority of people who come on Sunday are here because it's a significant meal in their week. A lot of people that are "living on the edge" get fed here at least once a week. A lot of them come during the week and ask for food and they're always welcome.

At what point in your life did you realize that you wanted to live full-time in an ashram environment? Was there a certain period of time when you said, "this is the life I want to have"?

I wouldn't say that it was ever a conscious realization particularly because, although we call this an "ashram," it's not what most people would think of as an ashram. There are not specific religious practices that have to be done for someone to be here. We're not "cloistered." I live a very normal life. I watch TV and go out to movies. I feel like I'm very privileged to be in the space that I'm in, because it is a very— maybe I could call it "rarified energy" here, because people come here to do their devotional practices. Generally speaking the energy here is very "Shanti" or very peaceful. I've been living here for most of thirteen years, and at some point in my life I realized "this is what I'm doing." It wasn't a conscious decision before I came here, to live here. I came to Taos because the Ashram was here, but I thought that I would be starting a tree nursery business. I came to the Ashram when I arrived and just never left. I feel very blessed to have spent all this time here. And it is not what you would consider easy being here, in the sense that every day I'm having to deal with a lot of different people. One of the sayings here is "if you have a 'button' to be pushed, it will get pushed." So everyday I feel I'm dealing with a lot of "pushed buttons." [Laughter]

So in this sense, living in an ashram is not "escapism," and there is a strong relationship with the world coming in from the "outside." There's a direct interaction and relationship with the world.

Yes. If anything I feel like I'm more exposed to the world here than I was when I had a "private life." Because there [in private life] when I shut my doors, they were shut. Here you can't close the doors. People are coming all day long. They bring their problems, their love and their other energies with them. I don't feel like I've escaped from the world at all. If anything I'm getting to see many, many more aspects or facets of it than I could possibly have seen in my private life.

What spiritual teachers aside from Maharaj-ji have had the greatest impact on you in terms of living a more spiritual life and helping others to do so?

There are so many. I mean—it would be hard for me to know where to begin. When I was much younger, there were many teachers from the Catholic tradition that really helped to move me along on the path. And then in the last twenty-five or thirty years, it's mostly been Hindu teachers. Ramakrishna's teachings really have moved me and helped me in my understanding of who I am and who God is. Ramana Maharshi—spending time with his teachings I think is the best way anybody could spend their time. Ananda Mayi Ma also. Papaji (H. W. L. Poonja) who I spent time with in India, brought me to a point where I not only saw the Divinity in everyone else but also the Divinity in myself. Siddhi Ma also has been one of my main mentors and teachers for the last twenty years.

Can you share with us a few essential spiritual experiences that have thus far shifted your perspective about reality? Do you recall any specific instances either being in the presence of someone or. . . .

My first recognition of Neem Karoli Baba was probably the most significant spiritual experience in my life. I was hitchhiking on the East Coast in 1968 and got picked up by a couple in a van. I'd never heard of Neem Karoli Baba before. They had a little picture of him on their dashboard. I was sitting in the back seat and kept being drawn to look at his picture. I felt very strong emotions building up inside me until I burst into tears. And I asked the woman, "Who is that a picture of?" She said, "Well that's our guru, Neem Karoli Baba." When they said his name, it was like all of a sudden I had a "recognition" of a certain aspect of the universe that there was "no separation, no where to go, and nothing to do." Right then and there, everything was "complete" and there was a total non-separate reality that I could exist in. I was given grace to see in that moment. And then they let me out of their car. And I carried that with me for another three or four years before I really found anybody else or found (the book) "Be Here Now," or anything to relate it to. That was probably the strongest "awakening" that I can think back to in my life.

The next really strong one was with Papaji. Sitting in his presence and having him ask me to give him "one second" of my time, brought me into another whole realization that was way beyond my mind and into an "empty space" where there was no suffering and no pain. This has carried me through ever since then and has really made my life very different.

Do you practice any other types of meditation or spiritual techniques in addition to participating in arti's and devotional singing?

On a daily basis I do a short meditation every day, sitting in silence and just watching my breath; very much like Vipassana [meditation]. I've spent time with Vipassana teachers and that's really about it. I spent many years practicing Hatha Yoga and various different forms of meditation. At this point in my life I feel in my daily activity, I'm constantly "remembering" and so I don't feel so much need anymore to set aside a specific time to do a practice. My life is my practice now.

How do you feel about the popularization of meditation or meditation techniques in these times as a means of gaining a deeper sense of reality or enlightenment?

I think it's incredible that it's become so available and so widespread. I think meditation is a good vehicle for anybody to get a deeper sense of who they are and what their relationship with the world is. I hope that it continues. My only thing is that I would caution people to not get too attached to their "practice" because you can get stuck even in meditation.

A famous Buddhist Master once said, "There is nothing which can be attained is not idle talk: it is the truth. You have always been one with the Buddha, so do not pretend you can attain to this Oneness by various practices. If at this very moment, you could convince yourselves of its unattainability, being certain indeed that nothing at all can ever be attained, you would already be Bodhi-minded. Hard is the feeling of this saying! It is to teach you to refrain from seeking Buddhahood, since any search is doomed to failure." On the other hand there are strong traditions of practice and striving throughout many traditions. Can you help us understand the meaning of the word "seeking" in each of these cases, and how does it fit into the context of spiritual liberation?

I think when you are still identifying yourself with your mind and your physical form, you're a seeker. To get stuck in that—in the process of "seeking" and not go beyond who we "think" we are, to recognize who we really are is one of the main traps to practice. And I think Poonja or Papaji was one of the best teachers for that because he would always tell people, "you are already enlightened, you are already free. You have always been free and you have always been enlightened. And it's only a matter of recognizing who you really are, recognizing that That is who you are." And any idea that you are not That is a wrong idea. It is only your mind that is keeping you from "knowing yourself."

Does that coincide pretty much with the way Maharaj-ji [Neem Karoli Baba] taught also? Were there aspects of direct realization in his teaching, or were there various practices he would give to people who were around him?

It's hard because his teachings were either very general or very individualized. He tried to make people recognize that there was no separation between them and the other person. I think that was where his teaching coincided with Papaji's. But I think mostly his [Neem Karoli Baba's] teaching was more of how to be in this world in the sense of relating to the world and everyone around you. His teachings were not so much concerned with "becoming enlightened." He just wanted everybody to love each other and to recognize that there was no difference between "myself" and "you." We're really just "One." One of his main things when people would ask him a question, he would just say, "Subek" which means, "Only One." And in that sense his teaching was that; it's all One and if we're all One, if I'm One with God then I must be enlightened, I must be Omnipotent and Omniscient. Because if there's "Only One" then "I Am That."

The concept of "enlightenment" seems to have taken on many definitions in these times. What does the term "enlightenment" mean to you?
Simply put, it is the recognition of "non-separate reality."

Some say that through silence alone one can realize peace or true liberation. Others say it's through action alone. How can we cut through this dichotomy?
Well, I think through either course you can find enlightenment. And I think that to say that, "through silence alone" is the way to do it, or "through action alone"—it's too narrow. Because I don't believe there's any one particular way other than stopping your mind and recognizing the truth within. It can happen like that [snapping fingers]. In any moment—you can be brushing your teeth and it will happen or you can be sitting with your eyes turned up in your head in quietude and it can happen. So I think it's by grace that it happens and it doesn't matter what you're doing.

Why do you think there remains so such confusion about the term enlightenment and liberation in these times?
I think that with concepts of "enlightenment" and "liberation," people tend to think that something is going to be different. Once you're "enlightened," the world is different or you are different in the world. And I think that is a real mistake to believe that. If somebody does have an "enlightenment" or a "liberation" experience they don't become any different. They still have the same body, they still have the same "personality." Their nature is still the same. The only difference is that they have a recognition of who they are. You're not all of a sudden going to start being a whole new being once you're enlightened. I think that people think "enlightenment" implies that all of a sudden

this person sitting here is going to be somebody different, something greater, something better. The truth is that there is nothing better to become, there's nothing greater to become. We are already That and it's not going anywhere, it's not "becoming" something, it's just recognizing who you already are and living with that recognition.

That's an interesting situation that has arisen in the West. There seem to be individuals who claim to have gone through some kind of great transformational experience, and yet on the other hand they still manifest what I would consider very typical "egoic" kinds of behavior. How can we understand this? In one sense they have basically been "translated" in realizing "That which is True," but on the other hand, in some instances there seems to be hypocrisy between who they say they are and their actions in the world.

And I think if you have to judge anybody, judge them by their actions, not by who or what they say they are. And I think that's where the hypocrisy comes in. If somebody says, "Oh, I am this and I am that" and continue to manifest contrary actions, then they haven't had a complete awakening or a complete awareness of what "reality" is.

For seekers it's really hard to sort it all out. In some cases those who claim to be enlightened act in a way that breaks the rules of traditional cultural or religious circumstances. Is it possible to have a "means" to see through someone's pure or impure motive and make a decision on what kind of relationship to have with a teaching or teacher?

It's difficult because it's true that many of the supposed greatest spiritual masters I can think of often times did things that were contrary to the norms of morality of the time that they lived in. So for us to discern which teacher is really enlightened and which one isn't is a really difficult thing. And at the same time I think since it is so important, before you submit or surrender to any teacher, you need to give it more time than an initial reaction like, "Oh wow, they're powerful; they're somebody." Maharaj-ji said that you should examine a spiritual teacher for at least twelve years before you submitted to them. But that didn't happen in my case because it was "immediate." (Chuckle) And that's the other thing. I think that when a teacher is "enlightened" and is meant to be your "personal guru" there is a certain connection that you can feel within yourself, whether you want to call it a "heart-connection," or something else. There's a very powerful, strong feeling that you'll have towards that person.

Then they may display behavior that seems like they're crazy or contrary to the teachings. In my case with Neem Karoli Baba, there's lots of things I've heard about him that people have told me, and I'm like, "Wow, if I didn't know that for me he is the Lord of the Universe" I'd be sitting here going, "Well who does he think he is?" [Chuckle] So it's not a question that you can just answer across the board. I think each person has to discover for themselves what an individual means to them and whether or not it's someone they should take as a teacher. Nisargadatta, one of the most incredible teachers of our time—if you looked at his "physical reality" you would forget about it. I mean he sat around smoking bedee's, swearing, and telling people off all the time. And yet I think he was one of the most amazing beings to be on the earth at this time. And his teachings cut through everything including his actions.

It's tricky business isn't it?
It's tricky business. [Laughter]

Along these lines, if someone were sincerely interested in a genuine spiritual teaching or teacher, what are the most important things to consider? I think you mentioned a couple of them; one is "give it some time." What are some others?
First of all do give it time. And at the same time invest yourself in that teacher in the sense that, O.K., you're not only giving it time, so you're in a way holding back, but at the same time let yourself go into a teaching and really see if it's working for you. Those things become clear pretty quickly. If I go to a Vipassana teacher and I sit for ten days, I usually can tell by the end of ten days whether that teacher is really there with me and taking me to a place I couldn't go without them. Also look at a person's life. I don't consider myself a "spiritual teacher" in any way, shape or form. But I do consider that I try to live the teaching that I know. And if that teacher is living in the same way that they are teaching, then it becomes obvious pretty quickly if you spend some time with them. You can then say, yes they are living their teaching. One of the people who came out of Papaji's teachings named

Gangaji, if you spend any time around her, you say, "yes, she's constantly living and teaching the same thing over and over." She doesn't change, she doesn't go home and be a different person. She's the same wherever she is.

There's real consistency.

There's consistency. And yes, there's always room for "crazy wisdom" so . . . nothing is the same across the board. The other thing is if you've gotten to the point where you're looking for a spiritual teacher, you have a certain amount of sensitivity and insight into it. You have to pay attention to it. And I think a lot of times people don't give themselves enough credit. You either get the warning signals or you get the "go ahead" signals. If you listen to your own intuition, generally speaking you'll go in the right direction. The best teaching I got from a teacher I had in the '70's was "follow your Heart in every situation." If you follow your Heart you'll be doing what's best for you and the rest of the world.

It's been said by some very well known spiritual teachers that enlightenment is beyond even good and evil, right and wrong, and that true realized individuals aren't even accountable to God. In our daily lives, what's the best way to deal with right and wrong decisions that we must make, or in dealing with destructive tendencies in others who want to cause wars and death and extreme suffering—which appear to most people to be very wrong?

For myself I believe that the best course of action is the action that is least harmful to everyone. And that's how I try to live my life. I look at a situation and I try to follow the course that is going to be the least harmful and the most helpful to everybody involved. As far as right and wrong, I think that's true. Once you're enlightened, joy and suffering—there's no separation. They're the same. Once you get into a "place" where you see the non-separateness of reality then pain and joy—what's the difference? There is no difference because it's all contained in "the One" and once you're there it doesn't matter. And as far as being accountable to anybody else, of course you're not because in that reality there is "only One" and you're not accountable to God or man because you're accountable to "the One" which encompasses all of it. There are those teachers I believe who use this concept to say, "Well I'm enlightened, and I can see beyond the concepts of good and bad and therefore I am not accountable for my actions." If I heard this said, my "alarms" would go off and red lights would start flashing. [Chuckle] I am cautious.

At the end of the question you said something that's going on in the world?

Yes, dealing with destructive tendencies. Some people have fallen into acquiescence. There's so much destruction and suffering in the world. People say, "Well, that's just the way it is." On the other hand, they might take one position or another and fight.

The Buddha said, "All life is suffering." But that didn't stop him from trying to alleviate suffering in every spot he saw it. And I think in our lives we can't affect the whole world and change wars or stop all the suffering, but every time we encounter suffering in our own personal interactions with people we can do our best to make it go away at least in that moment. As far as "changing the world," the best place to start is with ourselves. If we can change ourselves to where we're not creating suffering, that's going to ripple out. And eventually like the Bodhisattva wants, all suffering will be relieved and we will all be in that space of understanding and enlightenment where pain and suffering, joy and happiness are the same and therefore there's no more suffering.

What was Maharaj-ji's position on the comprehensiveness of God's will? Is there individual free will, and if there is how does it fit within the context of what God wills?

That's a good one. I couldn't really tell you what his position was. But from my own "trying" to live his teachings, I would say that all of us always have choices. And we have a free will to decide whether to take this path or that path. In the course of our lives we make a lot of different choices, some good and some bad. I think that because of the fact that there is a non-separate reality, in the end we're going to get to the same place. And it might take an extra lifetime or two depending on the choices we make. But we will wind up in a place of enlightenment or awareness regardless of the choices we make. And I think that's where God's will comes in. In God's plan we are all One. And we are going to all recognize that or become aware of that eventually. In that sense I think we are all "pre-destined" to come to a place of understanding and awareness where we all recognize that. But in the meantime we can choose to go this way and that way; make this mistake and that mistake, or that right choice and that wrong choice. And that's where free will comes in. But eventually we're all going to wind up at the same place.

Do you feel it is essential to have a spiritual teacher (living or not living) to realize liberation in this lifetime, or can people somehow do it on their own?

I don't think it's essential to have a spiritual teacher. I think as Papaji said, "we all are already enlightened," and if we just get out of the way, we'll recognize that. I think it's a matter of grace perhaps that at any moment whether you've been seeking or had a teacher or not, you can have that awareness and that recognition—and stay with it. I think it's helpful to have a spiritual teacher and a "path" that you're following because until you are to that point, at least you're living your life in a way that is probably more helpful to the rest of humanity and to yourself—but not essential.

Historically there seems to be either a patriarchal or matriarchal dominance. The patriarchal either ignores or idealizes the matriarchal, and the matriarchal seems to have rooted her too deeply in the world, in nature. Can there be a true fusion of these two great principles, and how would it best come about?

I think there can be a true fusion. In the Hindu tradition, Shiva-Shakti are the two ways they talk about the male and the female energies. One cannot exist without the other. Without Shakti, Shiva does not exist because Shakti is the energetic manifested forms and the actual energy. And Shiva is the formless unmanifest. As to how to bring those into unison—they already are. And I think it's a matter of our minds allowing for that and recognizing it rather than there's anything we have to "do" to bring them together. In reality they are already "One" and inseparable.

How do we bring that recognition or revelation about? Can we do anything about that in terms of taking action? Or is it really a graceful process of something that intervenes, that comes from "outside" of ourselves?" Is it possibly a combination of the two?

I think it's probably a combination of the two. And I do think that there are things that we can do in our own lives to recognize that. My own view of the Shakti or feminine principle is that everything in form, everything that I see here, feel and touch is "the Mother." And that she deserves my respect in every one of those manifestations. And so that's how I try to live my life—in respect, admiration and gratitude for "the Mother." As far as the paternal or the male principle, just that very act of giving respect is my male principle, recognizing that without all of this that is manifest before me, there would be nothing of me. There would be no way to even know who I am if it weren't for the manifest form, "the Mother" and all she represents.

If you could give one piece of guidance to individuals very interested in realizing freedom in this lifetime, what would it be?

Once again I have to go back to Papaji. He was constantly telling people, "If you will give just one moment of your time to stop your mind." That doesn't necessarily mean going and sitting in someplace quiet all by yourself. But it can happen at any point. And just when you're genuinely ready to say, "O.K. I'm just going to give one moment to 'the Self' and see who that is," that's one of the best things I think anybody can do for themselves. And beyond that, Neem Karoli Baba's teaching, "Love everyone." There's no qualification there. "Serve everyone." There's no qualification there. To recognize that love doesn't know any barriers or separation in any individual. Love is just a universal principal and a universal energy. Once you tap into that, it's a lot easier to recognize the God within each one of us. We all are That.

Hanuman, you have been living here in the ashram for many years now. What are some of the most important things you have learned from this experience and could recommend to others?

I think the most important thing I've learned is that our actions and how we live our lives affect people more than any words I could speak. It is the consistency that I've had to keep to be here and to continuously remember that my Guru's teaching was to "love everyone" and to bring that into every relationship that I have with people. And I think that it's just "remember." I guess it's "walk your talk" is how it's been put so simply and easily. That's going to affect your life and the lives of everybody around you a lot more than any words that I could say.

Hanuman, again thank you very much for spending this time with us today. We are very grateful for the opportunity to explore these important topics with you.

Thank you. It's been a pleasure.

JANE VENNARD

In an attempt to present a variety of spiritual teachers and teachings, I felt it was important to include someone with a strong academic background in religion and theology. Jane Vennard has a Masters in Divinity and teaches at the Iliff School of Theology in Denver. She has extensive experience facilitating workshops on various subjects including prayer and forgiveness, the spirituality of dissent, and women mystics of the Middle Ages: messages for modern women, to name a few. She is an expert on teaching others how to facilitate spiritual retreats and has a book forthcoming on the subject. I was delightfully surprised to discover that Jane was a former student of Zen Buddhism. She now finds Christianity to be her true calling and devotes her time and energy in this direction.

Since the West is dominated by Christianity, I wanted to explore with Jane some challenges that have recently arisen in this context. I found Jane to be very astute and open-minded as we probed into thorny topics related to Christian fundamentalism, women and Christianity, and religious tolerance. She has a marvelous gift for moving through mixed perspectives. Her eclectic background and spiritual perceptiveness serve us all in this regard. I found her to be very much in the moment which is an important foundation to her life. We are blessed to have Jane with us as we celebrate the great mystery of spirit.

❧ ❧ ❧

Jane, thank you very much for spending time to speak with us today. As a note of introduction, can you please share with us where you grew up and how it's impacted your perspective on life?

I grew up in Palo Alto, California. When I was six years old I moved there with my parents, my older sister, and my paternal grandmother. My father was a professor at Stanford. We were part of the academic community. I know the decision he made to move from New York City to California was very important in my life. Growing up in the late 40's and early 50's, I had an extraordinary amount of freedom.

Do you recall having any spiritual or deeply insightful experiences as a child?

I think I had a sense of "connection" but I wouldn't say that I had one moment, one major insightful experience as a child. I felt a lot of connection to nature. And I had a sense of belonging. I felt very interconnected.

Were you close to your grandmother?

I was close to my grandmother when I was young. She lived with us. I had a strong inter-generational understanding that I think was important. I was close to my father and mother as well, and close to the community through the church.

Did your parents practice any particular religion?
My parents were "religious" in that we went to church but I don't remember ever seeing my parents pray. Grace was said only at special occasions. We prayed in church. I remember my father saying to me one time, "I'm not a Christian, I just work in the church." I'm not sure exactly what he meant by that. But I think it had to do with the way he identified himself. "I'm a scientist, an intellectual. I believe in the church but I can't believe all those things that a lot of Christian's believe." He was very committed to social justice issues and the work of the church in the world. But I wouldn't say we were a "spiritual family."

Which church was it?
It was the Congregational Church, now the United Church of Christ, which is my present denomination or affiliation. The church we were in was very academic with a strong intellectual approach to religion.

You are currently a professor at the Iliff School of Theology. What spurred you on to choose this kind of work and how did it shape your educational pursuits?
Long before I became an adjunct professor at Iliff, I was an elementary school teacher. I went into adult education after I left the fifth-grade classroom. During that time I decided to go to the seminary. I had not been particularly religious in my young adult years. So it was my love of teaching, which has been there all along, my interest in spirituality, my pursuit of the academic training in a seminary setting. It just seemed like a natural thing. I'd been a teacher my whole life. First it was fifth graders and then it was public school teachers, and now it's religious professionals and interested lay people.

Was there a particular event that moved you to pursue spiritual activities?
Oh yes, very definitely. In my early thirties I was divorced and my life completely fell apart. Amidst the chaos and the pain, I seized the

opportunity to create my own life. That's when I returned, not to the church, but to that "longing" underneath, the spiritual longing, back to that "connectedness" I knew as a child. I needed to ask as an adult, "Where do I belong?" "How am I connected?" "What does my life mean?" I hadn't asked those questions in my young adult years. My divorce and my questions shifted everything. I began to pursue "meaning" more than "spirituality." I got involved in the women's movement, reading all the feminist literature I could find. I explored "depth psychology," and discovered that psychologists were talking about "the spirit." Carl Jung's work and Roberto Assagioli's writing was very influential. I explored Buddhist practice and some of the history of Buddhism. Finally, with great resistance, I began to explore my Christian heritage.

Do you have a religious or spiritual practice, and if so, how do you feel it impacts your everyday life?

I identify myself as a "Christian," which includes the importance of worshipping in community. So a "regular practice" is going to church. And although I belong to one church, I don't feel I always have to go to that particular church. I love going to a variety of churches. I like the liturgy of the Roman Catholic Church and the Episcopal Church. I love the music and soul of the African-American churches. I like the freedom and the openness of the United Church of Christ. I pursue worship in a variety of places. I have a regular dance practice, a "movement practice" that I do in community. That's been very powerful, finding the spiritual within the physical and the physical within the spiritual and not separating body and spirit at all. I don't have a "prayer practice" like some people do—twenty minutes daily at set times. But I feel very connected to the presence of God. God feels as close as my breathing. So I would say my "practice" is very much staying "awake."

Sounds very Buddhist! [Laughter]

I brought a lot of my Buddhist studies and practices into my Christian religion. I don't feel there's any quarrel at all.

What type of Buddhism did you practice? Was it Zen?

It was Zen. And mostly it was sitting zazen. I lived near a Zen community. So on a fairly regular basis I would sit zazen in community. Community, as much as I have sometimes resisted it, has always been important to me. I feel that my spiritual life is lived and enhanced by community, whether it was my family or church community as a child or my dance community or Buddhist community or Sunday worship. I find the "holy" in the people I'm with as much as in the transcendent.

As I've talked with various spiritual teachers and students over the past year or so, I've noticed that for some who feel they've gone through a real spiritual transformation, they've had to pass through the "dark night of the soul." In some cases it happened quickly, in other cases it was an agonizingly long period of time. Do you think a period of extreme angst must be passed through before the "truth" can be revealed, like what happened with St. John of the Cross? Or do you think there's another principle that comes into play that would allow it to be bypassed?

I don't think everyone lives their spiritual journey in the same way. I do think that some people go through what they and other people may call the "dark night of the soul." But the idea that everyone has to go through extreme angst feels antithetical to the surprising ways of the spirit. Some people move along and grow slowly into a mature spirituality.

If we go through the "dark night," it is something we look back on and say, "Oh, that's what that was!" St. John wrote about his experience after he had been through it. I've heard people say, "Oh, this is such a hard time. I'm in the 'dark night of the soul.'" Well, I don't think so. [Laughter] I think the "dark night of the soul" is much more interior. It's much more spiritual than psychological. What I went through after my divorce was psychological. I was broken open, broken apart. The spirit made good use of my brokenness. But I don't think it was a "dark night of the soul" the way St. John describes it. I'm not sure I've ever been there.

Believing we have to go through something to get somewhere else concerns me, for it implies that the spiritual life is getting somewhere else from where we are. I believe that true spiritual life is lived right here in the moment. So I don't think everybody goes through it or has to go through it. I sometimes find an elitism quality about the "dark night." "Well I've gone through the 'dark night of the soul.' Have you?" It's a little bit like the question, "Well I've been born again, have you?" somehow separating the sheep from the goats. I think St. John of the Cross' work is wonderful. It is very helpful to people who've been through the "dark night" as he describes it. I believe St. John of the Cross' writing is descriptive rather than prescriptive.

I think it was a Zen master who once said, "There's nothing to do and no where to go." On the other hand there's the biblical "Seek and ye shall find" proclamation. How do we cross over that dichotomy?

When I talk about "trying to stay awake," longing to be "present," that to me is "seeking." It's keeping my eyes open, keeping awake to whatever comes my way. But a "seeking" to get somewhere else from where I am is problematic. That form of seeking certainly takes me out of the moment. I believe the spiritual life is lived right here and now.

Could we replace the word "seeking" in terms of "eyes open" going into the world with the word "revelation"?

Yes.

Or with the word, just being "Open"?

Yes. Awake. Paying attention. If we stay awake and remain open and attentive, the work of the spirit is everywhere.

What spiritual teachers have had the greatest impact on you in terms of living a more holistic life and helping others to do so?

The writing of Roberto Assagioli, the Italian founder of Psychosynthesis, which is a form of transpersonal psychology, was instrumental in giving me an opportunity to experience myself as a spiritual being. He understood people to be "spiritual" as well as "psychological." Assagioli was a colleague of Jung's. But his model was educational as well as therapeutic. Being an educator, I found wonderful the idea that we can help people educate themselves about who they are and who they are becoming. His understanding of human wholeness was very impactful in my life.

When I moved back into Christian thinking, Thomas Merton became an influence particularly because of the connections he made between Christianity and Buddhism. Also because of his personal struggle to integrate contemplation and action. Now the writings of Thich Nhat Hanh touch me deeply.

I also believe that my colleagues, students, friends and family members particularly my two teenage stepsons, have been profound spiritual teachers. They all have called me into awareness of the spirit moving in my life. In addition, my spiritual directors have been inspirational teachers for me.

Were those teachers in the seminary?

No. People whom I basically found within a wider religious community, but not within the seminary. I think if we learn to listen, we find teachers everywhere.

Was there a certain point where you felt like you were going in a particular direction? For instance, you mentioned Buddhism was an important part of your life at one point in time. And then there must have been "something" that clicked for you, or something that happened which took you in the direction of Christianity.

Yes. There were a series of events that led to a moment of truth. As I studied Psychosynthesis and got my feet on the ground after my divorce, my intellectual understanding of the spiritual nature of the human person needed to be grounded somewhere. So the first place I explored "grounding" was in feminist rituals. That was wonderful until I realized I was building community and experiencing the holy with only half the population. That led me into the Buddhist community where I felt there was more equality between men and women than what I believed at that time about the Christian community. I loved learning about Buddhism and sitting zazen. I liked the simplicity of the practice. There seemed to be a deep truth about "being here now" and simply practicing that. Then at one Zen service with a priest and incense and chanting, I was moved by the rich tradition I was part of at that moment. Suddenly I got a strong sense that "this is a wonderful tradition, and it's not mine." I left the zendo that day thinking, "I need to go back to my Christian roots. I need to explore Christianity." I had left the church almost twenty years before. I knew things had changed, but I didn't know what had changed. And so instead of joining a church—people laugh about this—I went to Seminary! I come from an academic background. It seemed natural that if I wanted to know something, I should study it. I had no clue at that time where I was headed. I just wanted to go and find out. I really thought I would go to seminary and put my Christian heritage to rest so that I could truly embrace Buddhism. But what happened was I realized that Christianity was the place to ground my spiritual explorations. It was my tradition with all of its imperfections and problems. To leave it for something else didn't seem to have integrity. What I wanted to do was see if I could bring what I'd learned from other spiritual practices into my understanding and experience of Christianity.

Can you help us understand the difference between studying religion and studying philosophy?

I think that the only difference is the content. I think they both serve the same purpose, which is trying to structure or find meaning in our lives. Some people do it through philosophy. I know that when I was in college and left the church it was the philosophy and psychology classes that helped my search for meaning. And I think the study of religion is ultimately a search for meaning. To study religion is to open my mind and heart to what's possible and to discover who I am and who I am in relation to the world. I think the danger in any study of religion or philosophy is if someone is trying to convince us that their religion or their philosophy of life is the only one or the best one. The study of religion and philosophy can open us up to our own thinking and our own questioning. The study may even lead to a "dark night of the soul," because what we discover might throw us off of what we were so certain of into something much more mysterious.

Some people have said that philosophy is really the path of the mind and religion tends to develop more of a path of the heart. But there's a lot of crossover between the two.

I believe that a path of heart in religion which ignores the intellect can lead to trouble. We have to be able to think through and articulate our religious convictions. I also believe a philosophy that ignores the emotions becomes cold and unfeeling. My hope would be that the study of both religion and philosophy would use mind and heart. They are both valid ways of pursuing what I think all of us are longing for—the discovery of meaning in our lives.

What's the current thinking about how best to approach religious studies? Is there a growing tolerance for a broader view incorporating all religions in its examination, or has it become more specialized or focused?

The Iliff School of Theology is a liberal Christian seminary that is open not only to all Christian denominations but also to people of other religions. Ecumenism and interfaith dialogue are definitely the trend in liberal Christian seminaries and in most departments of religious studies in major universities. On the other hand, I think there are places where religious study is becoming much more narrow—places people sign on not for an exploration of religion but for the "party line." So I think some institutions are getting more and more inclusive and others are getting more and more focused. Some people are being left out of the dialogue or "choosing out" of the dialogue.

How do you feel about the popularization of meditation techniques or prayer as a means of gaining a deeper sense of the spirit, reality or realizing one's innermost nature?

Oh I think it's quite wonderful. Prayer and meditation have become much more popular. And I think the techniques are being used to find a deeper meaning and to discover a connection to the Divine. Materials are much more available for meditation, for relaxation, for self-discovery, for the discovery of the holy. I also think "that," like anything that's good—and a lot of material that's out there is good—can be used for "odd reasons." I think there are people who are using some really beautiful techniques not for self-discovery and more spiritual depth, but to make more money or to gain more power or to make others believe that they are "holy."

As more of a selfish reason rather than. . . .

Right. And I think some of the materials are being advertised that way. It's not just the people who are buying them, but "Read this book and you will have happiness." It's a little bit like some of the ads, "Buy this car and you'll be popular." I think the accessibility of a variety of prayer forms, meditation techniques, and teachings are wonderful because they open that world to people who might not find it in other ways. But some of these techniques are being used not to discover meaningful ways of living our human life more fully but rather for ego-gratification.

What's your impression of recent developments within Christianity of a more ecumenical approach coming from the Pope and the Catholic Church?

I think it's absolutely imperative. It's been coming from a lot of other Christians for a long time. [Chuckle] The Pope didn't get this started. He's "joined in" now and seems to see the importance of this kind of dialogue. And I love what's happening in Protestant denominations. The United Church of Christ was formed out of three denominations about thirty years ago. And now the Lutherans and Episcopalians are in agreement so that they are willing to share the Sacraments, and clergy can serve churches across denominational lines. I think we are saying, "There's room for everyone at the table and the table is large enough for all." It's been said before but not acted on. Now it's really being acted on. It's very exciting and I think the next step beyond the "ecumenical movement" is the "inter-religious movement."

I have to tell you a story. My wife and I were recently strolling through a public park and were approached by no less than four separate groups of teenagers wanting to know if we believed in God. We almost felt as if we were being harrassed in a public place. Evangelism has become a major activity with some Christian churches. In your experience what's the truest, most effective way to "evangelize" religious beliefs if someone feels they must do it, without giving the impression that the Crusades are upon us again?

[Chuckle] That's great. What comes to me is an old hymn I grew up with: "They will know we are Christians by our love, by our love, they will know we are Christians by our love." I think living our love is the best way to "evangelize." I think its living who we are to the best of our abilities. I do find, as a liberal Christian, that very often I'm a little leery to even tell people I'm a Christian. And yet I think it's very important that I claim the name "Christian." The young people I've spoken with are longing for a moderate liberal Christian voice in the world. I may not say much more than telling people I go to church on Sunday and this is my church and this is my faith. People need to know that there are Christians who think for themselves and attempt to live out the teachings of Jesus in inclusive ways. People need to be introduced to the paradoxical nature of Christianity and the living of the Gospel. A friend of mine told me that she had a bumper sticker that said, "Prayerfully Pro-Choice." She found that people would just be shocked at that. It seemed as if they thought, "No, if you pray you're on 'this side,' if you're pro-choice you're on 'that side.'" The idea that she was bringing these together in her life seemed impossible. I think it's important for me to name myself as "Christian."

What are your impressions of the growing religious fundamentalist movements sweeping across the world, not only in Christianity but also in other religions, and how are they impacting the pursuit of truth?

I find fundamentalism in any religion frightening. Because I think it does not "open" people to their pursuit of truth but closes them and oppresses them in some way. It feels to me that fundamentalism is based on a hierarchy of power and that any of that kind of dominance or hierarchical system is not good for the soul.

In your estimation, what's the most important religious studies development in the last few years?

I have to say a couple of things before I respond. A lot of people are studying religion, and that's different than living religion or living one's spiritual life within a religious form. I believe religious studies are beginning to include more and more "spirituality." The American Academy of Religion is filled with thousands of people who are studying religion. But there seems to be very little there in relationship to one's spiritual life. Spirituality is just beginning to be included in the Academy. I would have to say it is the most important development because it's just beginning. But I think the study of religion without the "lived experience" is problematic.

How has religious studies attempted to take students beyond what has been coined by one author as "mere intellectual voyeurism"? Direct spiritual experiences seem to be the keystone of genuine religious understanding. It sounds like religious studies are beginning to move beyond the province of intellectual exercise and into more of an experiential, spiritual side.

Well I think that's beginning to happen but there's a lot of resistance to that within the Academy. Does "spirituality" belong in religious studies programs? Does "spirituality" belong in a seminary? For example, at the Iliff School of Theology there is no full-time faculty person in "Spirituality." Some Protestant seminaries are doing more to integrate spirituality into religious studies. I do believe that's going to have to happen in religious studies. But there's a lot of resistance to it.

What is the Iliff School of Theology's religious inclination? You mentioned Protestant....

It's basically United Methodist. I don't know the figures, but probably about half the students are Methodist and then the other half are everything else. A number of people are there studying for the ministry, either in the United Methodist church or another denomination. But many people go to seminary to look at their faith, to study their religious heritage, to open themselves to a new way of thinking. Most students are very clear about wanting the spiritual dimension to be included in their religious studies. The students are the ones who have really been demanding more course offerings within the seminary structure.

The concept of enlightenment seems to have taken on many definitions in these times. What does the term "enlightenment" mean to you?

Well, [Chuckle] it's a term I avoid. Because again it has that sense that some people have "achieved" it and others have not.

So it's a buzz word....

It's a "buzz word." It's also a judgement. A lot of people are trying to become enlightened in ways that I think exclude them from the human experience. I think "enlightenment" to many people means, "moving beyond" the physical realm into some other "place." I believe true enlightenment is in the present moment. As a Christian that's my understanding of the incarnation. True enlightenment came into human form. The pursuit of enlightenment feels like dualistic thinking. You can probably tell I have a hard time with this term. I avoid "enlightenment." [Laughter]

What's your favorite analogy or metaphor in the field of religion that points to what the truth is about and how it is most effectively realized?
    Well, I guess I would have to ask the question of whether we're talking about capital "T" Truth or little "t" truth?

Let's say capital "T"....
    And I'm not sure there is such a thing. The best metaphor for "little t" truth has to do with "light." What I shine a light on, or what my tradition shines a light on, to help people to "see" more clearly so they can discover their own meaning and truth. So truth has to do with "light." This metaphor is from the Biblical tradition: "The light shines in the darkness and the darkness does not overcome it."

There seem to be a number of books written recently by spiritual teachers attempting to identify a common thread of truth that runs through all religions which promotes compassion and tolerance for other's beliefs. Is this a development that has value in bringing people closer together and broadening our understanding of how religion is perceived by others, or is it diluting the purity of various religious precepts?
    Oh I think absolutely the former. And I would even go so far to say that we're all worshipping the same God. When we believe that, acceptance of differences and compassion follow close behind.

Why do you think there remains such confusion about the relationship between God and the world?
    Oh, I think there always will be confusion. I think "God" is for me "mystery." The more we try to "sort out" and the more we analyze, the more questions come. For me the wonder of God is the mysteriousness. We can never completely understand. The real spiritual task and the religious task is living in the midst of the mystery with as much love and compassion as we can.

There are so many spiritual teachers and teachings coming about; some legitimate, some not. If someone were sincerely interested in a genuine spiritual teaching, minister or teacher, what are the most important aspects to consider?

I would say first off, congruence. Are persons living what they're teaching? Are their lives congruent with their words?—which is another way of asking, "Do they have integrity?" I would also look very carefully for humility. The humility of a teacher would be of utmost importance. I believe humility guards against the "guru" kind of mentality which can be so seductive to spiritual teachers. Humility tends to counter that danger. Another aspect would be to ask, "Are they out in the world or are they isolating themselves?" I am not equating isolation with people who are cloistered in prayer because their prayers are ultimately for the goodness of the world. They are deeply involved "prayerfully" in the world. But I would be wary of people who build walls around themselves, to protect themselves from the world, and remove themselves from any involvement with issues of justice and peace.

Is it possible to resolve the dichotomy between what's been referred to in the press as "the Jesus Cult" and the perception of Jesus as "the Christ"?

Are you talking about the Jesus Seminar and all that work or....

Well, basically there is no one else other than Jesus that is "the Christ," the "Christos."

A very influential teacher for me is Marcus Borg who writes and talks about the "pre-Easter Jesus" and the "post-Easter Christ" and looking at Jesus' life historically. In other words, "Jesus of History" and the "Christ of Faith." I believe the "Jesus Cult," the "Jesus is the Only Way," comes from a very literal rendition of scripture. I don't read the Bible literally although I take if very seriously. We read in the Bible that Jesus said, "I am the Way, and the Truth, and the Light; no one comes to the Father except through me." But we must ask whether Jesus said that or whether the early church writers wrote that. And so that understanding of Jesus as "the only Way"—and everybody else outside is damned—however you want to say that, feels to me to be very limited and literal. The people who are doing historical study on

Jesus, and who have also stayed connected to their Christian faith, are wonderful teachers if we can open our minds and hearts to them. They have a whole new way of looking at and understanding Christianity that is intellectual and faithful. This to me is very exciting.

Another apparent paradox within Christianity is the statement Jesus made in which he refers to himself as the "Only Begotten Son of God" and in other places within the Bible he states that there will be others who will follow Him. Help us with this one.

The stories of Jesus we read in the Bible were written after Jesus' life and death. They gave Jesus a lot of words that Jesus probably didn't say. This is what Biblical scholars are trying to sort out. There's quite a bit of controversy over whether Jesus knew himself to be "God's only child"; whether he believed himself even to be the "Messiah." Could it be his followers came to believe that about him and wrote the words into the story? The Bible was written by humans over a long period of time. Some of what was written was eliminated. Human writing is subject to error and bias. As a writer I know I bring my own bias to my writing.

Your bias may change over time. . . .[Laughter]

That's right, absolutely. So the contradictions in the Bible are what make the Bible so interesting. It's a little bit like the "mystery of God." It's what makes God so interesting.

It's been said that Christians have to help Jesus be manifested by their way of life as we mentioned before, showing those around them that love, understanding and tolerance are possible. And that this cannot be accomplished simply by reading the Bible and attending sermons only. It has to be realized by the way we live, as you mentioned. This has also been said by the Buddha, Mohammed and Krishna. Can religious fundamentalism work positively to assist people in living the principles of tolerance and understanding of other's beliefs, or does the opposite seem to be happening?

I think "yes" and "yes." I think the opposite does seem to be happening but I do believe that there are many people and teachings within what we want to call "fundamentalism" or a more conservative Christianity who are incredibly clear about their theology and religious beliefs and they are also extremely tolerant. So I think, as you said, it's not happening as much. Is it possible? I think it is. I think it is possible for somebody to have absolute certainty in what they believe at the same time they're tolerant of other people. And that would be my hope, because there are a lot of wonderful people who ascribe to some of the much more conservative Christian tenets of faith who are not condemning anybody. I think as liberals, one of our problems is we tend to categorically condemn "fundamentalists." As if, "Oh, he's a Fundamentalist so I can't talk to him." Well maybe we can. I think it's a real call for liberal Christians to look at our own intolerance toward Fundamentalist Christians.

From a religious perspective, what are the best ways to deal with daily right and wrong decisions that we must make, or in dealing with destructive tendencies in others who want to cause wars and death, and extreme suffering—which appear to most people to be very wrong?

By staying awake. I sound more like a Buddhist than a Christian but it has to do with what's in front of me. Also the willingness to think through the consequences. I think that in making decisions we do not look for the "right decision," rather we look at the particular and ask, "Given the situation, given what I know and who I am, what's the best decision at this time?" And then we must stay awake. If it wasn't the "best" [decision] now I can correct it. We can take a zigzag movement through life rather than looking for absolutes. I think at any moment all we can do is make the best decision given the information we have, but we don't always have it all. If we can remain spiritually grounded or "awake," or however you want to say that, then we can look at what effect this decision has. Then we make corrections as needed.

Some people believe that "everything is God's will." And if "all is God's will," as some spiritual teachings would have us believe, and some unscrupulous people use this as an excuse to do very bad things, where would accountability most appropriately reside for their actions?

No matter what we believe about God's will I believe that accountability ultimately lies within ourselves, and hopefully within ourselves in relationship with God. That's a hard question for me because I don't believe in "God's will" the way most people do. I think of "God's will" more as "God's promise." To align ourselves with "God's promise" for all of humanity is what connecting to God's will is about. And we must remember that God gave humans free will. . . .

Is that God's promise then?

When people say, "I've got to decide what God's will is for my life," they are usually saying, "What does God want me to do?" in a specific situation. "Do I marry or not marry?" "Do I take this job or that?" I believe God has a "promise," or a "dream" that all of us can become as fully human as we can be. And that there are many paths to that wholeness. So to blame something on "God's will," or to have my task to be trying to figure out what "God's will" is so that I'm on the right track, seems like a waste of energy to me. Rather I believe God has a promise for all of humankind—the possibility of goodness, peace and justice and harmony. Our task is to align ourselves with that promise, and act in accordance with that promise. If somebody uses the excuse, "I'm following God's will" to act without compassion, love and justice—it feels to me that they're trying to manipulate God or manipulate other people through their use of God.

Historically in religions there seems to be either a patriarchal or matriarchal dominance. The patriarchal either ignores or idealizes the matriarchal, and the matriarchal seems to be too deeply rooted in "the world," in "nature." The patriarchal accretions of two thousand years of what has been called by some, "authoritarian misinterpretations of the Christian message" is coming into question. It seems there was a very strong influence of women in the life of Christ, yet there's very little said about their lives, their thinking, their religious experiences during this most important religious time. Can you help us understand what the current thinking is on this subject?

I can tell you what my thinking is. [Laughter] Some people believe that the patriarchy has so taken over Christianity that there's no way to redeem it. I would not go to that extent. I believe that Jesus really did upset that power of the time, which was patriarchal. Although much of what women said and how they experienced Jesus has been left out of the Bible, the women's influence is still there. One passage relates how Jesus is traveling and preaching the Gospel with the twelve disciples and Mary Magdalene and Joanna and Suzanna.

Three women named in one passage! And then we read, "who supported him out of their resources." This very brief mention is very important, for it gives us a picture of women travelling with men, women with their own resources, women close to Jesus. This was radical for the time. Divorce laws were started for the protection of women. Those laws were not to keep women in marriages that were abusive, although the laws have been used that way by many churches. But Jesus' "laws" were to protect women who were being cast off by men for no reason. In that society, when women were cast off they had no life. So if you look deeply within the words, women are very influential in the Gospel. And Jesus' treatment of them was radically different from his culture. He touched them and spoke with them, healing them, befriending them.

But there wasn't actually much coming directly from the women as far as actual speaking and dialogue. . . .

You are right. We know little of their experience, their response to Jesus' teaching and healing. But the disciples' responses weren't very bright when you get into those stories. [Laughter] They kept missing the point. I wonder if, maybe silently, the women "got it."

And who was at the cruxificion?

Right. And who was there at the resurrection? And earlier the wonderful story of the Caananite woman who talked back to Jesus and said basically, "you can't treat me that way." And he listened to her and said, "Your faith has healed your daughter," or in another version he even says to her, "Well said," when she talked back to him. So we just have to look a little more closely at the stories—and use our imagination. There's a lot of wonderful scholarship right now about women in the Bible. . . . Women writers who are looking at these women and filling in the stories with knowledge about the time and the culture. The Jewish tradition of Midrash is to tell a story based on what we know and then to add and embellish. These Biblical women are becoming much more "alive."

If you could give one piece of guidance to individuals very interested in realizing a truly religious way of being in this lifetime, what would it be?

It would have to do with listening. It would have to do with being quiet, letting go, opening to whatever is in front of us, whatever those teachings are. It's the ancient tradition of Sabbath, a time of the heart. There are so many ways to say it but it has to do with "stopping."

Stopping the mind?

No, not stopping the mind. Because we don't want to stop the mind. The mind isn't supposed to be stopped. It's stopping getting hooked in the mind or getting hooked in my old "tapes"....

Patterns. . . .

Old patterns. Remember that old saying, "Stop the world, I want to get off"? I don't think we want to get off. I think we want to "stop" just enough to listen and breathe, to get into the world in a new way. But it has to do with the willingness to have some kind of discipline of silence, of listening, of stopping, of quieting, of stilling oneself. I think one of the things that happens in the spiritual quest is it can become driven in the same way that other things get driven. And so people are just reading more and more spiritual books, or thinking, "If prayer for twenty minutes is good, then prayer for an hour is even better." And if church one day a week is good, then maybe three times a week is better.

It's very "Western". . . .

Yes, very "Western." Rather than, "Can I stop just for a moment and trust that what I need will come to me? Maybe I don't need to be in this constant pursuit." And that's not to say that finding new books and reaching out to new teachers, and taking new classes are not good. I think learning is very enlivening to people. But it can become almost manic. And so I would recommend the willingness to "stop and choose, stop and choose." It doesn't matter how many books we read, we're not going to figure it out anyway. We might as well live in the mystery and enjoy ourselves.

Jane, you've been teaching at the Iliff School of Theology for a while now. What's the most important thing that you have learned from your experience working with students and the attending faculty?

Let me answer the students first. I think that the most important things I've learned from the students are their questions and their stories. People bring to the spiritual quest incredible stories of their lives. As a teacher in a seminary and because of the way I teach and the courses I teach, I get to hear some of these stories in ways that keep my sense of hope alive of how humans evolve and heal and move on. It's their stories. Being adjunct faculty I don't have a lot of contact with faculty on a regular basis like faculty meetings and retreats. I don't go on those because adjunct faculty are not included in those. But I think from the faculty that I know the most, it's the same thing, it's their stories.

Jane, thank you very much for spending this time with us today. We are very grateful for the opportunity to explore these important topics with you.
Thank you.

Publications:
Be Still: Designing and Leading Contemplation Retreats. Publishing date: 2000
Praying With Body and Soul: A Way to Intimacy With God. Augsburg Fortress Books, 1998
Praying for Friends and Enemies: Intercessory Prayer. Augsburg Fortress Press, 1995

Contact information:
Jane Vennard
C/O Iliff School of Theology
2201 S. University Blvd.
Denver, CO 80210

SANIEL BONDER

I've known Saniel Bonder since the mid 1980's. During this time, Saniel has evolved from being a long-time devotee of Adi Da Samraj into a spiritual teacher standing firmly on his own. It's been fascinating to observe the metamorphosis. We met for this interview in Marin County, California, where Saniel resides.

This is the longest interview in the book. After much rumination, I chose to include the entire interview in order to give you the full flavor of his teaching. While we were working on the transcription of this dialogue, Saniel aptly named it "The Making of an American Maverick: On Mutual Waking Down into the Paradoxes of White-Hot Freedom." Who Saniel is, what he teaches, and the way he teaches appropriately lends itself to a brimming presentation because of the profusion of spiritual "angles," detailed stories and free-flowing spiritual experiments.

As you will discover, there is a refreshing "feel" to Saniel and his teachings, which for many serves up liberation in a straight, no-nonsense manner. If you are looking for a "pedestal guru," you won't find him here.

If the interview appears daunting, you may want to spread it out over a few sittings. Or you might approach it as you would a long, hot bath permeated with soothing scents. Ease yourself in, start soaking, relax and enjoy!

᠀ ᠀ ᠀

Thank you very much, Saniel, for meeting with us today.
My pleasure.

I'd like to start out by asking you to recollect some of your earliest experiences with spirituality. Did you have any in your childhood? Were there any experiences that stand out in your mind that you might be able to share with us?

That's an amusing question, because I know a lot of people who have extensive memories of their childhood spirituality. And I don't have any! [Laughter]

My first moments of being aware as a human being came when I was three years old. I don't remember anything previous to that. I had a sudden, choking case of croup and had to be rushed to the hospital for an emergency tracheotomy. I remember being out of my body, looking down at it, at that time. But that experience didn't have any special spiritual meaning to me then. It was mostly bewildering. It was only much later in life that I was able to make any sense of it.

It's interesting that my first conscious experience of being alive was associated with almost dying. It just happened to work out that way.

I think for me childhood was a time of being very oriented to getting here materially, not of remembering or knowing anything of myself as a spiritual being. Before she died just a few years ago, my mother remarked that I was always very spiritual when I was a kid. But I think she was referring to my sensitivity, not to any particular experiences, insights, or other things like that. I was a loving, good kid who cared for people. And very sensitive—always cried very easily. Also too self-absorbed; I probably received too much praise and admiration for my own good. I was perhaps led to believe that I was, to use one of my dad's picturesque phrases, "the greatest thing since bottled beer." My sister later called me "Teflon Boy"—nothing ever stuck to me. I could do no wrong, or so it appeared.

The only thing close to a spiritual insight that I had, sometime well before my teens, now strikes me as a naïve picture of karma. I felt, for instance, that if I squashed a bug, then after my death probably some pretty big bug was going to squash me. [Laughter]

I did, though, receive some wonderful things from my parents. When our mother died, my sister summarized her in a way I've never forgotten: Our mother "always accepted everyone on their own terms." From my father, I learned that anything worth anything is worth persevering for, daring for, being willing to make sacrifices for. They both showed us an uncommon willingness to care for others and an intolerance of intolerance, for prejudices of any kind. So, for me, they were great parents. Our family had, and has, its problems, as all families do. But I was loved a lot by my family. That in itself is one of the outstanding spiritual experiences any child can have.

Were they religious? What actually drove you to getting involved with spirituality as an adult? Were there adolescent experiences later on?

No, my folks weren't religious. Like many of their contemporaries, they were second generation American Jews who didn't have an explicitly religious orientation but were very identified with being Jewish. I think my father is probably much more religious in his own inner life today than he or my mother were then.

So it was more cultural?

Yes. My parents did require my sister and me to go to synagogue, to learn about Jewish history and get steeped in the foundation lore of Jewish culture. This was in eastern North Carolina, where we had moved from New York in 1957. My dad was the vice-president of a garment manufacturing firm in a small town there. So we were surrounded almost entirely by southern Protestant Christianity. I think that may have been part of what motivated our parents and those of the only other Jewish kids in town to drive us forty-five minutes each way to Raleigh on Sunday mornings—just to make sure we got a good background in being Jewish.

I did have a Bar Mitzvah. Ours was a Conservative synagogue—not as loose as the Reform temples, not as straitlaced as the Orthodox synagogues. My training for the Bar Mitzvah was a good case in point. I did learn to chant the prayers in Hebrew, but my rabbi had told me, "You don't need to know what the words mean, just learn how to sing it." That said something about the whole orientation I was receiving. In other words, there wasn't any real training in the religious significance of it. It was pro-forma, it was something you did. And so I did it.

I'd had asthma with some frequency as a child, and then right before my Bar Mitzvah I had an attack so bad our family doctor insisted on hospitalizing me. I'd never had it that bad before. I got out of the hospital a few days before the ceremony. But then my rabbi's daughter became gravely ill with encephalitis. So she was in the hospital, and he was in a daze, the morning of my Bar Mitzvah. He couldn't even remember my name when it was time to call me forward to lead the prayers; someone had to prompt him. I felt pretty weird and a little lost.

Anyway, I got through it. Then that evening we had a big reception at the country club my parents were members of. Relatives from both sides of the family and business associates of my dad had come in from all over the East Coast and some from elsewhere. My local friends were there. It was a gala event. But my most impressive memory of it is of going out on the front lawn in some kind of enormous grief. The music's in there playing, everyone's having a grand time, but my dad came out and just held me while I wept my heart out, not knowing why. No idea.

At the time we figured it was all a bit much for me—the asthma, the hospital, the freaky things going on with the rabbi and his daughter, and just the big deal of a Bar Mitzvah. Years later, after my awakening, it struck me that I must have been mourning my lack of connection to my spiritual nature and the divine, and not even knowing that. I didn't have enough access to the sacred yet even to get that I was missing it.

Interesting.

A couple of years later I went away to a private school, and that was a very profound formative incident for me.

High school? Prep school?

College preparatory school—a private secondary school, then still mostly for boys. It's called the Webb School, in a little village known as Bell Buckle southeast of Nashville, Tennessee. It had been around for about a hundred years by then.

The founder was a classically educated Civil War veteran who had a particular bee in his bonnet for integrity and honor. And that was the core of what I got there. Many years later, long after I had left the school, gone through college and then my whole adult life of seeking, and begun my awakened teaching work, I went back to the school for the first time for my 25th reunion. A classmate who's now on the Board of Trustees asked me some intriguing questions. He said, "How do you feel about our experience at the school?" I said, "It's irreplaceable, one of the great things that has happened to me in my life." He said, "You know, as a trustee I've been checking it out. Almost everybody who went there feels that way—even guys who got kicked out."

He was pointing out that even many people who got expelled have become enthusiastic patrons. He asked if I were aware of anyone else who had such a feeling for their high school. I said, "Well, one person or another might, but very rarely, and most people don't even come close." So my friend then asked, "Why is that? What is it about this place that makes so many of us feel this way?"

As a trustee he had a vested interest in my answer, because we both had a sense that the school was changing in ways that might be eliminating some of its magic. He asked me to think it over and get back to him.

Well, with the benefit of my years of spiritual exposure, practice, and study of traditions of acculturation, eventually it dawned on me that being at that school was itself an initiatory ordeal. It was a real Bar Mitzvah into manhood—not specifically of a spiritual nature, but especially around the theme of integrity.

It was a hard place to be. It was in this little village out in the sticks. We didn't see any girls. There weren't even any in the village. And we had to pledge our word of honor in classic, archaic form that we would absolutely do some things and absolutely not do others. The rules and regulations were nit-picky to the extreme. Some of them were ridiculous, except that having your integrity ride on them meant that these things were larger than life. They were bigger than the apparent pettiness of promising not to be even one step off the property after nightfall and all the other things we had to promise.

I had a lot of friends both among the good-kid/high-achiever types and the more ragged crowd: the jocks, poets and wild ones. I was also on the school's honor council each of the three years I was there. I had the experience of having to deal with incidents where some guy, even a good friend of mine, lied or otherwise broke his pledge. Sometimes I had to agree to recommend to the headmaster that the guy be expelled. This was not a joke, and it wasn't a kangaroo court either. We had a real role there. Our recommendations were taken very seriously. So on more than one occasion I had to make room for the values of honor and integrity at what was, for my friends and me, a pretty extreme price—saying goodbye to a great friend and knowing very well I probably would never see him again.

Even among many of the guys who wound up being kicked out, there was a kind of manly respect for the authenticity and realness of all that. Years later I saw what a gift this was to me. That school really hammered in this matter of personal integrity at all costs, and that became a very significant part of my make-up. Perhaps we could call it more of a moral than a spiritual training. It means a lot to me to this very day.

Sunday school and the Bar Mitzvah helped me appreciate Jewish history and where I'd come from culturally. But I didn't really become either religious or spiritual until I got to college.

What school did you attend?

Harvard. I was awarded a National Scholarship—in my case "Honorary" because I didn't need financial help. They only gave them to 50 out of 1200 kids in the entering class, as recognition of intellectual and leadership potential. So that was a big deal for me, coming from this tiny southern prep school in a village in Tennessee, and having grown up in a small town in North Carolina. Getting into Harvard was rare even at Webb and had hardly ever happened in my home town.

It was also much more, culturally, than I could possibly anticipate. This was Cambridge, Massachusetts, in late 1968: the counterculture, the anti-war movement, rock 'n roll, sex, drugs, SDS; you name it, I got exposed to it.

I participated in the student strike that occurred at Harvard in spring 1969, in reaction to the university's brutal use of police against student protesters. I had strong feelings about the issues that were being debated that whole year—the war, racial issues on campus, and so on. But I didn't get, as we then called it, "radicalized," until one morning just after dawn when the University called in the police to get the kids out of the administration building they'd taken over. I was there watching as the riot police got out of their buses. So were hundreds of others. And there were maybe 50 kids in the building, and 50 or so others out sitting on its steps. Five or six buses full of cops in riot gear roll into the yard, and we're all thinking that the dean of the school is going to get up in front of everyone and say, "OK, see? We really mean it now. So you have five minutes to vacate the building before we cart you out of there by force."

Instead the police just got off the buses, lined up, got an order from someone, and then suddenly charged in and started clubbing people in the head and throwing them off the steps and out of the building. That blew my mind and got me to choose sides real quick.

I almost got kicked out of Harvard that spring. After an anti-Viet Nam war demonstration, the university officials confronted me with pictures of myself standing on what turned out not to have been Henry Kissinger's desk. They put me on probation and relieved me of my honorary scholarship. I'm still kind of proud of that, actually.

Even then, though, the political side was not my main focus. Some of us, led by teaching assistants, set up what we called "Harvard New College," which was an attempt to re-vision the actual processes of teaching and learning there. The university was clearly a corporate knowledge factory in collusion with big business and big government in all kinds of ways. From our perspective, it didn't have much to do with pursuit of the "Veritas," or Truth, it proclaimed in its motto.

But that all played out on the stage of my more basic experience that first year: culture shock. I spent a lot of time lying on the couch in the living room of the suite I shared in my freshman dorm, smoking dope and feeling miserable. In a lot of ways I wasn't close to ready for the experience emotionally.

By the beginning of my second year something began to shift in me. I can't put an actual date on it, but I began having an insight that was actually oppressive and disturbing. I just began seeing that everybody, on every side of every issue, was mostly devoted to shoring up their own self-imagery. The way this insight pictured itself to me was quite specific. It was as if everybody were encased in a shroud of self-concern, or like they were each walking around in a cage of mirrors—with the mirrors on the insides of their cages. So they, we, were each and all mostly only seeing ourselves. This was as true of the righteous student radicals as it was of the police, the university officials, the faculty, the bad guys at Dow Chemical, everybody we were complaining about. And it was definitely true of me.

This became gravely distressing for me. I began to feel that my only shot at getting out of that cage was somehow to find God. And I didn't know how to do that. I suppose you could say that my being itself became a prayer. I knew I needed a living connection to God, which I'd never had, and not just Someone to believe in, either.

This was now the turn of the decade. Very early in 1970 I began to feel that my prayer or need was being answered. I sensed that God was showing up in my life, that I was now in contact with some kind of superior Intelligence that was guiding me, creating all kinds of synchronicities or magical coincidings, and moving me in a mysterious process that would give me what I knew I required.

Were you reading things that were more spiritually oriented?

I began, actually, by reading Tom Wolfe's book on Ken Kesey and the Merry Pranksters, *The Electric Kool-Aid Acid Test.* From there I found Ginsberg and Kerouac, the Beats. Ginsberg remained a potent influence, mostly by his example. I met him once, shook his hand; I don't think I even told him my name, it wasn't much of an interaction. But through the way he lived—the honesty, the candor, the daring, the willingness to open himself to all kinds of situations and experiences, the compassion for these poor yearning suffering pleasure-seeking human bodies—he was and remained a great teacher and example for me.

Ginsberg and Kerouac had a strong Buddhist background.

Yes, I was aware of that at the time. Yet I knew I wasn't ready to turn to Eastern spirituality. People would ask me, "Have you read any Alan Watts?" and I'd say, "Maybe sometime, but not yet." I didn't know why exactly.

From there the first really serious philosophical and spiritual study that I did—I say "really serious;" it was nothing like what it would have taken to get a degree in philosophy, but for me in my quest it was quite serious—was in my exposure to Martin Buber and *I and Thou*. Buber impressed me deeply. His writings also exposed me to the original masters of Hasidism, and their lives and teachings had an impact on me too.

There's a story from Buber's life that I like to tell people. It ties into my own work in a beautiful way. I believe this incident occurred at the very beginning of the First World War. At the time, as a young man, Buber was already a renowned Jewish mystic. He spent a lot of time in ecstatic states. One day a young fellow sought an appointment with him, needing his counsel. But Buber was in an ecstatic state that day and sent word that he needed to cancel or postpone the appointment. So the young man went away.

Two weeks later Buber heard that the guy had gone off to fight in the war and had already been killed. That deeply disturbed him. I think it shocked him back into life. He realized he'd completely missed "the other" who had appeared before him, needing his help, while he was absorbed in a state of mystic union. Indulging his own ecstasy, he'd thrown away his only opportunity to be there for this needful soul.

Buber's focus then shifted. He became the great twentieth century teacher of "I and Thou," which he called "dialogue," the relationship of the self with the real "other" in all its forms, including the absolutely mysterious divine "Other." In an aggressively narcissistic, psychological age, he prophetically called on his contemporaries not to reduce others and the whole realm of otherness to some subset of one's self. And his teaching on really relating to the other as irreducibly other than oneself thus had a great impact on me, beginning in my second year at college.

I had my share of psychedelic experiences during that time, also. But as I became more serious in my spiritual quest, I already was starting to move away from that. I wanted whatever my spirituality was to be sustainable without artificial stimulation.

That summer I went out to Colorado Outward Bound, a wilderness training school. It was a very good experience for me. There was something cleansing and clarifying about spending an entire month mostly above eight thousand feet, away from life as I had known it, living with a small group of men who had never met before the course, and who now had to cooperate to survive.

When I came down from the mountains, in July 1970, I went to Boulder, Colorado, which had become one of the three or four Meccas of the American spiritual counterculture. Once again I came face to face with the many avenues people were exploring those days. And it was at that point that I became ready to turn East.

I had been deeply instructed, indelibly impressed, by Buber's Judaic emphasis on relationship to the other, especially the great "Other," God. But I had begun to feel an intolerable limit in that. It seemed like that emphasis on relationship to the other was somehow preventing the transcendence or ecstasy from becoming as full as I wanted it to be. Now I felt that I needed to turn East to find that. I sensed I was not going to find what I needed in Judaism or Christianity.

The first book that I picked up that really spoke to me along these lines was Paramahansa Yogananda's *Autobiography of a Yogi*. It was the gateway for many Western seekers in those days. I was staying at someone's apartment in Boulder—I don't have any idea now whose—and just hanging out, meeting people. I had no job or obligations. So I basically spent three days immersing myself in this book.

It was a revelation, the whole world of spiritual and psychic phenomena that Yogananda opened up for me in the clever way he constructed that story. One chapter described his experiences of this or that miraculous, mindblowing thing, and then the next one explained it in rational, scientific ways, citing everybody from Einstein to Luther Burbank. He was very carefully addressing the empirical Western mind while opening up the more classically Eastern realms of psychic and spiritual experience.

By the time I finished reading the book, the evening of the third day after I'd begun, I was supercharged. I was so happy to have discovered this whole new world. I was getting that this was a big deal for me.

So as I lay down to sleep that evening, in my sleeping bag on some guy's couch in his living room there, the thought ran through my mind, "I wonder if yoga is going to be part of my path." That was exactly the way it phrased itself. A question, in the form of a wondering.

And as soon as I was done asking the question, I heard, somewhere back behind my left ear, a high-pitched, oscillating sound. I immediately thought, "Well, that's like the 'sound current' that Yogananda talks about meditating on in the book, so I'll just meditate on it." I didn't try to figure it out. I knew it wasn't the kitchen plumbing or something. It was obvious—"Meditate on this."

The moment I put my attention fully on that sound—and I was quite relaxed, there was nothing intense about my response, just a very natural listening—I experienced it shooting through my left ear and then directly into the very center of my brain. Instantaneously I exploded up from there. I felt myself to be a very tiny form of myself, bodily, on top of what felt like a waterfall of current, except it was rocketing straight up at astonishing speed. The current just blew right through me. I could say it blew the top off my brain but I was not experiencing the having of a brain at the time.

Instantly I came into what appeared to be another world, a landscape with purple mountains and a deep blue sky. But there was no time to notice much about it; the current just kept shooting up right through that whole world, until it penetrated the very apex of that sky and went into what I could not know.

The only way, in fact, that I was able to make any reckoning at all of what happened was afterward, by inference. Suddenly I was re-coalescing, funneling back down inside the body again, as a kind of burst of light that illuminated my insides entirely. And then there I was back on the couch, my known human self again. My first thought was, "Oh! I guess yoga is supposed to be part of my path." [Laughter]

Immediately, or at any rate fairly soon thereafter, it hit me that I had just, out of nowhere, with no preparation except reading the man's book, experienced a clear instance of what Yogananda described to be the ultimate realization of yoga: nirvikalpa samadhi, the formless state of divine Being. I had been blasted to infinity: no self, no mind, no form, no color, no world, no identifiable "anything," but only this immense, absolutely unbound expanse of bliss and potency of freedom unlike anything I could ever have known before.

Well, boy oh boy, did I want to get back to that again! [Laughter] I remember describing it to a few people that summer. Immediately I began looking around. "What spiritual group or path could I associate with that will allow me to learn how to activate this 'at will' like Yogananda said he could do, and Sri Yukteswar his teacher could do?" I wasn't moved toward Yogananda's Self-Realization Fellowship, because I could tell it was politically and socially a rather conservative organization. I still had plenty of political radicalism in me. If I were going to be a "yogi," I didn't just want to do yoga to achieve samadhi and, in effect, get out of life. I wanted it to transform life—even all of life, not just my own. I needed an activist yoga, if such a thing even existed.

So I began looking for a path that would answer that need. Meanwhile, as the days and weeks went by, I grasped more and more fully what had occurred. "Here the first time in this life that I even read about this supreme nirvikalpa samadhi that yogis seek for lifetimes, and now suddenly 'I have it.' Gee, maybe I've got a talent for this!" [Laughter] It all prompted what would become a rollercoaster of further seeking.

That fall of 1970, back at Harvard, I was introduced to a yoga organization from India that appeared custom-made for me. I'd rather not name it here, for reasons that should become clear. It was very politically and socially oriented. In the West it emphasized social service, creating schools, serving health and healing, along with spiritual practice. In India, in addition to such laudable, charitable, service activities, there was also an explicit, spiritually socialist economic philosophy and revolutionary activism, which the people involved there were living out with a lot of intense dedication. So I took the initiation from one of the monks who'd come to America, and got involved.

Other influences had already touched me. I had spent a few hours at the Meher Baba ashram in Myrtle Beach, South Carolina, near my family's home in North Carolina. I felt Meher Baba's presence very strongly as a blessing on my path. Other spiritual figures had come to me in dreams and reveries; something was obviously cooking. But now this sort of socialist yoga work became my focus. I soon moved into a house of people in Cambridge near the Harvard campus, and became one of the active leaders of that work in the Boston area. I began making plans to go to India as soon as I could swing it, to meet the guru—whom, again, I'd prefer not to name—and get as deeply into the yoga as possible.

The illumination in Boulder had come in the summer after my sophomore year. I spent my junior year at Harvard mostly getting more involved in this yoga. The format was pretty much traditional ashtanga, or "eight-limbed," yoga: yamas and niyamas, asana, pranayama, various stages of dharana or concentration and refinement, working with the chakras, bringing the energy up, meditating on bringing light into the highest chakra, the sahasrara, and achieving profound meditative contemplation, dhyana, leading ultimately to realization or samadhi and moksha, liberation. That was the practice. The key to it was the relationship to the guru. His spiritual blessing was said to make all the difference.

He was a powerful, mysterious character who was also leading the group's revolutionary activities in India. We kept hearing rumors that he'd been arrested, that he was getting framed by the Indian authorities for this or that trumped-up charge. For an old radical like me, that was actually part of the allure.

With a loan from my best childhood friend, I arranged to go to India during what would have been the first semester of my senior year at Harvard. My plan was to complete my degree the following summer. And that's what I did. It was a wild trip.

Culturally or spiritually?

Altogether. Encountering India at the age of twenty-one was an event in itself. The first place my traveling companions—housemates from the Cambridge yoga center—and I spent any time in was Calcutta. Talk about another planet. Calcutta is indescribable, so I won't even try, except to say that there is nothing remotely, not even remotely, like it in the United States. There wasn't then, and I'm sure there isn't now.

On top of that shock, the very day we arrived in Calcutta the guru's wife, who was his spiritual partner and consort, a heavyweight in his work, and nine or ten of the top monks in the organization, held a public meeting, denounced the guru with allegations of heinous activities on his part—and left his work. That very night!

My friends and I were a little rattled, but we weren't altogether surprised. He had already been jailed more than once by the Indian authorities. The allegations against this guru were pretty bizarre, but my orientation and that of my friends was, "We've come this far, we have to find out for ourselves. Innocent till proven guilty."

Within a couple of weeks I was able to have fairly close contact with him, in sittings with no more than another twenty or thirty people. He was indeed a very charming and powerful, captivating character. He could speak many languages—legend had it, all languages—and he was certainly fluent in English. Whenever he spoke to me, he always seemed to be letting me know that I didn't have any secrets from him. He would ask me things like, "What's the Latin root of 'sanguine'?"—and I'd never mentioned to anybody there that I had even taken Latin.

So, in a variety of ways, I got that I was an open book to this man. I didn't have any secrets from him. Not everyone was having that experience, by the way; each person seemed to be on their own journey with him.

Well, just as it was becoming clear that he could read my thoughts and my entire past at any time, one of the women associated with our group pulled me and another man aside. She pled for confidentiality, and then told us that she had just started a sexual affair with one of the supposedly celibate monks in the organization.

The other guy and I weren't too fazed by that. We'd heard rumors for some time that these guys in the orange robes, the avadhutas, eventually graduated into tantric sexual practices, classic graveyard yogas, if they had what it took.

But then this woman said, "Well, there's more. He and one of the other main monks here want to leave the organization, but they're afraid that if they do and try to stay in India, their lives will be in danger. Will you guys help me help them escape to the States?" Their idea was that she would marry the man she was having the affair with, and we'd all find another of the American women to do the same with the other one, and then they could split to the States.

Well, what do you do in a situation like that? Here these people were begging for help and fearing for their lives. I felt no option but to help out.

Two other things were going on that made my choice obvious. The first was a crisis in my yogic practice and quest. I did indeed feel a strong devotional attraction and appreciation for the guru. But I was already starting to feel, after a year and more of this yoga, that if I were to make my way back up to nirvikalpa samadhi, it was going to be a long piece of work. [Laughter] I'd be lucky to get the kundalini up to my navel, maybe, never mind the kind of rocket shot which had actually started from the center of my head. It hadn't come up the body from the base of the spine; it had blown from the middle of my brain right up and out the top. So I'd already begun despairing of the yogic path I was being taught. It was becoming burdensome to try to meditate on the chakras and do the mantras and all the rest of that endless labor.

Even while I was receiving more advanced, and tantalizingly promising initiations, I was feeling, "What's the point?" I kept having this feeling. It grew in me the whole time I was in India and then especially when I got back to the States. I kept feeling, "If the Self really is my Self, there's got to be some way for me to 'be the Self' right now, even if I also have to mature in my capacity to live in that Self-nature."

So I was outgrowing, or in any case falling off the vine, of that whole yogic search. I wasn't going to be able to make it in that yoga world no matter how much devotion I felt for the guru.

The second thing, then, was my total relationship to him. My initial feeling, after getting a request for help, was that I couldn't deny or refuse them. But since I was an open book to the guru, and since he was such a tantric wild man anyway, when I encountered him in the sittings he held, my orientation inwardly was, "This is what I'm doing. If you don't want me to do this, if this is going against my most auspicious development, please find a way to let me know. I'm sure you can." And everything that I picked up from him said, unmistakably, that I was doing exactly what I should be.

Admittedly, my take on his disposition was entirely subjective. I just interpreted certain things he said and did, and other things he didn't say and didn't do—certain ways he'd look at me just when mentioning, for instance, that some people need to apparently oppose Krishna and his work in order for the dynamic flux of nature to really make room for Krishna; that was a good one. Such things indicated to me that he knew exactly what was going on, and that it was my dharma or calling to leave, even to help these guys escape from his control.

That blew my mind. First of all I was stunned that he might actually be operating outside not just political laws but also common moral principles. One of the questions that came up, John, as we discussed doing this interview, was, "Is enlightenment beyond good and evil?" Well, here was this wild character who was operating in a circumstance of virtually absolute power over others. And, if I were simply to take at face value all the information that was coming in about this man, it was pretty shocking.

I couldn't dismiss any of it. I also couldn't disprove any of it, in terms of the more negative allegations. My own experience with him was relatively positive. But it was requiring me to hold extremes of understanding that were way outside what I had previously been taught or learned on my own about religion and spirituality.

We did indeed provide some assistance to these people. It was quite an adventure.

There was another major event during my time in India that sheds light on these issues we're considering. In the midst of our scheming to get these former monks out of the country—hiding them in a large city, getting them shaves, haircuts, and ordinary street clothes, arranging to get them passports, and so on—the other American guy and I ran into Ram Dass (Richard Alpert) in Delhi. We went to an arati, a traditional Hindu evening worship ceremony, that Ram Dass and his friends were holding in honor of his guru, Neem Karoli Baba, also called "Maharajji," the "little old man with the blanket" in the book, *Be Here Now*.

I was actually taken aback by how powerful that arati was. During it I felt the most powerful spiritual presence I had encountered in India, including personal darshans or sacred "viewings" with the guru I had visited. It was very potent, very peaceful, and nurturing at a deep level.

My friend and I asked Ram Dass and his people if we could go see Maharajji. They were hesitant at first but eventually they gave us the address and directions, along with a warning that we might not be allowed to see him.

The next day I picked up a copy of the New Testament in a bookstore. This was the "New English" version. Having grown up surrounded by the Christianity of the American South, I was permeated with bits and pieces of the King James version of Jesus's life and significance. I can still sing Christian hymns that I learned in the prep school I attended, even though no one there was trying to make us few Jewish kids convert; it was just something we all did. But I had never read the Gospels. The language had always seemed opaque to me. I'd just never been interested.

Now, here I am in Old Delhi, a yogi and spiritual seeker, picking up a relatively easy to read version of the Gospels, and suddenly I'm thinking, "I wonder what it was like for those guys, the Apostles?" I mean, I'd just been dancing at pretty close quarters with a man considered to be a God-man, a great God-realizer. His display of being a human being was off the charts from anything else I'd ever encountered, though I'd read about characters like him in *The Life of Milarepa* and other books.

So I picked up the New Testament and started reading through it and it totally blew my circuits. I was encountering Jesus almost as if I were right there with him. Having grown up Jewish, I knew the meaning of certain things to the Hebrews who were around him. For instance, "picking an ear of corn on the Sabbath." To us, today, come on, who cares? To them—they feared going to hell for that. That would be breaking the Law of Moses. You don't do that.

The Jesus I was reading about just upset their good Hebrew applecarts every which way he could, every chance he got, right through to the end. Particularly at the Last Supper and then, not missing a beat, right into and past the crucifixion. It was utterly shocking. The sugar-coated, sweet, pure and lily-white Jesus I'd been hearing about all my life was almost nowhere to be found.

So I am having this amazing encounter with the Jesus of the hallowed texts of Christianity, and meanwhile my friend and I sought out this mysterious saintly yogi, Maharajji, and eventually were permitted to attend one of his darshans. We had been wondering if we might discover him to be the true guru for ourselves—but neither of us had any such feeling during our time with him. Afterward, we were both ready to head back to Delhi right away. Curiously, though, his interpreter tracked us down in the crowded town of Vrindaban that evening and insisted that we come back for darshan again the next morning. We

tried politely to wangle our way out of the invitation; the man would-
n't hear of it, so we agreed to return to the saint's temple.

That next morning I awoke with the inspiration to write a play, a
kind of *Waiting for Godot*, except instead of two absurd characters on
the stage, it would be eleven: all of the apostles of Jesus but one, Judas,
as they supposedly sat waiting or sleeping while Jesus prayed in the
Garden of Gethsemane. In the play they would try to figure out what
the hell had just happened in their lives over the previous three years,
culminating moments before at the Passover dinner—later known as
"the Last Supper"—when their Master assured them they would all
fall away from him, and that one of them would betray him, although
he wouldn't say who and they didn't and couldn't really know.

Even from the moment of inspiration I knew that writing this
would be a way of integrating the shock of encountering a God-man
who appeared to be beyond the law, who had his own reasons for
doing what he did that did not conform to the dictates of conventional society. I was now encountering a very similar kind of God-
man in the New Testament. And this was not in some apocryphal,
heretical story, like The Gospel of Thomas or the Dead Sea Scrolls.
This was right there in the canonical Gospels, around which Christianity had been built for two thousand years. This was the official
story of Jesus that Christianity had accepted in detail since at least 300
A. D., or whenever the Council of Nicea decided, "This is it. This is the
way it really was. These books are the ones that tell the true story of
Jesus and his times."

Well, that morning at darshan I finally got up nerve and asked
Maharajji if he felt writing this play about Jesus and his apostles was a
good idea. His response blew me away. He practically shouted, "You
must! It will be a great success, and you have my blessing!" He yelled
this in his own language, and his interpreter, wide-eyed, shouted it to
me in English.

I immediately began taking notes, imagining snippets of the dialogue and action between the characters. Within ten days or so I left
India. I finished an initial draft of the play within weeks and another,
fairly complete one within a few months. By early 1972 it was more or
less finished. After that I just tinkered with it. It remained very central
to my meditation. It was a way of encountering the guru, the God-

man, the real event of having your life be given over to such a person with no other real recourse, such as the laws of the state or an official religious hierarchy. You don't have any protections, no one else to appeal to.

That contemplation, through my creative work on *While Jesus Weeps*, was important. Other key things also occurred after India. When I came back to the States a sequence of events eventually led me to Ramana Maharshi's teaching. I'd heard of him in India, but I became more fully aware of his life and teaching that spring, 1972. While on a trip to Canada—actually, with the same friend with whom I had helped the yogis escape India, and with whom I'd traveled to meet Maharajji—I found a book that presented his teachings on the meditation he offered, called *Self-enquiry*. In the collection of teachings, this sage, who had died in 1950 just days before I was born, urged seekers to ask or feel into the question, "Who am I?," while focusing attention on a place in the right side of the chest. He asserted that this spot was the real seat of Consciousness in the Heart.

I'd never heard of such a thing. I had only heard of the central chakra, the anahata in yogic literature, also the heart center of the soul in mystical and devotional traditions such as Sufism and esoteric Christianity. But I felt strongly attracted to Maharshi, especially the radiant intensity of his eyes in his photos. And I so wanted to find a path that would establish me directly in the Self, without having to engage in yogic gymnastics of seeking. This was what he seemed to promise. I felt I had nothing to lose by attempting the meditation technique he offered.

My friend was with his girlfriend, and I was—once again—camping out in the living room in my sleeping bag. Before going to sleep, I sat down by myself to meditate as Maharshi prescribed. At first nothing special was happening. Periodically I asked his recommended question, "Who am I?" trying to feel what might be beyond my thinking mind, while also trying to feel toward whatever this center might be somewhere in the right side of my chest. Suddenly I felt this extremely intense, infinitesimal point, deep, deep in the right side of my chest, just open up. Then it was as if an extremely bright and hot laser of energy and feeling leaped up and forward from an unfathomable depth in my heart. This was followed by a wave of bliss.

Though my external awareness didn't completely disappear, I understood in retrospect that this was a kind of samadhi, an initiation of the intensely consuming feeling of the Self in the true seat of the Heart. While it didn't entail as complete a dissolution of phenomenal awareness as what I had gone through in the ascent to samadhi when I first read Yogananda, it was in some ways even more profound for me. At the time, whatever its depth or meaning, I was just astonished. I felt, "Oh my gosh! I must be close to enlightenment, Self-realization at last!"

I accepted Ramana Maharshi as my guru on the spot. Over the coming days and weeks I devoured all of his teachings and the stories of his life. My focus on him and his approach led to spiritual loneliness. Most seekers in America were either into yogic experience or mystical union, or else Buddhist approaches to insight. Nobody I knew had ever heard of or felt that power seat on the right side of the chest. None of my yogi friends could relate. I wound up rather isolated, trying to take refuge in a place of ultimate Consciousness that, for all I knew, was actually located maybe underneath or perhaps behind my right lung.

Years later, with Adi Da, I learned that the right portion of the physical heart organ is actually located to the right of the sternum, and, sure enough, the physical, biological source of the heartbeat is in what is called the sinoatrial node, at the back of the right atrium, there in the heart organ itself. At the time, I didn't know how to make sense of this opening and illumination. The feeling of it continued from that moment on. I didn't feel it as strongly as I had in the moment of initiation, but from then on it was always there at the physical as well as spiritual center and ground of my being, no matter what was happening. So I couldn't deny it, but I also didn't know how to comprehend it.

Armed with Maharshi's writings and talks, I tried my best to "dive into the Heart," as he had instructed. Over the following year and a half many insights and intuitions of the nature of consciousness, and further wellings up of the deep bliss of the Self-nature in the Heart, occurred for me. But by the early fall of 1973, I began to feel disturbed. I would have these blissful intuitions in meditation or while reading the teachings, but in the very next instant, I'd be a basket-case in my life. What to do about diet, sex, relationships, career, family—life? I didn't have a clue.

And Maharshi wasn't much help. He'd say, in his talks, that others didn't need to renounce the world as he had. But he didn't offer much by way of useable advice to a kid trying to realize the Self in the wild and woolly trenches of America, a generation after his own death in the last vestiges of traditional India.

To my chagrin, I had to admit to myself that I was suffering at least as much as I had been when I started seeking several years before—if not a good deal more. I sensed that I really needed a teacher, but where in the world was I going to find one? Maharshi had not appointed anything like a successor. In his identification with the One Self, he refused, for the most part, to acknowledge relatedness to "others" in his speech. He wouldn't even acknowledge having disciples or being anyone's guru while he lived, though he obviously acted out the work of transmission and instruction, and tears of compassion would often stream down his cheeks. So Ramana had not provided a successor. I meanwhile felt I could not possibly accept anyone who had not realized the Heart as he had. And no teacher I'd studied was talking anything like the language of realizing the Self in the Heart.

I had, however, heard about one man, an American actually, who supposedly claimed that Maharshi was something of a spiritual father to him. He was named Franklin Jones, and he had started an ashram out in Los Angeles in 1972. I'd seen ads for his first book, The Knee of Listening, *but hadn't felt moved to get it.*

Did you find it in a bookstore?

Yes, I kept dropping in to this spiritual bookstore all that early fall. I never asked for it, but I was always keeping an eye out for that particular book.

Was it in Cambridge that this happened? Where did you actually find the book?

At the time, fall 1973, I was teaching in a private school near New Orleans, Louisiana. I was trying to save up money to go to Maharshi's ashram in India during the summers.

So you took on a teaching career after you graduated from college?

Yes, I guess you could say so. I didn't know what else to do. After graduating I went back home to North Carolina to live with my family. I was there for three quarters of a year or so, working as the grunt on a construction crew, trying to figure out what to do next. It dawned on me, "You're going to have to earn a living somehow while continuing with your quest." I figured the only thing I might have a shot at doing was teaching at a private school, which didn't require a state teaching credential. So in the summer of 1973 I sent my resumé around to about fifty private prep schools, and one of them, outside New Orleans, happened to need somebody on very short notice. I headed down there to teach Civics and Ancient History—reading it at night, teaching it the next day. [Laughter]

Every week or two, that fall, I'd drop into the local spiritual bookstore. I knew I wanted that book, *The Knee of Listening*, but I still didn't want to order it through the mail and pay extra for the hardback version. I figured it would come out in paperback some day. When it did, his second book, *The Method of the Siddhas*, arrived at the bookstore at the same time.

I found them on a Friday afternoon. I was supposed to grade a briefcase full of mid-term exams. Instead, I spent the weekend devouring those books and recognizing that this American man, just a decade or so older than me, was my guru. It was obvious to me that he had realized the Heart, though he was living it in a different way than Ramana Maharshi had. And, he had just started a spiritual community a year and a half earlier, out in California. I was thrilled. This was the answer to more of a prayer than I had even dared to conceive.

I immediately contacted his community out here in California and became what was then called a "corresponding student." I received volumes of information on what to do about my diet and every other practical aspect of my life. [Laughter]

What were some of the things that were not addressed in your earlier spiritual pursuits?

Well, certainly not by Ramana Maharshi, who had become my most profoundly initiatory guru though no longer alive bodily. His spiritual presence had been very active for me, but I hadn't been able to find helpful practical guidance. Also, his teachings, when all was said and done, contained a profound bias toward the unmanifest. A good indication of how deeply I'd gotten into the classic Oriental bias through his influence showed up in my initial take on Adi Da's prescription for enquiry. Adi Da had used, and now taught, the enquiry question, "Avoiding relationship?" When I first read it in *The Knee of Listening*, I thought he meant you were supposed to be checking to make sure you are avoiding relationship—not opening up into its inherent reality in Being. Later I grasped the error of my initial interpretation.

In contrast to Maharshi, Adi Da—then "Bubba Free John"—was saying, "I'm going to tell you exactly how to live." Sure enough, in *The Knee of Listening* and especially *The Method of the Siddhas*, he made it clear that he was going to be a demanding and sometimes wild teacher. Having done my homework in India and in writing *While Jesus Weeps*, I saw what I was signing up for, I accepted it, and I was looking forward to it.

I came out here to join his community in California in January, 1974, and quickly became involved as a writer and editor. That is how I developed a close personal connection to him for the first several years. I certainly had lots of spiritual experiences, but I have to say, in retrospect, that there were only a few that equaled what had occurred for me before I came to him. Most of my time with Adi Da was about getting humanized, getting "here" as much as I could, and getting an immense education in many aspects of human life and culture.

In terms of his own work, Adi Da in those early years was trying hard to pull us out of what he called "vital shock."

Which means?

The shock of being alive, how the sheer fact of it dissociates us from our own organismic existence. Much of his early work was just getting people to feel into being their own bodies. Of course there were many sides to it, but this was one. At the same time, while I had and have no regrets about having participated in that experiment— well, that's not true, I wish I hadn't needed to stay there so long—and though I'm pleased and proud in some ways to have been in that school, in hindsight I can also see that Adi Da's wild man's way of conducting himself with people was reinforcing that shock at the same time he was trying to help us understand and transcend it.

That's one of the dangers of what he and others have called "crazy wisdom" teaching methods. The shock treatments that such teachers administer may well guarantee that only the hardiest of souls will be able to fulfill the spiritual quest for awakening in their company. Others might very well fulfill something upon leaving—which is what happened with me. [Laughter]

I don't want to diminish the gifts I received from Adi Da. They were huge. I continue to have great appreciation for what I regard to be his pioneering work, following on Ramana Maharshi's. To me those two are like the Liebnitz and Newton of evolutionary spirituality for the human future, at least from the twentieth century forward. Liebnitz and Newton independently invented the calculus within a generation of one another. That gift has transformed science, technology—thus, the world as we know it. Ramana and Adi Da have given humanity both the wisdom and the transmission of the living link between infinite Consciousness and finite embodiment. They are the progenitors of something great. I don't think that "something" is well understood yet, or even very well elaborated in our individual and cultural lives. I think my work will in this respect point back to them with great homage. It will help clarify and bring perspective to their immense contributions. In effect, it will be saying, "Hey, everybody, take a look. We haven't yet gotten what these men have given us."

It's like the scientists who followed Einstein. He was a brilliant physicist, but others then stood on his shoulders to see what could be revealed by further study of physics.

Right. That's how I regard my relationship to these two great masters. I've written of it in exactly that way—that "standing on the shoulders of giants" quotation is from Isaac Newton—in my book, *Waking Down*.

How many years did you spend with Adi Da?

About nineteen.

What did you get from that relationship and his teaching that you feel is true?

One of the main things was, in my attention to and study of him personally, seeing a man living a life that embodied the realization of transcendental, divine Consciousness. Watching that life not negate but rather fully embrace the body-mind and the play of relationships. Seeing him allow his own awakened body-mind all of its natural display, including his feelings, reactions, and desires, in ways that many more orthodox spiritual approaches would view as negative or inappropriate to either the aspiring or the realized life. Being around Adi Da I got to see someone live a very vibrant realization that appeared to me to be an advance upon the more orthodox, restrained, traditional demonstration. I saw him bring realization to life in a vigorous, profound, and vulnerable way.

Something happened, then, after nineteen years which either gradually or suddenly suggested it was time to pursue some different kind of activity?

I think it's important for me to respond to that question in some detail. First, I want to say that another great thing I got from Adi Da only became apparent to me after I had left him and gone through my own autonomous awakening. It was this: I saw that, in the force field of fundamental Existence, for lack of a better phrase in the Satsang of the capital "H" Heart, he had continuously nurtured me all along and prepared me for my freedom.

Now, of course, this does not jibe with his stated teaching or with how orthodox Daist practitioners might view a person like me, but it is true to my own experience. Underneath all of the storm and fury, the wildness and the theatricality of his ways of working with people, and other qualities that I now very intentionally depart from as best I can in my own work, something much more profound was happening. All that was like storm waves on the surface of the ocean. Underneath was this five-mile deep current, wider than the mouth of the Amazon, that was and is always sustaining existence, freedom, life, truth, love, Being. I can't talk about events on the surface without acknowledging that vast current.

Well—what would induce me to leave there? Over the years, Adi Da despaired of eliciting or evoking in us a capacity to duplicate his own radical, free exploration of existence and experience. In the early years, he was confidently teaching "the Way of Radical Understanding" in the context of devotion to him as one's guru. The idea was that our relationship to him as guru would provide necessary transmission, counsel, aid, and instruction. This would allow us to mature in our own free exploration of existence so that eventually we would understand reality as he did and does—on the basis not of intellection, but of realization.

As the years went on, however, Adi Da concluded, I think with some bitterness, that no one else would be able to understand in this profound way. And with the great transition that occurred in his life in 1986—what he referred to as his "Divine Emergence as the World-Teacher," which came to be the title of my biography of him—as of that time, he shifted gears.

From that point forward, the priorities were reversed. The focus of devotees' practice became guru-devotion: worshipful love of him and self-surrendering obedience to him. In the midst of that life of energetic attention and devotion to him as guru, to his bodily person as well as his universal spiritual presence and transcendental divine Consciousness, each one's radical understanding would, he now taught, come forth quite naturally. Devotion became the way, and understanding of one's own existence and experience, a by-product.

Bhakti?

Yes, bhakti, but also seva, service. In other words, it wasn't only the exercise of devotion, but the principle of devotion as the context for a whole, guru-oriented or guru-centric life, first, foremost, and always.

I didn't get this until years later, but it was at that point, beginning in the later 1980s, that I began falling off the boat of his work.

Part of what didn't work for me was his increasing insistence on renunciation, which began in 1986. In earlier years of my life, for instance when I went to India in 1971, if someone had assured me that you have to become a monk to awaken, I would have said, "Great. Where do I sign up?" I might have been scared and uneasy, but I would have done it. And, like many of Adi Da's devotees, I had some pretty remarkable, grace-given moments of renunciation, especially in 1986. There were times of quite natural relinquishment of concern for sex, preferred foods, and other preoccupations of the desiring body.

But, by the beginning of the new decade, I was not interested in that. As he began insisting on a more austere life of renunciation of small-"s" self in embrace of devotion to him as the exclusive foundation of one's life, I wasn't able to do it.

A couple of things occurred that propelled me out the door. One had to do with the issue of my integrity. At one point in late 1990 and early 1991, I was on the East Coast. I did not want to be involved in the leadership of Adi Da's work here in California. I knew from experience that every time I got involved in some leadership role, I'd manage to screw up. Then Adi Da would get angry at me and mete out disciplines that would help me get straight and fly right—until I screwed up again. I didn't want to even get near that whole potential cycle any more.

But then in early 1991, he found out I was on the East Coast and requested that I come back to California and take up just such a leadership role again. He hadn't known I was on the other side of the country, and frankly, that had been fine with me. [Laughter] Whereas in the past I would always leap for such an opportunity to serve, and in any case would obediently comply, this time I dug in my heels. I did not want to do it. Eventually, though, with my friends back in California twisting my arm in a variety of ways, I capitulated.

Sure enough, despite my best efforts, within a few weeks the exact kind of scenario I'd experienced too many times before occurred— which I had dreaded, and had predicted in letters to friends. My job was to communicate his wishes and requirements to, and to bring news of relevant responses back to him from, a particular sector of the organizational management team and the general community. And the way I always wound up doing that was nerve-wracking and demoralizing for me.

Adi Da had two rules for communications to him: Only bring him the truth, and only bring him good news. These were his precise requirements. And his demands upon people and the organization were extremely difficult to fulfill. I'd say that is putting it lightly, maybe even euphemistically. So, particularly after a few experiences of getting castigated for bearing bad news, my orientation was, I would always try to make sure the news was good, and if I had to fudge on its truthfulness while getting it to make the shift from bad news to good, I was more willing to risk that than just lay out bad news.

Again, sure enough, within a few weeks of my tenure in leadership in early 1991, Adi Da caught me in a lie. As on similar occasions in the past, I received some stern communications from him and was given a variety of corrective additional disciplines to observe.

This time, though, something different took place. My response was different in a fundamental way. Typically, in the past, I'd bemoan my fate and wonder and scheme about how I could get back into the guru's good graces. There was a little of that in me, yes, this time around—but where I really went with the riot act he read me about myself was, "He's right. I did lie. I lied."

Even though it seemed to me, as always, that this was how most people were agreeing to live who tried to conduct communications with him—even though it seemed to me on some level that he wouldn't have it any other way, really—nonetheless, my reflections pretty much sidestepped all those concerns. This time around, I was looking at the event face on. "I did lie. In fact, I have become a liar. A kind of spiritual bureaucrat, as he often complains I am. I lie as part of my way of doing what's supposed to be done around him. It seems to me that my truth, the truth, the actual factual state of things, is to be subordinated to the greater principle of service to the guru in the form of bringing him 'good news.'

"But—is that me? Is that who I really am? No. This is not who I really am at all. So what am I doing?"

That reflection took me back to the training I received at that quaint, old-timey Southern prep school as a boy. And, at that point, I began to realize that there was something about the way Adi Da's work was set up that appeared to evoke lies, subterfuge, and something like ruthless, egoic court politics in the well-meaning spiritual seekers who became his devotees. It certainly did in me. This incident was my first serious look at what I had become, as a man, in the process. I didn't like what I saw. It was like looking into a dark chasm.

That was the first of the things that occurred that eventually prompted me to leave his work. The second came later that same year. It had to do with sexuality and in particular, celibacy.

For years Adi Da had been trying every which way to help people realize intimate sexual love and marriage as truly transformative yogic sexual tantra—a process that would increasingly release and refine their available energy and attention for their primary, all-encompassing spiritual relationships with him, their divine guru. That summer, after another concerted but, from his perspective, fruitless effort along these lines with the people closest nearby (he was living at the time on the island sanctuary his work maintains in Fiji), in exasperation he gave up.

Word went out, directly from him I can assure you, that everyone involved in spiritual leadership on his behalf in all the sub-communities of the work around the world should immediately embrace what he was calling "celibate renunciation." In other words, we should all just give up these marriages and intimacies we'd been trying to sustain all these years.

In his classically extreme way, Adi Da left no room for partial responses. He had tried for twenty years or more to help us truly spiritualize our sexuality and intimacies. The experiment clearly had not worked. Now we should all just bite the bullet and leave our partners, once and for all. From his point of view, none of us were capable of "yogic sexual sadhana," or truly liberating practice as sexual tantrics. Therefore, since we were all getting older, and so was he, we should say goodbye to our partners, give him a vow of lifelong celibate renunciation, and get on with the work at hand. From his point of view, two decades of attempting to manifest heroic tantric capacity was plenty. Our experiment was over.

It's not that the notion of celibacy was new. Though it was anathema in the early years of his work, Adi Da had been giving it more and more credence as a practice for his devotees especially since the mid-1980s—for the very reasons I've just indicated.

Nonetheless, I personally freaked. I didn't want to do it. Not because I had a great relationship that I wanted to keep—on the contrary, I was in a terrible relationship that I was still hoping my wife and I could fix. But more that that, I just felt, in the most primal way, "This is not me. I can't do this. It's not who I am and it's not going to be who I am, either."

Well, given my central leadership role, my resistance was not smiled upon. I went back and forth several times over the course of several months. First I capitulated. Then I reneged—I just said I couldn't do it. I promptly got my arm twisted, along with my then-wife and other renegades, and capitulated again. Then I reneged again. The cycle repeated itself three times.

Finally Adi Da got so upset with me and a few others in key leadership roles that at one point we were excommunicated from the community. Then the very next day he insisted we just had to accept a slightly less stringent form of discipline he was offering at that time—a minimal form of intimacy, where you would only have a few minutes each day with your partner, and only stay together one night a month. I had recently written, and we'd published with much hullaballoo, a full-length biography of him; another of the renegades had just published another major book about the work—it was unacceptable to him that the two of us, as visible as we were, not get with the program he was calling for.

In addition to the sheer shock of being expelled, I also saw clearly that my intimate relationship could not possibly be healed under the conditions we were now having to enter. How in the world could my partner and I work out our intimate problems when the very fact of having a relationship was the cause of our expulsion and disgrace? We were checkmated, from my point of view. Along with the others, I capitulated one final time.

"Checkmated" probably sounds pretty cold and calculating in relation to one's beloved guru, the revealer of divine truth to one's heart. True. I won't pretend I was thinking very much like an ardent, loyal devotee at that point.

For some time—even long before the incident when I was caught lying, some months earlier—I had become increasingly cynical about the actual, political workings of my teacher's community and organization. I didn't suspect anyone of malicious intent. Everyone, I felt strongly, had only the best and noblest of intentions. Starting with him. But the way we all lived left so much to be desired. And I was beginning to sense that it was never going to change. The day was not going to come when we would all become true devotees at last and the whole tenor of the community life around him would change. I began to admit to myself that that terribly-longed-for transition was not going to come. Ever.

That acknowledgment in itself was extremely disturbing for me. After years of being frequently criticized by him as an incompetent "failed case," a self-glamorizing sycophant, a double-minded (that is, extremely ambivalent) ego with no real capacity either as a devotee or as a communicator, I had managed to write and publish a full-length biography of Adi Da that was fairly well received. It was not authorized in the sense of his having read it in advance of publication; indeed, when he read it I was already on tour promoting it around the U. S. and other countries. It was in a way my last and best service to him. Word got back to me that he had said it was "basically fine," which, coming from him, was like "triple A plus." Then he had listed six or seven typos he'd found in the text, which I felt was his way of saying to me, "I read the whole thing; I'm not saying 'basically fine' on the basis of skimming through it. Good work." So putting that book out was a huge achievement.

As it happened, the publication date—mid-April 1990—was just before my fortieth birthday. So here I am, very much a Jewish-American guy in mid-life, and I get a taste of what it is to accomplish something. And I feel and know that I am here to accomplish a lot. Yet I am getting the sense, now in late 1991 and early 1992, during and after the celibacy wars, that if I stay in any way centrally involved in serving Adi Da's work, I am never going to be permitted to accomplish much at all.

After writing the biography I had, for fun, started writing a fantasy sci-fi-type novel, with spiritual themes of course—and had wound up setting up a little company around its publication with financial investors. Yet there was a problem there too. Everyone who knew about it knew very well that if we ever told Adi Da about it, he'd shut the project down in a heartbeat. A lot of people liked it, had high hopes for it, even invested little chunks of money in it—some not so little—but it was nothing we could possibly bring to the guru's attention. For years he had berated me for a lack of creativity. But now my creativity was coming forward in ways that he would never permit if he were informed of them.

So all of these currents were swirling around in me, but in the final analysis they were secondary to something much more fundamental. Sometime after leaving Adi Da and his work, which I finally did in August 1992, I saw that, after that day I'd spent in the limbo of being kicked out of the community for six months' probation and discipline, I had never really come back.

Yes, the next day we received something like clemency—but I never quite got back in the door. Somewhere in that whole crisis of my relationship with Adi Da, I began to suspect that his greater interest in me, or for me, was in my obedient ongoing practice and service to him and his mission. It no longer had much to do with any hope or intention on his part for my actual liberation, at least not in this lifetime. I felt he had given up on me as a potential realizer, whereas I could not possibly give up hope for myself even though my prospects were bleak indeed.

To this day I could never prove this. But it wasn't about proof or anyone else's conviction. I began to grasp that I was no longer really bowing to him as my divine guru. When I would try to make what he called a "full-feeling prostration," even if I could get my body down onto the ground, there was a big part of me still standing with my arms folded across my chest. As I recognized more and more that this was so, I fell off the truck, or out of the boat, of the work that I had assumed I would be committed to for eternity. And after about eight months, in 1992, of laying low and not practicing much at all, but just trying to make sense of what was going on with me, I formally discontinued my membership there.

How long after that did you begin actually teaching on your own? Was there a time of "sorting"?

Oh yeah. There was a time of sorting things out.

Particularly after nineteen years of involvement.

Yes. My awakening occurred almost immediately after my leaving Adi Da's work, and the changes it entailed and prompted made for a huge transition.

In one sense it was a huge transition, over some time. But in another sense, as you have reported your experience of recognition in a restaurant, something happened to you that was a dramatic, sudden shift— not a gradual transition at all.

Yes. It was quite unexpected, though I could tell something remarkable was brewing. But that's getting a little ahead of the story here.

Back at that time, in 1992, anyone who was tempted to leave Adi Da's work was forcefully presented with the warning that they were breaking their eternal vows and severing their eternal bond with him as the God-man and Source of grace in their lives. We had signed literal, detailed vows of eternal devotion and practice along these lines. What prospect could one expect, then, other than "hellish karmas for lifetimes"? I'm not exaggerating for effect. That was the precise phrase that was used

Well, I knew the history of those vows. I knew exactly when and why Adi Da, frustrated with people's coming and going from commitment to the practice, had insisted that these vows be written and signed by every single member of his community. It was in part an attempt to get people serious about their commitment, so they would understand the seriousness, the gravity of the connection, and not casually either enter or leave it.

This wasn't just a fear-based, fire-and-brimstone political device for keeping people in the corral. It had immense significance on all kinds of levels, and it was, I suppose, his adaptation of a very traditional form, a good example of which is the Tibetan Buddhist samaya vow of loyalty and fidelity to one's guru.

When I left, one of my very good friends called to ask me to please reconsider. He brought up these vows and the likely hellish karmas that would accrue to me for breaking them. His words didn't fall on deaf ears. I mean, I had seen Adi Da with my heart and whole being as the great GOD-MAN, the Supreme Divine Being in Person.

In particular, there had been one occasion with him, while I was living on the island in October 1989 writing that biography, that was a greater samadhi than anything I had ever experienced or lived before, either with him or previously. It was so supernal that it actually took years after my awakening for me to grok altogether what had occurred in that incident. It was an ultimate revelation of the evolutionary future of everyone and everything, such an extreme intensification of Conscious Love that the entire cosmos literally dissolved in infinite Bliss; in his own language, an instant of "Outshining" or "Divine Translation." I had been drawn into this, I had seen that he is This, and I wasn't even able to recollect its most auspicious and intense aspects in the mind until years later. I guess that was the last gift that I needed from him spiritually during my years as his formal devotee.

On some level then, did you know you were going to move on from that point?

It wasn't in my head at all. But in retrospect I can see that, as I write in my book *The White-Hot Yoga of the Heart*, from then on I "did everything wrong." Not literally so—I finished the biography, went on a successful tour speaking about it and him and his grace, and kept trying to practice until the crises I spoke of a few moments ago, which came a bit later. But I think I was on a trajectory in Being that was taking me out of his work.

What occurred, John, was that during that eight-month free fall before I formally took my leave—or, between my day of being excommunicated and when I finally got up and walked out the door—I connected with a couple of old friends whom I'd known in the community. The woman had been a formal devotee briefly, and the man had been what was called a "Friend."

This guy had become a shamanic teacher and mentor himself. We spoke a few times that summer of 1992, before and shortly after my formal departure. He proposed he could be of some help to me. His orientation was, "You didn't fail. You graduated. Now it's time to view Adi Da not as your 'teacher' but as your 'example.' This is about Self-realization. You have to find your own way into it—just like he did."

In many spiritual cultures I think there is a tradition for that. Those last steps have to be done alone.

Yes, that's right.

In some cases, spiritual teachers or gurus will literally throw you out of the ashram at the right time in order for you to actually gain that realization.

Right. And for all I know, something like that is what happened to me. [Laughter] Of course Adi Da would never say such a thing; it's not his style. But that in effect is what did happen.

I began doing some shamanic work with this man and a small group of people here in the Bay Area who were linked up with him. Again to condense a detailed story into a few sentences, I did some journeying with them using psychoactive substances. Early on, we used a combination of ecstasy and psilocybin; later he replaced the ecstasy with ayahuasca.

I hadn't used any substances since very early in my years with Adi Da. It definitely set a different tone for part of my new life. But the substance journeying, I need to say, was really quite a secondary aspect of that new life and the awakening that soon blossomed in it. Prior to awakening I only did a couple of those journeys, one in late August and the other in early November. I left the Daist community that August, began this shamanic work at more or less the same time, and awakened in early December.

The primary thing that occurred, from my perspective, was not journeying. It was shoehorning myself out of the tight lock that Daism represented for me. It was risking everything to extricate myself and to recover my integrity as a man no matter what the consequences, hellish or not. As I put it in a discussion with this shamanic mentor, the real empowerment came from "daring to grasp the means of my own realization." Leaving such a supreme God-Man against the odds of "hellish karmas for lifetimes," daring to grope my way toward and then into my own direct realization of infinite existence—all of that turned out to have been most empowering for me.

Did you really feel there was an official stance that Adi Da had taken regarding people who were going to disavow his teaching? Or do you think that stance was created by his community?

It was his explicit stance, at least at that time. It was one of those official stances that neither he nor they will perhaps acknowledge. Even then, it never came out in print under his name. But it was most definitely understood by people around him that he was espousing precisely that orientation to people's prospective departures.

Since then, perhaps things have changed a bit. But I think that Adi Da and the people closest to him still hold it in essentially the same light, whatever the official disposition is. He is regarded to be the supreme and only God-Realizer of his stature, not only in this but in any historical time, ever. Having written his biography, not just once but many times in many published forms, I still understand the esoteric logic of this claim. I don't agree any more, but I do understand it.

For one who is convinced of the truth of that claim, what can leaving him be but a leap into hells of self-absorbed narcissism? If he is the supreme and only real source of divine grace, where else could true grace possibly be found?

At that time, I bet everything I had, everything I was, on finding true grace elsewhere. I did leave. And for me, as it turned out, the cautionary warning about the fate of hellish karmas for lifetimes worked superbly. It crystallized things. Whatever relief I might have felt superficially upon leaving, in my heart of hearts I felt like anti-matter. I felt like God must be allergic to me. And yet somehow I had to dare to find grace and to find myself. My shamanic friend was saying, "Go for Self-realization." I'm thinking, "Yeah, right. Let me just recover my basic integrity as a man. Best case scenario, let me find Spirit again and be able to take a breath." The shock of leaving and uprooting myself from the most profound source of grace that I was aware of anywhere in all the worlds was, in a paradoxical way, most catalytic for me.

Without knowing it, I had embarked upon the "fulfillment stage" of my quest. Without knowing it, I invoked the living Goddess in a kind of humorous, side entrance way. Someone recently asked me why; all I can say is, it was time. My invocations were not even intentional. She just began showing up in ways I couldn't altogether figure out. Luckily, my mental comprehension proved quite unnecessary. It was beside the point. I knew something was going on, something big and fundamentally out of my control.

My inquiry into the Self-nature of consciousness became instantly sustainable and profound as soon as I regenerated it, that Fall. I had been enquiring into consciousness on and off since 1972, often for hours at a time, trying to realize the "witness consciousness" and beyond. Now, "Bang!" The first time I earnestly asked my particular enquiry question—which is one I had come up with during my Daist years, but had never seriously permitted myself to acknowledge as such until leaving—well, all I had to do was ask one intense time, and I fell into that witness consciousness for keeps. The question was, "What is it that is conscious of everything arising?" The answer, on that occasion, was not any kind of thought but the reality of consciousness itself.

It took awhile for me to grok that that's what had occurred. It was a wild time of learning on a whole new curve, where there were no rules except the ones that revealed themselves at the time. I was having to find all that out my own way. The finding was itself the Way.

Very quickly my work yielded a fundamental awakening, through both profound investigation of the Ground of Consciousness and also this mysterious dance with the Goddess. Not so much in any archetypal form—though She did reveal herself in one particular form, which I only recognized at the time of the awakening—but more in material forms. One was the mountain here, Mt. Tamalpais. I've named my organizations after this mountain, because, as I later realized, it had attracted my attention, captivated and caught me, you might say, and held me here as I was free-falling out of my entire previous life. It was a divine form for me.

Like the mountain Arunachala for Ramana Maharshi?

That's how it feels to me, yes. Arunachala has been revered as a direct expression of Shiva or Consciousness in India since ancient times. It's a bit different with Mt. Tam. A lot of people love her and many feel she's a sacred, living being. I regard her as a touchstone of embodied Consciousness.

More obviously to me at the time, a number of special women showed up in my life. Periodically during the months of my awakening journey, there were these moments of flat-out darshan nearly as profound as anything I had ever experienced with my guru or anywhere else.

With these women?

With these women. It was very captivating. We were all aware something magical was happening. I was beyond moved by it—I was awed. My years with Adi Da had exposed me, more as an observer than as a real initiate, to some of what can go on when the living Goddess is active in a spiritual process. Now I was able to grasp that that is exactly what was happening, in these encounters I had with these women friends. Still, it was blowing my mind.

I should add that though, on a couple of occasions, these encounters were sensual, they never involved full sexual intercourse. I had not been sexually intimate, fully, with anyone since leaving the Daist community. Just before I left, my marriage to my second wife in the community had ended.

Now, in the first couple of days of December, I began an intimacy with one of these women I was getting to know in this special, intense way. That consorting was, obviously to me and I think to her, a tantric spiritual initiation. I had never experienced anything like it.

This precipitated the incident you mentioned earlier, when I was sitting one morning at the local Good Earth restaurant, waiting for my breakfast. I looked out the window and realized the seamless "Only-ness" of reality. It was immediately obvious that this was the fulfillment of my quest. I felt, "Oh, right! This is what I've been trying to do. This is what I've been trying to get at all this time, who knows how many lifetimes."

It was at once clear that my heart had broken open to infinity and it wasn't going to get stuffed back in. It was the simplest kind of transition. There was no experience associated with it. It was the most bare recognition, and yet the most profound. I was sitting in a restaurant. They brought my pancakes and eggs, and I ate them. It was nowhere near as dramatic for me as so many other spiritual transitions had been.

It sounds like a Zen type of transition.
Yes. It was very simple.

Before enlightenment you saw the mountains, and after enlightenment you saw the mountains.
And ate the pancakes. [Laughter] The feeling-tone associated with it was not, "Oh my God! How amazing!" It was, "All right! Good. Hey—not bad. About time!" And then, following right on that, was, "What in the world am I going to do in relation to Adi Da and the whole community I came from? This is outside that entire universe of possibilities." [Laughter]

More to the total point, the question was, "How am I going to live this?" That, sure enough, has remained the consuming question of my personal life. There is no fixed answer to it. Answering it is my moment to moment, day to day life-work.

Within about a week the transmission process became activated forcefully through me, and other people began noticing it. I felt, "Hm, I may have a talent for this. I definitely feel a calling. If I could awaken, and I don't consider myself a spiritual hotshot at all, then probably lots of people can, maybe lots and lots and lots of people."

During my years as a Daist, I had only rarely been considered an advanced practitioner. Most of the time there, I was in the "failed case" category. Then I had left in dis-grace, literally, and had been most likely to face the fate of "hellish karmas for lifetimes." So now I figured that if I could make this transition . . . well, who couldn't?

Then my questions became more focused. "How can I do this in such a way that other people can have access to their own divinely human Self-realization in Being—very directly, bypassing anything and everything in the politics and culture of how we interact that might wind up inadvertently hobbling them, or sabotaging their efforts?" That kind of question has been the focus of my work ever since.

Please speak about the main points of your teaching as it has evolved since the point of recognizing that it was something you wanted to do? What is it that you are actually teaching and sharing with people?
First, in terms of how I got into it—it wasn't something I thought about and decided to do. I felt I had no choice. That's what I mean by a "calling." I was, you could say, helplessly radiating this awakening force of Being, and I had to take responsibility for it. It wasn't something I could turn on or off. It was happening. People were being affected, they were noticing something going on with me and then, through my presence, in themselves. Like an 800-pound gorilla in the living room, it was something we just had to take into account.

In terms of the offering itself—we call it "Mutual Waking Down." Sorry, I don't have a nice little two-syllable acronym for it. Another name I use is "The White-Hot Way of Mutuality."

I didn't pop through my awakening with this approach ready-made. In fact, the most important work I did that distinguishes this offering from others all occurred after that incident and time of awakening.

There are many different kinds of realizations and illuminations, you know. The different paths don't lead to the same peak. They lead to different ones.

From the moment of awakening, I saw that my former guru Adi Da's description of the realized condition corresponded more closely to what I was living than any other teaching I was aware of. I want to emphasize here that I am NOT saying this awakeness I live and transmit is what Adi Da calls "the seventh stage of life (which is the highest stage in Adi Da's teaching)." Not at all. The qualities of the body-mind of a devotee who might enter that stage through the practice Adi Da offers are not at all what either I or others who've awakened with my help demonstrate. And his description of his own state, at this point, reflects several decades of his own divine incarnation. The reason he's changed his name so many times is to reflect wholesale transformations of his being.

So I just indicate that there are analogies, parallels, points of similarity. And that was obvious to me from the outset. I knew that if my realization was real and was going to mature, it was going to take me in some specific directions that his teaching and life suggested. I was also getting pointers from the people around me at the time, particularly several of these same women who had been so close with me and helped facilitate my transition.

We had a kind of standing joke. I called myself "The Rent-A-Shiva Corporation," because, whoever of them I was spending time with, I was always wanting to talk about the direct awakening of free Consciousness—the real meaning of the "Shiva" archetype. But more often the reality was, every time I would visit one of them, I felt like I was on a hospital gurney being wheeled from one operating room to another. A number of these women were, and are, dynamic, pioneering psychotherapists. All of them were and are profoundly intuitive. So their communication to me was, "Fine, yes, Consciousness, well and good—but come on in to your human person here. What are you feeling, Saniel? And don't tell me about the wounds of the whole world. I want to hear you talk about your personal shadow, not just the collective stuff." [Laughter]

Gradually I got that they were revealing a gateway into the deep, unprotected, chaotic, feminine reality of our—ahem, my—existence. And they became my greatest teachers after realization. They helped me to humanize myself and to allow the divine current of Conscious Being to "wake down."

Down into the body?

Down into the body, down into the material world, down into the limits of "self" and "other" and "object" that are so confining and painful for us. I remember way back in 1970, after that initial rush upward into samadhi, the thought literally went through my mind, "If I could just get back to that state at will, whenever I want to, I wouldn't have to be so damned vulnerable."

These women were inviting me back into vulnerability. I knew that was exactly where I had to go, with no escape. I could enjoy the bliss of the Self, yes, but not as a hedge against vulnerability. I talk about this to this day with people. Sometimes I get asked, How did I know this for myself? Well, I just did. I had seen in others that there is no more powerful shield in all the worlds than a good, impermeable realization of infinite Consciousness. A lot of people who enter such realization act as if it entitles them to become immune to others in all kinds of ways. They may be very sensitive in some ways, but they use the awakeness as a kind of straight-arm to keep others at bay.

In that respect, one of the great moments in my post-awakening life came when one of these women who meant so much to me in those early years said finally, "You know, Saniel, every time we talk these days, I can feel you being right here with me, really owning your own personal stuff, just present and available." That was like a religious confirmation. A real Bar Mitzvah—but this time the "rabbi" was a woman.

My mentor and I talked about how what we were trying to achieve was a true partnership. It was in our work together, and with others, that I began hearing and using the word "mutuality," which has become another key thread of my teaching.

It's not only an orientation toward being awake as Consciousness and incarnating, being "down here" in your own subjective, human personhood. It's also an orientation toward interplay with others, in your objective life. It tests your capacity for what winds up being an immense, profoundly tantric paradox: being that infinite, "Only" Spirit-Identity and yet also continuing to encounter the "other" in many forms. And not just in a way where those others are only a subset of your Self. It entails granting them space to really be "other," even while you both might also realize and enjoy the mystery of "sameness."

Mutuality, then, is about granting others permission to live in a basic equality with you in Being. It also honors the natural eldership of different generations of growth, and different forms of expertise and seniority. It's not just raw, across the board egalitarianism.

What mutuality means, practically for my friends and me, is that everyone is accountable, including me. People get to tell me what they feel about how I am doing my part—and they do, frequently. I also get to say back, in turn, how I feel about how they're participating. If someone tells me they feel I am not getting something important about who they are or am failing to respond, we have the opportunity to work that out.

The same is true for all the other participants. It's challenging. Not everyone feels they're able to speak up for themselves very well. But the very opportunity, even the cultural sanction to do so, is tremendously empowering. It's like a dysfunctional family suddenly starting to function a little bit; a lot of energy and attention are liberated from the previously suppressive dynamics. But, whew, does it take work.

In some spiritual traditions they say that ultimate enlightenment means that there is the revelation that "there is no other."
Right.

How does that fit into the mutuality you describe? You mentioned still being able to relate to someone as an "other."
Well, using some of that Zen language—"first there is a mountain, then there is no mountain, then there is"—the great paradox of that third "is" accommodates the simultaneity. In true Onlyness, yes, there is no existentially isolated "other." There also is no existentially exclusive self.

No exclusion of the world to hold some kind of non-worldly samadhi?
Right. And no treating of the world as if it did not really exist. That, it seems to me, tends to be the great violence of many of the transcendentalist traditions, for which all humanity and all life on Earth are now paying dearly. Such world-denial has been enshrined in what I call the "hypermasculine" era of human sensibility, which has had to dissociate the self, even violently, in order to be able to control nature, or to achieve what I regard to be an evolutionary cul-de-sac of liberation from embeddedness in the karmic play of phenomena. So many great masters and teachings propose that ultimate liberation is some kind of cessation of the appearance of phenomena. I disagree. I think such liberation, if achieved, is a kind of false summit. For the seemingly liberated individual, it may appear to be supreme liberation because it points nowhere beyond itself. But in the larger picture, it may prove to be a less than ultimate liberation. And because it seems so sufficient to the awakened Self, that subjective awakening may very well stagnate the current of our species' real-growth.

If your realization really is so all-fired immutable and free, then why not embrace the play of phenomena? What power can it possibly have to confine or fundamentally enslave you? In archetypal language, if you've realized that you are Shiva, don't kick Shakti out of your life—embrace her, love her, dare to dissolve in her and find out what she shows you next. In other words, if you've realized unconditioned Consciousness, don't abandon the living Spirit-Energy and all of its manifest, conditioned, changing phenomena. Dare the embrace, the union, and take that ride!

Some traditions say that in order to go into complete realization you must first enter into that world-excluding Self-knowledge, or "Jnana Samadhi." Then you go back down into the world with that. Eventually the two principles, the world and consciousness become One. Another traditional saying from India is, "The world is unreal; Brahman [the Supreme Reality] alone is real; and Brahman is the world."

Yes. And I am saying, let's take that third stipulation fully for real. The way traditional Oriental sages have tended to live it suggests that, yes, philosophically or in principle, Brahman is the world, but in practice, let's be careful because the world is not really real.

Which goes back to that first principle, "The world is unreal," even though . . . ?

Even though a kind of lip service, perhaps a very awakened, compassionate, and in some ways world-embracing lip service, is paid to the more inclusive understanding.

In the midst of all this dharma debating, I have to affirm again, just for the record, that I view all of this as work in the great science of not just human but cosmic and earthly evolution. Though I may have points of adamant dispute with various teachings, teachers, and traditions, I also have great respect for everybody who is doing and has done their work, who've carried on and made their contribution however they were moved.

That having been said, to me, if you are going to take the Brahmic realness of the world most seriously, you are going to wind up not only in "Self-realization" but in "Other-realization" as well. And not just the capital "O" Other—that is, some obviously divine Being—but also the small "o" others of people, animals, objects, things. You go beyond holding all others as only subsets of your great Self, or of the impersonal Absolute Reality into which you have dissolved. This becomes a tantric paradox of living the Onlyness of what Is and simultaneously encountering, and allowing yourself to be touched, moved, changed, even disturbed, by all kinds of others.

I speak of basic awakening into the Onlyness as "the second birth." That transition into the awakened condition is like a moment of being born, truly. Then you have to get a life. As in the first birth, which brought you into this world to begin with, the early time of the second birth is an opportunity to become invested in the human life organism. Optimally, I suggest this is so. It's not optimally focused, for most people, on psychic and subtle, otherworldly kinds of experience. Such things may come and go without the individual's search or effort. But the best, most integrative, most all-inclusive focus of his or her attention at that stage is on "getting here" more and more. It's on learning what it takes to discern, live, and speak one's truth, humanly, in this earthly realm, while also, a lá mutuality, making room for real others to really do the same.

Meanwhile, you are no longer what and who you were. You remain a person, yes, with all your "stuff" there, your shadow conditioning and patterns still very much alive in you—but you know your body and life now also as a living force-field of this divine radiance of Being. The unconditional, unqualified dimension of who you are is working an awesome reconfiguration of the organism you are, achieving a more and more fundamental and profound integrity. If that sounds abstract, well, try living it.

On a cellular level . . .

On a cellular level, on every psychic level—you name it; it just doesn't let up. We're careful to say, "People, beware: This process really works!" That's as good a reason to be careful about getting into it as any doubt or hesitation you may have.

You have to be ready to have the light shined into every aspect and area of your life, and it's the strongest light available?

Well, it certainly is for us! [Laughter] It is for those who find themselves choosing it. Other people have other lights that they turn to, other inspirations and paths to take, and that's fine with me. This is not for everyone.

This awakening, this simultaneous realization of infinite Conscious Being and finite personhood, is attuned to the esoteric revelations of Ramana Maharshi and Adi Da, with respect to "the Heart" and the "Amrita Nadi." The Amrita Nadi is, most simply, the Heart alive and active in and as your finite person and All that Is.

Beyond passage into awakening, there is this further process that I call "the Wakedown Shakedown." It is in some ways analogous to what Adi Da refers to as "Transfiguration" or "Divine Transfiguration." So there is a life cycle in the realized condition that naturally stimulates various capabilities. It puts us through cycles of growth and change much like what we went through to become adults in our first-birth lives as still-separate individuals.

There is a Sanskrit saying in the Bhagavad Gita, "yogastha kuru karmani," which means, "established in Being, perform action." It sounds like there has to be some establishment of that pure consciousness or that Beingness in order for it to effectively and most efficiently "wake down" into the body. How do you establish that platform of pure Beingness or pure consciousness in the process, since it seems to be a prerequisite at least for this stage of it?

Great question. Establishing that platform is, for that very reason, the first significant stage of our work. My colleagues and I have been continuing to refine how we as individual transmitter-teachers and also as a cooperative group serve this establishment in Being in people who are truly hungry for it. Our cooperation is important, because there's an alchemy in having many different bodies who are able to manifest such effortless awakeness and to facilitate it in others. And people have to be hungry. Hunger for direct awakening is an important qualification. In most cases people have grown weary of enthusiastic, programmatic, willful seeking of the kind they've often been doing for years—the mantras, the prayers, the daily exercises of energy and breath and observation, and so on. We call this weariness and disillusionment "the Rot." Rotting out of all that, despairing of it, resigning themselves to non-success at it, prepares the ground. They've fallen off the vine of seeking, and now they're composting.

When they get into this work with us, then, they're receptive to the direct transmission of that condition of establishment in Being. We use silent, meditative sittings and also what we call "gazing," a form of the traditional adept practice of transmission by glance. And plenty of conversation and interaction—your adept has to listen to you as much as you need to listen to and hear him or her. All this is managed in a dynamic balance or "tantric tension" between formality and informality. We try to keep it very personable with people. Nonetheless, boundaries are necessary if each person is to feel properly respected and taken into account.

I should say a little more about this. Many people who come into our work have already gone through periods of conforming themselves to protocols of all kinds. They were taught, in those passages, that the conformance was absolutely necessary for their desired transformations. But, though they attempted the disciplines, often with great success, either they never achieved the sought-after transformations, or the achieved transformations at last proved unsatisfactory.

When they get here, such individuals begin to decompress from the pressure of all that conformity and structure. For many who've been through excessively formalized programs of seeking and spiritual acculturation, it's really liberating just to be able to call your teacher by an ordinary first name—and be called one, personally, back. At the same time we look to offer each other forms of mutual acknowledgment and respect that allow the transmission to function with optimal effect. One of the dangers of excessive informality is that it can tend to stifle or inhibit an aspirant's receptivity to what the adept is radiating. People can get distracted by too much "personalness" in the mix.

As the transmission of "establishment in Being" takes hold in the individual, he or she shows signs of what I call "Being-initiation." One of the first signs is a re-dawning of hope. A hallmark of the Rot" is a loss of spiritual hope, even to the point of despairing of ever awakening. Spending time in the presence of teachers established in Being resurrects hope in your heart of hearts—particularly if they are offering a process that they and many others demonstrate really works for everyday people. Then, gradually, working with one or more of the adept-helpers here—which many people do by email and phone nowadays—you make the awakening process more and more your own. You conform it to your own life.

I like to say that fundamentally each of us can practice only in one tradition, that of our own whole body. The adepts and others here can only help you find and clarify your own unique yoga of establishment in Being. There are some general guidelines, there are wheels you don't have to reinvent, yes—but, as it was for me, the finding of your unique way is itself your Way.

One of our unbendable principles is that each aspirant must have access to someone who is committed to working with her or him personally. Really human, intimate, direct access, not membership in a crowd of five hundred people.

In that sense, and in certain qualities of the work that gets done, our process bears similarities to psychotherapy. You can't be an effective therapist for a giant crowd of people. You've got to be able to go into the depths, into the trenches, with each one. You've got to be trustable and reliably present there to help them get their bearings, find their sea legs.

It's similar in our work. This transmission is alive, it's potent. It activates a spontaneous process of changes in people that go on day and night from that point forward. Most initiates in this work, then, don't have much reason or much time to wonder if it's actually happening for them. They're trying to learn how to cooperate with what amounts to their own unstoppable, customized process of becoming established in Being-realization. The adept-helper has to be there in a hands-on way, ready to help them through.

In that respect it also bears similarities to parenting. You can provide such intimate nurturance and loving challenge only to a very finite number of people. Done right, it produces "adults," which, in the case of the second birth, are people who really are established in their own autonomous awakeness in Being.

Through this mutual, cooperative enterprise—mutual listening, mutual support, mutual commitment—the Conscious Principle becomes self-aware in the aspirant. In other words, he or she awakens. This tends to happen rather directly. It usually takes at least a few months, and not often longer than a few years. In most cases, within two to three years, the person has at least realized what we call "the embodied feeling-witness consciousness."

Does that mean, in that stage, that there's a "Self separate from activity" that is "witnessing" the activity being seen?

Well, it's simultaneously separate and not. It's the beginning of this tantric paradox of living as That which is utterly transcendental and simultaneously "right here." That is the nature of realized consciousness.

And eventually that "gap" will close?
Exactly.

Based on what principle?
You continue to live in mutuality with not only the world as a total configuration of phenomena, but also human "others" who are coming to you right out of that material realm of limits and pressures and saying, "Hey, I can see you, I feel you, I get what you're going through, bravo!"

Much of what is most liberating in our work is counter-intuitive to our previous training about what's spiritual and what isn't. Let's say you come here and, at some gathering we're having, you wind up having an emotional outburst. It could be anger, sorrow, some kind of jealousy, numbing fear, whatever. People who are hip to this process will be right there saying, "Good for you. We don't have a problem with that part of you. We know it's there. That part is every bit as inherently divine as the part of you that speaks up and says, 'I am becoming aware of myself as immortal consciousness.' So you don't have to fight to overcome that reactive, miserable, confused part of you. And bravo for daring to bring it out into the room!"

Those parts, you see, aren't transcendental by nature—they're part of the changing flux of phenomena. But we are changing phenomena just as we also are the unchanging principle that gives rise to changing phenomena, or in which those phenomena mysteriously appear. So in this work both principles, the changing and the unchanging, are given a green light. Much as in my own awakening, when literally those several women came to me out of the configuration of phenomena and shined the light of divine presence to me, attracting me into love and union and embrace and communication. All the parts are embraced and embrace one another, somehow.

So Shiva and Shakti then have an opportunity to have a mutual relationship with each other.
Assuming an esoteric understanding of the terms "Shiva" and "Shakti" as, in this discussion, the unchanging and changing principles, respectively, yes - that is exactly what happens.

Or the Shiva element, which is that transcendental consciousness, and which seems to be separate from the world, which is the Shakti element . . .
Right . . .

So what I hear you saying is, when those women appeared in your life, that Shakti element became much more apparent. When you're introduced to the Shakti element, then the Shiva element, which is the "moveless," moves in that apparent direction, even though by definition it's moveless. The "moveless" moves.
Yes. That exact paradox reveals itself alive. That which is utterly transcendental and unattached mysteriously embraces. And that which is moving, attached and attachable, is also attracted to the principle of its own freedom.

It's like the ocean. There is the vast, deep silence of the ocean, and there are the waves on the surface, but the fundamental constituent is H_2O.
Yes.

And in recognition of that principle, it doesn't matter if the waves are flopping around at high speed or if they are silent. It is still recognized as the ocean or that Oneness.
Right. And at the same time there is both the Self-realization and the sacred Marriage to the Other in all her/its/his forms.

And there's a delight in that . . .
Yes, and that delight achieves in each organism, as each divine or divinely human person, a fundamental wellness, an "OK-ness," a great relief from separateness. It's great relief even from the pressure of the extremely subtle separateness experienced by infinite consciousness in its preliminary forms of Self-realization, when dynamic union with the Shakti, or the Spiritual play of phenomena, has not yet been realized as a seamless Onlyness.
We're very pragmatic about this. I mean, my orientation is, I'm deeply disturbed by the history of human spirituality, by the fact that it absolutely has not transformed human nature and culture in a most fundamental way. I'm always looking, always tinkering. "What am I doing, what are we doing, that might inadvertently be bringing for-

324 ~~~ Dialogues with Emerging Spiritual Teachers

ward some supposition, some presumption, that actually hamstrings people? How can we do this better? What are we failing to notice?" We're just very attentive to this. We want to achieve results that are real. And we want to keep on achieving results that are real.

I need to say, here, that the Mutual Waking Down process is not therefore merely heading toward some kind of earthly utopia. I'm a realist on that score. One of the big cosmic jokes for me, which came to articulation in my mind sometime after my awakening, was that I have realized "hellish karmas for lifetimes!" The very fact of infinite conscious spirit impaling itself, as it were, in organismic embodiment, and being willing to endure those limits while also remaining limitless—this is an embrace of a hellish situation by that which is heavenly.

So you live the paradox of simultaneous heaven and hell. And human beings who awaken and live this way wind up noticing that their very nature is a living out of the "Bodhisattva" orientation: to serve the awakening, transfiguration, and ultimate "white-heating" of all beings and things. My realization is not complete without yours, and everyone's. And there is no way out without that completion for All.

Where then do we go from here? What I'm pointing to is presaged in a lot of esoteric detail by Adi Da's great, pioneering contributions on the question of "Divine Translation" or "Outshining." But many people, Teilhard de Chardin being a good example, have had intuitions or intimations that we are heading for a wholesale transmutation, an ultimate cosmic epiphany, that may be the birth of this whole cosmic display into Whatever Comes Next.

From that perspective, it's important to emphasize that the Mutual Waking Down work is not just about getting spiritually chummy with each other. It's not just moving us toward being able to communicate and feel really enlightened together here. It's a fire of inconceivable transformation. Curiously enough—and I say that because there's so much "greenlighting" of the person here—that fire is not really "a respecter of persons." It's a transformer of persons, no less ruthlessly so despite the fact that we are free to be as loving, caring, and gentle with one another as possible.

Yes, I wanted to address that also. Ken Wilber writes about personal spiritual development activities and successes versus truly transformational spiritual work, which I think is what you're referring to. How can people best sort through the differences? If you're involved in spiritual activities, many times when you see something that happens in your life as a result of that spiritual activity, so that "your life is getting better," some people would say this is more of a "personal" kind of "success program." In that case, you're going to be a better person in the world, you're going to have more money, better cars and houses, and so on, and you're also going to have better and more meaningful relationships. But it sounds to me as if there is something beyond that.

Yes, certainly. I begin one of my published tapes, Our Risky Experiment in Total Transformation, with a reference to Wilber's distinction between ways of translation and ways of transformation. By "translation" I gather he was implying the translation of spiritual blessings into betterment of things you were already wanting for yourself as a separate ego or soul.

I think he calls it "transitional."

Okay. Whereas the ways of transformation pretty much radically upends your life and winds up devoting you to a greater principle. [Laughter]

Once you get into that vehicle, you're going to be taken along for the ride.

That's actually a lot of what is happening in the post-awakening stage of our process. I call it the Wakedown Shakedown, which is a humorous title for something that's no joke. It's as if the Y-O-U of you were shaking down into, but also shaking out and dispersing, the previously developed karmic patterning of the organism, including your basic sense of who you were. It's often quite disorienting for people and very challenging in every case.

Well, it's good there's a sense of humor that underlies it in some sense. Otherwise it would be such a serious affair, no one would bother to do it. [Laughter]

Yes, well, we have to remind ourselves sometimes! [Laughter]

But it's interesting to take the perspective that actually going through such a process is really an "opportunity." It's an opportunity for us to actually use the patterns as compost, as something that we can see as an advantage to ourselves. "Oh, I have another opportunity to get through that particular bit of compost and use it, burn it up, penetrate through it," rather than seeing it as something negative: "Oh my God, here we go again! I have to pound through this again."

Thank you. My orientation is that the stages we might call transitional or translational, the stages of separate personal and soul growth, are part of our natural evolutionary journey. And then at some point we become capable of a much more radical transformation. Then, however, if we keep growing—and the orientation to do so, in some sense the conscious choice to do so, is enshrined in my work as much as my friends and I can get it there—then the two become a singular event.

The radical, ultimate, transformational principle is always senior in some sense. In other words, the concerns of the personal growth principle—more rest, more pleasure, more personal satisfaction and rich experience, deeper relationships, and so on—are always being naturally subordinated to the divine principle of unconditional transformation. We have to be careful not to override the personal, transitional values. But what winds up happening is that people who are indeed established in Being, helplessly and perpetually so, do perform action that always weaves the unification of the two great principles more deeply. This produces a simultaneously more grounded and humanized and more sublimed or divinized character.

That marriage of these two principles eventually opens us into what I call that "White Heat" of transfigured, divinely human existence. This is a form of nirvikalpa samadhi that is not dependent upon any kind of ascent of energy and attention out of life, nor any resolution of energy and attention away and back, we might say, down into the Heart-Ground of being. The Conscious Being is already being lived as infinite or utterly unpressurized feeling space, at peace and in love, indeed effortlessly identified, with all Matter, all Phenomena. The way that this natural state intensifies into formlessness feels as if that Conscious Love were superheating. It feels like everything is melting into the evolutionary future of all that exists, which is at the same time the original source and eternal ground of it all, too. Who knows what to call it? It makes you babble.

Here's what actually happens. You are already living in the paradox of simultaneous form and formlessness. The "sahaja" or naturally "twinned" condition that you have realized is an unshakably felt intuition of infinite formlessness simultaneous with all forms, in other words, with the whole field of perceived phenomena. And now that formless unity intensifies so as to dissolve attention at its roots, destroying all awareness of distinct forms. The extreme dissolution of the samadhi is temporary. In my experience, once entered, it recurs thereafter with some frequency. Coming back from it into subject/object forms of perception and participation, you get that you are now, in some way, established in that White-Hot quality of the Mystery. You feel yourself to be it, and it to be you.

You thus become a divinely human, White-Hot transformer of everyone and everything, even while walking around and doing ordinary things, with all your typical human limits and foibles intact. This is an even greater consummation of the union of Shiva and Shakti than the basic awakeness and non-separation you've already been enjoying. And it relieves you, progressively, of every kind of residual psychic and cellular imprinting of separateness and unreality. It deposits you more and more in the unforeseeable Peace toward which the cosmos itself may be evolving. Who knows?

Those are things that you've articulated quite clearly in your book, Waking Down. You might want to say more about that book, although I think we've covered most of the main points.

I guess one that I could emphasize is that, from the outset, my orientation is that the problem human beings feel being alive is not "sin," it's not "evil." It's what I call "the core wound." As natural beings it's a given for humans to be very much aware of confinements and limits, mortality, separation, and so on, while always also sensing or feeling, "There's got to be more than this. It could be much better than this." Or, "This is exactly how I want life. How do I keep it this way?" That's sort of another way of saying, or voicing, the same thing.

Eventually this factor becomes an intuition not only that there is or may be a limitless principle, which we might call "God," "Being," the "Unconditional," but also that our own nature is of that limitless nature. And so we have to resolve that paradox—that we appear to be both limited and limitless, and neither can really most fully be realized to the complete exclusion of the other. Falling into that paradox in the real, concrete, messy, even fucked up conditional limits of your own particular human life is what I mean when I talk about falling into the core wound.

I suggest that the core wound may well prove to be the supreme realization of our first birth. After all the samadhis that appear to distill limitlessness out of all limits but then somehow leave you or others here smothered by still more limits, to live in the paradox that you are simultaneously infinite and finite—both principles realized, not just being thought about—that's a profound, tantric awakening. It's the comprehension that this is the way it's going to be at least until death and whatever appears thereafter, that while we're here neither principle is going to completely give way to the other. For many people there is enormous relief in accepting that this is so. It permits them to end the struggle of one part of themselves somehow trying to overcome the other part or parts, as if the very existence of the body, desires, negative or reactive emotions, and the feeling of separateness, were itself proof that you are a sinful, unspiritual being.

It's an infinite dynamic that goes on between the Self, or you might say that infinite, transcendental aspect, and the material, relative world of limitations. There's an infinite process of transformation or we could say transcending, that goes on forever; a "widening" or "expansion." There should be great joy in that, I would think?
Yes.

It's a revelation, a constant, perpetual revelation, moment to moment.
Right. Exactly. And that's how individuals live it here. Part of my assumption, which is certainly in the *Waking Down* book and everything else I've published, is that there really is only this Onlyness. Therefore, every human being is struggling to incarnate as That, though they may not know it at any given stage. Nobody is absolutely and only evil, or a sinner, though there are some god-awful, terrible ways to be living that in effect are violent, sinful, and evil in relation to life and the total world of self and others. We're in a school here in this life.

I've been doing my work ardently for seven years or more now. We're still in the early stages of this revelation, of which, being a mutual event, my own work is only an initial, founding demonstration. As you and I are talking today, the work is in a kind of transition. Not only I but a number of others, men and women, have moved into what may be the initially maturing phases of this Shakedown. It's taken us into the pits of our broken zones, what I call the "primal insanity" that we've needed to make into survival strategies just to stay alive. So much of that has had to be covered over and cut off from our rational ego-awareness—again, just so we could survive. But when you awaken you have the anchor of infinite consciousness, so you can encounter these other aspects of your identity and not just go completely insane. This permits a reconfiguring, a release and realignment of energy and attention from the old patterns by in some sense re-inhabiting them. It's like a homeopathic dose of your own poison. You go into it and through it.

But you go into it with very good light to begin with, so whatever is there can be seen through more quickly?

Yes, though "quickly" means some time to do the work carefully, well, thoroughly. Now some of my friends and I are at a stage where that kind of level of intense purification, which is often cathartic, dramatic, and messy, is beginning to yield to more of the balancing or harmonizing process. As a cultural event, we're going through transitions that are allowing more of the obvious ecstasy of divine Self-abiding and communion with the mysteries of the Other in all its forms. And these shifts are transforming the quality of our lives together.

To get to this transition, I had to be very careful not to override or hasten the messy phases of purification. Both for individuals and our informal gathering, it has amounted to an immersion in the deep, dark chaos of the feminine principle. At times it's had to go at what seemed like turtle speed. And it continues to in some ways for all of us, and for many individuals. As a result, some people get the impression that this often difficult exposure to the wounds and broken zones of our deep psyches is what my work is all about, or that it has been and always will be helplessly fixated there. But that is not the case, and I think the transition that is now underway—especially as we've entered the new year—will become more and more obvious in the coming months and years.

I'm wanting to point out that we are in continual transition, and that our expression at any moment is only a phase in an ongoing evolution. Every person who comes into our work transforms it, because each one is such a unique event. And though I especially, and others in their own ways, have special and in some sense prominent roles, it

really is stimulating a democratic dissemination of these great transcendental principles. It's triggering a mutual, cooperative, White-Hot
embodiment that no single person or group could possibly control,
even if they wanted to.

By the time your book comes out, then, not only I personally but
we, as a loose-knit and already far-flung community, will be down the
line from what I can describe today. I wrote in another of my books,
The Conscious Principle, that it's going to take us a generation of time
just to begin to reveal, in our bodies and our cultural interplay, what
this White-Hot Way of Mutuality can become. Even so, I also understand that we, today, are a rather crude, primitive transitional generation of our own evolutionary process. These bodies are refugees from
a lot of battering and shattering just to survive in this world. There is
only so much scar tissue we're going to be able to soften and bring
back to healthy life. Obviously I mean that emotionally and spiritually, in every way, and I do also in many cases mean it physically.

The principle of trust of self and others is very central to this
unfoldment, and boy oh boy, it cannot be legislated. It can't be man-
dated, it can't be superimposed, people can't be armtwisted, brow-
beaten, or even willfully inspired to trust. Trust grows exactly like any
living thing that is not and cannot be forced. In the most esoteric
sense, the divine intensity or current of Conscious Being is made, I
suggest, of "love-trust." Where there is love and trust, bliss not only
manifests naturally but magnifies quite apart from all effort.

Well, I've come to see—the hard way, with lots of heartbreak, disappointment, and disillusionment—that our generation is only going
to be able to go so far into what I feel is the true amrita, the "Immortal Nectar of Conscious Love-Trust." People following us will be able
to build on our foundations. No doubt they'll have to do some reno-
vation and repair work here and there, too. But they'll be able to look
back and say, "Whoa! Those guys were like people in the covered wag-
ons. Talk about primitive modes of relating." [Laughter]

Here I need also to acknowledge that I have made many mistakes
in my work to try to bring forth into the world this, this what? this
event. And I continue to make mistakes. I am quite fallible. I am by no
means beyond the purifying stages of my own transformation. I think
they will go on always in this life. The same is true of everyone else
who gets into this adventure with me and those friends who already

find it sustaining to work with me. Life is messy. We're messy. I think we humans are only barely beginning to find out who we are and how to live as individuals and pairs, groups, clusters, communities. I certainly include myself in that observation.

Some people find many faults with me and my work that have led them to take or keep their distance. I'm an unusual person in some ways, and some people find aspects of my character—for instance, my occasional outbursts of anger—or my lifestyle—for instance, my non-monogamous heterosexual approach to intimate commitment and fidelity—a little hard or even impossible for them personally to deal with.

While some of those reactions are inevitable, I always try to stay open to both questions and criticisms and to take them seriously into account. I take great pains to help people realize that they are fundamentally safe here, and that means safe from my and everyone else's power to manipulate, coerce, or impose on them in any intentional way. Life is difficult enough without adept teachers trying to make it even weirder!

So, with respect to sexuality, for example, I am absolutely not the kind of tantric male adept who presumes a sort of divine right of access to women. No way. I'm not going to hide what I have found to be my own nature, which emerged during the, to me, miraculous tantric sexual process of my awakening that I described earlier in this interview. I think it's extremely important for people not to encounter such aspects of a teacher's life only after they've already invested themselves in a teaching. I want to be outfront about it. I don't want to get in people's faces with such things, and I treasure privacy and intimacy. But I've learned that even too much reticence can appear to be a form of hiding. People have a right to a basically full disclosure from someone as important as a prospective spiritual teacher.

To look at it in another way, I never disempower men and fascinate women with an alpha-male game of sexual power. I never have done that, and I never will. Those who come here are seeking their own realized autonomy and strength and their own fullest opportunity to create truly transformative intimacies. Recognizing the liabilities of my inevitably alpha presence in my own life-work, which is so much about invoking others' fullest presence in life with me and others, I pull my energy way back to make room for everyone else's. Not just sexual energy—my whole personal energetic field. I recognize that my transmission of the White-Hot force of Conscious Being is very yang, very penetrating and forceful. I'm not in a position to manipulate or mute it. To balance it out, to make sure that I am not overwhelming others, as so many teachers with strong personalities do, I try to manage my social behavior and personal interactions with as much yin energy as I can.

So, in the arena of sexuality, I am extremely careful. Even if I were monogamous, I would be that careful. I don't even get close to anything like flirting. To me, the conditions under which sexual intimacy might become appropriate are most profound. As it happens, I am presently living with one intimate partner, Linda Groves, who has been with me for more than five years and is a brilliant adept of this Mutual Waking Down work in her own right. Another partner, Fay Fields, recently found it necessary to discontinue an intimate partnership with me and a sisterly partnership with Linda. She had been with us for two and a half years. What we were trying to create together proved, at last and for many reasons, to be unsustainable.

I can tell you that during that time Linda and Fay have anchored my life's work. Fay also is an awakened adept of this yoga, currently on a kind of sabbatical for health reasons. They have been the primary forms of the Goddess for me. Their sacrifices and dedication have made much of this Mutual Waking Down process possible for others today, in ways that could not have occurred otherwise.

I want people to know that, to my view, the Goddess incarnating in her union with me provides the magic, the spirit, the juice that "Mater-ializes" all the miraculous conscious embodiments and transformations in this work. On some level this is true of everybody, female and male, who is working with me. It's also true of my own material body! But it's especially true of my closest intimates. From the day of my awakening, this has always been my truth.

Thus, while Fay remains very close to me spiritually and deeply committed to our work, losing her has been tragic, and a terrible blow. Yet the total Waking Down process is only continuing to evolve. This unproveable God-Goddess event is materializing in many awakened, continually self-integrating men and women. So perhaps that unconventional form of my divinely human intimacy has birthed what it needed to, and is now no longer viable.

In any case, at this point I don't know if Linda and I will ever again have the energy to try to bring in another partner. Knowing myself as I do, it seems to me it would be auspicious; but I don't know if it is necessary or even really possible. Not only for me but also of course for Linda. She has her own very autonomous integrity and voice and, by our agreements, one hundred percent participation in all such choices. Then there's everyone else around us, and what they have to deal with. I don't want to burden people with excessive unconventionality on my part. "Unnecessary weirdness," you know? So my service to others may require me to relinquish all opportunities, at least for the foreseeable future, to activate the unconventional kind of tantric lifestyle that would feel most natural to me. I really don't know.

All of this leads me to emphasize that I don't recommend any aspect of my personal nature or choices to anyone else. I don't recommend specific forms of sexual intimacy to everyone any more than I recommend a universal practice of meditation. I never have, by the way. Each one of us must discover our own truth and how to fulfill our real needs and wants. That discovering is the Way! Therefore what I do recommend, and always have, is continual self-investigation, with no holds barred. And I recommend and try to practice living one's continually self-refining truth with utmost integrity while also really cooperating with others who are doing the same themselves.

That is the essence of mutuality. When people are awakening directly and then exploring the startling challenges of an inherently awakened existence in relative proximity to others doing the same, such work in mutuality is not only demanding but most rewarding. It exposes all our shadow stuff, to ourselves and others. Through that deep integration and gradual, cooperative healing of our cut-off and broken parts, it also accelerates our evolutionary brightening. What emerges is mutually sustainable, White-Hot freedom.

From that perspective, dealing with our shadow material is not an unfortunate chore. It's central and crucial to the whole practice. And if the teacher or teachers are openly doing that themselves, everyone else gets empowered to as well. I mentioned my anger a few moments ago. In that yin spirit I described, I work very hard to make sure that people are not fundamentally knocked back into their own psychic recesses by any of my reactions. Sometimes I fail, it's true. I wind up doing a lot of sincere apologizing. I have to eat a lot of crow, which I try to do with class. And I know that working things through with people helps empower them to stand up for themselves, even sometimes in opposition to me.

As Ken Wilber said about our work, it's messy, yes, and who knows how well it will work at large? But it makes for real openings and transformations. Sometimes I can literally feel people's circuitries getting rewired when I or some other adept here does that thing that historically has been almost unthinkable for "Awakened Beings"—getting down and just flat out apologizing and asking to be forgiven for having misunderstood, hurt, or been insensitive to someone you are supposedly helping.

That's the best I can promise: to try to keep my ear to the ground and to be receptive to the currents of auspicious growth, release, and change, for myself and everyone. I try to be open about who I am, how I live, my faults and failings. I require the other teachers working closely with me to do the same. We are accountable to our aspirants and the other teachers who are apprenticing with us. In this day and age, people shouldn't settle for less from any teacher or helper, and I think that's a big advance for us all.

I also try to make sure there are many others here to whom individuals can go for direct adept transmission and counsel. Your awakening in this approach of Mutual Waking Down is no longer dependent on your personal involvement with me. And that, to me, is a great victory for this particular experiment in human Being!

If someone were seriously, genuinely interested in exploring your teaching and work, what can you advise them to do? What kinds of things should they consider if they're going to approach your teaching?

In *Waking Down* I have a chapter called "Due Diligence and the Essential Practices of Mutuality in This Way." I might make some minor revisions today, but that pretty well says it. I invite people first of all to a spiritual or transformation-process version of "due diligence." In the business world you investigate who you're getting into a contract with, and every aspect of the contract and the arrangement, in detail before you proceed. Both parties expect and require that of each other. I think that kind of care and mutual examination is most important in a spiritual work of this type.

In practical terms, if people contact us through our office or the website, we'll always have free information and at least one free, introductory audiotape that we will happily send out to you.

Waking Down, in both print and audiobook forms, is a good general introductory overview. It speaks especially to seekers with some background in the rather rarefied, transcendentalist traditions, especially those coming out of the Orient and appearing in the West over the last generation.

At some point over the next year or so I hope to bring out another introductory book, *Great Relief*, that will be much more plainspoken. A draft of the first forty percent of it or so is already posted on our website. It opens up the whole consideration of healing the core wound for everyday folks who haven't had exposure to Advaita Vedanta, Vajrayana Buddhism, Daism, and so on. It'll come out in an audio format also.

We're just now getting our digital video act together, and intend to put out lots of videos so people can see us and feel us at closest-to-direct personal contact. This work is so much about human bodies coming alive and awake together. By the time your book is out, John, people will be able to purchase videos of my sittings, and perhaps those of other teachers in our work as well. We hope soon to make video contact with us available on our website.

So I recommend people start with these introductory books and tapes. I am committed to making unabridged audio versions of all my major writings so that people can have the oral, auditory transmission as well as that of print. It makes a big difference for a lot of people.

If, after at least reading *Waking Down*, you feel a pull to explore more deeply, you can contact us for my more tantric teachings, *The White-Hot Yoga of the Heart* and a two-volume work now in progress, *The Incarnation of Mutuality*. These are big, live-wire, Goddess-juicy, up close and personal, down and dirty as needed, sometimes dense and intense, sometimes serene and sublime, other times flat-out silly, comprehensive, potent, transmission-masterworks. We're currently doing a major course on *The Incarnation of Mutuality*, one course for each volume, a twenty-session, six-month project that we're also putting onto audio and video tapes. Quite a number of people are already signing up to take the course on tape, and some people are creating study groups around it in their own areas.

I decided that it was time to let the White Heat of this process out the front door!

You also offer seminars and workshops?

We're beginning to do our workshops outside the Bay Area, in addition to our regular monthly offerings here. Our "Waking Down Weekend" is the best intensive initiation into the Mutual Waking Down process, but it's a major commitment of time, energy, and money. So we're now developing one-day workshops on topics such as "Healing the Core Wound," which are proving to be very successful ways for people to take gentle steps toward more serious exploration. Many of the adepts hold sittings regularly. People can always check out the website for an updated schedule of events. And they can order publications through the site, contact us by e-mail, fax, write, and of course call.

We welcome people to get in contact with us. Many of our other adepts are now doing a lot of their work by phone with people all around the U. S. and in some cases overseas. You can meet as many of them as you like this way. They'll work out fees and such with you.

In all these ways, you can do your due diligence and see if there's a fit for you here. See if this feels like what you need to do, or where you next need to focus. If it does, it will feel more like finding something that really meets your needs and welcomes you to be yourself, rather than a "joining" of and conforming to something outside and foreign to you. The due diligence, which should take some time if you are going to do it well, will give you the opportunity to see if this approach serves your current needs.

Saniel, if you could make a summary statement about your teachings to people seriously interested in realizing freedom in this lifetime, what would it be?

What I would say is that your fundamental feeling of lack, or of not-quite-rightness, or of everything-wrongness, whatever it is that has driven you to seek, is at last to be discovered as not really a problem. You wind up, then, relaxing back into that anxiety or disturbance that has motivated your whole quest. When you do that, if you have competent help—and we've talked about the forms that takes, in terms of transmission of Being-force, wise counsel, and good company—you can rather directly complete your quest for fundamental freedom and begin to live in it in this lifetime. I can't make promises, but in most cases this can occur in the course of at most a few years, rather than a few more decades or even lifetimes.

It's not going to be a freedom that is sheer, uninterrupted, unlimited bliss. It is a limitlessness that will coincide mysteriously with all kinds of persisting limits. That, to me, is what it means to embody while alive the supreme or ultimate principle of "Being in action." So you can thus live the rest of this life as such a free, fundamentally awakened, divinely human person, and go through the spontaneous, unpredictable changes that life will certainly bring. This is indeed a "second birth," a radically renewed "second life," compared to everything you have ever known before.

This kind of freedom is especially attractive to those who, as in the old cliché, want to have their cake and eat it too. The joke, of course, is that you are not only the eater but also, in many ways, the cake. If you get to eat life in your freedom, then life and the world also eat you—and not always in ways you find pleasurable. As we have talked about, realistically, what that means is that you wind up finding out how you need to conform your ordinary human desires, wants, needs, reactions, and impulses, to this great conscious principle that is also always recognizing that nothing is permanent, everything is changing. The changeless principle does exist, but not as any kind of thing or state that stands out and somehow quells the flux of changes. So, the great wisdom and freedom still obtain in that harsh reality.

This, then, is the possibility of a life in which that which is inherently free or unattached is realized and permits that which is limited and attached or detached to continue, and to be conformed to itself. It's also a possible life in which the free, unconditional principle somehow mysteriously embraces and dies again and again in its embrace of what is conditional and apparently bound and binding. It is a life of conscious love, freedom, and peace. It remains to be seen whether it turns us into living gods and goddesses. It definitely makes us into authentic human beings. It makes us capable of integrity, and of dignity; it imbues us with humility and joy; and it opens the eyes of our hearts to marvel in the Mystery forever.

Saniel, thank you very much for spending time with us this morning. It's been very insightful. We certainly hope to have the opportunity to meet with you again as your teaching unfolds.

You're welcome, and thank you, John. I look forward to that myself.

Postscript as of late March, 2000: Saniel Bonder wrote the following letter to me, which both he and I think is an important afterword to his interview:

March 21, 2000

Dear John,

I know you'll be interested to hear, and I expect many readers will also, that I recently proposed marriage—of the exclusively committed, monogamous variety—to my partner Linda. And, to my great delight, she happily accepted!

In our interview I mentioned that perhaps the non-monogamous, "unconventional form of my divinely human intimacy has birthed what it needed to, and is now no longer viable." Well, since then I came to the firm, clear conclusion that that is indeed the case. As I also implied in the interview, I don't want Linda, myself, or anyone else, and certainly not my and our work as a whole, to be "penalized for unnecessary weirdness" on my part! I'm done with that stage of my own necessary exploration of who I am in this world.

It's not that my nature has fundamentally changed. It's that I can and do choose to live differently now and into the future. I have made a yogic choice to commit to Linda as my beloved, the one divinely human woman whom I now embrace exclusively in tantric intimate partnership. She is a magnificent being, and a brilliant heart-companion for me. She gave her all to our exploration with Fay (for whom we both continue to care deeply), though it became increasingly obvious to Linda that she would not choose such an atypical intimate form herself. I honor her, I cherish her, and I'd have to be an idiot to jeopardize the very human and very sublime love we have together. Divinely human fool that I may be, that much of an idiot I am not!

Linda, by the way, was totally taken by surprise by my proposal. (This is documented—I was clever enough to set up our camcorder and get the moment on film; she had no idea what was coming.) She has always seen and understood my unconventional tantric nature and has never, ever tried to change me. For years we have endured this burn together of being, in that sense, very different people. And now she deeply appreciates that I am freely, fully making this yogic choice of marriage with her.

We don't have a date yet, but the fact of our engagement has somehow already changed my and our whole lives and our work from the core—in a wonderfully bright, delightful way. All our friends are thrilled. As one woman e-mailed me, "I'm SOOOO happy! Welcome to this world!" That's how it feels to me. I've gone to heaven and hell and back to be able to bring this "White-Hot Way" into this world. In choosing to marry Linda, I am also, in the mystery of my relationship to the living Spirit of the Goddess, choosing to marry my entire time and place. I am choosing to accept the limits my time and place require of me if I am to be here and do my work for humanity in the most congenial, harmonious, and effective way.

I wasn't planning anything of the sort—had hardly even thought of it—but there you have it. It's a new calling in Being. Though I have to cop to being a little disoriented, in accepting this calling I am relieved, overjoyed, and amazingly renewed.

And what a lucky guy I am to have such a woman in my life! All discussion of "embracing limits" notwithstanding, I truly feel I must be the most blessed man on the planet to be so loved by Linda. I hope a lot of the people who read my interview will have a chance to meet her. It won't take them long to see why I feel about her the way I do. She and I are now traveling a lot, doing introductory workshops together on the White-Hot Way. Along with other adepts in our work, we want to help people get jump-started in this yoga wherever they live.

Anyway, I thought you and our readers would want to know of this most unexpected and very happy turn of events. Thanks for letting me tell the story, John.

Blessings,

Saniel

Publications

Books/Publications written by Saniel Bonder available through Ma-Tam Temple of Being and retail bookstores:

Waking Down: Beyond Hypermasculine Dharmas: A Breakthrough Way of Self-Realization in the Sanctuary of Mutuality

While Jesus Weeps: Conversatioins in the Garden of Gethsemane

The Conscious Principle: Talks on Recognition Yoga and Mutual Embodiment

Great Relief: Healing the Core Wound of Your Existence: A Message of New Hope for Frustrated Seekers and Anxious Hearts

Healing the Spirit-Matter Split

All publications are published by Ma-Tam Awakenings, Inc.

Contact Information

www.wakingdown.org

Mt. Tam Empowerments is the private publishing and personal services company of Saniel Bonder and his wife, Linda Groves-Bonder.

Ma Tam Empowerments
369B Third St. Suite 162
San Rafael CA, 94901
1-888-657-7020
www.sanielandlinda.com

PAMELA WILSON

W hile researching various candidates to interview, I came
upon a loose-knit collection of Western teachers aligned
with the spiritual tradition of non-dualism. For the
most part they are informally associated with the teachings of
Ramana Maharshi and Nisargadatta Maharaj. These two luminaries
of nonduality lived during the late 1800s and early to mid-1900s. They
lit the fire of awakening and liberation in a handful of Eastern and
Western followers. Over time, nondualism spread rapidly in the West
resulting in a flourishing number of Western-born teachers.

One of the challenges in talking about non-duality is that if one
tries to describe "it," it is then not nondual. The basic premise of spiritual nonduality is that the separation between "I" and the "world" is
ultimately false. In other words, the knower and the known are in reality not separate. Shankara, the eighth century Indian sage of non-dual
Vedanta or Advaita, held that as a function of beginningless ignorance, we superimpose illusory conditions on the non-changing, non-

dual, eternal context which underlies and is prior to all conditions. Liberation or enlightenment is seeing through or transcending this ignorance. It is through the revelation of nonduality that one uncovers the state of liberation or enlightenment that is eternally present.

I first heard about Pamela Wilson from a friend who had spent a great deal of time with various western teachers of nondualism and recommended that I contact her. There were dozens of other Western nondualistic teachers I could have chosen who have gained a greater level of notoriety than Pamela. That, in and of itself presented the possibility of a diamond in the rough. Pamela was a devoted student of Robert Adams who as a young man fortuitously spent precious time in the presence of Ramana Maharshi.

What intrigues me most about Pamela is her lightness and laughter coupled with a pervasive presence of openness and love. Pamela presents nonduality through the essence of silence. Those who attend her meetings are met with a motionless gaze that immediately puts the mind at rest in fathomless being. While looking at someone, she sometimes smiles, giggles and then gives a one-liner that cuts right to the core of who that person is. She has written a small book titled *The Ocean, The Fish and the Buddha*. It contains a collection of aphorisms that spontaneously came out of her meetings. The book gives everyone a smile coming directly from the heart. There's nothing formal about Pamela's teaching. She always looks relaxed yet very alert. She is totally with whatever is happening or whomever she's with. Pamela is a pleasant reprieve from stiff ritualism that may be a prerequisite to having a relationship with a spiritual teacher.

Pamela, thank you very much for spending time to speak with us today. Can you share with us your experiences growing up as a child?
I had a very blessed childhood. My parents divorced when I was six. But it was very beautiful, my childhood because my mother was quite kind. I now refer to her as a saint. She was pretty much resting in acceptance most of the time. Of course having three young children and raising them on her own was challenging. But she actually was my

first spiritual teacher. Because I would watch her, and she was open and welcoming with everybody. It didn't matter who they were, she treated everybody equally. Everybody felt at ease around her. My experience was more that I felt I had an aversion to people. I was quite a loner and a recluse even as a child. I would spend most of my time in my room reading. I was very joyous but preferred to be alone rather than in the company of people. I was overwhelmed at school by other children. As I grew up I realized that she had been the role model and that all my spiritual work originally was so I could be like her—at ease with everyone, welcoming. She was always peaceful, except on occasion our role as children was to try and see if we could test her imperturbability. So it was very nice.

Do you have brothers and sisters?
    I have a younger brother and older sister. My older sister is also quite a saint. She's amazing, like my mother.

How does your family react to what you're doing? Do they have an understanding. . . .
    They don't really know. I told my sister that there had been a shift or realization. But she felt it was just like a nature epiphany, a sense of Oneness you get in nature that is true and is always present from moment to moment. I told my Dad there's a church that's been set up to support my work, so I told my Dad I was a minister. [Laughter] My Dad has always been very religious.

What religious activities did you participate in while you were with your family?
    We would always go to Episcopal Church. I would get into these altered states in church. I would look at God, or these images of what I was told was God—which was Jesus, and then the Father—and even when I was five and six just pray. It's almost as if I was having Darshan [a visionary meeting] with Jesus and I would just fixate very strongly on the form, this big statue in church. And I would always say, "I want to help, I want to help, I want to help." It was very beautiful.

Do you remember any particularly powerful spiritual experiences you had as a child? Something that stands out?

Mainly just those ones in church. And I also had a very extreme affinity for animals and nature. I was often wandering off by myself. We were blessed to be able to go to Lake Tahoe and Stinson Beach every summer. That happened more when I was older and wasn't going to church you know, as a pre-teenager. Relating was more to nature. I would feel Oneness with animals and nature so that was how it was experienced.

What spiritual paths did you find most useful to explore and which teachers or teachings had the greatest impact in terms of realizing the truth?

I'd have to scroll backwards a bit, because when I was fifteen I was very confused and felt very separate. And so one night I prayed, I prayed. I said, "If there's anyone out there that knows anything, please come here." And I prayed for two hours. It was the cry of a teenager for some help. And in the middle of the night I woke to this Light in my room and there was an Indian man sitting. And I didn't know who he was and I got scared and threw a pillow at him and he disappeared. And again when I was eighteen in college, the same thing happened.

Was it the same man?

Yes, it was the same man. And once again I threw a pillow at him and screamed. [Laughter]. It was only many years later that I recognized it was Ramana Maharshi.

Very interesting.

I felt he was looking out for me and didn't appear to mind the pillows. [Laughter]

What happened after that?

My sister had gotten involved with TM, Transcendental Meditation. My sister was older than my brother and me. My brother and I were naughty. We'd run into her room while she was meditating and would start ringing cowbells [Laughter] being generally irritating. Then she finally took me to a TM introductory lecture. I took TM and it was just exquisite. I found what I was looking for. I found peace in that twenty minutes in the morning and the evening. But there was a recognition even after I took the Siddhi [special abilities] program that I needed something in between. I needed a walking meditation because peace was present in the morning and evening during the meditation, and then of course it was obscured or destroyed by what we call "life." I'd go out into the world and do my work or studies and become instantly perturbed. So just in this asking for something during the day, a friend introduced to me the "Release Method," the Sedona Method. And that was very helpful. That was my practice for almost twelve years.

What is the "Release Method"? I'm not familiar with it.
Lester Levenson realized the Self in the 1950's and then created this method. It's based on Buddhist teachings, which is from moment to moment you just let go of all desire. So he took every thought or feeling to its underlying desire and then you would just release it. The problem with that, like any practice, is that I got caught up in the practice and forgot why I had entered it, which was freedom. There was a moment to moment returning back to peace, but I got caught in the practice, and there was recognition of that. Lester died; left the form in the late 80's. And then a friend brought me to Robert Adams who also was from Ramana Maharshi. I had never been to Satsang before, because my other teacher Lester wasn't into any of that. Since he had "awakened" on his own he didn't value the guru-devotee relationship. He felt it was unimportant and that everyone could do it on their own.

The moment I walked into Satsang with Robert Adams there was this inner laughter that rose up in me because I looked at him and went, "Ah!" When I was young I had an image of what God the Father would look like. He'd have white hair and a white beard. And he'd have these immense sky-blue eyes. I walked in and there was Robert. And so it was very clear he was my Master. The first message I heard at the first Satsang (he had Parkinson's at the time so it was sometimes hard to hear him), was "It's not in the words; it's never in the words, it's in the space between the words." From all of the letting go there was an innocence in me that took direction very well. So I entered the space between the words, and much to my delight and wonder, there was peace.

It was a different peace than you experienced in doing TM. Was there a qualitative difference?
It seemed like a more fresh, innocent peace because there was

nothing done to achieve it. There was just an entering into the space between the words in Satsang, which is a very sacred place, I feel.

Satsang means . . . .

Satsang is a gathering to honor truth. So it's beautiful. The highest teachings are always "Do nothing. Just come here and rest." That was Robert's teaching. He said, "There's nothing to do. There's nothing to do." That was such a welcome invitation, because before there was always this sense that I had to "effort" and I had to "practice" and somehow I was impure or not whole and complete and therefore had to make extreme effort to become more pure or more complete. And these are the final teachings; nothing to do; just come here and rest.

What happened after you met Robert?

Well, at the time I was not living in Los Angeles, which is where these Satsangs were held. I was living in Northern California. So I wasn't in continuous Satsang with him in bodily form, though of course once you sit with such a magnificent one, you're always under their wing. I was still very immature. My heart valued Robert but my mind would take me away from him. So there wasn't the complete honoring of the attention he gave me.

Did you have a job at the time?

I was teaching the "Release Method."

So the "Release Method" became something that you shared with other people in addition to being a practitioner?

Absolutely, yes. And it was very beautiful to share. But as soon as I found Satsang then I realized, " Oh no, Satsang is much more important." I was living in Marin at the time while Robert was giving Satsang in Los Angeles. So I would go back and forth. I was blessed by being able to be with him occasionally, just the two of us. And as he would do with everyone, he gave me very loving attention. It was the only time I had ever experienced unconditional love except with my mother. It was just so exquisite. I really knew I had come home. Meanwhile, living in Marin I would also go to Gangaji's Satsangs and to see Catherine Ingram and Francis Lucille. I was once again reminded that Satsang was home. That it was the only place one could truly just go and rest because there was nothing to learn. There was no "doing-ness" required. So it was a refuge. It was my refuge. And then I would see Robert. At one point he was wanting to move out of L.A., so I suggested Sedona [Arizona] to him, because that's where a large community of friends lived near a retreat center that had been Lester Levenson's. So Robert moved to Sedona and I would fly to be with him. But mainly I would stay in Satsang up in Marin and I listened to his tapes and other beloved Satsang speakers' tapes. Then I heard that Robert was leaving the body. He had announced that this upcoming Satsang was going to be his last, so I went and made reservations to fly from Northern California to Sedona.

I set my alarm that morning for about three-thirty to catch a six o'clock flight. The alarm went off and I was resistant. I didn't want to go. And this voice just yelled inside me, "Get up! Get up! Get up!" I said, "Oh, I'm tired." And the voice said, "If you want to sleep you can sleep for the rest of your life. Get up!" So I got up, drove the car to the airport, got on the plane, went to Sedona and I was late. Everyone was already in Sedona so I didn't have a ride. I was trekking up this hill to go to Satsang, the last Satsang with Robert. When I arrived there was a big crowd. I had to sit in the back. Once again this voice yelled at me in the middle of Satsang, "Get up! Get up!" I said inside, "You can't get up. It's Satsang! You're supposed to sit here." And all of a sudden I felt the body rise up and move towards Robert. People were coming up to me, saying "Sit down, sit down, you can't." But I went anyway, and he motioned to come sit next to him. I sat as his feet and he asked me, "How are you?" And at that time I had started just to go into what I call samadhi for about half-day periods. I was so immersed in Satsang. But it would never last. So I just looked at him and I said, "Robert, I've been merging with the All!" like a little kid would say. He was a little taken aback. He looked into my eyes and said, "Good, Good." He kept his hand on my head for the rest of the Satsang. There was just this immense showering of love and blessing on me. Then Satsang ended and he left. That was the last time I saw him in bodily form. Then there was a recognition, "What a fool I've been." He had asked me to come be with him in Sedona and I said, "I don't like Sedona, Robert." [Laughter] There was recognition of how immature I had been. And then there was this fierce dedication for freedom. I knew my life depended on it.

Even though you felt like you had merged with the All, there was still something missing. There was something else . . . .

The ocean would recede, this sense of immense peace, so I knew it wasn't finished. Then I would return to Satsang and I was very blessed to be taken to a beautiful lady named Neelam. It was right after Robert had left. I had a beautiful time in her Satsang because it was just pure love; not much speaking. Just love and laughter.

Where did this take place?

In Berkeley I went up to her after Satsang and said, "Would you come to Sedona because Robert Adams Sangha is hurting. They miss him so much." She said, "Yes, I'll go to Sedona." So we went off together to Sedona. The Satsangs were very beautiful. And I could feel this presence in me but there was still a sense of separation. Then one day in Neelam's Satsang, two months and two days after Robert had left the form, there was just a falling away of the separation, very exquisitely. There was a "knowing" that I had never been separate; that that was also just an illusion. So I went up to her and said, "It appears that the bundle has been set down." And she said, "It is your love that has brought you here." And it's true. It was the love of Satsang and Truth.

What's happened since then?

Well, then there's something called "unfoldment" that kicks in. For two weeks there was this sense of being wiped clean by the grace of God, by the grace of Robert and Neelam and Poonjaji and Ramana, all of these beautiful beings.

Could we call this an awakening?

Oh absolutely! Because it's an awakening to, "Oh, I've always been This. This is who I AM."

Then the rest is simply a revelation from that?

Yes. And there was a bit of chaos in the unfoldment. I was in a crisis when this realization struck. Francis Lucille says the unfoldment takes two years. Papaji used to say it took seven years. The unfoldment of the past falls away like old chunks of stucco. The remaining tendencies or things of the persona fall away. And sometimes it's uncomfortable and there's suffering, but there's always the recognition that peace is present.

How would you define what is "real," "reality" or "truth"?
Well, reality is just That which doesn't change. That's the good news, because if we were bodies that die, then we would die. If we are our thoughts and feelings then we'll have endless torment. We must be something else. So the good news is that the only thing that doesn't change is what they call "substratum" or "peace." So that must be who we are. [Laughter]

There are two ancient yet contemporary ways of thinking about realizing the truth; and we've touched on this before, but possibly we can go into it a little further. One way emphasizes that there's no need for practice or striving for the truth, and the other requires an incredible intensity to practice in order to prepare one for the Truth or to realize the Truth. Can you give us your insights into this apparent paradox?
Often a teacher gives a student practice. But often that teacher isn't the final teacher. A final teacher would never give a student practice.

A person might possibly be served by going to an "intermediary teacher," who gives some form of "practice" to begin with?
Absolutely. Practice has value in that it keeps you out of trouble and it keeps the attention from moment to moment on the object of the practice. So always people go into practice with some idea of freedom, and they think freedom is a "thing" or an "object." Basically it appears that "practice" is designed to exhaust you until you get so exhausted and so frustrated that you stop. And then there's a huge chuckle in the universe and the true teacher appears and gives you a final "Welcome! Come here, just sit, rest."

Is it possible to have a relationship with a "final teacher" in the beginning?
Oh, absolutely. That's what's happening now.

They may say there is "no practice," or possibly give you a "practice"? Or would they refer you to another teacher who would give you a practice first, and then ask you to come back and see them after a certain period of time?
I can't really speak to that because I can only speak from my experience. In truth there was through the Releasing Practice a great

amount of returning the little personality back to resting. When Nee-lam first met me she said, "What do you do? You're so released." She felt I was so at rest inside the form. And I started laughing and said, "That's funny. I do this 'Release Technique.'" So inquiry is a light form of practice. And Ramana Maharshi and Robert Adams always invited those that sat with them to just ask, "Who am I? Who am I?"

Do you think that spiritual seeking is an obstacle to enlightenment?

It's both obstacle and aid. As an aid it exhausts you and frustrates you until you realize there's nothing you can do. Absolutely nothing. So in that it's definitely a benefit. But it does obscure the fact that free-dom is here right now. It's just an idea that it's not—just an idea that you're separate.

Do you think it's possible to use concepts to rid oneself of concepts, like using a thorn to remove a thorn?

Lester Levinsen's teachings were using the mind to release the mind. Robert's just allowed the awareness to return back to the silence. It just brings the attention once again back into that quiet, benevolent presence inside. But practice isn't necessary. [Laughter]

The concept of enlightenment seems to have taken on many definitions in these times. How would you define enlightenment or awakening, and is this the final destination where living the Truth becomes an every day reality?

I would say "enlightenment" is a big word, it's just a fancy word for "Being." The reason why anyone enters into any meditation prac-tice, spiritual practice or any spiritual seeking is the promise of peace. There's this notion, "O.K. if I do this practice or if I go sit with some-one, there'll be this transmission of peace and then I can just rest and Be." So it's funny, this idea of "effort" being the gateway to no effort.

Some say that through silence alone one can realize enlightenment. Others say it's through action alone. How do we cut through this dichotomy?

The fastest way, from my experience and through many of my friends' experiences, is to go sit with someone who's already "resting." Robert Adams used to say, "It's the vibratory rate. It has nothing to do with knowledge, it has nothing to do with any practice." It makes sense. Silence and love vibrate at an immense vibratory rate. It's immense. And anything that comes in contact with it rests and comes into harmony or at One with that higher vibratory rate. It's much faster just to go sit with a friend who's resting.

So would you say that a teacher is necessary for that to take place?
I always quote a higher authority. Ramana Maharshi said that if one was just doing practice on one's own it would take twelve years. It's funny, it was twelve years exactly of releasing on my own. That was realization. But I totally attribute it to sitting with Robert Adams and the grace of Neelam and her master Poonjaji. So why wait? It's so much easier. So many young people have done no practice and they simply come to Satsang and realize who they are.

You mentioned Ramana Maharshi. He once said, "That which is not present in deep dreamless sleep is not real." From this statement, can you help us understand what he is referring to as "real" in that condition as distinguished from what is "not real"?
In our day to day life we think what is real is our problems, our thoughts, our feelings, our physical sensations, our body. That's what we take to be the sum total of reality. So what happens is when you go to sleep at night, Robert and Ramana both said, "The small 'I', that notion of separation, returns back into the spiritual heart on the right side of the chest and rests." And in deep sleep there's not even any notion of world; there's no notion of body. There's certainly a resting prior to any idea that "I" have problems. So that's what they mean when they say " If it's not there in deep sleep, it's not real." The only thing that's present is this nourishing sense of well being and rest.

So there's an awareness there even though it's in deep dreamless sleep?
That's it. So what's sleeping is the body and the mind. But the awareness or consciousness, is the one who speaks first thing in the morning before the small "I" awakens and says, "I rested very well." It's aware of deep rest even though the mind and the body claim, "That's my thought." They take ownership of it as soon as they wake up.

Ramakrishna, a very famous Indian saint once did an experiment where he tried to give a running commentary on his highest spiritual experiences. He succeeded in describing his changing mental and phys-

ical sensations, but suddenly in mid-sentence he stopped, and his body became still in wordless rapture. Afterward he retold a story about a salt doll that went to measure the depth of the sea. The salt doll wanted to tell others how deep the water was. But it could never do so, because no sooner did it get into the water than it melted away. Now, who was there to report the ocean's depth? Is it really possible to obtain a report? Yet this crowning experience literally demands expression. How does this expression best come about in your teachings, knowing that at some level it is unspeakable?

I just always let "the mystery" speak, because I know nothing. There's still a form present but it's not "my" form. There's still a brain left but it's not my brain. All of that gets returned back to its rightful owner which is the "mystery" or the silence or the love. And I just sit for a long time in silence until any trace of this "me" is extinguished and then I let the "ocean" speak. And the ocean knows the ocean. Only the ocean could speak about it.

There is a term used by St. John of the Cross, a famous Christian mystic, called "the dark night of the soul." It refers to extreme angst that many beings have passed through before realizing the truth. History shows us that many famous spiritual figures have gone through a monumental internal and/or external crisis at some point. What was your experience, and is this form of deep angst or suffering really required in order to realize the Truth?

From my experience how I entered heaven was through hell. There was an immense crisis, utter devastation. The entire life fell apart, complete abandonment by family and friends. That's how I was thrown into the refuge of Satsang. Often when life is exquisite and beautiful there isn't a seeking of the Truth. This is not always the case, and this is a very unusual time now that many friends are just coming to Satsang without needing that sort of fierce "kick" from within through suffering. They just fall into silence and peace. So it's definitely not required. And I can say that [Laughter] often some of these sages experienced suffering for the ones who came after them. So they would dive right into the heart of suffering or austerity or renunciation so that the Beloveds that came after them wouldn't have to. When Robert Adams went to Ramana and asked him, "Should I do tapas and austerities?," Ramana said "No." He laughed and said, "I have done these for you!"

Did Robert Adams also go through a crisis that he shared with other people?

He realized when he was fourteen taking a math test in New York City. So who's to know? Often there's this notion that suffering has to be in this life to realize the Truth, and that's not true. Papaji says, "Thirty-five million years we've been suffering. I think that's enough." It's not required.

So, again in some cases there could be a spontaneous awakening without going through the "dark night of the soul?"

Oh, absolutely. Absolutely. There's really just one consciousness. And I think as a six billion faceted jewel, we've had enough suffering. It's no longer required.

Where does humor fit in to realizing and living the Truth? And do you find it manifesting itself in your teachings?

Yes, I have a friend who says, "Reverence without irreverence is religion." And I think it's so nice to be light-hearted with these teachings. Any spiritual teaching sometimes has a tendency to become serious. And Robert was such a good teacher about that. He once put carrots in his nose and ears when somebody was getting too serious. What could be more humorous than Buddhas everywhere thinking they're separate? This is very funny. It's high drama and it's incredible humor. [Laughter]

How do you see art, music and theatre or the fine arts fitting in to realizing or expressing the truth?

Satsang doesn't need to be formal. Satsang just means resting and honoring the Truth. That also is present in music. I mean, all music and all art comes from the same source, the silence and the love. It's very beautiful. I love music now more than I ever did. And both Ramana and Robert said that Shakespeare was realized, and he enjoyed "the play," writing about it, acting in it.

Why do you think there remains such confusion about enlightenment teachings in these times?

Confusion is only present if there's not direct experience. Of course, what happens is, the brain or the mind comes to Satsang and tries to figure it out. Satsang or Truth is sometimes veiled in paradox and confusion, and the trust that is required is to be able to "not know." That's the gateway to all wisdom, to be able to "not know."

What does it mean to be a spiritual master, and once a person is a spiritual master is there anything more to realize?

Often in Advaita we quibble a little bit about language, because if there's someone left, then there's no master. The Truth is that if there's no one left there's no veil of separate self, little "self" left. Then all there is is Truth that's left. But my experience is more of being a servant of the master.

And the master is . . . .

The master is silence and love and also the beautiful beings, you know, Robert, Ramana, and Neelam and all the beautiful teachers. I'm happy to be a servant of the Self. I would never claim mastery of anything.

If someone were sincerely interested in a genuine spiritual teaching or teacher, what are the most important things to consider?

That you can trust Satsang and the Sangha. They always say, "Keep holy company." That's also pointing to its vibratory rate. There's really nothing for anyone to do. You just come and you rest in Satsang. Papaji used to say, "Keep quiet," but he didn't add what the rest of it was. He used to say, "Keep quiet," and also he meant, "let me do the work." Many teachers that give out practice are very fierce about the student doing a lot of effort and work. But that's not required. When you go and have a massage you don't help the masseur. You just go and you trust Beingness, in the Self, or Grace. Let them do the work. That's their job, not ours.

And when you say that they're doing the work, you're not really referring to them as a "person." You're referring to them as an instrument of That?

That's it, yes. It's grace. When I went to Neelam and I thanked her for this freedom, she said, "Oh, don't thank me." There was a picture of Papaji on the wall and I said, "Do I thank Papaji?" and she said "No." And there was Ramana and I said, "Do I thank Ramana?" and she said "No." And I finally threw up my hands and said, "Well then who do I thank?" She said, "Grace. It's only Grace that brings us here, brings us home."

It's been said by many well-known spiritual teachers that enlighten-ment is beyond good and evil, right and wrong. In our daily lives, what's the best way to deal with simple right and wrong decisions that we must make, or in dealing with complex destructive tendencies in others who want to cause wars and death, and extreme suffering—which appear to most people to be very wrong?

What they mean by that is that freedom is untouched by dual-ity—duality meaning male/female, night/day, up/down, good/bad. Freedom exists prior to that. Peace is the substratum or the movie screen that all good/bad, all of lila or life plays upon. So in our daily life it is just as the Buddha said, "The invitation to be harmless." It doesn't mean to let yourself be abused by people but to be harmless in your actions and in your words. That's kindness. And that's being a master from moment to moment.

How would we define "the Divine?" If by definition "the Divine" can-not stand apart from anything, then is there anything we can say or do that is not "Divine"?

I'll go to the beginning, what we call "Divine," "God," "the Beloved" or "Love" or "Silence" which is definitely omnipresent. There's nowhere it could not be because it's all there is. Yet in this play of separation there is apparent destructiveness or harming others or being harmed. So what I say is always return back to the Heart. You know that often the mind or brain in its misguided notion of protect-ing the body will cause chaos or destruction. But if you just bring any questions inside into the Heart, then that's where the Sat-Guru is, and it gives the best advice.

And the Sat-Guru is defined as . . . .

It's that presence that's resting in the Heart. Not the heart that pumps the blood but what Ramana called "the spiritual Heart on the right side of the chest."

So there's a location for this in the physical body?

Yes. If there's identification with the body, then there's a very obvious presence you can feel on the right side of the chest. Once identification falls away with the body, once there's not a notion that it's "your body" but it's just "a body," then you can't really find it there anymore because it's revealed itself to be everywhere.

What do you feel is the most appropriate way to hold ourselves and others accountable for actions that occur?

That's interesting. Because you have to go prior to that question to find who's accountable. Love sees this play, even the harming and the beauty as love. It's a mystery. Yes, there is great suffering and great war and great chaos. But even at the heart of it, prior to the action, it's just love. It's strange sometimes to speak about it.

If all is God's will, as some would believe—and some unscrupulous people use this as an excuse to do very bad things, how would they be most appropriately held responsible for their actions?

If there's identification with body/mind there's karma and karma is very fierce. It doesn't let anybody get away with anything. So in the Eastern countries there's an awareness of this. In the Western countries there isn't. So often there's this notion, "Oh, I can get away with murder" or I can get away with anything.

And call it God's Will, even.

Yes. There's a little extra karma for doing that, too. I don't like to speak of this, because it has nothing to do really with Advaita, but it's true. If there's identification with body/mind, then there's karma.

You used the term Advaita. What does Advaita mean?

[Laughter] Advaita is very simply that there is no "other." There's nothing separate from this One Heart, this One Consciousness, this One True Self, Non-duality.

It seems that in Advaita, there is some sense of predestination. If everything is predestined and there's no choice on the individual level, it may be viewed as a strong case of reductionism. Everything is already set in place. There's no human heart acting, there's nothing we can do and nothing we can change. Could we also say that it's God's will to give individuals free choice to make their own decisions?

It appears the only free choice is either to seek within or to constantly run around looking for happiness or peace outside. That seems to be the only choice. What's present in the heart is the chooser. You know it's the real "doer." So the only thing I would say to reassure people is that you can trust the power that knows the Way. That was the sum-total of Robert's teaching; trust the power that knows the Way.

And in trusting that, it's trusting it absolutely. Could we say then, that one's life is not a willful act any longer as a separate individual?

That's what you see as you mature, as you become an adult. Often when you're young and arrogant, and you think you can do anything, life slaps you. It's like the ultimate Zen stick. And as you get older you see, "Oh my God I of myself really can do nothing." And that's humility and that's when resting happens, when you see, "I can only apparently do so much." Even all my giving-ness, or my service, or my loving can only help so much. Truly it's all God's Will.

It's difficult for some people to agree that it's all God's Will because of what's happened with some spiritual teachers who have been abusive toward their students and have caused an incredible amount of chaos within their communities. It's challenging to try to figure out how people can be held accountable for their actions without rationalizing it away as simply "crazy wisdom," or something that is "divinely ordained." How do we deal with situations like that? It's hard to say "yes" to unorthodox teachings, yet there might be a choice not to participate. Where does the choice come from?

That choice comes from the Heart. When there's enough suffering, you're going to realize that maybe I'm not with a true teacher. There's going to be recognition, "I am suffering." You know you want to sit with someone who brings you to silence, who evokes devotion and love.

What if they evoked the "Dark Night of the Soul"? How do we determine whether someone is leading us to that crisis point in order to transcend it, or if they are simply leading us down the path of more suffering and delusion?

Once again you need to go in and have Satsang with the Heart, because the Heart knows. In some traditions there is very much of the Zen stick, or some harshness. It's often very appropriate, because in this notion of "separation," persona or personality, there's often a lot of arrogance thinking you know more than the teacher. And what happens is, that arrogance glues and cements the separation. So often the teacher will smack someone verbally. And in that there's a shock. There's a shock and then there's a stopping. Now, what happens is, there can be recognition of peace in that stopping. Or the brain or the mind can try to regain control and start to say, "Well, you should leave because this person doesn't know you," and that sort of thing. But the Heart knows a true teacher. The Heart knows often that even that fierce smacking can come from Love itself.

Some people have suggested that a lengthy period of time should be spent with a teacher to ascertain whether or not they are teaching from the Truth. Would you recommend this?

The good news about Advaita Vedanta and this lineage, and also beloveds like Francis Lucille and Adyashanti that come from other lineages, is that there's enough trust that's been built that you know you can sit here and you won't be hurt. That's the gift of lineage. Lineage is really just pointing to the form. And also it allows you to trust. It's a funny thing, because time isn't required with a teacher. These are very unusual years now where people who have done no practice, who haven't sat long just come to Satsang and there's full unshakable realization. This is the invitation now. For some reason, due to the grace of all those that have walked before us, nothing is required now, not even time.

Historically there seems to be either a patriarchal or matriarchal dominance. The patriarchal tends to over focus on the transcendental aspect of life leaving the world as something separate from reality and to be dismissed as a grand illusion or dream. On the other hand, the matriarchal seems to have rooted reality deeply in the world, in nature, de-emphasizing the transcendental. What would a radical fusion of the two look like, and how would it best come about?

I think it's happening right now. It's as I keep saying, it's a very unusual moment in what we call history. Papaji used to say that in some traditions there's only silence and emptiness. And then he would laugh and say, "That's not my experience. In the depths of silence there's love." That's the feminine principle. Silence is the male Shiva, Shakti is female. So in this beautiful tradition there's a complete unification of that. There are some teachers that express jnana, knowledge or wisdom. And others are going to just say come here, rest in the heart, rest in love itself. Let love dissolve any separation.

So love is sufficient wisdom?

At the depths of love rests all wisdom. Either way always leads you home.

How long have you been giving Satsangs now and where does the motivation come from to continue to do them?

Arjuna who comes from Poonjaji's teaching asked me to give Satsang, and I said at least fifteen times "No." I felt I was resting in cluelessness. I hadn't any idea of the mystery other than that it is a vast, exquisite, loving mystery. I felt, "No." And then finally I realized this invitation was coming from the Self. So I said, "Yes." And then there was the delicious discovery that Satsang is never given by the form. It's given by the mystery that resides outside and inside the form. That was a great relief. [Laughter]

What plans do you have to expand the Satsangs in other parts of the world or around the country?

That too is great fun, because it's also part of the mystery. You are somewhere and someone says, "Will you come to Mexico City?" and then of course there's a "Yes." That's how it works. It just comes from the mystery. So I'm getting organized, but to say I'm making plans would be inaccurate. [Laughter]

If you could give one bit of advice to individuals very interested in realizing freedom in this lifetime, what would it be?

Make it your first priority. It doesn't mean that you have to renounce family or loved ones or your work, absolutely not. This is a Western freedom that's available now. Just make it your number one priority. I found it to be of great benefit to read books from these beloved teachers, all the lovely Satsang books from Papaji and Ramana and Neem Karoli Baba. In bringing the intention from moment to moment to Truth, you merge with Truth. What could be simpler? Listen to tapes, and if you have Satsang in your area, sit in Satsang. If there's not Satsang in your area, you just e-mail the Satsang givers and they'll show up. They have to. [Laughter]

Pamela, thank you very much again for spending this time with us today. We are very grateful for the opportunity to explore these important topics with you and hope to have the opportunity to meet with you again in the near future.

Thank you, John.

Publications:
The Ocean, the Fish and the Buddha. 1999.
Mountain Heart, 2000.

Contact information:
Pamela Wilson
360 Staggs Loop Road
Sedon, AZ 86336
Website: www.pamelasatsung.com

JOHN DE RUITER

J ohn de Ruiter was raised in Stettler, Alberta, Canada. At age seventeen John had a spontaneous awakening to an "innermost contentment" that revolutionized his consciousness. This awakening mysteriously disappeared after one year. During the following six years, John embarked on an arduous journey attempting to recapture the truth of what he had previously known. Searching through a myriad of spiritual and philosophical teachings, nothing seemed to work. Finally, after reaching the pinnacle of seeking in all directions, he simply relinquished all effort and found himself unexpectedly consumed by pure Being.

John is a skilled orthopedic shoemaker by trade. He currently resides in Edmonton, Canada, is married and has three children.

In the summer of 1999, I first met John during one of his public meetings in Boulder, Colorado. I was immediately struck by his unfathomable eyes and intense silence surrounding his physical presence. John's primary message is that truth and honesty will set you free. "When you've let in TRUTH to the point where it has replaced everything in you that is untrue, then at that point you come in to TRUE FORM, which is actually the REAL YOU."

Our interview took place in a modest apartment on the south side of Boulder. John seemed the same in a casual situation as he did when he was holding public meetings: quiet, peaceful and yet very vibrant. Following the interview, I attended several of his public meetings. A wide variety of people were present who wanted to explore a variety of spiritual topics with John. In a very calm and patient manner, John addressed each person's questions with exceptional sincerity and openness, adeptly moving through and beyond any false concepts or conditioning that might have arisen from the questioner. The audience seemed actively engaged and was given the opportunity to look deep within.

As mentioned in a brochure introducing John's teaching, his main message is: "Surrender, through openness and softness of heart, unfailingly releases the false, leaving behind just Truth." Enjoy John de Ruiter's "core-splitting honesty."

John, thank you very much for spending time to speak with us today. As mentioned in one of the publications about your teachings, you were propelled into a deep spiritual experience at the age of seventeen. Can you help us understand what that experience was for you and how it might have come about at that point in your life?

Someone had talked to me about God at a job interview. And it meant nothing to me at all. I went home, and that night all of a sudden something started to open up inside. It was like a universe opened up inside as well as a universe "outside"—a different universe than the one that we see. It was like a whole universal awareness. And these two universes, inside and outside, were intimately connected. It was like they were the same. There was just as much outside as there was inside. And I didn't know what it was. I just knew that it was real and it was true.

What exactly happened after this experience? You embarked on a spiritual journey that lasted many years. During this time, what spiritual paths did you find most useful to explore, and which teachers or teachings had the greatest impact on you in realizing the truth?
There was nothing that really worked. That was my frustration. This first experience lasted for about a year. And then it passed off. And when it was gone, I knew nothing was worth living for until I was back in that first state. In looking, I tried everything outside of me, and I ended up exploring everything inside, trying to find out how to get back to what I had experienced. And not just know it again, but know the source of it.

How did you go about doing that exploration? Was it more on your own? Did you go into Christianity, Buddhism, Hinduism, or any of the other traditional religions, or did you go to any particular teachers to try to have them mentor you or help you through that process?
At the time, I was involved with Christianity, but there was nothing in it that really touched what I knew.

From your previous experience?
That's right.

How would you define what is real? What is reality or truth?
Reality or truth is something that can't be understood by the mind alone; can't be realized through mental exercise or mental focus. Reality or truth is something that originates from one's innermost. And that touch of reality or that movement of truth comes up from your innermost and touches what is like the underside of your heart. If the topside of your heart were everything to do with your vehicles of expression such as the mind, emotions and will, and if you were to use all of these resources to try to attain truth, then you would end up being pulled out of what touched you, instead of letting in this "touch." So truth is more like a way of being. It has a flavor to it that moves your whole being. At first there is no comprehension of what is happening other than a clear knowing that it is real and true.

Did it have any physical sensation that went along with that opening or awakening? You mentioned the heart. Was there something there that you felt even physically that was opening, moving?

It affected my whole body. It was like my body turned into something different. It became alive. It was like my whole body was one giant heart. My whole body was a conductor for something that was bigger than anything I had ever known before that.

A Buddhist Master once said, "The statement that there is nothing which can be attained is not idle talk: it is the truth. You have always been one with the Buddha, so do not pretend you can attain to this oneness by various practices. If at this very moment you could convince yourselves of its unattainability, being certain indeed that nothing at all can ever be attained, you would already be Bodhi-minded. Hard is the feeling of this saying! It is to teach you to refrain from seeking Buddhahood, since any search is doomed to failure." On the other hand there are thousands of years of traditions suggesting that spiritual practices, devotional prayers, and meditation techniques be employed which is epitomized by the biblical statement, "Seek and ye shall find." How can we distinguish between actively "seeking" for the Truth, and a choiceless vigilance that is propelled by the truth itself?

It all has to do with the state of a person's heart. When there is any measure of dishonesty of heart—seeking to find for yourself, seeking to find because that will make you happy, seeking to find because you are wanting something such as enlightenment or awakening—then you will never find it. The most you will ever find then is more of what it is that you want, that you can't get. But when there is a seeking for the purpose of surrendering to whatever it is that you would honestly know is real and true, then the moment you touch what is real or true, there is an absolute surrender. Then, when you seek, you do find. So it's like the truth or reality is only hidden to those that want it for themselves. But to those that seek to know reality just so that they can give away their "everything" and their "all" to that reality, it is easily found.

The concept of enlightenment seems to have taken on many definitions in these times. How would you define enlightenment or awakening, and is this the final destination where living the truth becomes an everyday reality?

The terms awakening and enlightenment have been used synonymously. And they are not the same thing.

What is the difference between the two?

Awakening is when the eyes of consciousness open so that consciousness begins to see what is real, instead of consciousness seeing only an illusion, or what it wants to be real. When consciousness chooses only to see a want and a need, then it only sees its own self-created understanding. It can't see what really, really is. When there is an honesty of consciousness, a core-splitting honesty of heart, then the eyes of consciousness begin to open. Then we really begin to see. When that real seeing happens—seeing reality, seeing what is true, really knowing clearly what is real—then that is awakening. Then there is awakening to everything that is real versus only being awakened to what we want to be real or to what we think is real. Awakening is like true seeing.

Enlightenment is becoming functional in this reality that we can see; it is gaining the capacity to "do" what is seen. At first we only see it. When we see it, it is unspeakably amazing. Totally life changing. It causes real transformation. And as such, we as consciousness still don't know how to do what it is that we see. We only know how to surrender to it, how to love it, how to enjoy it, how to swim in it. But we don't know how to transmit it, how to "do" it. The "doing" of that reality is enlightenment.

Who is the doer then?

Consciousness.

Consciousness itself? So there is no "doer" in terms of a personal someone who's actually "doing" it?

There's not a somebody. There's not a someone or a somebody that's doing. It's consciousness itself that does. So as long as there is a someone there, or a somebody that relates to any kind of doing, then enlightenment is much more impossible than awakening would have ever seemed to be.

Some say that through silence alone one can realize enlightenment.

Others say it's through action alone. How can we cut through this dichotomy?

Awakening can happen with much action or only silence. Awakening can happen even through thinking, provided that there is an absolute honesty in the silence or in the action or in the thinking. Where there's an absolute honesty of consciousness, then there is a willingness of consciousness to open its eyes to what really is true, regardless of the cost. In that case, anything works. But if there's any measure of dishonesty of consciousness, any agenda to "have" something, then years of silence or years of action or meditation or years of nothing, will not accomplish anything. It is that little bit of dishonesty, that little bit of having an agenda of getting something—that's the energy that blinds us and hides us from being able to see. There is no technique that will ever work. It is the honesty of consciousness that does it. If you take that ingredient and insert it in the midst of meditation, you will awaken.

Is there an intention on someone's part to choose that honesty of consciousness?

There is.

So there's a choice on the part of someone to lean into it? I'm just using my own terms here. There's a "doing" on someone's part in order to have that honesty of consciousness?

It is a choice, but it is honesty choosing instead of "you" choosing.

So honesty of consciousness chooses itself?

Yes. A person can "think" that they have much sincerity, and they can "feel" as though they are being as honest as they possibly can be, and yet the agendas that are underlying that can still be endless. True seeing requires a kind of honesty that splits right through the very core of everything that we think or feel we are. And unless that core gets split by an honesty of consciousness, there won't be any true seeing.

How is that honesty of consciousness then brought about in someone's life if it comes from consciousness itself? Is it something that comes through grace?

The grace is always there. It is always there for everyone.

It seems that there are only a handful of people in history who have actually been able to receive the grace enough to have that true honesty of consciousness and be able to take it into true enlightenment.

The grace is really there for everyone. What happens is that countless people will begin to open up, begin to awaken. And as soon as they start to see a little bit, then through their mind they realize some of the implications of how this will affect their life. And then everything shuts down.

So there's fear that comes in.

There is a fear of what they will lose. When you begin to see a little bit, then the first thing that you realize is that there is absolutely nothing in it for you. The "you" that you think and feel you are will entirely disappear. When your eyes begin to open, then you begin to experience the disappearance of yourself. And if there is any agenda to acquire something for "you," then it's that part of "you" that will keep you from opening your eyes further.

So it tries to own that experience, then, or tries to take it to itself and incorporate it within its own limited ego or conditional state?

That's right. So then instead of awakening, one just goes on a path, seeking something that one has already tasted.

Ramana Maharshi, a famous Indian saint once said, "That which is not present in deep dreamless sleep is not real." From this statement, can you help us understand what he is referring to as "real" as distinguished from what is "not real"?

Everything that we are familiar with, everything that we think, does not represent what is real. It represents only what we are thinking. Our feelings represent only what we are feeling. What it is that we actually know is true, that represents what we do know and what is true. But we cannot come to that point of knowing what we do know is true until we have relinquished all of our mental constructs, all of the emotional constructs, all of the intuitive constructs. In terms of what we are familiar with, it is relinquishing everything. There would be nothing left. When that has been relinquished, then what is left over is what was always real.

So even in deep dreamless sleep that consciousness and awareness is there. It's always there?

It's always there.

Underlying even all waking, dreaming, sleeping, relative states of awareness?

It's there all the time. But we are so accustomed to relating to what we think and relating to what we feel, relating to our intuition, our will, our body, that we can't see what we do know. If we were to begin to see it, then we would refuse to believe it. We would realize that if this is true as we know it to be true, then all life as we presently know it, would be over.

That's a pretty scary thought for a lot of people.

It is. It's the end of everything. And then that reality that we actually know is true, that would replace our life. And we don't want to be replaced. We want to fix ourselves. We want to find reality so that we can repair what we think or feel we are, and make it better. And that is why so few will ever find it.

Ramakrishna once tried an experiment where he tried to give a running commentary on his highest spiritual experiences. He succeeded in describing his changing mental and physical sensations, but suddenly in mid-sentence, he broke off and his body became still in wordless rapture. Afterword he recalled a story about a salt doll that went to measure the depth of the sea. It wanted to tell others how deep the water was. But it could never do so, because no sooner did it get into the water than it melted away. Now who was it, John, that was there to report the ocean's depth? At that particular point of melting away is it really possible to explain it? Yet this crowning experience literally demands expression. How does this expression best come about in your teachings knowing that at some level it's unspeakable?

To know the ocean is easy. To describe its depth has no meaning. To connect with the ocean floor—that's easy. But when you are connecting with the ocean floor or with any part of the ocean, then to measure the depth of what it is that you are connecting with has no meaning.

That's when it falls into that unspeakable realm.

Yes.

John, does the "dark night of the soul" or extreme angst need to be passed through before we can realize the truth? It seems that most famous spiritual figures have gone through a monumental internal crisis. What was your experience and is suffering really required in order to realize the truth?

Suffering is not required. It is not required to know the truth. However, because of our illusion and the lies that we live in, because of the emotional and mental attachment to everything that we are familiar with, then to know the truth while having a false base like this, makes suffering inevitable. We will experience the loss of everything that we have made to be so real. When there is mental or emotional attachment to something, then that attachment has to die. It can only die in the place that it was brought to birth. For that attachment or that valuing of something to die in the place that it was brought up, then a deep loss is experienced. There is mental or emotional suffering in that. But the greater the honesty of consciousness, the more quickly the attachment is pierced right through, and there is little time invested in the suffering. Then what happens is like a piercing, like an arrow going through you. And when there is an absolute honesty of consciousness and there is no resistance to that arrow at all, then it is letting oneself be completely, cleanly pierced. Any aversion to suffering always holds you in the suffering because of a resistance to that piercing. Then instead of being pierced, you get torn apart.

So the more that someone hangs on to those false assumptions, the greater the suffering? Some people are fortunate enough to be able to dive into that honesty of the truth and consciousness deeply enough to allow that to pass quickly. That's what I hear you saying.

That's right.

Where does humor fit in to realizing and living the truth, and how do you find it manifesting itself in your own teachings?

I find humor in everything. Much of it I don't use because it would be an affront to people's sensibilities. It would offend them. Humor is seeing the lightness in something of what one makes serious or heavy. So then humor is seen in everything. It is not a laughing at someone—an internal laughing at someone. It's like a warm endearment in tenderness, watching something that is most warmly not true made to be so real and so true.

What's the proper perspective on having thoughts and emotions?

Thoughts are worth having, emotions are worth having. And they are never worth trusting. They are never worth living for. Thoughts are harmless until you trust them. As soon as you trust a thought to tell you what is true, then all you are left with is a deeply rooted opinion of something that you think. And then you are even farther removed from reality than when you first trusted that thought. If you are having thoughts or emotions, but there is a very tender non-trust in those thoughts or in those emotions, then they are just thoughts, and they are just emotions. Then you are free to see in the midst of those thoughts and in the midst of those emotions what it is that is real. As soon as you trust a thought or an emotion, then you cover up what is real and you can no longer see. Then all you can see is what is in your mind or in your feelings.

Do you see art, music and theatre being valid avenues to realizing the truth?

Every avenue is valid. What makes it work is the energy that moves through it, the measure of awakening that is in context of the use of art, music or any kind of medium. The greater the awakening, then the more profound the energy of truth or reality that will be there. It is that energy of truth that does it.

Why do you think there remains such confusion about enlightenment teachings in these times?

The greatest confusion is because of individual's teaching on awakening or enlightenment and at the same time having an agenda; a "somebody" still being there. Then there are amazing words that are being spoken and there is truth in them because the one who is speaking is awakened. They are really knowing what they are saying but at the same time, there is a "somebody" there to reap some kind of benefit in being able to speak those things. So then there are two energies happening at the same time and there is an incongruency of energy. That is what confuses people. And those who come to listen to teachers, for the most part, initially have an agenda as well. People are seeking personal happiness. So then both of the incongruent energies are plugged into; they are plugged into by the teacher and by the student.

Both have an agenda. If a teacher has an agenda then it makes it O.K. for everybody else to have one, regardless of what is being said. There will be an unspoken communication that you can have the truth and you can still keep you; you can still have truth for you, even though the words that are spoken are the opposite of that.

Or the behavior possibly.
Yes.

If someone is genuinely interested in spiritual teachings or a teacher, what are the most important things to consider?
It is not even so much the focus on the teacher that is the primary consideration, but rather the focus within oneself…an intention to know what is true just so that one can surrender to it, and to never go beyond that. If there is no intention to awaken or to be awakened, no intention to get something, no intention of acquiring, no intention of healing, of anything being fixed, of life being made better, but rather only an intention to know what is true just so there can be an absolute surrender to that, then that is of the greatest importance.

It's been said by many well-known spiritual teachers that enlightenment is beyond good and evil, right and wrong. In our daily lives, what's the best way to deal with simple right and wrong decisions that we must make, or in dealing with even complex destructive tendencies in others who want to cause wars, death, and extreme suffering – which appear to most people to be very wrong?
The best way to deal with all decisions is to very gently lay down all of your own judgments; no longer trusting what you think and what you feel to tell you what is true, regardless of how that seems to be affecting you or other people. It is letting go of your own issues. Behind every issue there is a whole belief system that is emotionally backed by what we want to be good or evil. You can't keep your own judgments, you can't keep your own ideals.

John, what is the Divine? If by definition the Divine cannot stand apart from anything, then is there anything that we can say or do that is not Divine?

There is everything that we could say or do that has nothing to do with the Divine. As soon as there is a dishonesty of consciousness, as soon as there is a choice to make something true that we know is not true, and we do so just because we want to, then that is a misuse of something that we really, really are, such as the Divine. That power is being used to create something that is not true. It is like usurping a power and using it for something that we are not. Then there is really nothing of the Divine in that. There is no essence of letting go, there is only this energy of hanging on; the energy of control and the energy of hardness.

So then there is something that is not Divine, and there is something that is Divine. There are these two things.

What there is, then, that is not Divine, is only an illusion. It is not something that is real.

But we can't deny its existence. Like a mirage that we see in the desert: it may not be real, but we can't deny its existence even if it is an illusion.

But it doesn't have a real existence. It is manifested because of want and need. It is not manifested as a result of something that is already real. With an illusion, as soon as you let an illusion go, it ceases to exist. When you let reality go, it only deepens. Then it will move even more into form. An illusion has no existence on its own. It only has an existence when you give it one. When you believe in a lie knowing that it is a lie, then you give that lie an existence. As soon as you let go of hanging onto that lie, as soon as you let go of its usefulness, it is no longer there. It never did exist.

So it doesn't have a Divine quality then?

That's right. It is not real. It is not there. It is only believed to be there because we wish it so.

What do you feel is the most appropriate way to hold ourselves and others accountable for our actions? You mentioned being totally honest with ourselves. What about others? How do we hold them accountable for their actions? There are such terrible things happening in the world.

First, by not getting "you" involved with an issue. Then there is nothing to labor with regarding other people. There is nothing there to change. And then tenderness has room to address the situation. [Note: tenderness means the essence of Truth. Ed.] As soon as "you" address the situation, then it is a "somebody" who is making "something" of an issue. And then it is really not about the subject matter anymore. Then it's about "me." It's about what "I" think; it's about what "I" feel concerning a given situation. So then "I" would only be using that situation to give life to something that "I" am presently thinking and feeling. We end up having an edge inside, a hardness inside. We are holding on to something; it matters now that "I" change something outside of me. When tenderness deals with an issue, when tenderness deals with a circumstance outside of itself, then all that happens is a flow of tenderness. There is no grasping, there is no holding, there is no edge, no hardness, no "somebody." But when "we" address a circumstance, we do so to accomplish something within ourselves. It's basically done for ourselves. It is not really done for what we make it appear we are doing it for – another person, unless it is tenderness that is doing it. When tenderness does it, then "you" are not in the picture.

If all is God's will, as some spiritual teachings believe, and some unscrupulous people use this as an excuse to do very bad things, how would they be most appropriately held accountable for their actions?
The first thing that makes them accountable is their own suffering. What they do to other people, they do to themselves on the inside.

Historically there seems to be either a patriarchal or matriarchal dominance. The patriarchal tends to over-focus on the transcendental aspect of life leaving the world as something separate from reality and to be dismissed as a grand illusion or dream. On the other hand, the matriarchal seems to have rooted reality deeply in the world, in nature, de-emphasizing the transcendental. What would a radical fusion of the two look like?
It would be a relationship with what we are as consciousness being formless, and also being in context of form. As soon as there is a gravitation to being in what is formless, then there is a denial of what is presently existing in form, such as the mind, the emotions, the will, the intuition, the body, and a denial of the context in which all of

that exists in this world. A relationship of consciousness being form-less and existing in form is an absolute honesty of consciousness, existing in a way of tenderness, accepting the form as is, and accepting what it is that it knows but does not understand, as is. So then there is a relationship between what is formless as consciousness and the context in which that exists, in form. Then both are equally and warmly received. There is no preference of one over the other.

So there's no exclusion.
    That's right.

All is included.
    They both come alive.

If you could give one bit of advice to individuals very interested in real-izing freedom in this life time, what would it be?
    To warmly let go of ever needing to be free. The more we want freedom, the more we will be held captive or imprisoned by that want. Then the value of freedom increases, and the depth of our own cap-tivity as its opposite increases. As soon as there is a warm letting go of ever needing to be free, then that separation or that distinction between the two dissolves. If there is an absolute letting go of ever needing to be free, and if that is done in a way that is really warm, then the first thing that you become free of is wanting freedom.

And then you have an opportunity to settle into that place which is always already free to begin with.
    That's right.

John, prior to this year you have primarily been giving satsangs in the Edmonton, Canada area, but this year you have begun offering meet-ings throughout the world. Can you share with us the meaning of these meetings, and why it's important in terms of realizing the truth?
    The only reason that these meetings are important for me to do or participate in is because that is what I know is true. That's it. That stands on its own. If what I knew to be true was to no longer meet with people, then it would be over. There would be no amount of per-suasion that could ever change that. The importance for others is to

be in an energy where there is a consciousness that sees, where there is a consciousness that cannot be manipulated, cannot be bent to shape what people want to be true or need to be true. Anything that addresses a consciousness like that is always replied by a clarity, a cleanness. And it is that energy that pulls up exactly the same thing within each person that hears.

Then there is a matching of consciousness that happens. There is a pull. What gets pulled up within the person who is sitting in the presence of an energy like that, is exactly the same thing, the same energy. But it is deeply covered up. On his or her own that person would likely never "get it" because of all the sediment that he or she would have to move through—all the garbage, all of the illusion, all of the lies. That person would have to cut through all of that and never draw back regardless of what it would cost them, but without any outside influence of the same energy pulling them through. In terms of realizing truth, the two energies are working together to bring a person's heart through… it's of incredible value.

John, I know you're married and have three children. How do you manage to balance a very busy teaching schedule with the obligations of being a family man and a householder?
I let tenderness take care of that.

Is there a summary statement that you'd like to leave us with that has to do with the breakthrough and teachings of the truth?
For people to let go of ever trusting "themselves" again: trusting what they think, and trusting what they feel to tell them what is true … to let go of what they have ever acquired inside as teachings or learnings gained from all of life's experiences, gained from reading, gained from talking; to let go of absolutely everything. It is not throwing it away; it is not negating it. It is just simply letting it go. Whatever is in fact real, will still be there. And whatever is not real, or not true, the moment it is let go of, is gone. It never was real. What will be left over if a person does this, is a very, very small little bit. From the perspective of the mind, it is like losing absolutely everything, to have nothing. But to the heart that loses that "everything," there is a knowing that all of that is nothing. And the nothing that is left over, is in fact really, really everything.

You're not suggesting that we try to use a mental technique of "letting go" as opposed to not letting go. There are many teachers who ask students to take that on as a technique and say, "just let go, just let go." But the mind itself doesn't really want to do that, or it may take it on as a strategy for its own improvement or self-gratification. When you are referring to "letting go" are you referring to that as maybe transcending or going beyond, looking beyond....

It is going beyond "you" and you can't go beyond "you" if you are hanging on to what you need or want to be "you." So it is letting go of all of your emotional attachment to everything that you think and everything that you feel, everything that you are presently familiar with. And it is not throwing that out. It is just releasing the attachment that makes you identified with that. Then, what is left over is what you really are, separate from the thoughts and feelings.

So in that case, then once that's finished then we've let go of letting go.

That's right. One of the things that has to be let go of is the need or the want to let go.

John, thank you very much again for spending this time with us today. We are very grateful for the opportunity to explore these important topics with you.

Thank you.

Publications:

Unveiling Reality, John de Ruiter, Oasis Edmonton Publishing, 1999.

Contact Information:

Oasis Edmonton, Inc.
Box 78029 Callingwood
Edmonton, Alberta, Canada T5T6A1
Phone: 780-487-8781
Fax: 780-486-7870
Website: www.johnderuiter.com
E-Mail: truth@johnderuiter.com